THE ANGLO-KUKI WAR, 1917–1919

This book explores the Kuki uprising against the British Empire during the First World War in the frontier of Northeast India (then Assam-Burma frontier). It underlines how the three-year war (1917–1919), spanning over 6000 square miles, is crucial to understanding present-day Northeast India. The chapters in the volume examine several aspects of the war, which had far-reaching consequences for the indigenous population, as well as for British attitudes and policies towards the region – including military strategy and tactics, violence, politics, identity, institutions, gender, culture and the frontier dimensions of the First World War itself. The volume also looks at how the conflict affected the larger dynamics of the region within Asia, and its relevance in world politics beyond the Great War.

Drawing on archival sources, extensive fieldwork and oral histories, the volume will be a significant contribution to comprehending the complex geopolitics of the region. It will be of great interest to scholars and researchers of South and Southeast Asian Studies, area studies, modern history, military and strategic studies, insurgency and counterinsurgency studies, tribal warfare and politics.

Jangkhomang Guite is Assistant Professor at the Centre for Historical Studies, Jawaharlal Nehru University, New Delhi, India. He has specialised on the history of the tribes in Northeast India, and he has published scholarly articles in both national and international journals and in edited volumes.

Thongkholal Haokip is Assistant Professor at the Centre for the Study of Law and Governance, Jawaharlal Nehru University, New Delhi, India. He was formerly with the Department of Political Science, Presidency University, Kolkata, India. He has authored *India's Look East Policy and the Northeast* (2015), and edited *The Kukis of Northeast India: Politics and Culture* (2013). Dr Haokip is the editor of *Journal of North-East India Studies* and Executive Editor of *Asian Ethnicity*.

THE ANGLO-KUKI WAR, 1917–1919

A Frontier Uprising against Imperialism during the First World War

Edited by Jangkhomang Guite and Thongkholal Haokip

Routledge
Taylor & Francis Group

LONDON AND NEW YORK

First published 2019 by Routledge

2 Park Square, Milton Park, Abingdon, Oxfordshire OX14 4RN

52 Vanderbilt Avenue, New York, NY 10017

Routledge is an imprint of the Taylor & Francis Group, an informa business

First issued in paperback 2019

British Library Cataloguing-in-Publication Data

A catalogue record for this book is available from the British Library

Library of Congress Cataloging-in-Publication Data
A catalog record has been requested for this book

ISBN: 978-1-138-50704-3 (hbk)
ISBN: 978-0-367-47948-0 (pbk)

Typeset in Sabon
by Apex CoVantage, LLC

FOR

ALL THE HEROES AND HEROINES OF THE
ANGLO-KUKI WAR 1917–1919

CONTENTS

CONTENTS

CONTRIBUTORS

Arfina Haokip is a lecturer at Moreh Higher Secondary School, Moreh, Manipur, India.

D. Letkhojam Haokip is Assistant Professor at the Department of History, Gauhati University, Assam, India. Formerly he was at the Department of History, Don Bosco College, Maram Manipur, India. He is the author of *Thempu Ho Thu* (Priestly Charms of The Kuki) (2000) and editor of *Documents of the Anglo-Kuki War 1917–1919* (2017).

Hoipi Haokip is Assistant Professor in the Department of History, Y.K. College, Wangjing, Thoubal District, Manipur, India.

Sonthang Haokip is Assistant Professor of History at Moirang College, Moirang, Manipur, India.

Ngamjahao Kipgen is Assistant Professor of Sociology at the Department of Humanities and Social Sciences, Indian Institute of Technology, Guwahati, India. He was formerly with the Department of Humanities and Social Sciences, National Institute of Technology Rourkela. He has primarily worked on identity politics, ethnic nationalism and hydropolitics in Northeast India. His research interests fall in political sociology and environmental sociology.

Seikhohao Kipgen is Associate Professor in the Department of History, Manipur College, India. He did his PhD as UGC's Junior Research Fellow from Manipur University in 2006. Associated with various academic bodies, Dr Kipgen has presented papers in various state, regional and national level seminars/conferences. He has authored, *Political and Economic History of the Kukis of Manipur*, published in 2015. He has also co-edited *Ageing in North-East India: Manipur Perspective* vol.5 ICSSR-NERC, published in 2009.

Ningmuanching is Assistant Professor at Sri Venkateswara College, University of Delhi, India. She is the recipient of a PhD from the Centre for Historical Studies, Jawaharlal Nehru University.

Pum Khan Pau is Assistant Professor, Department of History, Visva Bharati University, Santiniketan, West Bengal, India. He was Raman Post-Doctoral Fellow at Arizona State University, USA (2014–2015). He has published in the *Indian Historical Review, Strategic Analysis, Journal of Imperial and Commonwealth History, Journal of Religion and Society, Journal of Burma Studies, Journal of Borderlands Studies, Small Wars and Insurgencies*, etc.

Hoineilhing Sitlhou is Assistant Professor at the Department of Sociology, University of Hyderabad, India. She completed her PhD (Sociology) from Jawaharlal Nehru University, New Delhi, India. She is a recipient of the M.N. Srinivas Award, 2016 and has published two books: *Kuki Women* (ed.), 2014 and *Deconstructing Colonial Ethnography: An Analysis of Missionary Writings in North-East India*, 2017. She has also contributed articles in *Economic and Political Weekly, Indian Journal of Gender Studies, International Journal on Religion and Spirituality, Indian Anthropologist, Asian Ethnicity* and chapters in edited books.

David Vumlallian Zou is on the faculty of the History Department, University of Delhi, India. He did his MA and MPhil from Centre for Historical Studies, Jawaharlal Nehru University, New Delhi and completed his PhD from Queen's University Belfast, UK. His publications on the history of Northeast India have appeared in *Journal of Asian Studies, Contributions to Indian Sociology, Indian Historical Review, Economic and Political Weekly*, etc.

ACKNOWLEDGEMENTS

This book is an product of the Kuki Research Forum (KuRF), a collegium of the Kuki intellectual community, in an attempt to commemorate the centenary of the Anglo-Kuki War 1917–1919. It has been long in the making, with the involvement of several people within the Kuki Research Forum and other organisations such as the Anglo-Kuki War Centenary Commemoration Committee, the Kuki Inpi and Kuki Students Organisations endorsing the project. The Kuki Research Forum had given the task to us. We began the project from scratch, collecting source materials from different archives and libraries and inviting scholars to contribute to the volume. Out of a good number of papers received from different scholars, 11 essays have been selected for this volume.

This work would not have been possible without the constant cooperation of the authors of the chapters in the volume. We are indeed thankful to all the authors for their consistent support till the last minute. We will, of course, be fully responsible for the errors and interpretations made in the volume, which we did so purely in our understanding of the sources at our disposal. The views expressed by the authors in the volume do not necessarily represent the view of the Kuki Research Forum and any other Kuki organisations. We are also grateful to the officers and staff of different archives and libraries for their cooperation and necessary support during the consultation of primary sources.

Last, but not the least, we are thankful to the editorial staff of Routledge India, particularly Brinda Sen, for their continuous support and cooperation in the process of bringing out this volume.

INTRODUCTION

Jangkhomang Guite and Thongkholal Haokip

100 years ago, when other parts of India were busy assembling combatants, non-combatants, labourers, funds and materials for the Great War, the Kukis of the Northeastern frontier of India declared 'war against the King-Emperor'.[1] Initially provoked by the 'forcible' recruitment of a labour corps for France, the opposition turned into an armed resistance, partly because of the intemperate local officers – who were incompetent to handle the situation – and partly because the Kukis were overawed, as intelligence reports acknowledged, by the revolutionary ideas from the valley of Manipur, from Bengal in the west and from the China/Germans from the east.[2] Though such influence cannot be overstated, the fact that it had happened made the Kukis bold in their war against the 'Sahibs' and the 'Sarkaris' and the local governments becoming extremely careful in dealing with them. Unlike the previous expeditions in the region – when media attention was fully drawn on – the news of operations against the Kukis was kept under cover of darkness throughout, save one 'press communiqué' released by the Assam government in February 1918 during the early phase of the war. The report belittled, as Colonel Shakespear (1929: 235) noted, 'the hard show carried' out by the combined Military Police forces of Assam and Burma as the 'outings of Political Officers and their escorts'. This small report, however, revealed the violent character of colonialism that immediately evoked a series of criticism from Indian nationalists who termed the actions as a 'tragic inhumanity' and the 'brute force in all its hideous nakedness'.[3] This led subsequently to the concealment of ongoing military operations from public scrutiny.

The invisibility of the 'small war' carried out in the frontier in the public domain and in the nationalist political discourse need not, however, demeans the 'hard show' given by the Military Police as well as the Kukis. The official reports (mostly confidential) were filled with the 'hard show' given in the mountain massif of India's northeastern and Burma's northwestern frontiers. An extract from the proceedings of the Chief Commissioner of Assam was, for instance, lucid in this respect. It described the 'Kuki rising of 1917–1919' as 'the most formidable with which Assam has been faced for at least a generation', covering an area of 'over some 6,000 square miles of rugged hills surrounding the Manipur Valley and extending to the Somra Tract and the Thaungdut State in Burma'.[4] Whereas the opposition started in March 1917, an active warfare and counterinsurgency operation went on for more than one year (December 1917 to May 1919), suspending two agriculture seasons and ending with the systematic destruction of villages, properties and all sources of livelihood. The military operations, carried out with 'continuous active service in mountainous country', was carried out by the combined forces of Assam and the Burma Military Police – 6234 combatants, 696 non-combatants, 7650 transport carriers, etc.[5] It was the 'largest series of military operations' in the eastern frontier of India, eclipsed only by the Second World War in the region in 1944 (Shakespear 1929: 235–236). It costs the government rupees 28 lakh in total.[6]

Casualties on British troops were 60 dead (including one British Officer), 142 wounded (including 3 British Officers) and 97 dead due to diseases. Interestingly, only seven coolies were killed by the Kukis, the figure which could have been higher had the target of attack been them. Many coolies died but due to diseases; the total figure of dead on this count (mainly the pneumonia epidemic) was 393 people. Official estimates of Kukis killed by the troops were 120 persons (much less from the Kuki's version), and 576 mithuns (a much more conservative estimate from the Kuki estimate, along with large numbers of goats, pigs, fowls, etc.) were destroyed or eaten. A total of 126 Kuki villages were burnt to the ground, 16 villages were permanently declared 'barren' and deserted and 140 villages were coerced to surrender.[7] No official estimate was available on the amount of food-grains (mainly rice) and other food-stocks (such as root crops, vegetable, oilseeds, beans, etc.), which were also systematically destroyed or looted, not only from the village granaries, but also from the 'hidden stores' in the jungle. Food reserves for one year, for an estimated population of 40,000 persons were inarguably high; all were destroyed by the military columns. Kuki villages normally contained large amounts of cotton and other products for their home and trade; the raging fire of colonial violence consumed them all.

After the rising was forcibly suppressed, the Kukis were compelled to pay rupees one lakh 75,000 (the exact amount disbursed was Rs. 1,67,441/-) as war reparations (officially termed 'compensation' to friendly villages destroyed by military authorities to prevent being used by Kukis, along with those destroyed by Kukis).[8] This amount was recovered from them in instalments during the period of about five years, partly in cash (rupees 25,000–30,000), and partly in the form of penal labour in the construction of bridle paths across the hills of Manipur, cutting government roads, construction of government offices and other official establishments, porterage and so on.[9] Large numbers of Kuki population (both 'rebels' and 'friendlies') were also uprooted from their ancestral villages and moved to the various grouping centres under the new sedentarisation programme. Manipur, so far unadministered (except by an annual political tour by the Political Agent in Manipur or hill *lambus* collecting house-tax) and the unadministered Somra Tract in Burma, were finally brought under direct administration. Administrative subdivisions, military outposts, construction of communication lines (750 miles of bridle path were constructed during the operations) and so on, were established.[10]

The concern of this volume is how we might understand this 'small war' in India's frontier during the Great War. The collected chapters are not concerned with the connectedness the Anglo-Kuki War has with the wider political and military discourses around the world, but they are in themselves bringing a new understanding to the rising. Based on the existing literature on the subject, which mainly focussed on 'causes' and 'consequences' of the war, or of the flaming romance of the liberation movement, the present chapters go further in exploring other important aspects of the war based on new approaches and fresh source materials at their disposal. With a new conceptual framework and methodology, the subject under study comes under full interdisciplinary scrutiny. The authors in this volume enrich the subject matter at the material grounds as to its conceptual height. In short, the subsequent chapters represent a new genre of researches undertaken by young scholars in the present day. There is a general agreement among the authors that the 'Anglo-Kuki War' was a people's war against elevated discontent under colonialism, ignited by labour recruitment for the Great War. The conflict aimed at achieving a clear objective of freedom from colonial yoke. This dispels the received wisdom of the rising, undoubtedly derived from dominant colonial discourse, that the war was the 'chief's war' and it was fought only by the Thadou-Kukis. The chapters point out the role played by all sections of the Kuki population including the women, aged and so on. It has also become clear that besides the Thadou-Kukis, many other non-Thadou-Kuki tribes also participated in the war – some directly, some indirectly – assisting them by supplying foods and other materials. People took part in the war not for their chiefs or for any pecuniary gains, but as 'men of one country', the patriotism which certainly centres on a territory free from colonial control.

The chapters are thematically arranged and touch upon the less known aspects in the scholarship of anti-colonial movement. The new themes range from the role of traditional institutions such as *sathin-salung-neh* and grand chiefs-in-council (the war conclaves), *som* (bachelor's dormitory), the war tactics, technology and symbols used by the Kuki hillmen as well as by the British, of the role of women and their conception of the war. The role of these traditional institutions and the war methods and tactics in organising and sustaining the war vis-a-viz the colonial modern military measures is profoundly clear from these chapters. Besides, important additions on the conventional themes like cause, course and consequences of the war are given with fresh insight and new source materials collected from different archives. Two more chapters deal with the section of the rising carried out by the non-Thadou tribes, namely by the 'Manlun-Manchong Kukis' (today Zou tribe) of southern Manipur and the Haka tribe of the Chin Hills, adding to our understanding of the war. These two chapters show clearly how the rising was not a Thadou war but had a wider participation across the eastern frontier. While the Zous fought the British side by side with the Thadous, the connection between the Haka uprising and that of their brethrens in Manipur is also clearly visible. These chapters, if not complete, have brought new insights into the frontier war during the First World War.

The chapters broadly take what is understood in academic scholarship as a subaltern approach and a methodology that brings both historical and other like disciplines together so that the views of the subaltern Kukis come to the fore in explaining the subject. The general argument is that the Kukis rose up in arms against the constituted authority 'on their own, that is, independently of the elite'. Instead of being incited from outside, the chapters look at the way the Kukis understood their situation based on their own consciousness under colonial regime. In this respect, the war was seen as a conscious, pre-meditated, and deliberate action against the shared grievances under the colonial state and directed towards a specific local objective of freeing their territory from such rule. Overall, the volume represents what Mayaram has called the 'counter-perspectives from the margin' (Mayaram 2003). They insisted on reading the

colonial sources, as Guha suggested, 'against the grain' to the elitist 'body of evidence' which took the form of what Sahid Amin has
called 'to interrogate the interrogators' (Guha 1994: 336–371; Guha
1983: chap. 1; Amin 1995: 'Prologue'). The obvious method they
employed to combat colonial or archival bias was what Guha has
called 'to summon folklore, oral as well as written, to the historian's aid' (Guha 1983: 14). Upon this corpus of written materials,
the chapters also touch upon a profound position of the Kukis and
in many cases by 'summoning folklores' or by taking a 'historical
fieldwork' to excavate historical facts from the 'bearers of history'.
In so doing, the chapters represent an in-depth understanding of the
subject quite different from the existing literature. A brief discussion
of the existing literature on the Anglo-Kuki War and its broader connection with the wider world and the First World War is given in the
following sections.

Writing on the Anglo-Kuki War

Some serious work has been produced on the subject, although they
are relatively little known in the wider scholarship. Thematically, they
are however mostly concerned with conventional themes like cause,
course and consequence. While some of these studies are coloured by
'nationalist' sentiments, others remain clouded by colonial percep-
tions of the war in their treatment. An exception to these was an in-
depth analysis given by some scholars like Gautam Bhadra and Lien
Sakhong (both discussed on the cause of war). Bhadra explains that
the colonial policy of sedentarisation was central to the dislocation of
Kuki polity, economy and social structure, which largely depended on
their freedom of migration. Migration not only provided them fresh
soil for the *jhum* economy but had also been 'the political safety-valve'
through which the custom left scope for their own expressions of
grievances and thus stabilised the workings of the chieftainship institution. Whenever the chief becomes unpopular, people could freely
move to another village or set up a village of their own so that such
migration immediately evaporated their sense of protest against the
office of chieftains. Thus, the bar against migration and formation of
the new villages not only 'hampered' the Kuki mode of production,
but it also 'destroyed' the 'safety valve' of their political organisation
(Bhadra 1975: 10–56). Therefore, the Kuki's opposition to colonialism was laid in a deep-seated grievance against the colonial policy of
sedenterisation programme, which had charged six rupees against the
usual three rupees if any village was below 20 houses.

In his study on *Lai Ral* (Haka uprising), Lien Sakhong locates the cause of what he called 'Anglo-Chin War 1917–1919' to their fear of death in going too far from home (France). He laid this fear deep into their cultural worldview of crossing the boundary of their village (*khua-hrum*): 'our Khua-hrum cannot protect us in a foreign country'. The idea of the fading power of their village gods over individuals beyond their *khua-hrum* was, to him, central to their opposition to labour recruitment for France. For this reason, they said that 'they would commit suicide rather than go' to France (Sakhong 2003: 154–175). Ranju Bezbaruah has also shown how the Anglo-Kuki War has also been caused by their fear of death, the rumours circulated by the Manipuri *lambus* (Bezbaruah 2010: 165–175). However, he could not give any cultural explanation as to why the Kukis feared death in France while they were willing to die at home fighting the British. This crucial point will be explained by Ningmuanching in her chapter in this volume.

The colonial discourse on the war had been taken for granted in general and a much less critical tool was employed to find out the truth, just as the Kuki views on the war have been either left out completely or taken with hesitation. Asok Kumar Ray, for instance, provides a chapter of this war, but his overall analysis was purely based on colonial presumptions of the war. He gives four causes of the rising: labour recruitment, corrupt *lambus*, customary payment to hillmen on *pothang* or foreign service and house-tax (Ray 1990: 63–85). Similarly, John Parratt also felt that there were some genuine grievances behind the rising besides the commonly found labour recruitment. Of these, one serious cause of grievance was the emergence of *lambus* in hill politics. The emerging influence of hill *lambus* as hill advisors and administrators, who were often open to bribery, gradually demeaned the authority of Kuki chiefs and hence caused considerable resentment (Parratt 2005: 43).

S.M.A.W. Chishti also gives the immediate cause of the war with the labour recruitment without giving any explanation on why the Kukis had to oppose labour for France while they never oppose such recruitment earlier (Chishti 2004). Besides, his objective of discolouring the hard show given by the Kukis against colonialism is clear by selecting some instances where the colonial accounts put them as 'raids on friendly villages'. By completely denying any mention of the two massive operations launched by the British for two consecutive winter seasons and the various fierce resistances given by the Kukis in different parts of the hills, his idea of reducing the Anglo-Kuki War to an act of what he called 'terrorism' is incomplete. Such a writing, driving on the malicious sentiments of present ethnic relations, was not only in bad taste but was completely unhistorical.

A good number of writings also slowly appeared from among the Kukis (Haokip 1984; Gangte 1993; Haokip 1998). While some plainly took the colonial view to explain the subject, some works clearly came out of such hostages only to be engulfed with a present romance with the anti-colonial movement and nationalism. Explanations from Kuki points of view have been coming up slowly; there are a few unpublished theses at different universities (Kipgen 2005; Haokip 2011). While few of these works will appear in this volume, one interesting work was done by a non-academic with a strong, empirical approach. P.S. Haokip brought to light much of the oral versions of the rising by the Kukis. He maintains that the Anglo-Kuki War was fought against the intrusion of colonialism in what he called *'Zale'n-gam'* ('the land of freedom'). Some of the important war conclaves and episodic battles fought by the Kukis have also been discussed in detail (Haokip 2008: 141–269). This is, so far, the most detailed discussion on the Anglo-Kuki War based on both colonial and local accounts. However, while the projection is well understood, it can also be said that the work mainly concerns the political character of the rising, whereas other aspects of the war are given little attention. Overall, the existing literature on the Anglo-Kuki War drew up many crucial points, leaving some unanswered, and drew on some important questions that formed the foundation of the chapters in this volume. Yet, they discuss this frontier event in an isolated and unconnected way that the importance of it hardly becomes significant to scholars. This volume intends to undo this as much as possible. Three points are summarised here.

On the question of 'small war' or counterinsurgency (COIN)

We have a rich corpus of literature on colonial counterinsurgency 'theory and practices'.[11] Thus, when a regular army engaged with irregular forces, it was not treated as conventional war but described to be 'small war' or 'little war' or 'insurgency'. Across the globe, regular state forces were consistently engaged with irregular forces, ranging from the fluid tribal rebellion to more organised 'communist insurgents'. The core issue in this scholarship was the place of strategy, tactics and violence. As the objective of 'small war' was to restore 'law and order', the question of violence was often relegated to the background. By treating 'small war' outside the 'conventional war' and hence outside the laws of 'civilised warfare', the former is said to be governed by the doctrine of 'minimum force' aimed at winning the 'hearts and minds' of the people. Thus, we have the dominant narrative of COIN that offered a 'humane' and 'civilised' stance on warfare, whose aim is peace and stability in the insurgency affected region.

What was often considered unimportant, and in most cases taken for granted, in the debate was the question of 'moral effect' and its alter ego: violence. What emerged from the various COIN operations around the world was that the combination of 'minimum force' and 'moral effect' doctrines eventually displaced and defeated the very objective of winning 'peace' and the 'hearts and minds' of the people. Some theorists even granted importance to a 'moral effect' doctrine that calls for violence to end the insurgency. Callwell, for instance, insisted that 'moral effect is often far more important than material success', and COIN operations may be 'limited to committing havoc which the laws of regular warfare do not sanction'. Thus, he felt that 'the regular troops are *forced to resort* to cattle lifting and village burning and that the war assumes an aspect which may shock the humanitarian' (Callwell 1906: 42). Martin van Creveld approved actions like the 'Hama Massacre' of 1982 and advised the government that 'refusing to apply necessary cruelty' when needed 'is a betrayal of the people', and when it decided to strike 'it is better to kill too many than not enough' (van Creveld 2008). Everywhere, we see that the 'moral effect' doctrine, rather than 'minimum force', dominated colonial COIN operations. Be it the 'razzia' in French Algeria, the 'butcher and bolt' in the northwest frontier of India, the 'blockhouse' or 'cordoning and raking' in South Africa and elsewhere, and so on, were the result of the'moral effect' doctrine that involved so much of violence. Violence was so taken for granted in colonial COIN operations that it became the 'natural order'. This also amounts to racial order. Thomas Mockaitis rightly contended that even when the 'colonials were subjected to excessive force Victorian racial attitudes insured that there was likely to be little outcry over the brutalisation of non-Europeans' (Mockaitis 1990: 17).

If the Victorian racial attitude towards the Orients was unkind, of which humanitarians always accused them of being 'inhuman' and 'barbaric', the case with the 'savage' tribal people was even more unsympathetic. The case of the 'North-East Frontier of India', is instructive. Since the British occupation of Bengal (1765) and Assam (1826), one witnessed a series of 'military expeditions' into the surrounding hills, sometimes annually. The objective of these expeditions was to 'punish' the hillmen who had created trouble – termed savage 'raid' – in the 'civilised' plain. These 'punitive measures', as they were officially known, followed that the only effective form of punishment was to burn down their villages and destroy their properties, particularly their grains. These measures were considered a 'barbarously expedient' form of punishment, as there was no other way to punish the recalcitrant hillmen, they being untraceable in the wildness of the highland jungles. Hence, to the British government of this eastern region, the 'systematic' burning of villages and the wholesale destruction of properties has become the usual form of 'minimum force' doctrine. Militarily, such rapid escalation over the highland destroyed their properties or lives, and then after withdrawing again in the plain, was normally termed as 'mobile/flying columns' or the 'butcher and bolt' tactics. The idea was, to recall Callwell's famous line: 'If the enemy cannot be touched in his patriotism or his honour, he can be touched through his pocket' (Callwell 1906: 40). Although such policy was often called 'successful', the truth is that such a 'barbarously expedient' form of punishment, instead of stopping 'raids', enhanced them and thus transformed the peaceful frontier into the geography of violence. Only permanent occupation of the hills ended the tribal war of 'raid'.

The highland region of Northeast India was never completely occupied throughout the colonial period; Northeast Frontier Area/Agency (NEFA, today Arunachal Pradesh state of India) and the Tuensang Area of Naga Hills continued to remain 'unadministered'. Until the Anglo-Kuki War 1917–1919, the hills of Manipur state, Thaungdut state and Somra Tract, remain outside the purview of direct colonial administration. The hillmen of Manipur and Thaungdut states, besides paying house-tax and impressed labour, were left to themselves in terms of administration and so on. Somra Tract falls under 'unadministered area'. The Kukis were the dominant tribe in all three hills. If the discontented hearts often burst out into open 'rebellion', they were rapidly rubbed off by force of arms. Already in 1910, a military operation was conducted against the Kukis of the Aishan area in northeastern Manipur, known as 'Aishan rebellion' under the leadership of Chengjapao, chief of Aishan. Similarly, in 1911–1912 we have the much publicised Abor Expedition in NEFA. In 1915, another major military expedition was carried out against the Kachins of Kachin Hills.

The Anglo-Kuki War 1917–1919 was the last major COIN operation in eastern India and, as noted, was 'the most formidable' and 'largest series of military operations'. What makes this COIN operation different from the earlier military operations was not only its arduousness and extent in time (two years) and space (about 7000 sq. miles), but more importantly the military strategy adopted to quell the rising. We have noted that the operations went on for two consecutive winter seasons, hence two broad phases of operations with different tactics. In the first phase, we will see that the military tactic employed was the usual one in the region, the 'flying' or 'mobile columns' which come within the infamous 'butcher and bolt' type. Thus, a rapid mobile military column will go around the 'rebel area' and commit 'systematic' destruction of villages, properties and all sources of livelihood. The idea was to enforce 'submission' by cutting out food supplies and settlements. When such usual tactics failed them, a new tactic was introduced in the second phase.

There was no exact equivalent to the tactic employed elsewhere, but it relates closely to the 'blockhouse' tactic employed in Boer War 1899–1902, or the French system of 'cordoning and racking' tactics. Officially known as 'area' or 'section' systems in Assam, it draws largely from the tactical principle laid down by the sixteenth-century military theorist Lazare Hoche for a counter-guerilla operation. T. Haokip (chap. 3) and J. Guite (chap. 1) in this volume will give the details of this tactic. It involved massive amounts of violence and destruction, which would shock humanitarians. Systematic destruction of 'livestock', driving the civilians implicated to be helping the insurgents to 'concentration camps' and punishing the general Kuki population with communal penal labour seems an addition to the general tactical principle. The idea of 'chastising' the whole community or 'collective punishment' was a new addition to the general policy of pacification in the region.

Overall, the 'moral effect' doctrine was so freely used across the colonies that the question of violence had hardly become a question. Yet, violence as a 'natural order' in the colonial COIN operations is clearly visible in all cases; the case of the Kuki rising is just a tip of the colonial violence in it 'hideous nakedness'. In fact, some scholars and humanitarians kept challenging the legitimising idea of 'minimum force', the 'hearts and minds' principle and the claim of 'humanism' in all 'small wars'. For instance, *The Advocate of Peace* (1901) regarded the colonial COIN measures in the colonies as an act of 'civilised barbarism and savagery'.[12] David French, in his recent work, also argues that British justification of their actions under 'minimum force' was just to hide the use of naked force behind a carefully constructed veneer of legality. In reality, they commonly used wholesale coercion, including cordon and search operations, mass detention without trial, forcible population resettlement and the creation of free-fire zones to intimidate and lock-down the civilian population. The British COIN campaigns were generally nasty to the people (French 2011). Similarly, Douglas

Porch also challenges the contemporary mythologising of COIN as a 'humane' way of war and argues that the 'hearts and minds' doctrine has never achieved a lasting peace and stability but shattered and divided societies and unsettled civil-military relations (Porch 2013). This is the argument clearly visible in the context of the Anglo-Kuki War 1917–1919 as well. We will see that the rising was brutally suppressed with 'inhuman' colonial COIN strategies, and the 'restoration' process failed to bring real peace in the hills, and discontentment once again burst out during the Second World War, a subject addressed in S. Kipgen's essay (chap. 11).

On the question of leadership and tactics of Kuki war

In the colonial civilisational narrative, all other forces are yet-to-be-modern except the modern western imperial army. In this line of thinking, the tribal forces were the least organised forces, lacking leadership and the forces being fluid, defused and erratic. Hence, their 'war' never constituted a 'war' but was dubbed as a 'raid' or 'rebellion' and at most 'guerilla/irregular war'. It was true that the tribal Kukis did not developed an organised and 'regular' army just as they did not procure sophisticated modern weapons like the British forces. However, to say that they lacked organisation, leadership, command and discipline is only to swallow the dominant civilisational narrative. The truth is that Kuki forces during the rising were scattered across the hills in small groups, yet they were connected to each other through their respective regional or area central commands. Each of these areas, under the command of the clan head (*pipa*), was in turn connected to each other by a clan network. Thus, for instance, all the Haokip clan members who fought in different areas were first connected to their sub-clan *pipa* in that area, and in turn, connected to their clan *pipa* at Chassad on a wider scale. The organising principle across the hills was therefore the clan network and relationship. Thus, each and every individual Kuki was connected by a clan network through which his/her loyalty and discipline was oriented towards the clan head. Leadership was therefore intrinsic to the clan. D. Letkhojam Haokip's chapter (chap. 4) in this volume will show this formation clearly. N. Kipgen (chap. 8) traces the role of the Kuki traditional institution *Som-Inn* (bachelor's dormitory) in shaping the spirit of unity, courage and discipline among the Kuki men, which played a crucial role in the rising. We will come back to this point shortly. The question of leadership draws attention here.

One serious confusion in the existing literature on the Anglo-Kuki War is concerned with leadership. In most historical scholarship on war and movement, one central point of the discourse was who led the war or movement. We develop certain notions that there cannot be a war without a leader. This is what may be understood as the pyramid notion of war and movement, where there is one leader at the top and one central command under his control. It is true that all wars or movements require leadership for organisation and strength, but it hardly crosses the mind that there can also be *leaders* in such wars/movements, not only *a leader*. Thus, in many wars and movements fought around the world in history, there were always leaders on equal footing commanding different command centres. This becomes particularly significant when we deal with tribal warfare. The pyramid notion of war often leads certain scholars to distortion by declaring a certain person as the one leader of the Kuki war when he was not in reality. The Anglo-Kuki War had also been often subject to this notion of war in the existing literature.

One disturbing case among the Kuki students in recent time was that certain study material for competitive examinations put Jadonang as the *leader* of the Anglo-Kuki War. The use of this name was doubly mistaken. First, giving a leader to a war, which has not one but many leaders, is a complete displacement of facts. Second, Jadonang was a Kabui Naga, who led the 'Kabui Raj' movement in Manipur in the 1930s and was completely unrelated to the Anglo-Kuki War. The truth about Kuki war, and for that matter most tribal warfare to the scale one witnessed in the case of the Anglo-Kuki War, is that the war was fought on an egalitarian line – connected, organised and sustained by a clan dynamic and kinship relationship – not on a central leader. Since many clans of the Kukis fought together, each clan member saw each clan head (*pipa*) as their leader. Thus, in each area the *pipa* of the clan that dominated the area emerged as the leader not only over his clan members but also eventually assumed the leadership to all other clan members in that area. He was therefore the leader of that area geographically and politically; his decision was final in that area unless his fellow chieftains in the area disagreed with him.

Therefore, the leader of the war in the eastern hills was Pache, the chief of Chassad, because he was the most powerful chief and *pipa* of the Haokip clan who dominated that area. As the *pipa* of all the Haokip sub-clans, he was also the head of all the Haokip clans in other parts of the hills, but was not necessarily the leader of all in practice. Thus, Ngulbul, chief of Longya, as the *pipa* of the Mangvum Haokip sub-clan, who dominated the southeastern hills, was the leader of that area under which all the other Kuki clans also came.[13] This was also the case with the Ukha chief (Semchung), the Henglep chief (Pakang) and the Laiyang chief (Tintong) in their respective areas, although they all belonged to Haokip. Jampi chief Khutinthang was also the leader of the Jampi area as the *pipa* of Sitlhou clan who dominated that area and under which all other Kuki clans also fought together. It was also the case with Chengjapao, chief of Aishan, who was the leader of the northeastern hills, and Longjachin, chief of Behiang, in the southern hills. In this way, many leaders emerged in the Anglo-Kuki War, and they all fought in their respective areas and occasionally helped each other when needed. They were not bound together by a single leader and a common central command, as we are often shown with other warfare. They all fought together for clan and country based on an agreement and vow taken at their traditional war council. The Kuki adage *'phung ngailut jalla chang tumbu poh'* (lit. 'carrying paddy-load for the sake of clan') becomes the governing principle in the war.

Thus, what appeared to be fluid and disorganised forces were inherently well connected and deeply organised. The organising principle was, as noted, the dynamic of the clan in which each individual was connected and disciplined to the minutest detail not under a central leadership and command but by centrally ordained clan heads who decided to stand together at the grand Chiefs-in-Council (*upa* or *pipa* council). This aspect is discussed in detail by Sonthang Haokip (chap. 6). We will see that, before any war can take place, the various principal chiefs consulted each other and then came together in a grand Chiefs-in-Council (officially, 'Assembly of Chiefs') which acted as the customary War Council/Conclave. Kukis normally resorted to war councils only when they were preparing for a major war, and the size of this council depended on the strength of the enemy and the area to be covered. This council was democratic in nature, where all the important chiefs came together on equal footing and freely deliberated and decided on issues. Although the elder clan member was normally given the final say in all matters by the younger clan, the former hardly acted as the king or president of the clan. Resolution was normally taken on majority opinion, and if certain chiefs disagreed with it, he has the choice to opt out. Once a common decision was reached and the leadership for each area agreed upon, the meeting was customarily solemnised by a sacred ceremony called *sathin-salung-neh* ('feasting on the liver and heart of animal killed for the occasion'). This ceremony bound all the partakers together with a bond that could not be broken unilaterally. Such war councils and the resolutions taken formed the bedrock of the war, its connection and its central command. Under the circumstances, one can only talk about the *leaders*, instead of a *leader*. As the *pipa* of the Thadou-Kuki clans, Chengjapao chief of Aishan assumed the overall leadership role and called himself the 'King of Kuki'. By taking clan precedent, the British government also recognised this and extended his confinement at Sadiya for one more year. This clan connection among them can be gleaned from the statement of Haonek Kuki, chief of Nabil:

> I am Lunkhel clan. Our *piba* is Tinthong. His *piba* is Hlupao of Hinglep. His *piba* is Pachei of Chassad. Hlupao is *piba* of all the Songthat clan. Pachei's *piba* is Khuthinthang of Jampi. Khuthinthang's *piba* is Chengjapao of Aishan.[14]

This is the line in which clan network and relationship flows, especially in decision-making process on major issue that concerns the whole community such as the war now fought. Based on this clan precedent, the British were somehow able to form the conclusion that Chengjapao was the leader of the Anglo-Kuki War. This is fine by the Kukis, to the extent that there was at least one recognised leader of the war. Yet, on practical ground, it should be remembered that the Anglo-Kuki War was not fought on this pyramidical notion of organisation.

While clan precedent was undoubtedly an important factor in the decision-making process, the actual control of warfare was co-opted to an immediate clan *pipa* of each clan in different areas. Thus, Chengjapao was no doubt the *pipa* of all, but he did not directly control the areas. Factoring the harsh geography and their capability to control over the area, power to carry out the war was distributed equally to multiple areas under different leadership. With a provision to circulate warriors from one area to another, there was therefore no paramount central command. Thus, each of the war leaders in their respective areas was not under the control of the other leader. While they all had to fight simultaneously, they were independent from each other in terms of command and control. They all fought separately until they could withstand the heat of colonial military forces. This was the strategy adopted at the War Council. Thus, the 'surrender' of one leader did not cause the surrender of another or the collapse of the whole war. For instance, the surrender of Chengjapao on 23 August 1918 and Khutinthang on 24 September 1918 did not lead to the end of the rising, which went on until March 1919. Pache chief of Chassad surrendered on 5 March 1919, but Ngulkhukhai, his trusted lieutenant, continued to lead the rising in Somra Tract until he also surrendered on 15 March 1919. This make Kuki war, and for that matter the tribal warfare, most difficult to control and perhaps different from other wars based on central leadership. This reinforced the idea of a fluid regime, but it was to be sure not unorganised and undisciplined or erratic.

The idea that the 'hit and run' or 'guerilla warfare' tactic of the Kukis, or for that matter all other guerilla warfare, as 'primitive', is therefore only to swallow the colonial civilisational narrative on 'war'. Despite the advancement of military technology and war tactics, guerilla tactics continue to remain popular among many state and non-state elements fighting regular forces across the globe. The question is why 'guerilla' tactic remains an evergreen method for 'irregular' forces? The efficacy of guerilla warfare to irregular forces is a familiar case. To the tribal Kukis, this choice was certainly a new tactic, not purely borrowed from outside but a synthesis of old and new. It was certainly not the old tactics of 'rushing' and 'surprise', but the idea had a strong presence in the present 'guerilla' warfare. There was some form of guerilla in the traditional tactic of ambushing the invaders on the way, which found a strong visibility in the new 'hit and run' tactic. Kukis normally choose this tactic in a defensive war against a powerful enemy. The fact that the mighty British forces were not beatable by any offensive war makes guerilla tactics most attractive to the Kukis. The role of few Assam Rifle return Kukis like Enjakhup, one of the tactical leader of the war, is apparent in the choice of such tactic.

Yet, the fact that they also combined the 'guerilla' tactic with fortification of their villages and construction of a series of stockades along the routes, combined with their traditional stone traps, *panjies* and so on, makes their war unique. This is visible in the context of the weapons used, ranging from Western-made firearms (flintlock, muskets, etc), local 'leather cannons' (*pumpi*), bows & arrows, etc. The use of traditional methods of communication to send out different messages across the hills such as *sajam* ('piece of meat'), *thingkho-le-malchapom* ('king chilli bound with burnt wood'), swords, bullets, etc. are also significant. D.L. Haokip (chap. 4) examines these aspects of Kuki war tactics in detail and argues that Kukis chose defensive tactics, waiting for the enemy in their hill stockades and fortresses, harassing them on the way and targeting the British officers leading the march. The difficulties in dealing with such tactics and their demoralising effect on the regular troops were reported from various field diaries. Thus, while the tactic saved casualties on both sides, the guerilla tactic shows its efficacy in dealing with a powerful enemy. The Kukis did not win, but their tactics remain valid to this day among the various insurgent groups in the region. The harsh geography, such as the Northeast mountain highland, best suits the tactic, and its apparent fluid formation of the forces was at its best. Such choice also made the Kukis receptive to a new idea of war available around them.

'A humble part of the Great War'

Another important point that draws attention in the existing literature is the idea that the Anglo-Kuki War was an isolated, disconnected and unimportant frontier tribal 'uprising' like any other 'rebellions'. Yet, the connection this war has at the time and the way it was taken seriously by the colonial state is testimony of the war being an important event. Three factors draw our attention in this respect. First, this war was fought in connection with the larger world order, being influenced from the west and east, and also from the valley of Manipur and other hill tribes. Second, the Indian nationalists had well recognised it as one important event; lack of information made the event go unnoticed. Third, and more importantly, the Anglo-Kuki War was directly connected to the First World War, partly, because it has been incited by the labour recruitment in the region for the war, and partly, the military operations to suppress the rising was considered to be part of the war and hence persons connected to the operations were awarded the two war medals. We will briefly discuss the three connections it had.

In May 1918, when a military column was assembling at Tamu (Burma) before breaking up after the first phase of operations against the Kukis, the Medical Officer, going through the sepoys' huts, found some Sikh soldiers tearing papers which they said 'they would not want anymore'. The Officer looked at the papers and discovered the photos of 'one or two white men' which Shakespear said was 'obviously Germans, one being in uniform'. On the photo, he said, it was written, in 'Hindustani' – 'If you fall into the rebels hands show these and they will not harm you'. The sepoys said that when they leave Bhamo (a frontier town of Burma with China) for the Kuki operations 'a sahib had given them these papers' (Shakespear 1929: 236). At the outbreak of 'Kuki rebellion', intelligence was also received that emissaries from Bengal revolutionaries have a hand on the Kuki rising, but no clear discovery was made if strict surveillance was kept to intercept such influence in due course (Shakespear 1929: 210). Col. L.W. Shakespear, the DIG, Assam Rifles, was deeply involved in the suppression of the Kuki rising throughout the operations. He had become the official historian of Assam Rifles later. To both these evidences, he wrote:

> Allusion has been made earlier to the belief that the [Kuki] rebellion had been still further fomented by emissaries from Bengal seditionists, but any idea that the hand of the Hun [Chinese] could possibly have been in it occurred to none.
>
> (Shakespear 1929: 236)

Surely, nobody knows for sure the wider networks and connection the Kukis had created in their 'war against the King-Emperor' and in fact, little expectation was given to them. It is also difficult to reconstruct from oral sources of the Kukis, unlike those from the Second World War.

Yet, seen from the situation across the colonial world, during the First World War, where information about the war reached all the corners of the earth, certainly the people of this frontier knew the name of the Germans as well. We have information from different parts of the hills that even the sleepy hill villages have been thirsty of information about the war. The news of the War have been asked, told and circulated in different formats till it stopped at the corner of the earth. The news they received were dominated by the strange imagery of the weapons of destructions used in the War such as submarine, bombers, tanks, poison gases, cannons and artillery, etc. which have been understood in different registers.[15] The news of these deadly weapons eventually translated into the idea of death. Thus, when labour recruitment started, most hillmen were initially unwilling to send men because the idea of death was so pronounced, and they preferred to die at home. It was through such formats that Germans were also known to them, as the archrival of the British Empire. It was therefore expected that they developed some feelings about the Germans, as enemy, friend or neither. In this context, the response of Haka Chins to British officers is instructive. Laura Carson recorded that: 'They said that their people absolutely refused to go to France; that they said they had no quarrel with Germany and why should they go and fight the Germans? They said they would commit suicide rather than go'. This was the line of thinking the Kukis of Manipur also had when they told the political agent in Manipur that 'they feared to go so far from their homes and that if they had to die they preferred to die in their own country and would be prepared to meet force with force'.[16] It was within this line of assumption that the Kukis support of the Germans and their war against the British should be located.

It was surprising to note that 1,158 guns were confiscated from the Kukis after the suppression of the rising.[17] This is surprising because between 1907 and 1917, colonial authority had already confiscated 1,195 guns from the Kukis.[18] Where have they got all these guns? We have some information that certain Mawson from the Chin Hills had supplied guns to the Kukis during the war.[19] If the information of their connection with the eastern (Chinese) and western (Bengal) worlds was correct, it was also possible that the Kukis got supplies from these areas. Besides, one is also surprised to find that the Kukis were able to offer large amounts of money as a term of surrender (Pache, for instance offered Rs. 3000/-) or able to pay their house-tax or war indemnity after the war, even after their whole properties were destroyed during the war.[20] Where did all this money and guns come from? Nobody knows, and it may perhaps remain a mystery.

If the influence of the wider world, especially from the Bengal revolutionaries, is not clearly definable in the Kuki war, the latter was well recognised as one powerful anti-colonial movement by Indian nationalists. The operations against the Kukis had incited furor among Indian nationalists, especially in the Home Rule Movement group. Its mouthpiece, the *New India*, for instance, makes a frontal attack on the British Empire for its double standard on 'war' and 'civilisation'. It considered the action against the Kuki hillmen 'barbaric', revealing the 'brute force' of colonialism 'in all its hideous nakedness'. It drew similarities to the 'tragic inhumanity' committed by the 'agents of the British Nation' in India on the Kukis to that of what the Germans had done in France and Belgium. All 'civilised' nations, it urged, should condemn the brutality and appealed the Viceroy and the Secretary of State to 'order an immediate cessation of the brutality' and to institute 'a searching enquiry to find out who are actually responsible for initiating them'.[21] Another London based newspaper called '*India*', criticised British government for their actions. It argued that instead of 'endeavouring to allay their [Kuki] fears and suspicions', government used force in haste. It ridiculed the government idea of 'pacification' through burning of villages and properties and proclaiming such proceedings as 'satisfactory'. 'Satisfactory' to whom?' it bluntly questioned.[22] The sharp reaction from Indian nationalists however led to screening the 'tragic inhumanity' from press after its first appearance. Their spirit of freedom, if not broken at heart, had to be brutally suppressed without being known to the world.

Closer to home, from the valley of Manipur, however, a connection was clearly noticeable. Seeing the boiling political situation in the hills, a Manipuri revolutionary, Chingakhamba Sana Chaoba (whose world of munificent spirituality has very soon attained him a millenarian reputaion among the large number of hillmen and valley population), took the wind of dissent to revive the Manipur *gaddi* to its old strength, free from colonial control. He told the Kukis that 'the Kingdom of the British is coming about an end' and the Kukis should start fighting against the British from the hills and he, with his three companies of sepoys, will fight from the plain.[23] In fact, the Kukis had helped him in attacking the Manipur State Ithai toll station on 19 December 1919. The Manipuri revolutionaries were immediately arrested and suppressed, and its leader Sana Chaoba Singh was captured later in Burma by the Thaungdut Sawba and sent to Imphal jail. It was also reported that:

> The Kukis are in touch with some sections of the Manipuris themselves, and that certain villages of Lois . . . have contributed rice and rice-beer to the Kukis. It seems also that some Kukis in the Naga Hills have been acting in concert with their brethren in Manipur, and the Kukis have even been trying to stir up the Nagas to join them in resistance.[24]

Certain valley traders have also been arrested for sacretly trading with the Kuki 'rebels'. Nothing further come from the valley population apart from what Chingakhamba had promised, but for a time the spelt of a religious man, of the invincibility to bullets, of his flying sword that could cuts people into pieces if they refuse to join the rising, and so on, seems to strike a magical note and a comforting sense among the Kukis.[25]

Besides, in this war against the King-Emperor, the Thadou-Kukis were not alone, as some studies would like to make it known.[26] Instead, we have evidence that shows that all the Kuki tribes were part of it. While it is true that some Thadou-Kukis had abstained from the war for some reason or another, many other Kuki tribes had also joined in the war. For instance, when he was at Sugunu, Higgins was informed that the Anals and Lamgangs of the southeastern hills were also supporting the Mangvum Kukis. He reported:

> My informant said that the Anals were supplying rice to the Kukis, but that with the exception of Torjang, Khubung Khulen & Khubung Khunow, which had joined the Kukis, the rest of the Anals were loyal at heart, though they did not dare to come and see me.[27]

An Anal man from this village was moving among the Anal villages and asked them to provide their guns and join the rising, 'saying they all were men of one country'.[28] The Koms of Langkhong Chongmang, in the western hills, had also demanded licenced guns from Kabui village, 'as they were about to make war with the sahib'. [29] The Vaipheis of Bongbal Kulen areas had also taken an active part during the war, and many of them had been arrested.

Perhaps the clear case that this war was not fought only by the Thadou-Kuki is best illustrated by the case of what was known as Manhlun-Manchong Kukis (today, the Zou tribe). They were in close alliance with the Ukha Kukis on the one hand and the Mombi Kukis on the other. For instance, it was reported that when the military column under Higgins attacked Ukha Kukis, the 'sons of Haokip chiefs in the vicinity of the operations were friendly, the rebels were being reinforced by a large body of Manhlun Manchung Kukis with many guns from near the Chin Hills border'.[30] There was also a large gathering of 'the Haokips and Manhlun Manchong Kuki association' at Tuidam (in Haobi ching) to decide on certain matters about their war against the British such as, besides other, the 'stringent measures' to be taken 'to breakdown the stockades of the British Government' during the rains and to punish the friendly villages.[31] In fact, the Zous were at the forefront of the war is illustrated by their attack on Nepali *gots* of Khuga Valley at the start of the rising, military columns going round their villages with systematic destructions, the fierce battles with them such as near Khailet (Gotenkot), Hengtam, etc., which went on till the Chiefs of Hengtam and Thirgodang were captured on 17 January 1919 in an encounter.[32]

The connection of the Anglo-Kuki War with their brethrens in Chin Hills was also clearly established. When war preparation was taken up among the Kukis in different parts of the hills, Higgins reported certain Kuki villages such as Mueltom and Tungjang [Tonjang] 'were endeavouring to stir up the northern Chin villages to join in the armed resistance of the Manipur Kuki'.[33] Reports were also received from Burma that 'a large force of Kukis' was gathering at the border areas on Manipur side, that rations were being collected in villages above the Kabaw valley, and that the Kukis of Manipur 'were in communication with the rebel Chins of Haka'. [34] The DC, Upper Chindwin also reported that:

> Sellers from Sandin Chin village Manipur side state word was given them by Kinki Chins to have 8,000 baskets paddy ready as about 8,000 Kukis with arms and equipments are coming shortly. . . . Kukis from Haka also told Chins on Tomu frontier to collect paddy as much as possible.[35]

It was also reported that the Kukis provided shelter to the refugees from Chin Hills, who were reluctant to send men for the Labour Corps. Cosgrave reported one small village near the Paldai stream 'built by some Kamhows who ran away from the Tiddim sub-division' so as to escape labour recruitment.[36] The Kukis also received large amount of firearms from the Chin Hills from a person called Mr. Mawson.[37]

Further south, with the the Hakas of Haka Subdivision, there were also evidences to show the connection. If direct assistance in terms of manpower sharing is not clear, one can draw the connection from circumstantial evidence. One may first ask why the Hakas took so long to come into open uprising, which broke out in November 1917. Like in Manipur, recruitment had started in Chins Hills as early as May 1917. The Teddim Chins had already supplied their share, the Falam Chins had also given theirs. Haka was supposed to be the last to do so. However, before any such recruitment could start, they broke out into open rebellion. The local officers were stunned because there was, unlike Manipur, no sign of trouble or agitation against government until it broke out. What could have, therefore, influenced their decision to go for a war at this point in time? Here, it is important to remember the situation in Manipur. In Manipur, the trouble was brewing against the labour drafts since the month of March 1917. The burning of Mombi (Lonpi) on 17 October 1917, however, changed the situation from peaceful negotiation to war-like preparation. We have information that emissaries were sent by the Kukis to different parts of the region – to Naga Hills, North Cachar Hills, Somra Tract and Chin Hills. It was during this time that the Kukis of Manipur 'were in communication with the rebel Chins of Haka'.[38] The Haka Chins eventually broke up (about the last week of November 1917) probably seeing the war-like preparation of their brethren in Manipur against the British government.

Perhaps the connection of the Anglo-Kuki War with the First World War is direct and visible. On the one hand, this uprising was ignited by the labour recruitment for the war. On the other, those who participated in the 'Kuki Operations' were awarded with the two war medals, the British War Medal 1914–1919 and Victory Medal, making it 'the humble part of the Great War'. If the Kuki rising was not known much to the general Indian public, it was well recognised among the colonial officialdom as 'the most formidable with which Assam has been faced for at least a generation' and 'the largest series of military operations conducted on this side of India' (Shakespear 1980: 224, 235–236).[39] The 'hard show' given by colonial military forces, described to be 'most difficult', disconcerting, thankless and

21

disagreeable jobs, was also highly commended by the Imperial government. Already during the first phase of operations, most of the field officers were insisting for the inclusion of these frontier operations as part of the Great war. W.A. Cosgrave, for instance, wrote that 'in consideration of the hard marching done by the men of the Assam Rifles in the various columns', and 'in view of the fact that a considerable numbers of sepoys have been killed or wounded', the GOI should give some money allowance on the analogy of *batta* and 'to sanction a medals for these operations'.[40] After the first phase of operations, the DIG, Burma Military Police and Lt. Col. Ffrench-Mullen also asked the government to recognise the Kuki operations as part of the war: 'It is hoped by those who participated in them that they may be considered worth of recognition as a *humble part of the Great War*'.[41]

After the Kuki rising was fully suppressed, many rewards were awarded to officers and other ranks – one C.I.E, one O.B.E, five Indian officers and nine riflemen the I.D.S.M, one Indian officer the King's Police Medal, several of them were promoted, and a numbers of 'Jangi Inams' were granted. The question of war medals was then taken up by the GOI with the British War Office which eventually accepted to include the Kuki Operations for both the British War Medal 1914–1919 and the Victory Medal. The matter of medals was also raised by some Parliamentarians like Sir C. Yate in 1921 and Sir A. Holbrook in 1923 in the British Parliament.[42] The latter was told by the War Office that 'the grant of the two Great War medals would seem to have been *the more favourable* alternative' for the Kuki Operations.[43] This decision ideally recognised the operations against the Kukis in the Northeast Frontier of India as one of the theatre of th First World War or the 'humble part of the Great War', as Ffrench-Mullen puts it (see Figure 1.1). Thus, all the ranks and files, including combatants, non-combatants, coolies, clerks, dhobis, sweepers, barbers, etc., who were fulltime employees, paid from military funds and came under the enemy 'fire zone' during the Kuki Operations were honoured with the two war medals.[44]

The chapters in this volume

Considering the weaknesses we have charted out in the existing literature as the starting point, this volume strives to come out with some more new insights on the subject under scrutiny with an interdisciplinary touch and with fresh materials. It is divided into five sections. The first section covers the conventional theme, such as the course of the war in chronological order, but with fresh materials from the

Figure 1.1 Form for medals (showing the Political Officer J.C. Higgins' claims for British War Medal and Victory Medal puts 'Manipur, India, Kuki Punitive Measures, December 1917 to May 1919' under the column 'theatres of war in which served with dates of service').[45]

perspective of the Kukis. The first chapter by Jangkhomang Guite deals with the progress of events during the Anglo-Kuki War, starting from March 1917 to the lives of the Kuki 'State prisoners' at Sadiya and Taungyi and the general conditions of Kuki population in the aftermath of the war. Most scholars have touched upon this subject in the past, but no detailed discussion has been so far given in a systematic manner. From the Kuki perspective, the course of the war is seen from three broad phases – period of passive resistance (March 1917 to October 1917), active resistance period (October 1917 to April 1919) and the period of Kuki tribulation (May 1919 onward). The active war period is also divided into five phases – war preparation period (October to December 1917), the first phase of the war (December 1917 to April 1918), the period of punishing the 'friendly villages' (April to July 1918), the second phase of negotiation (August to November 1918) and the second phase of active warfare (November 1918 to April 1919). With fresh historical materials and different insight on the course of the war, this chapter will serve as the background information for the other chapters in the volume. Pum Khan Pau discusses separately the case of the same war fought in the Chin Hills in his chapter on 'Haka uprising'. The two will form a complete picture of the Anglo-Kuki War 1917–1919 and the extent of its geography. We have already touched on the connection between the two areas, and it makes sense to bring the two together into one larger war fought at the time.

The second section concerns the tactics, technology and symbols used by the British and the Kukis. Thongkholal Haokip's chapter discusses the various tactics employed by the British military forces to quell the Kuki war. Although the two phases of military operations were equally 'barbaric' in character, the methods employed were different. In the first phase of operation, the method employed was variously known as 'flying' or 'mobile' military columns that moved around the 'rebel' areas and committed wanton destruction to the Kukis by burning their villages to the ground, destroying all their properties, foodstuffs and livestock. The idea was to compel the Kukis into submission. But when such method fail to bring any Kukis to submission as it used to be in all other cases of military expeditions in the region, a new method was eventually invented in the second phase. The method invented in the second phase of operation in practice amounts to the military occupation of the Kuki hills. The whole Kuki country was divided into six 'areas', each area was enclosed by a chain of military outposts and each area was provided with substantial numbers of flying columns whose duty was to hunt the Kukis from pillar to post, burn down their villages, destroy their properties, foods and livestock and frustrate cultivation and any attempt to rebuild their villages. Construction of roads as a pacifying agent, disarmament of the country and finally imposing a new administration were also the objectives of the operations. Besides, Haokip also discusses the modern weapons used by the military forces. In the first phase, the dominant weapons of destruction were Martini Henry rifles and a few 7 lb. mountain guns. In the second phase, the military forces were better equipped with .303 rifles, Lewis guns, stokes mortars and rifle grenades.

D. Letkhojam Haokip discusses Kuki war tactics, technology and symbols of war. He explains the way in which Kuki used 'guerilla' hit-and-run tactics to fight against the imperial military forces as the best method, and he shows the effectiveness of such tactics on their enemy. He also points out that the Kukis did not want to kill large numbers of their enemy, but they were committed to inflicting minimum casualties with maximum harassment in the rugged hills. Therefore, instead of meeting the military forces in their villages, they built a good numbers of 'stockades' in strategic points and through sniping harassed them. He points out that this was in keeping with their inferior technology (muzzle-loaders muskets, Kuki leather cannon, *panjies*, stone traps, etc.) against the more advanced weapons of the enemy. The Kukis did not defend their villages, although they erected village fortifications which were meant to preventa surprise attack. He also discusses the various traditional Kuki symbols of communication during war. Some of the important symbols for passing information and so on are *sajam* ('piece of flesh'), *thingkho-le-malchapom* ('smouldering wood with king chilli, etc. as their "fiery cross" '), beads, swords, bullets, gunpowder, etc. They were sent around the hills at different times during the war and had specific messages for the receiver.

The third section includes some completely fresh themes on the Anglo-Kuki War, based on some recent studies by young researchers. They discusses on subjects ranging from centrality of land and territoriality in the war, of the cultural notion of death, of being under oppressive control, and the role of traditional social and cultural institutions like the Kuki 'war conclaves' or 'chiefs-in-council', and the *som* (bachelor's dormitory) institution. David V. Zou sets out on the question of land rights and contestation over territory among the Kuki chiefs and locates the intervention of colonial state as one source of discontentment to certain chiefs. On the same question, he argues that while the whole Kuki population fought during the Anglo-Kuki War for the protection of their land and territory, in peace time such land become 'merely a romantic home of his or her ancestors, but not a piece of real property that can be validated in law'. Only an over-whelming sense of patriotism against 'White Imperialism' during the war, land was real to them as 'the land of my birth'. The chiefs contin-ued to hold such lands protected by the people from outsiders as their legal tenement never to be shared with the people. The strong mes-sage of the war is that the common people who had fought for their land as the land of their birth should have their due share of property rights over such land. Thus, when the Kuki masses fought against the colonial state in defence of their territory, they were not only fighting against the government but also against their chiefs, who controlled the land their ancestors had occupied over the ages and demanded such landholding rights which are yet to be given.

On the same notion of the war as a people's war against colonial-ism, Ningmuanching also contends that multiple regimes of oppres-sive systems under colonialism led to the outburst of Kuki war. She pointed out the general economic grievances of the hillmen, besides the declining authority of the chiefs, the infamous *pothang* (forced labour system) and general indebtedness in the aftermath of bamboo famine, as some major factors for the outbreak of the Anglo-Kuki War. She argues that their refusal to go to France was not only a spark, but it was also a serious one for the Kukis. She locates their refusal from the deep-seated cultural notion of death which make them com-pletely resolute not to go to France. She shows that dying in foreign land (like far away France) would deprive the Kukis not only the usual death ritual but to their much longed nether-land, the land of the death (*mithi-kho*) which demanded a proper death ritual. These are fresh insights into the causes of the Anglo-Kuki War, with large amounts of unexplored archival materials.

Sonthang Haokip studies an important part of the Kuki war, the 'war conclaves'. He explains why such a war conclave, commonly understood as the chiefs-in-council, was so important for the Kukis as their highest decision-making body on the question of war. No war to the scale witnessed during the Anglo-Kuki War or even smaller one cannot take place until it was resolved by the war council. He shows that this war council is a peculiar Kuki traditional institution for mak-ing decisions concerning, mobilising for and sustaining the war. An interesting aspect of this Kuki war conclave is that it was deliber-ated upon egalitarian principle, unlike the King's war council. All the prominent chiefs who participated in the war council expressed freely of their opinion, and the decision was taken on a majority view. If any chief chose to go against the majority opinion, he could do so. Decisions on such a war council was concluded and solemnised with a sacred ritual of bodily performance by feasting over the liver (*sathin*) and heart (*salung*) of the animal killed on the occasion. This ritual is called *sathin-salung-neh* or *hansa-neh* in Kukis, and the partakers are bound by an unbreakable vow on the decision taken. Thus, Kukis can declare war or start fighting the enemy only after such council and its associated ritual is performed. It was such war conclaves that gave the war unity in dimension and character over the vast territory. This very tradition show how the Kukis, in line with the modern notion of War Council, normally do war, and Haokip argues that instead of committing a 'savage warfare', they had traditionally practiced a form of 'civilised war'.

On the same line of projecting the important role played by traditional institutions and ideas, Ngamjahao Kipgen's chapter is concerned with the role of the traditional Kuki institution of *Som* (bachelor's dormitory) in organising and sustaining the Kuki war. If the chiefs decided and declared the war, the Kuki warriors fought it. In the absence of a regular standing army, as in the state and kingdom, one wonders how could the Kukis withstand against the well-armed and trained army. Kipgen shows how the principle of warfare and the *esprit de corps* has been imparted in the Kuki *som* comparable to the military line of training. Young boys who are supposed to stay in the *som* until they get married, were guided and supervised by senior supervisors there. He was trained not only in the art of warfare, such as in the use of weaponry and fighting tactics, but also in the principle of cooperation and unity. The idea of selflessness, discipline, responsibilities and duty towards their fellow men and their community (*tomngaina*) was one central principle that defined and governed the *son*. It was under such circumstances, Kipgen argues, that every Kuki men became a born fighter, a skilled craftsman and a selfless and dedicated patriot for the community. This is what Kipgen called the 'militariness' of the Kuki *som* institution that organised and sustained the Kuki war. Thus, in spite of the absence of a regular trained army, the Kukis could withstand the British military forces for almost two years of continuous active services.

The fourth section concerns the role of women in the war. The two chapters bring out the role played by the Kuki women in the Anglo-Kuki War. Besides noting the hardships caused to women by the war, both chapters came out with the burgeoning responsibilities that the women had to take up in the absence of their fellow men, who went for the battles or in prisons. Hoineilhing Sitlhou discusses the role played by the chiefs' wives after their husbands were kept in prison, such as in the administration of the village, besides other normal chores of the family, like attending domestic and cultivation works. Interesting aspects of women's lives after their husbands, sons or brothers were killed or transported are discussed from the women's narratives. On the same line, Hoipi Haokip and Arfina Haokip also discuss some interesting ways in which Kuki women joined the war. They called the women the 'invisible confederate' in the war, who were always beside their male folks, 'implicit rulers' who guided their young sons in the governance of the village and they discuss what they called the 'unspoken sufferings', especially when they were hiding in the jungles during the chilling winter. The two chapters are not only a new addition to our knowledge of the Kuki war, but also a new genre of writing in which the local narratives (which are normally excluded in the official archives) are taken on a serious line of scholarly argument. While the role of women is generally excluded in the colonial archives and also in the male dominated local narratives, works such as these are required intensive 'historical' fieldwork. The role of women in the Anglo-Kuki War certainly needs further investigation, but the little work we have so far from the two chapters are a pioneering endeavour that could provide further impetus to researchers in the future.

Section five mainly concerns the aftermath of the Anglo-Kuki War. Seikhohao Kipgen's chapter discusses the consequences of the war on Kuki society and the new regime of control that came about in the shape of military outposts and new administration in the hills. He notes the untold suffering caused by the communal penal labour system, the cultural sock that the war had caused to Kukis leading to massive conversion to Christianity and the dwindling power of their principal Kuki chieftains, leading to the political disintegration of the Kuki people.

Notes

1 In the following pages, we will use the term 'war' (*gal* in Kukis), which closely followed the way the Kukis had understood the 'rising' viz., *Sap gal, 'Thadou gal', 'Haokip gal', 'Zou gal'* and so on. The term 'Anglo-Kuki War', which some authors applied to the rising, is found most suitable as it conveyed the 'war' between the Kukis and the British colonial state, the fact accepted by most colonial authorities. The quotation 'war against the King-Emperor' was commonly used in the colonial records which considered the Kuki as 'enemy'. See for instance, J.E. Webster to Foreign Secy. to the Government of India, 6 December 1918, IOR/L/PS/10/724: 1917–1920, File No. 483/1919: 'Burma-Assam Frontier: Disturbances among Kuki Tribesmen in Manipur', British Library, London (BL), Asian and African Collections (formerly Oriental & India Office Collections) (hereafter AAC), Indian Office Records and Private Papers (hereafter IOR&PP)

2 The drafting of Col. Cole for the Great War was greatly lamented by Assam as his influence over the hillmen of Manipur was soon felt after he left Manipur. His wife tried very hard to bring in the Kukis to negotiation table but it was too late. Government intention of labour recruitment was purely 'voluntary' but the local officers in Manipur used threats to bring in the hillmen who were opposed to sending men for France and faltered out into open uprising. See, for instance, Manipur State Archives, Imphal (hereafter MSA), R-2/231/S-4: 'Tour Diary 1916–1918': *Tour Diary of J.C. Higins* (hereafter *Higgins Tour Diary*), 6 & 7 April 1917. See also Shakespear 1929: 236.

3 The *New India* newspaper, the mouthpiece of Home Rule Movement, for instance, had criticised the actions against the Kukis as the 'brute force in all its hideous nakedness', 'barbaric' and a 'tragic inhumanity', similar to what the Germans had committed in France and Belgium. See the extract of *New India*, 5 March 1917 in BL, AAC, IOR&PP, IOR/L/PS/10/724: 1917–1920, IOR, File No. 1880/1917: 'Burma-Assam Frontier'.

4 BL, AAC, IOR&PP, IOR/L/PS/10/724: 1917–1920, Mss. Eur E 325/13: 1920, 'Extract from the proceeding of the Chief Commissioner of Assam in Political Department' by A.W. Botham, 27 September 1920.

5 BL, AAC, IOR&PP, IOR/L/MIL/17/19/42: 1919: 'Despatch on the Operations Against the Kuki Tribes of Assam and Burma, November 1917 to March 1919', Brig-Gen. CEK Macquoid, General Officer Commanding Kuki Punitive Measures to Lieut-Gen. Sir Henry D.U. Keary, Commanding Burma Division, Controlling Kuki Punitive Measures, 27 April 1919, Appendix – I.

6 BL, AAC, IOR&PP, IOR/L/PS/10/724: 1917–1920, Mss. Eur E 325/13: 1920, 'Extract from the proceeding of the Chief Commissioner of Assam in Political Department' by A.W. Botham, 27 September 1920.

7 BL, AAC, IOR&PP, IOR/L/MIL/17/19/42: 1919: 'Despatch on the Operations Against the Kuki Tribes' Macquoid to Keary, 27 April 1919, Appendix – II & III. See also Shakespear 1929: 236–237.

8 National Archives of India, New Delhi (NAI), Foreign & Political Dept., 1919, Nos. 4–14. See also BL, AAC, IOR&PP, IOR/L/PS/10/724: 1917–1920, Mss. Eur E 325/13: 1920, 'Extract from the proceeding of the Chief Commissioner of Assam in Political Department' by A.W. Botham, 27 September 1920.

9 NAI, Foreign & Political Dept., 1919, Nos. 4–14.

10 While three hill subdivisions were established in Manipur (part of it was brought under direct administration by the Sadar subdivision at Imphal), Somra Tract along with part of Thangdaut state inhabited by Kukis were brought under Upper Chindwin District.

11 See Callwell (1906), Galula (1964), Thompson (1966), Mockaitis (1990), van Creveld (2008), Kicullen (2010), French (2011), Porch (2013). On India's Northeast see, for instance, Nag (2002), Waterman (2017).

12 'Civilised Barbarism and Savagery', *The Advocate of Peace (1894–1920)*, Vol. 63, No. 3 (MARCH 1901), pp. 51–53.

13 Ngulkhup, chief of Mombi (Lonpi), by his sheer strength practically looked after the affair of war and mobilisation in conjunction with the Longya chief.

14 Assam State Archives, Guwahati (hereafter ASA), Political Deptt., Political – A, February 1920, *Annexure B,* as cited in Bezbaruah 2010: 166.

15 Sainghinga, for instance, informed that once the news of the war reached his village 'it became the main subject of conversation in all gatherings', and all those who went to Lunglei brought the news of the war put up in the notice board of the shopkeepers by the missionary and reported back home. People told about 'the ship that went underwater to destroy ships' (submarine), the 'flying machine' (bombers) that dropped 'things that explode' (bombs), 'dirty smelling air' (poison gases), 'molten iron that can fight the enemy' (tanks), large cannons, etc. (see Pachuau and Schendel 2015: 189–190).

16 BL, AAC, IOR&PP, IOR/L/PS/10/724: 1917–1920, File No. P-383/1918: Webster to Secy GOI, 7 November 1917.

17 BL, AAC, IOR&PP, IOR/L/MIL/17/19/42: 1919: 'Despatch on the Operations Against the Kuki Tribes' Macquoid to Keary, 27 April 1919, Appendix – III.

18 MSA, *Manipur Administration Report, 1918–1919*, p. 2.

19 ASA, Political Department (PD), File No. M-33P of 1918, Political – A, December 1919, Nos. 1–144: 'Surrender and trial of the Kuki rebels in Manipur': *Meeting notes between CC, Cosgrave, Shakespear*, 5 September 1918 by Webster, Surrender, p. 11.

20 ASA, PD, File No. M-33P of 1918, Political – A, December 1919, Nos. 1–144; 'Surrender and trial', No. 11, Political Agent, Manipur (PA) to Chief Secretary to Chief Commissioner, Assam (CS), 11 July 1918.

21 See the extracts in BL, AAC, IOR&PP, IOR/L/PS/10/724: 1917–1920, File No. 1880/1918: 'Burma-Assam Frontier: Kuki disturbances in Manipur'.

22 See the extracts in BL, AAC, IOR&PP, IOR/L/PS/10/724: 1917–1920, File No. 1880/1918: 'Burma-Assam Frontier: Kuki disturbances in Manipur'.

23 The same memo also claimed that he organised a meeting of chiefs of Henglep, Mombi, Longya, Songphu, Nabil, Tingkai, Khabang, Phaibong, Jownai and Gowthang and asked to join the rebellion against the government. The tribunal also accused him of circulating bullets and other articles with the intention of stirring up armed rebellion. He sent dao to Tintong, Khutinthang, Ngulbul, Ngulkhup and Pache 'with an orders in each case to make war or the Government and to cut the telegraph wires'. See for detail the 'Memorandum' of Kuki political prisoners to Commissioner, Surma Valley and Hill Districts', as appended with the letter (and also this letter) of J.E. Webster to Foreign Secy. Government of India (GOI), 27 June 1919, BL, AAC, IOR&PP, IOR/L/PS/10/724: 1917–1920, File No. P-6933/1919.

24 BL, AAC, IOR&PP, IOR/L/PS/10/724: 1917–1920, File No. 3931/1919: Webster to Foreign Secy. GOI, 14 (15) December 1917.

25 Certain Kuki chiefs, such as Henglep, had even said that he joined the rising for fear of Chingakhamba Sena Chauba's warning.

26 See for instance Bhadra's paper where he was slightly hesitant to use the term Kuki. He explains that it was basically a Thadou war and hence he put 'Kuki (?)'. This is more of a problem now than ever before. On the one hand, there are people among the erstwhile 'Thadou' who do not want to recognise themselves as such now. On the other, there are also people among the erstwhile 'Kuki' who do not want to recognise themselves as such now. This volume, therefore, maintains those terminologies adopted by the colonial archives.

INTRODUCTION

27 ASA, GSC, Sl. 260, File No. M/64-P of 1918, Political – B, March 1919, Nos. 1–397 (Part-II), 'Progress of events', No. 134: *Tour Diary of JC Higgins, Pol Officer Southern Kuki (Shugun-Mombi) column No. I,* January – February 1918.

28 ASA, GSC, Sl. 260, File No. M/64-P of 1918, Political – B, March 1919, Nos. 1–397 (Part-II), 'Progress of events', No. 135: *Statement of Sugnu resthouse chaukidar (an Anal of Kareibung).*

29 MSA, R-2/230/S-4: *Higgins Tour Diary*, 1 November & 1 December 1917.

30 See BL, AAC, IOR&PP, IOR/L/PS/10/724: 1917–1920, Webster to Foreign Secy. GOI, 14 January 1918.

31 ASA, PD, File No. 9C/M-61P of 1918, Political – A, March 1919, Nos. 1–255: 'Arrangement', Cosgrave to Webster, 13 May 1918: *Statement of Waishon Kuki, Chief of Leirik, Lam No. 4.*

32 See MSA, R-2/230/S-4: *Higgins Tour Diary*, 1 January 1918, *Tour Diary of WA Cosgrave*, 18 March 1918; BL, AAC, IOR&PP, IOR/L/PS/10/724: 1917–1920, File No. 1783/1919: Webster to Foreign Secy. GOI, 13 February 1919.

33 *Documents of the Anglo-Kuki War 1917–1919*, edited by D.L.Haokip, 2017, chapter 3: J.C. Higgins to CS Assam, 24 November 1917 (hereafter *Documents of Anglo-Kuki War*).

34 MSA, R-2/230/S-4: *Higgins Tour Diary*, 7 December 1917.

35 BL, AAC, IOR&PP, IOR/L/PS/10/724: 1917–1920, Telegram from Chief Secy. Assam to Foreign Secy. GOI, 8 December 1917.

36 MSA, R-2/230/S-4: *Tour Diary of WA Cosgrave*, 16 March 1918.

37 ASA, PD, File No. M-33P of 1918, Political – A, December 1919, Nos. 1–144: 'Surrender and trial': *Meeting notes between CC, Cosgrave, Shakespear*, 5 September 1918 by Webster, Surrender, p. 11.

38 MSA, R-2/230/S-4: *Higgins Tour Diary*, 7 December 1917.

39 BL, AAC, IOR&PP, IOR/L/PS/10/724: 1917–1920, 'Extract from the Proceedings of the Chief Commissioner of Assam in the Political Department', 27 September 1920.

40 ASA, PD, File No. 9C/M-61P of 1918, Political – A, March 1919, Nos. 1–255: 'Arrangement': Cosgrave notes on 'Proposals for strengthening temporarily the Garrison in Manipur', 13 March 1918.

41 BL, AAC, IOR&PP, IOR/L/PS/10/724: 1917–1920, File No. P-2686/1919: Lt. Col. JLW Ffrench-Mullen, DIG, Burma Military Police to IGP Burma, 17 September 1918.

42 See 'Kuki Hills Operations (Medal)', Hansard, 1 June 1921, http://hansard.millbanksystems.com/written_answers/1921/jun/01/kukihills operationsmedal (accessed 5/6/2017) and 'Indian Frontier Operations (Medals)', Hansard, 30 April 1923. http://hansard.millbanksystems.com/commons/1923/apr/30/indianfrontieroperationsmedals (accessed 5/6/2017).

43 'Indian Frontier Operations (Medals)', Hansard, 30 April 1923. http://hansard.millbanksystems.com/commons/1923/apr/30/indianfrontier operationsmedals (accessed 5/6/2017).

44 See ASA, PD, File No. 142/1925, Military Branch, Mil-B, June 1925, Nos. 83–175: 'War Medals in connections with Kuki operations', No. 123: Officer Incharge, Medal Distribution, Army Department, Calcutta, to Under Secy. Assam, 1 September 1923, 'Memorandum'; No. 90:

31

'Definition of the term 'fire zone' by BWM, 22 November 1921; No. 91: 'Definition of the term "fire zone"' by BWM, 15 August 1922. For all the claims of medals and others, see Nos. 83–175; for Manipur, see No. 98: L.O. Clarke to Under Secy. Assam, 16 June 1923. For the receipts of medals in Manipur see No. 153: JC Higgins to Under Secy., Assam, 28 July 1924.

45 ASA, File No. 142/1925, Military Branch, Mil-B, June 1925, Nos. 83–175: 'War Medals'.

References

Amin, S. 1995. *Event, Metaphor, Memory: Chauri Chaura 1922–1992*. New Delhi: Oxford University Press.

Bezbaruah, R. 2010. *The Pursuit of Colonial Interests in India's North East*. Guwahati: EBH Publishers.

Bhadra, G. 1975. 'The Kuki (?) Uprising (1917–1919): Its Causes and Nature', *Man in India*, 55 (1): 10–56.

Callwell, C.E. 1906. *Small Wars: Their Principles and Practice*. London: Harrison & Sons.

Chishti, S.M.A.W. 2004. *The Kuki Uprising in Manipur: 1917–1920*. Guwahati: Spectrum Publications.

French, David. 2011. *The British Way in Counter-Insurgency, 1945–1967*. Oxford: Oxford University Press.

Galula, David. 1964. *Counterinsurgency Warfare: Theory and Practice*. Westport, CT: Praeger Security International.

Gangte, T.S. 1993. *The Kukis of Manipur: A Historical Analysis*. New Delhi: Gyan.

Guha, R. 1983 [reprint 1999]. *Elementary Aspects of Peasant Insurgency in Colonial India*. New Delhi: Oxford University Press.

Guha, R. 1994. 'The Prose of Counter-Insurgency', in N. Dirks et al. (eds.), *Culture/Power/History: A Reader in Contemporary Social Theory*, pp. 336–371, Princeton: Princeton University Press.

Haokip, J. 1984. *Manipur a Gospel leh Kuki ho Thusim*. Private Circulation.

Haokip, P.S. 1998. *Zale'n-gam: The Kuki Nation*. KNO Publication.

Haokip, S. 2011. 'Anglo Kuki Relations', unpublished PhD Thesis, Department of History, Manipur University.

Haokip, V. 2013. *Pu Tintong Haokip: Unsung Heroes of the Kuki Rising, 1917–1919*. Private Circulation.

Kicullen, David. 2010. *Counterinsurgency*. London: Hurst.

Kipgen, S. 2005. 'Political and Economic History of the Kukis of Manipur', unpublished PhD Thesis, Department of History, Manipur University.

Mayaram, S. 2003. *Against History, Against State: Counterperspectives from the Margins*. New York: Columbia University Press.

Mockaitis, Thomas R. 1990. *British Counterinsurgency, 1919–60*. London: Palgrave Macmillan.

Nag, Sajal. 2002. *Contesting Marginality: Ethnicity, Insurgency and Subnationalism in North-East India*. New Delhi: Manohar.

Pachuau, J.L.K. and W. van Schendel. 2015. *The Camera as Witness: A Social History of Mizoram, Northeast India*. New Delhi: Cambridge University Press.

Parratt, J. 2005. *Wounded Land: Politics and Identity in Modern Manipur*. New Delhi: Mittal Publications.

Porch, Douglas. 2013. *Counterinsurgency: The Origins, Development & Myths of the New Way of War*. Cambridge: Cambridge University Press.

Ray, A.K. 1990. *Authority and Legitimacy: A Study of the Thadou-Kuki in Manipur*. New Delhi: Renaissance Publishing House.

Sakhong, L.H. 2003. *In Search of Chin Identity: A Study in Religion, Politics and Ethnic Identity in Burma*. Copenhagen: NIAS Press.

Shakespear, L.W. 1929. *History of the Assam Rifles*. Guwahati: Spectrum Publications.

Thompson, Robert. 1966. *Defeating Communist Insurgency: Experiences from Malaya and Vietnam*. London: Chatto & Windus.

van Creveld, Martin. 2008. *The Changing Face of War: Combat from the Marne to Iraq*. New York: Ballantine.

Waterman, A. 2017. 'Compressing Politics in Counterinsurgency (COIN): Implications for COIN Theory from India's Northeast', *Strategic Analysis*, 41 (5): 447–463. http://hansard.millbanksystems.com, 1 June 1921, 30 April 1923, and 30 April 1923. (accessed 5/6/2017)

Part I

UNDERSTANDING THE ANGLO-KUKI WAR

1

'FIGHTING THE WHITE MEN TILL THE LAST BULLET'

The general course of the Anglo-Kuki War

Jangkhomang Guite

*The Sahibs are not made of stone. They will bleed the
same as us. We will kill them.*

— Enjakhup

Different scholars understood the course of the Anglo-Kuki War in
different ways, and even among the colonial officialdom, there was a
much disagreement on it. While some scholars and official historians
started when it actually broke out into open armed uprising in December 1917, the majority started from the time they started opposing the
labour draft in March 1917. Disagreement was also ensued on the
very outbreak of 'rebellion'. For instance, 19 December 1917, when
Ithai toll station was attacked was taken as the beginning of an armed
resistance by Assam government. The Burma administration fixed it
on 21 December 1917, when the 'revolt' broke out. It was, however,
agreed that the rising ended on 31 March 1919, when the operations
were officially closed. Yet, it should be remembered that all these dates
are base on the understanding of the war by colonial officialdom. It
may not necessarily represent the way the Kukis understood their war,
and there is no reason why one should necessarily stick to the colonial
understanding of the event. This chapter attempts to see this important frontier event from the Kukis' perspectives. After all, it was the
'Kuki war', and to see the war in their eyes makes much sense.

Interestingly, the official account of the Assam administration puts
the course of the Anglo-Kuki War into five phases, beginning from

April 1917 to the end of 'reconstruction', which went on until about the end of 1920. The five phases are:[1]

1   April to December 1917, during which the trouble was brewing;
2   December 1917 to mid April 1918, during which the first attempt at the suppression of the rebellion was made;
3   April to October 1918, during which the Kukis raided and harried loyal tribesmen and interrupted traffic;
4   November 1918 to April 1919, when operations under military direction were in progress and the rebels were systematically attacked and disarmed;
5   The stage of punishment and reconstruction.

This division is broadly fine, but the fact that it is based on colonial state dealings with the Kukis missed out on some important landmarks the Kukis would have given more importance. Besides, the very idea of division, such as their notion of 'raids' on friendly villages, of the division between military and non-military, of active service period and rainy season, and of punishment and reconstruction, were a little disturbing to the Kukis, whose understanding of the same were quite different. Therefore, it becomes necessary that this important frontier event during the First World War needs to be understood from the perspective of the Kukis. An attempt is, therefore, made here to understand this war from the Kuki point of view in the following section.

The course of the Anglo-Kuki War

The Kukis understood their war against the King-Emperor quite differently from the way it was known in the colonial archives. According to this, the phases of the Anglo-Kuki War can be broadly divided into three, with some subdivisions within.

1   Non-cooperation and passive resistance (March to October 1917)
2   Active resistance (October 1917 to April 1919)
3   Trial and tribulation (April 1919 onward)

1. Period of non-cooperation and passive resistance (March to October 1917)

The first phase broadly covers the period when the 'trouble was brewing' in colonial parlance. It was the period when one witnessed passive resistance against colonial labour recruitment. It was passive in the sense that the Kukis did not indulge in any violent resistance. In the early months of 1917, when the War Office called on 50,000 Indian labourers for France, the Assam government promised to supply 6,000 to 8,000 men.[2] The Maharaja of Manipur also promised to supply 4,000 men.[3] The announcement was followed by a rumour saying that no one return from France. The rumour was serious, for the Political Agent was not able to convince any hillmen even after announcing many inducements such as liberal pay, exemption from house-tax, *pothang* and *begar* for life. The only way to bring them into agreement was the use of threat, although it was supposed to be voluntary. Other tribes eventually gave in and some Kukis from the southwestern hills also did it, but the majority of the Kukis stuck to their guns.[4] In early March 1917, Chengjapao, chief of Aishan, killed a mithun: 'send round the flesh to other Kukis, inciting them to swear an oath, sealed by eating the flesh, not to go to France' and 'to resist efforts to recruit by all means in their power'.[5] Aishan's announcement was followed by a series of meetings held in different parts of Kuki hills – Chassad, Jampi, Taloulong, Mombi, Ukha, Henglep, etc. For instance, Col. H.W. Cole, the Political Agent (PA) in Manipur, reported 'some four of our most truculent Kuki chiefs are said to have taken an oath after killing a mythan (mithun) that none of them would go to France or send any of their people there'.[6] The four chiefs were Chengjapao (chief of Aishan), Khutinthang (chief of Jampi), Pache (chief of Chassad) and Ngullen (chief of Khongjang).[7] Khutinthang even 'refused to permit state Lambus to enter his villages'; the baggage of 'one Lambu was seized by him and his personal effects scattered'.[8]

It was wrong to assume that Kukis had persistently avoided meeting the PA or refused to talk, as the official account would like us to believe. In fact, they were keen to resolve the tangled question by peaceful means. They sent three of their principal chiefs to meet the PA, but they were badly treated. Chengjapao went to Imphal in May 1917 to settle the problem with the PA, but he was arrested and detained at Imphal jail. Somehow, he managed to escape by pretending to parley with other Kuki chiefs.[9] Ngulkhup, chief of Mombi, also met the PA at Kakching in July 1917.[10] Pache went to Imphal in early August 1917, but he was also arrested and put in jail 'as a hostage'. He also managed to escape when on parole at Imphal.[11] These were the stories of treachery that all the Kukis were well aware of. Hence, their refusal to come to Imphal was not without any substance. In their earnestness to resolve the tangled question by peaceful means, the Kuki chiefs (between 30 and 40 of them) of the northwestern hills met the PA at Oktan (in the hills), 26 miles from Imphal, from 10 to 11 October 1917.

The meeting went on for about two hours but failed to reach any conclusion:

> Two hours of argument failed to move them and they proved obdurate against threats of punishment. They persisted that they feared to go so far from their homes and that if they had to die they preferred to die in their own country and would be prepared to meet force with force.[12]

The air was filled with hostility. PA refused to accept a sum of Rs. 1500, three gongs and one mithan as *salam* from the Kukis; the Kukis refused to drink his offer of 'Rum'. The next morning, before they dispersed, the Kukis told him that 'they could not give any men' and the PA told them to surrender all their guns, pay Rs. 10 per house as house-tax and he promised to convene another meeting shortly with them.[13]

On 14 October, barely two days after the Oktan meeting, the PA took 50 rifles to Mombi (Lonpi) to arrest its chief Ngulkhup. About 1½ miles away from Mombi was a small stockade where they found four men. Higgins reported that they 'parleys with them, and after asking us not to frighten the women and children by firing, they promised to bring the chief, Ngulkhup, to speak to us and retired'. While approaching the village, they saw lights moving, and when they reached the village at 9.30 pm they found that it was 'completely deserted'. The chief's and some of the nearby houses were occupied for the night, and on the next day *lambus* were sent out to inform Ngulkhup to give himself up. His military column savoured the pigs, goats and chickens of the villages, which were said to be 'plenty'. When the chief refused to give himself up, Higgins, before his party returned home, burnt down all the houses and properties of Mombi on the morning of 17 October 1917.[14]

The burning of Mombi immediately invited anger from the government of Assam and India. They had not contemplated the use of force for labour recruitment. The Chief Commissioner of Assam, therefore, immediately issued orders that:

> [N]o further punitive measures are to be taken without the previous sanction of the Local Administration.
>
> [N]o punitive expedition that can by any possibility lead to a requisition for Military assistance will be undertaken without the previous sanction of Government of India.

[N]o further requisitions for drafts for the labour corps should be made unless the Political Agent is satisfied that they are not likely to provoke opposition.[15]

Government of India (GOI) concurred the order and instructed that 'no force should be used except for the purpose of preserving order'.[16]

The burning of Mombi, on the other hand, so displeased the Kukis in general, and the Mombi Kukis in particular, that the whole course of their relationship with the government changed. Ngulkhup, for instance, said before the Advisory Committee at Kohima that 'he was not aware of the reasons' put against him by the PA for burning his village, such as stopping the Anals and Lamkangs from sending men for coolies.[17] The memorandum of the 'Political prisoners' to the chairman of the Advisory Committee also claimed that they took up arms after 'the Political Agent burnt the Mombi Kuki village without calling us to consult again as previously arranged'.[18] Truly, Higgins's action was a breach of trust to the Kukis. It was the first time violence was use against them by the government, and that too committed soon after they were promised for another conference. It therefore invited anger and indignation from all Kukis leading them to a violent showdown. Overall, the burning of Mombi marked the watershed between two broad phases of the Anglo-Kuki War, between passive and active phases. Tintong was particularly explicit. He said that 'he was driven to the war by the burning of Ukha' (read as Mombi). The Advisory Committee also noted that Tintong 'made up his mind to fight' after the burning of Mombi.[19]

2. Period of active resistance (October 1917 to April 1919)

Even if I am alone, I will fight the 'white men' until my last bullet and gunpowder.

– Tintong

The active resistance period can be further subdivided into five phases: the phase of war preparation, period of active engagement with colonial forces, punishment to the friendlies, second phase of negotiation and the second phase of active engagement. These phases are not a strictly compartmentalised segregation; each of them in the series overlaps with the previous one and the one that follows. Thus, when war preparation is going on one area, battles were fought in other places. Similarly, when the Kukis eventually fell on the friendly villages after the withdrawal of military troops, they also continued to attack government establishments and sepoys wherever possible. When the second phase of negotiation was on, there were also incidents of violence in certain areas. When the second phase of active military engagement was happening in one place, some chiefs engaged in negotiation in others. Thus, each of this subdivision should not be considered as a strictly demarcated phase. Yet, the fact remains that these subdivisions signify a broad policy/method followed by the Kukis to handle the war situation. These phases will be briefly taken up in the following sections.

The autumn conclaves and war preparation
(October to December 1917)

The burning of Mombi was followed by a hectic phase of consultations, mobilisation and war preparation across the Kuki hills. The Mombi people went back to their charred village and rebuilt it. The chief Ngulkhup (probably after convening a war council) declared his country 'closed' to the Sahibs and Sarkaris and issued an order to all hillmen that no one should go to the plain. He had communicated his decision to fight the British to his *pipa*, Pache chief of Chassad.[20] The burning of Mombi was also followed by the 'assembly' of Kuki chiefs in different parts of Kuki hills. On 31 October 1917, it was reported that '22 chiefs of the Haokip villages round Moirang had met at Ukha with 40 guns and decided not to send coolies to France and *to resist forcibly* any attempt to arrest them or burn their villages'.[21] They also informed their *pipa*, Pache of Chassad, of their decision.[22] It was also reported that Tintong asked the Kabui villages to 'mend the roads or to supply him and his men with provisions' as he was visiting his *pipa*, Pakang chief of Henglep (undoubtedly for another round of consultation).[23] Similarly, it was also reported that Khutinthang, chief of Jampi, had 'recently been in communication with the chiefs of Mombi and Chassad with a view to concerted resistance to any attempt at coercion or arrest, and the latest information to hand indicates that Pachei chief of Chassad had called him to a council [at Chassad]'.[24]

After the consultation process, Pache eventually convened the traditional Kuki War Council, the grand Chiefs-in-Council at his capital Chassad. The Council was attended by 150 Kuki chiefs from all parts of Kuki hills (Burma, Assam and Manipur). This grand council, known as 'Assembly of Chiefs', took place at 'the end of November or beginning of December' 1917. Based on intelligence sources, J.B.

Marshall, Deputy Commissioner, Upper Chindwin District, reported on the Chassad war council as:

> About the end of November or beginning of December [1917] also a big meeting of the Kuki Chiefs was held at Chassad. About 150 chiefs are said to have been present including Pase [Pache], chief of Chassad, Ngulkhup chief of Mombi, Ngulbul, another south Manipur chief, and Shempu, chief of south Somra. At this meeting, it was *resolved not to obey any orders or summons* from Government and *to fight* if Government tried to enforce orders.[25]
>
> (Emphasis mine)

'Not to obey' and 'to fight' should be read as declaration of war against the British. This resolution to fight was solemnised with a customary war rite called *sathin-salung-neh* ('feasting on the liver and heart of animal killed on the occasion'). This ceremonial performance and its associated utterance marked the highest form of vows among the Kukis that is sacred and cannot be unilaterally broken.

The significance of the Chassad War Council can also be seen from the song composed by Pache to commemorate the grand occasion, a normal practice among the Kukis:

> *Phai chungnung kol kimvel'e;*
> *Kolmang tolkon;*
> *Ikal lhangphai thin eisem gom me;*
> *Phai thin sem gome;*
> *Lheppon bang kitho tin;*
> *Nam cham khat in vabang pao tadite.* (as quoted in Haokip 2008: 151–152)

Translation:

> From all around the valley of Manipur;
> From beyond the horizon of Burma;
> The valley storm[26] brought us together;
> The valley storm had brought us together;
> Let us stack together (stand together) like the folded clothes;
> Like the birds, let us speak (fight) as one free nation.[27]

The depth of this song, put in poetic form, is especially interesting. It makes clear that the 'valley storm' (*lhangphaithi*), referring to the

British government, was the paramount enemy to be reckoned with. As the common enemy brought them together, it urged all to stand together 'like folded clothes' and speak in one voice like the birds. The song also defined the Kukis as 'one free nation' and the war they called was to defend that freedom from the British. Thus, the Kuki war, which goes on until March 1919, was founded on, and sustained by, this resolution taken at the war council at Chassad. I would prefer to call this magnetic and a moving song as the Anglo-Kuki War song not only because of its wide political ramification but also its poetic originality and expression through which their ideas of the war, how they were to do it, and for what objective, can be known.

The importance given to traditional War Council is significant at least on two important grounds. On the one hand, it signifies the importance the Kukis had given to the Anglo-Kuki War. Unlike the way the colonial archives understood them, it was the traditional idea and practices, which the long history of the Kukis would tell, that the decision to go to war like this was a grand public affair. They normally made such important decisions at the highest level of their political body, the grand Chiefs-in-Council. In this sense, it would be unfair to reduce the hard show given by the Kuki fighters against the colonial military forces as a mere outburst of some hotheaded young men, lacking any political objective, which the use of the terms like 'raid', 'loot' or 'murder' and so on connote. On the other hand, such a War Council was a well-established institution among the Kukis that they only invoked when there was a major war, or when some common enemy had threatened their existence. The Kukis invoked on this occasion as they were fighting the mighty British Empire, whom they knew was considerable and required a common concerted effort to combat. This also means in terms of tactics, which now largely assumed a modern form.

Following the War Council, mobilisation for the war immediately took off on a massive scale. As the host of the war council, Pache subsequently sent bullets to all the Kuki villages to inform them of the resolution taken for a war with the British. Higgins, for instance, reported:

> Subsequently, I learn from a good authority that he [Pache] sent a bullet to the chiefs of Jampi, Ukha, Songphu, Henglep and Loibol with instruction to resist forcibly any attempt to impress coolies or to burn villages.[28]

Emissaries were sent to different parts of the hills, guns (mostly flintlock, musket, muzzle-loaders, etc.) were collected by flying parties from all possible sources, old guns were repaired, leather cannons (*pumpi*) and other weapons were also manufactured.[29] Gunpowder was produced in large quantities in each village through their traditional processing method. Village fortifications were erected. Stockades (*chang*), stone traps (*songkhai*), *panjies* (sharp bamboo stack) and other necessary means to encounter the invading forces were also put up on all the roads leading to their hills and villages.[30] Foods were gathered from the fields; large amounts of them were stored up in the 'hidden granaries' in the jungle. The Kuki forms of 'fiery-cross', such as *thingkho-le-malchapom* ('chilli with smouldering wood'), gunpowder, bullets, beads, swords, etc. (all having different and definite messages), were sent out among the Kukis and other tribes in Manipur, Naga Hills, North Cachar Hills, Chin Hills, Thaungdut State and Somra Tract.[31]

Tintong was reported to have been touring through the Kabui villages, north of the Cachar road, with an armed escort, and 'inciting them to refrain from paying their housetax and to join in the rebellion'.[32] The Koms of Langkhong Chongmang, in the western hills, had demanded licenced guns from Kabui village, 'as they were about to make war with the sahib'.[33] An Anal man was touring around the Anal villages and asked them to provide their guns and join the rising 'saying they all were men of one country'.[34] Reports were received from Burma that 'a large force of Kukis' was gathering at the border areas on Manipur side, that rations were being collected in villages above the Kabaw valley, and that the Kukis of Manipur 'were in communication with the rebel Chins of Haka'.[35] It was during this time that emissaries from Bengal revolutionaries (not definitely clear from sources), and from the valley of Manipur, reached the Kuki Hills.

There was 'a good deal of unrest', and the situation was described to be 'extremely grave and difficult'.[36] Manipur authority was seeking an approval from the government for military action against the Kukis 'for deliberately organising armed resistance'. It insisted that 'undue delay in taking action' would result into 'state of lawlessness and anarchy'.[37] The GOI approved the plan in their telegram dated 11 December 1917.[38] *Parwana* was then sent out to the Kuki chiefs saying: 'If you come in immediately on receipt of this parwana, and obey my order and carry out the punishment imposed upon you, your village will not be burnt'.[39] Along with this, preparation for punitive action was also taken up at Imphal. The Kukis had already decided 'not to obey any orders' but fight if the government entered their country. Therefore, not a single chief surrendered, and in many cases, they refused to accept even the *parwana*.[40] Given a free hand now, a series of military columns were planned out to go against the Kukis, and thus began the hard show in the rugged mountain ranges.

The Kuki winter war (December 1917 to April 1918)

While war preparations, on both sides, were going on, the boiling political temperature in the hills broke out into some local incidents. It began with the sepoys firing upon a group of 12 Kukis who were sent out by the chief of Ukha to collect his mithuns from Kangvai (foot-hills).[41] It was possible that the action of sepoys so enraged the Kukis in this area that they joined the Manipuri revolutionaries in attacking the Ithai toll station on 19 December 1917.

> Kukis from Ukha, Hinglep and neighbouring villages, headed by 4 or 5 Manipuris, raided the Manipur State forest toll station at Ithai. This raid is found to have been planned by Chingakhamba Singh, a Manipuri of bad character with reputed magic powers, living by his wits.[42]

From the official point of view, this instance was the beginning of the Kuki rising. Yet, it is still doubtful whether it can truly be counted as part of the Anglo-Kuki War, although many Kukis had taken part. The fact that the Kuki war council urged for a defensive policy, not an aggression like the Ithai attack, and that it was planned and led by Manipuris, places this incident in a different light.

The attack on the Ithai toll station was followed by a series of local incidents in the frontier villages where the Kukis had collected provisions for the war. The fact that not a single casualty was reported, and not a single bullet was expended, in these incidents also shows that they were just part of the general process of war preparation in the hills, which might have spilled over into the frontier villages. Yet, these incidents had incited fear and excitement in the hills and valley of Manipur.[43] Rumours of Kuki attacks soon flooded the whole valley. Higgins took 160 rifles under Capt. Coote for Ukha hills on 22 December 1917 only to return back from Bishenpur the same day, with speed, when he heard that 'the Kukis intended raiding Imphal and looting the guns of the garrison'.[44] It was a mere rumour, but the city residents remained nervous. Higgins noted one interesting incident at Imphal on 23 December where an electrifying alarm was raised across the city that 'the Kukis were looting the bazaar'. Enquiry found that the alarm started from the women's bazaar where a woman 'started a shout that the Kukis had come' when one hillman took away her vegetables without paying for them. There was so much confusion that the bazaar was shut down for the day.[45]

When he was still at Imphal, Higgins received information of a 'large concentration of Kukis' in different parts of the hills and the roads to the hills were fortified.[46] On 25 December 1917, he set out again with his sepoys to punish the Ukha Kukis. On 28 December, he reached the foothills of Thangting where he saw a 'war-like preparation' and had therefore ordered 'to fire on any Kuki seen with a gun in his hand'. It was here that they met the first Kuki attack (possibly by a leather cannon or *pumpi* as the description given below shows) and indeed the first bloodshed on the military troop. Higgins reported,

> The Kuki's bullet splintered on a branch, and two of the splinters lodged in Captain Coote's sleeve, while one hit him on the side of the face, drawing blood. . . . While the column was passing through the stockade a few stones were sent down the hill from the stone traps.[47]

Higgins's diary went on narrating the series of 'incessant sniping and attacks' from Kukis along the routes until his column withdrew in the valley (on 7 January 1918). He admitted that he came out of the hills with 'much difficulty' after 'a long and difficult march under the most trying conditions'. On many occasions, hundreds of bullets were expended on the way just to keep away the Kuki snipers from harassing the party.[48] He had burnt down some Kuki villages, including Ukha, and destroyed all their provisions and livestock, but he could not arrest, or bring to submission, any Kuki, as he had hoped earlier. Instead, Higgins reported several casualties among the government troops and coolies.[49]

On the other hand, W.A. Cosgrave, the new Political Agent in Manipur, took 100 rifles to the Mombi hills. Even before climbing the hills, they were beaten back by the Kukis at the foothills of Tuiyang Karong on 4 January 1918. Cosgrave reported that when they had gone

> a little way across the river suddenly shots were fired from the jungle on the far side of the river and we ran back to join the main body of the escort who were still on the Shugunu bank of the stream and who were opening fire.

The column withdrew to Shuganu (then to Imphal) 'having some difficulty in taking back wounded sepoys and coolies' and 'one sepoy and one temporary Manipuri Interpreter' gone missing.[50] The failure of these two military columns stunned the local officers. Higgins was particularly outraged. He had hoped that the 'threatened resistance will disappear as soon as the Kuki see a large forces opposed to them and that not a shot will be fired'.[51] However, to his great amazement, he found that 'the Kukis intent to make a strenuous resistance'.[52] Cosgrave also declared that 'as the Kukis have fired on both Higgins and myself, the time has passed for peaceful negotiations'.[53]

With this, Manipur authorities now proposed for multiple military columns to deal with the Kukis. The expedition against the Mombi Kukis was to be carried out from four directions by four military columns: one each from Sugunu, Lenakot (Chin Hills), Kabaw valley and Palel-Tamu road. Similarly, another column would revisit Ukha area until the Manlun-Manchong hills and a column would guard from Lushai Hills boundary. Two columns, one from Imphal and another from Silchar, would also go against Kukis of the Henglep area and Cachar road. Two columns, one from Imphal and another from Burma, would attack Chassad Kukis. One column from Naga Hills would attack Jampi Kukis and another the Aishan Kukis. One column would also deal with Kukis of the Somra Tract and Thaungdut state. With this mounting requirement, more riflemen were called in from Naga Hills Battalion, Lushai Hills Battalion and so on. The Burma government was also called in to cooperate in the war. As it was difficult to get coolies from Manipur due to the threats of Kukis, the Naga Labour Corps who were recruited for France were soon diverted to Manipur for Kuki operations. Thus, altogether 15 flying or mobile military columns were planned, and then sent out, against the Kukis during the first phase of operations.

Due to a need for space, it is not possible to narrate the unfolding events in the hills. Few instances are given to provide the general picture of the war. Kukis met the military columns on their various stockades erected at strategic points across the hills. Like in the Ukha hills, the British military columns were harassed by Kuki snipers. For instance, when Higgins took a military column against Mombi Kukis in January 1918, he found that his party was, despite being well prepared, harassed by the Kuki's sniping attacks throughout the hills. At the battle near Gobok, he reported:

> Three or four shots were fired at the advance guard from a small ridge commanding the path, from which a line of retreat led sheer down into the valley, and the advance guard replied. Three sepoys were hit, fortunately with large shot and not with bullets.[54]

At Khailet, the column under Lieut. Stedman was 'repulsed' or 'reversed' after a fierce encounter from the Kukis. Stedman was 'seriously/dangerously wounded' with many casualties in his column; eight killed and eight wounded. He retired to Lenacot for refit.[55] At Hengtam, Cosgrave reported that his party was 'fired on by the enemy' whom they found 'in very strong forts behind a long and substantial stockade'. He said that the 'enemy kept up a brisk and well directed fire from the stockade', and they could not be dislodged from it until several shells from seven-pounder mountain gun, and bullets from magazine rifles were deluged into it at close range. He reported:

> The defence of Hengtam village was far the most stubborn and well organized fight I have seen the Manipur Kukis put up, and there is every sign that our present foes the Manhlun Manchong Kukis are a more formidable foe than the other Kukis with whom No. 2 column has so far dealt. Our column had to fire some 1300 rounds of .303 [rifles] and Martini Henry ammunition.[56]

At Maokot's 'Kuki stockade', Higgins reported that the stockade was defended by about 100 men with 50 guns from the villages of Maokot Chingsang, Maokot, Lakhan Khaihol, Langja, Mattiyang and Khulen Bongbal. The encounter went on for more than three hours.[57] Besides these, there were many other encounters in the Jampi and Aishan areas against Hutton's military column. The troops were also met with similar strikes in the Cachar road area (under the command of Tintong and Enjakhup), in the Henglep area and in the Somra Tract.

Besides meeting the invading military columns, the Kukis also attacked, once the war began, the symbols and persons related to the *Sarkari* (government) such as the police station, telegraph lines, rest houses (bungalows), *dakwallas* (postmen), *lambus* (hill peons) and so on. On all sides, the hills were 'closed' down to the 'Sahibs' and 'Sarkaris'. The roads leading to Burma and Cachar were patrolled and closed, and the main line to Assam through the Naga Hills was also threatened. The government *dakwallas* (postmen) and *lambus* were intercepted, captured, threatened or killed and their *daks* destroyed. On 10 January 1918, three parties of Kukis attacked the Sugunu military outpost from three directions at midday; there were no casualties but 'the Manipuris of Shuganu village were very frightened and deserted their houses'.[58] It was also reported that the Kukis sent a *dao* to the big village Maram 'with orders to cut the telegraph line'. They blocked the Cachar bridle path at various places 'so as to bar the passage of Government officers', prevent the Kabui Nagas of the roadside from repairing the road and threaten the big village Kaupum 'because they worked for government'. A reserve body of 25 pensioned and *Nam Khat* sepoys armed with muzzle-loader was raised to defend the valley.[59]

It was also reported that there was a band of 30 Kukis near the Laimatak River headed by Thangkhulet Chief of Khoiru. They took away the *perwanas* and others from *dakwallas*. Hill's peons were also killed and his decomposed body discovered. The *daks* of Kuki *dakwalla* were also taken away and burnt on Tamu road.[60] Tengnoupal civil police *thana* was attacked on 20 January 1918, killing one Havildar, one constable and a Gurkha chaukidar of the bungalow and wounding another constable.[61] The Tengnoupal inspection bungalow was also burnt down later. On 19 January 1918, the Kukis killed the bungalow chaukidar at Kaupum.[62] The chaukidar of Makru bungalow was 'chased away' by the Kukis.[63] It was reported that the Kukis had gone towards Jirighat to attack the column coming from Silchar; they have threatened to cut the Barak bridge, and drove away the chaukidars of Yangoupokpi and Lemjanglung rest houses.[64] Thus, from all sides, the Kukis rose up in arms against the Sahibs and Sarkaris. So much of fear was created among the government servants that when Higgins visited Waikhong bungalow he found its chaukidar in a state of unusual drunkenness 'having been drowning his sorrows consequent on being told by the Kukis of Aihang that the bungalow and himself would suffer the same fate as the Tengnoupal bungalow and chaukidar'.[65]

Although no attack was committed on civilians, the general populations, especially in the hills and the villages at the fringe of the valley, feared a Kuki attack. Coolies for transport of foods for expedition parties were not procurable, as all the hillmen were afraid of enlisting due to fear of reprisal from the Kukis. Cosgrave, for instance, noted that 'the hillmen as a whole are becoming so frightened of the Kukis that it is difficult to get coolies and harder to keep them'. Hence, the Naga Hills labour drafts were diverted to Manipur.[66] At Palel, he has noted:

> All round Palel, the quiet law-abiding Marings and Aimols people are frightened of helping me with coolies as they say that the Kukis will kill their women and children as a punishment and they correctly point out that the Kukis can swoop down on a village like hawks and be off again as they do not have to prepare camps and carry rations like sepoys.[67]

Many hill people also took refuge in the valley for fear of the Kukis. Moyang Khulen people, for instance, took shelter in the farmhouses of the Shans near Tamu in Kabaw valley of Burma because they were threatened by the Kukis 'on account of their refusing to supply the men to fight against the sahebs at Mombi'.[68] The whole Manipur valley, as also Kabaw valley in Burma and Cachar frontier in Assam, were also in fear of the Kukis. They sought protection from the government or evacuated their villages or moved their women and children to safer places. The Manipuris of Palel, for instance, sent away their women and children to a large Manipuri village of Kakching; Moirang people kept their women and children at Thanga for safety; Jiribam residents buried their rice and stayed in the jungle at night.[69]

However, it is significant to note that during the first phase of operations the Kuki war was clearly directed to the 'Sahibs' and the 'Sarkaris'. No attack was made on innocent people nor against any plainsmen or other hill tribes although everyone was dreads of Kuki attack. An attack on Tengnoupal *thana* on 20 January 1918 was revealing. Cosgrave informed that the Kukis had selectively killed government servants and desisted from indiscriminate killing, the fact shown by sparing the life of the Gurkhali chaukidar's wife and children. He said that 'this confirms my previous impression that the Kukis are only out against Sarkari people and are not indulging in any indiscriminate head-hunting orgies'.[70] This impression was further confirmed by two instances. First, he found that the Manipuris of Palel remain calm and peaceful because they said that the Kukis do 'little or nothing to harm the Manipuri villagers'.[71] Second, he was stunned to see that three large parties of Manipuri traders returned from Kubo valley without meeting any molestation from the Kukis. He remarked: 'This confirms my opinion that the Kukis are not up against Manipuris but only against the sahebs and their subordinates'.[72] J.B. Marshall noted that 'There can be no doubt it was part of the settled policy [of the Kukis] to try always to shoot the British Officers'.[73]

If the Kukis were difficult to get in person for war or arrest, what the 'flying' military columns did in the hills was, as Lt. Col. Ffrench-Mullen put down as their objectives: to overrun the rebel country with suitable columns, harrying the tribesmen, preventing them from cultivating and inflicting all the damage possible on them and their property, giving them no rest whatever until the rains broke out.[74] This policy, it was argued, 'has always subdued rebellious savages and semi-civilised races'. The result of this strategy under various military columns can be seen from the report of J.B. Marshall: 'Consequently, the destruction of grain and cattle was very thorough, the punishment of villages by burning was systematic, and the rebels were driven out and had to take refuge further north'.[75] Thus, the military columns, having no other ways to punish the Kukis who usually deserted their villages for their jungle hideouts, eventually fell on their villages and properties. Their villages were systematically burnt down, all their grains and livestock were looted or destroyed and all their properties destroyed. These brutal actions amount to what *The Advocate of Peace* would call the 'civilised barbarism and savagery' of the colonial states.[76]

Despite this wanton destruction, the officers were surprised to see that the Kukis had not submitted but continue to resist the invading forces with 'incessant sniping and attack'. It was eventually admitted that the flying columns failed to defeat the Kukis and therefore new tactics became necessary. At the end of the first phase of operations, W.A. Cosgrave, for instance, reported:

> Personally, I am now inclined to think that the suppression of the Kuki rebellion is too big a matter for our Assam Rifles and that the operations next cold weather should be made over to the Military Department.[77]

In countering Maj. Vickers's demeaning description of the Kuki as 'a few robbers armed with rusty muzzle-loaders', Cosgrave remarked:

> In spite of their armament, they have managed to kill more of our poor sepoys than we know we have killed on the other side, and at the present time in the greater part of the 7,000 square miles comprising the Manipur Hills tracts, the Kuki is master of the situation.[78]

If the systematic destruction of villages, properties and livestock normally quelled similar risings in the colonial world, this was not the case with the Kukis. Lieut. Col. Ffrench-Mullen, for instance, remarked: 'Punish the Kukis we did certainly, but we did not break their morale as we did elsewhere'.[79] This gave a new rethinking of their strategy to 'reconquer' the Kuki hills. Most officers agreed that military occupation of the Kuki country was the only answer. The Chief Commissioner of Assam, for instance, felt that:

> [I]f we are to reconquer this tract we must get rid of the idea that movements in certain localities are possible only at certain seasons; the enemy moves everywhere at all seasons and that is why he is 'top-dog'.[80]

Similarly, Lieut. Col. Ffrench-Mullen felt that 'there is only one way to conquer the savages [Kukis], and that is occupy their country for a longterm or permanently'.[81] Major Vickers came out with his military strategy to suppress the Kuki rising. He suggested military occupation of the Kuki country.[82] His suggestion was accepted with some modifications and hence the next winter operations were planned on this line.

The Kuki monsoon (April to July 1918)

With the arrival of monsoon rain, the military columns withdrew in the plain to refit. The government policy was to bring down all the friendly villagers in the valley until the war is over. For this, they set up a big concentration camp, 2½ miles from Imphal. However, it was able to collect only about 2,000 refugees, 'which have been raided or are likely to be raided by the rebel Kukis'.[83] However, most of them were forced to return to the hills due to unhealthy conditions in the concentration camp, the epidemic, which broke out in the camp, killed several of them.[84] In June, another 'concentration camp' was opened up at Ukhrul. On the other hand, the Kukis plan for the rainy season was to make a concerted attack on the military outposts and to punish the British's 'friendly villages'.[85] When the last military columns were still in the hills, a band of armed Kukis burned down the Palel bungalow on 10 May 1918 and the Manipuris of Palel village temporarily fled to Kakching Khulen.[86] Cosgrave reported that the situation 'has changed very much for the worse'.[87] The Maharaja of Manipur, for instance, ordered his guard of 35 Manipuri sepoys to shift from Waikhong to Kakching Khulen 'as that big and important Manipuri village is afraid of being raided'.[88] On 23 May, the suspension bridge over Thoubal river on Imphal-Ukhrul bridle path was burnt down.[89]

On the other hand, the withdrawal of military columns in the hills gave the Kukis a playing field to punish the 'friendly villages'. Official figures of friendly villages attacked by Kukis was 19, killing 193 persons and 21 missing. An extract from government proceedings put it thusly:

> Up to March 1918 the animosity of the rebels seemed to have been directed solely against the British authority . . . but by the end of April a series of brutal outrages began, and in the next three months 19 friendly villages were raided by the rebels with the loss of 193 persons killed and 21 missing.

Some of these outrages appear to have been in revenge for grudges of old-standing and others because the villagers either had refused to help the rebels or were suspected to having helped the expeditionary columns.[90]

In certain cases, we have reference of non-payment of the usual tribute normally given in the past by some villages.

It should be remembered that such attack was clearly directed to some selected 'friendly villages', not an indiscriminate attack on villages belonging to a particular community or tribe. The reasons for the attack can be clearly definable within the different causes noted above. The devastated 'friendly villages', therefore, belonged to both the Kukis and the Nagas. For instance, in June, a Kuki village Mechangbung was raided and its buffalo looted. The Kukis also attacked the Dulin military outpost and the three Kuki villages of Dulin, Senting and Yopi were raided and burnt down. The reason was that these villages had surrendered to the British before others did and become 'friendly' to the British against other Kukis. Dulin outpost was created to protect them. During the same month, a Kuki village of Khongde was attacked and its chief, who was the brother of Pasut who served Mr. Hutton as Kuki guide in his recent expedition into the Lapvomi country, was killed. [91]

When the situation become 'undoubtedly serious' in June, the government was seriously mulling over the idea of negotiation and peaceful settlement again. It was thinking of utilising the 500 Kuki labourers who returned from France.[92] The Chief Commissioner of Assam also visited Kohima on 7 June 1918 to take stock of the matter. In the conference there, it was pointed out that the offer of reward for certain chiefs 'dead or alive' was a mistake and need to be substitute with 'life spared with voluntary surrender'. In the meantime, the chiefs of Chassad and Jampi made an overture to surrender by offering to pay their house-tax, licenced guns, two elephant tasks and Rs. 3,000, *if they are pardon*.[93] The overture was immediately taken advantage of. Order was issued to the Kuki chiefs that if they surrender within two months, pay their house-tax and give up all their guns, the lives and property of themselves and their tribesmen will be spared, and no one would be punished except after 'a full and fair trial'.[94] In June (18–27), the Chief Commissioner of Assam visited Simla to consult on the matter with the Viceroy. He was told that the GOI was ready 'to go great lengths in the direction of clemency', and he should make use of France-returned Kukis for the purpose. It was also decided to put the operations in the next cold season under one military control without deploying regulars. At the same time, Assam was instructed to explore the possibility of a peaceful settlement to obviate the operations and 'tide over the period of war'.[95]

The autumn alternative (August to November 1918)

The policy of leniency was vigorously taken up from July. It immediately brought down the temperature of violence in the hills. Except for a few cases of long-range fire on the stockade of Kaupum village, the hills remained calm.[96] The month of August also shows only a few incidents of attack on military outposts such as at Saji-eng and Dulin. Instead, the new leniency policy brought Chengjapao, chief of the Aishan, into submission on 23 August 1918.[97] In September, violence came to almost nil. On 16 September, five chiefs of the Jampi area, including Lunkhulal of Chongyang, surrendered with three guns and revenue.[98] On 24 September, Khutinthang, chief of Jampi, also surrendered.[99]

Some influential France-returned Kukis and trusted interpreters were instrumental in bringing these chiefs to submission. For instance, for bringing the chiefs of the Jampi area, an influential France-returned Kuki interpreter Ngulhao Christian Kuki was instrumental for which the Political Agent recommended money reward, a certificate signed by Chief Commissioner, and, after the war, the post analogous to Mauzadar.[100] Another France-returned Kuki labourer, along with Yamkholun chief of Aibol, was also sent to Laiyang to induce Tintong and his followers. Another Kuki interpreter Thangkhong, accompanied by a relation of Khutinthang, was sent to Ngulkhup, chief of Mombi.[101] No wonder, the Political Agent of Manipur felt that the political situation, on the whole, was 'distinctly improving'.

The month of October also witnessed relatively no violent incidents directly related to the Kuki rising. Several emissaries have been sent out to the hills to induce the chiefs and some responses were also received. Semthong, chief of Songpi, was sent to Henglep, Ukha, Nabil and Paosum. Hlunthanga, a very powerful chief, was sent to Manhlun Manchong chiefs. Khamzamanga, head of the Guite clan, and a man of considerable importance among Lusheis and Kukis, was sent to Chassad chief; Lala, another France-returned Kuki, was going with him.[102] The Mombi chief demanded that they should not be sent to France and should not be put in jail as conditions of their surrender, while accepting other punishments.[103] On 4 October the PA received information from Yamkholun, who was deputed to go to Tintong, that he returned as he was afraid to proceed because the sepoys of

Dulin outpost had attacked his village Aibol and killed four persons there. He also received information from another Kuki whom Ngul-hao had sent earlier to Tintong that

> Tintong's men had started for Imphal with some guns, but turned back on receiving news of the attacks of the Dulin sepoys on Aimol (Aibol). They are reported to have said that 'it is no use to surrender as villages which had already surrendered and paid revenue were being cut up by the Dulin guard.[104]

No response was received from Ukha area, who later attested before the Tribunal that they did not receive any such *perwana* from anyone.

Longjachin, chief of Behiang, surrendered on 22 October at Imphal.[105] Thangkhong also reported that Mombi chief Ngulkhup was willing to surrender with his licenced guns 'provided that he is assured that no more Kukis will be sent to France and that he will not be sent to jail'. Accordingly, another *parwana* was issued to him on 12 October that

> if he or the other Mangvum Kuki chiefs surrender with their guns and revenue within 20 days (i.e. by 1 November) they will not be hung or transported, but will be detained in Imphal jail till the rebellion is suppressed.

They were also told that they would make bridle path from Sugunu to Lenacot and Witok via Mombi as punishment for rebellion.[106] Thangkhong Kuki interpreter returned on 23 October, reported that the Mombi chief was afraid to surrender alone, and hence called a big gathering of Kukis on 25 October, which he was waiting for the result at Sugunu. He also reported that he met at Mombi the chiefs of 17 rebel villages 'who all expressed their desire to do punitive labour on roads provided that they are not sent to jail'. Therefore, another *parwana* was issued which says that 'they will not be put inside the ordinary Imphal jail but will be detained in a stockade while the Kuki operations are in progress'. For this purpose, a temporary stockade containing barracks was built as an annexe to the Imphal jail.[107] Lala also reported that Pache told him that he would not surrender unless Ngulkhup of Mombi and Ngulbul of Longya surrendered and also threatened to commit suicide if sepoys went again to his village. To this response, the Political Agent felt that Pache was planning to 'fight to a finish'.[108]

Despite this vigorous efforts to bring in the Kuki chiefs, the policy of leniency fail to obviate operations in the winter of 1918–1919 because many of the important Kuki chiefs remain at large. This failure was mainly due to policy of leniency itself which many Kukis disliked it. Most Kuki chiefs wanted unconditional pardon and restoration of pre-war condition such as payment of house-tax and *pothang* and against imprisonment. Some of them even wanted to face some punishment like penal labour. However, the government stuck to its policy of imprisonment and 'a full and fair trial' besides communal labour, which the Kukis could not accept. Hence, another phase of active engagement took place in the winter of 1918–1919.

The winter of 'civilised savagery' (November 1918 to April 1919)

Based on the new scheme of operations, the whole Kuki country was now divided into six operation 'areas' with sufficient numbers of military forces. In his 'Plan of Operations against the Kuki rebels', Lieut. Gen. Sir. H.D.U. Keary, GOI, Burma Division and who now took up the overall command of the operations, spelt out this scheme as 'to divide up the entire hostile theatre of operations into [six] areas' each of which are to be 'enclosed by a chain of outposts [54 posts in total] of a strength of 50 rifles. Each outpost was to furnish active patrols and to act as supply depots for mobile columns which will be 'constantly on the move within the enclosures'. He went on noting that:

> The post patrols will keep close touch between posts and endeavour to hem the rebels inside the enclosed area wherein the stronger mobile columns can hunt them down and at the same time destroy rebel villages and sequestrate or destroy livestock and supplies. The rebel will be given no rest and attempts at preparing ground for cultivation or running up temporary villages will be frustrated.[109]

The objectives of the new scheme of operations were, he noted:

> To break the spirit of the Kukis to such an extent that they will become completely weary and demoralized and be ready to surrender themselves, their guns and property, agreeing to suffer such pains and penalties as, aided by the advice of the Chief Political Officers I may decide to inflict.[110]

Besides, it aims to enforce fines and other punishments, establishment of posts to hold the country after the operations, and to drive bridle paths throughout the rebel areas. In other words, the objects of the operations were, he noted, 'to end the Kuki revolt by force of arms, break the Kuki spirit, disarm the Kukis, exact reparation and pave the way for future administration of their country'.[111]

The operations actually began from 25 November 1918.[112] Once the operation started, all the schemes of 'civilised barbarity' were carried out with impunity and the military occupation of the hills by 'force of arms' was made. The Kuki villages were systematically burned down to the ground, all their livestock and supplies were 'sequestrated or destroyed', and every effort to cultivation and new settlements were 'frustrated'. At the end of the operations, it was reported that a total of 126 Kuki villages had been burnt down, 16 villages deserted and 140 villages surrendered. Official figure of mithuns killed was 576.[113] Besides these, the military columns had also destroyed a much larger numbers of other livestock such as goats, pigs, fowls, etc. No official figure was given on the amount of food-grains (mainly rice) and other food stock (such as root crops, cereals, oilseeds, etc.) which were also systematically destroyed or eaten. Food reserve for one year was inarguably very high. Kuki villages normally contained large amount of cotton and other produces for their home manufacture and trade, besides a much larger amount of properties and family heirlooms; the raging fire of colonial 'barbarity' consumed them all.

Besides this scorched-earth policy, the whole Kuki population was harried and hunted down from pillar to post, giving them no rest, inside the enclosed area. Those hapless Kukis such as women, children and aged, or even their fighters who were captured in the hunt, or who had surrendered, were put into the various 'concentration camps' closed to military outposts. They were used as bait to the 'rebels' to submit and as human shield against their attack. While most of the leading men were incarcerated in the 'prison of war' annexed to Imphal Jail, hundreds of women, children and other men were kept in different 'concentration camps'. There were Kuki concentration camps at Tengnoupal, Ningel, Bongmol, Mombi and Nunglao. It was here that their suffering had become outrageous. They were made to do many odd jobs under severe conditions and many of them died in the most pitiable way. The nature of torture and oppression in all these concentration camps can be gleaned from their accounts of the tragedy at Kuljang (near Mombi)

concentration camp, recorded by the Consultative Committee of
Kuki Leaders (1963):

> The Kukis kept in this camp were tied together with one
> another by their loins (the distance of the next being two feet
> or so) and made to proceed in a long chain. Heavy loads of
> rice bags were put on their backs and shoulders, and they
> were then driven in herds as beasts of burden, up the steep hill
> along the road for about a mile. The process was repeated sev-
> eral times for a stretch, right from sunrise to sunset when they
> were given several lashes on their rear ends. Unable to bear
> this torture, many Kukis succumbed to the pain. Even to this
> day Kuki elders who experienced these worst days cannot but
> hold back bitter tears, when they relate the sad tale of those
> punishments and torture meted out to them.
>
> (Haokip 2008: 246)

The conditions of those Kukis who were kept at Imphal 'prison of
war' were equally harsh. Many of them died due to the hardship, officially said to be 'sickness'.[114]

The harsh military tactic, officially known as the 'enclosed area' system, a tactic popularly known in colonial counterinsurgency theory
'cordon and search' or 'cordoning and raking' operations, was now
so drastic that the Kukis were, one after another, compelled to surrender or be captured by 'force of arms'. Already in December 1918,
some Kuki chiefs of Mattiang (Matijang), Maokot, Somararam,
Maudam, Paipum, Monglam, Hinglep and Twishun had been forced
to submit before the military troops. In January 1919, there was an
active military engagement in all the areas. Many of the leading rebels
had been killed or captured, and large numbers of Kukis also surrendered. On 15 January, the GOI reported that 44 Kukis had been
already killed, 48 villages were burned down, 54 villages surrendered
with 89 guns and 40 mithuns and large quantities of grain had been
destroyed. Since then, among many captures and surrenders of less
importance, Longya has been occupied, its chief Ngulbul and his son
killed and his brother and 55 men of his village captured. The Chief
of Ukha had also been captured. Eight Kukis, including the Chief of
Bukshao and Lumpum, were killed, and 48 were captured, including
the Chiefs of Hengtham and Thirgodang on 17 January in an attack
on Lumpum. At Umdum 210 men, women and children surrendered,
and Ngulkhup of Mombi was also vigorously pursued from hill to

hill, and having no place to move on, submitted at Tamu before Burmese officers.[115] Pache, the Chassad Chief, was harried from pillar to post in which he always had a narrow escape. The month of February also witnessed active operations in many parts of the hills. Pache and his band of fighting men were surrounded and finally dispersed only to start fresh fighting in the Somra Tract. Tintong of Laiyang, in the western section, and his henchman Enjakhup, had also been harried from hill to hill, but they were successful in evading the columns. Tintong was finally captured on the night of 11 February and Enjakhup on 13 February 1919.[116] Military operations continued throughout February and many more of them surrendered and gave up their guns to the columns. On 21 February, GOI reported that the Imphal-Silchar road was open to traders without escort. On 25 February, the Somra north sub-area was said to be practically cleared with the surrender of Vumngul and Howkhupao of Molvailup with four other chiefs. On 5 March, having no place to hide, Pache chief of Chassad also finally came down to Imphal with his wife and child and submitted there. Active opposition was reported to be practically over, and during the latter part of February it was reported that the columns were busily engaged in road making and building stockades.[117]

Active operations during March were practically confined to the Somra Tract where Ngulkhukai led the rising. He also eventually submitted on 15 March with his wife and family. This completed the tally of Kuki leaders on the 'special list'; one of the 15 having been killed in action, five captured and nine having surrendered themselves. The military columns were busy throughout the month of March making roads, building and rationing stockades and collecting guns. While all political and civil questions was handed over to civil administration by the 15 April, demobilisation was completed on 1 May 1919.[118] This was how the operations finally ended.

3. Period of trial and tribulation

The capture and submission of all the prominent Kuki chiefs and the eventual suppression of the armed resistance was followed by another phase of Kuki tribulation. On the question of punishment, much disagreement cropped up in British officialdom. Local officers wanted capital punishment or life deportation to their leaders as if they were 'murderers'. The Assam government (concurred by GOI and Burma) felt otherwise and urged to treat the Kuki war as a political matter. The Chief Commissioner of Assam, for instance, felt that the Kukis were 'enemies in arms' rather than mere murderers. He said:

> Everyone would agree that murderers and their abettors should be hanged, but the question was who should be treated as murderers, *i.e.*, how far should the [Kukis] people who fought against us and shot the members of expeditionary forces be treated as *enemies in arms* and how far as murderers.[119]

The GOI also maintains that the 'offence in question' was in the nature of 'acts of barbarous warfare than of ordinary murder and should as such be dealt with tribally'.[120] Both these views excluded capital punishment.

Assam government eventually came out with the proposal to treat the matter under Bengal Regulation III of 1818. It was legally known as 'State Prisoners Regulation' which stipulated that for 'reasons of State' individuals can be place '*under personal restraint*' against whom 'there may not be sufficient ground to institute any judicial proceeding, or when such proceeding may not be adapted to the nature of the case, or may for other reasons be unadvisable or improper'. It also stipulated that the 'President of the Union' (i.e. Viceroy) should determine the punishment. The local administration was therefore required to provide information to the Viceroy from time to time for his decision. It also required the administration to give 'due attention' to 'the *health* of every State prisoner' and 'suitable *provision* be made for his support according to his rank in life and to his own wants and those of his family'.[121] The Regulation excluded capital sentence. On the period of detention, it was virtually left in the hands of the highest office in the country, the Viceroy.

The pronouncement of this Regulation was a wise decision on the part of the CC of Assam to get away from the vindictive sentiments of local officers. Considering all the facts related to the 'origin and early stages of Kuki revolt', the CC recommended to the GOI that the Kukis were 'more sinned against than sinning'. His argument was that the Kukis were wrongly coerced to supply labour recruits and that they were not properly informed of the government's policy. In the GOI, it was also felt that the Kuki war was caused by 'somewhat injudicious methods of recruitment for Labour Corps'. Therefore, concurring on the opinion of the CC, the GOI had finally decided that the Kuki 'State prisoners' should 'be placed under personal restraint at Sadiya and within a radius of two miles from the offices of the Political Officer, Sadiya Frontier Tract'.[122] Out of the 15 persons on the 'special list', Ngulbul died while fighting, whereas Semchung and Lunkhulal died at Kohima jail. While three of them (Ngulkhukhai, Enjakhup and Chingakhamba Sanachaoba) were kept in the Dibrugarh jail, the remaining nine chiefs (Chengjapao, Khutinthang, Pakang, Ngulkhup, Leothang, Pache, Tintong, Heljashon and Mangkho-on) were kept 'under restraint' at Sadiya. Similarly, 13 Kuki chiefs (Vumngul, Nohjang, Haokhopao, Kamjahen, Tongkholun, Letkhothang, Semkholun, Jalhun, Sonkhopao, Tukih, Kondem, Letjahao and Nomjahen) were detained at Taungyi, Burma under Chin Hills Regulation 1896.

The story of their detention at Sadiya and Taungyi has been often misunderstood as 'jail' or 'prison' by many scholars. It should be remembered that the Kuki chiefs, except for some names noted above, were not put inside the prison cells. They were detained, as the 'warrant' shows, within a two-mile radius from the office of the Political Officer, Sadiya Frontier Tracts, where a proper accommodation for them was built, their health being taken 'due attention' by medical officers, and 'suitable provision' such as food, clothing and so on, were given 'for their support' as important chieftains of the Kukis. The place where they were put under detention was said to be an 'open country', not inside a jail. The report of the Assam government notes that the nine Kuki 'state prisoners' were 'now specially housed in the open country at Sadiya'. It also reported that the CC of Assam, Sir Nicholas Beatson Bell, had also 'recently visited these chiefs at Sadiya and was pleased to find them all in excellent health and (in the circumstances) wonderfully happy'.[123] The official notes in Assam administration clearly noted that 'the Kukis in Sadiya are not kept in jail, though there is a guard over them'; they 'enjoyed certain measure of liberty and only restricted to Sadiya'. They were found to be comfortably housed, looked healthy, happy and contented. Some of them 'expressed a desire that their wives should be brought down at Sadiya; but if they should be released within a few years they did not press the request'. Footballs were supplied for them, but it was not known to what extent they used them.[124]

In this context, the place where they were detained was certainly not a prison; they were comfortably 'housed in the open country', which may be best understood in popular vocabulary as 'house arrest'. In fact, it is interesting to note that the Kuki 'political prisoners' often use the terms 'Sadia tuikol' (lit. Sadiya water island, meaning a river island in Sadiya) and 'henkolkai' (lit. hen is detain, kolkai is round fence, probably by river); they hardly use the term 'Songkul' (prison), in their songs and narratives. Their various songs and narratives related to their lives at Sadiya and Taungyi are instructive in this respect. From their narratives, one can surmise that they lived in separate houses or rooms in an open country and apparently cooked separately. They used to hunt or trap deer, birds and other wild animals (Haokip 2013: 67–69).[125] Tintong, for instance, once caught a deer and took it to Khutinthang. This upset Pache, who considered himself the rightful person to receive that honour as *pipa* of Haokip clan. The next time Tintong caught a deer, he took it to Chengjapao, which annoyed Khutinthang. Tintong then felt so confused and asked: 'Who is the eldest of all?' Khutinthang responded that 'Guite is the eldest of all of us'. This comment then upset Chengjapao, who considered himself the *pipa* (eldest) of all the Thadou-Kukis, and in response he composed a song:[126]

Mang leh chunga mang chang hi ing,
Nigui Guite nitui a peng,
Kaselung jaona umponte,

Free translation:

Government and ancestors recognised me as the eldest;
Guite was born of sunray;
I will not feel lesser [by Khutinthang's remark].

While Chengjapao understood 'sunray' in a negative sense, Tintong felt it otherwise, probably in the sense of a royal birth. Thus, while accepting the headship claimed by Chengjapao because of the leadership he assumed in the Kuki war, Tintong responded with another song.[127]

Namtin velkhupna lhung joulou
Nitui ja pendem?

Free translation:

One who could not lead the nation,
Can he be born of the sunray?

This kind of narrative provides an insight into the lives of Kuki 'state prisoners' at Sadiya.

On the other side, Taungyi in Burma, it was said that the Kuki prisoners used to brew rice beer and their traditional drinks (*vaiju*). When they got drunk, they used to dance and enjoy. Chief Nohjang was said to be a very handsome man, and the daughter of the British Officer there, they said, was attracted to him and used to come when they danced. Nohjang, then composed a song:[128]

> *Noi mangpa Boro sab chanu,*
> *Napa laihen kahi'e nei deicha hih in.*

Free translation:

> You! Daughter of British Officer
> Do not like me, I am your father's prisoner.

One day they went to Taungyi bazaar. There, a young Shan lady of the place asked them in Burmese '*Tongyi sann dalar?*' which means 'Is Tongyi cold/comfortable?' Other Kuki men did not understand Burmese, so they asked Nohjang 'What did the lady say' and 'How should we reply to her?' Nohjang replied, 'She said she wants to sleep with me, tell her "Nohjang mayabu" [Nohjang refuse!]'. When they told the young lady '*Nohjang mayabu*', they said, 'she laughed'. They came to know later what the lady had actually asked them and realised how Nohjang was lying to them. Since then, '*Nohjang mayabu*' became the most popular catchphrase in the detention camp to express one's disagreement. Until this day, the phrase has become one of the most popular catchphrases among the Kukis of Burma (Myanmar) that signifies disagreement to what one is being told or what one has done (Kipgen, n.d.).[129] Although the Kuki prisoners of Burma were trialled under Chin Hills Regulation, the GOI treated them in such a way as their counterparts in Assam. Overall, they were also treated as political prisoners. The above few accounts provided an insight into the daily lives of 'State prisoners', which is full of lively stories that provided a good sense of social life and a life that was without prison cells. Due to the want for space we skip the narratives that depict a life that was far away from home, the melancholy life, a life studded with dreams.

Enjakhup was transferred to Kohima in December 1920 only to be released there due to his ill health. He was suffering from tuberculosis, and the government did not want him to die when he was in prison. He died on 18 December 1920, the day he was released from Kohima, at the village of Khonoma, while being escorted home by his relatives.[130] Chingakhamba Sanachaoba was transferred to Shillong jail on health ground. After two of his companions were tranferred, it was proposed that Ngulkhukhai should also join other Kukis at Sadiya because he could not speak any of the languages spoken in Dibrugarh jail. As the GOI was opposed to what it called 'undue leniency', he was accordingly transferred to Shillong jail so that he could share the company of Chingakhamba Sanachaoba.[131] As the situation at home improved and there was no danger of any uprising again, the Kuki 'state prisoners' were released after three years, except Chengjapao who was released after four years.

On the other hand, the general Kuki population continued to work on different government road projects on communal penal labour. This was besides the war reparation amounting to one lakh 75,000 imposed on them which they paid partly in money and partly in labour. The Kukis were, therefore, freely impressed to cut the bridle paths and other roads connecting all important places in the hills with the valley of Manipur, Burma and Assam. They were also impressed to build new buildings and other official establishments in the hills which came up after the war. In this communal penal labour, the Kukis worked for about five years after the war. Perhaps one of the most important changes brought about by the war was the extension of direct administration into the hills of Manipur and the Somra Tract in Burma. This aspect of the administration will be taken up in a separate chapter in this volume. Here it is important to note that the new scheme of administration was, as the Chief Commissioner of Assam told the Manipur Darbar after the war, 'to ensure that they [Kukis] shall not again embark on a mad course of rebellion'.[132] This was carried into effect by the four subdivisions, which came up in the hills of Manipur under British officers. If the 'clouds of war had rolled away' and 'a peace with happiness and a peace with honour', as the Chief Commissioner put it, returned to the people of Manipur, that was not the case for Kukis, whose daily life had been now subjected to colonial control.[133] To the Kukis, the new administration was truly not a 'thoughtful and sympathetic administration' as it was said to be, but only an instrument of oppression and exploitation. Most Kukis spent their days on communal penal labour in the jungles and their growing poverty and hardship went on for a long time. This made them even more discontented, and therefore they were constantly looking for an opportunity to tide over their sufferings under the colonial yoke. The Second World War brought new hope, only to be faded away into oblivion.

Concluding remarks: military estimation of the Kuki war

The Kuki war was brutally suppressed and their leaders eventually captured or surrendered not because they lacked courage and skill

JANGKHOMANG GUITE

but because of the brutality the military operations had perpetrated against their villages, properties, livestock and to their hapless population. Lt. Gen. H.D.U. Keary, for instance, admitted that the defeat of the Kukis was not due to the lack of courage and skill but due to the superior weapons of the British forces.

> The extraordinarily few casualties, taken in conjunction with the complete collapsed of the Kukis, might lead one to suppose that the opposition offered by the Kukis was negligible. The Kukis, who numbered at least 8 to 1, were fighting in country that *neutralized* to a great degree our superiority in modern weapons. Moreover, they were *not lacking in courage or skill*.[134]
>
> (*Emphasis mine*)

The experience gained in the first phase, the introduction of Stokes mortars, rifle grenades and Lewis guns, was decisive.[135] Gen. Keary even went on recommending to the Army Headquarters that Kukis should form part of the colonial armies in the future.

> There is fine soldierly material in the Northern Chin, and I have every reason to anticipate that they and the Kuki will in time make a useful addition to our local irregular forces, and ultimately to the Army.[136]

Col. Shakespear also similarly wrote on the Kuki war later:

> The rapidly spreading rising amongst the Kuki clans was disconcerting and most difficult to deal with. . . . It grew therefore into the largest series of military operations conducted on this side of India since the old expeditionary days . . . eclipsing them all in casualties and arduousness of active service.
>
> (Shakespear 1980: 224, 235–236)

Various field reports also show how fighting Kuki tactics of 'hit and run' or 'guerilla warfare' was most tedious and demoralising to the troops. Lieut. Col. J.L.W. Ffrench-Mullen, for instance, reported the enervating and demoralising effect of Kuki tactics on government troops.

> There is nothing more disheartening to troops than chasing the elusive savage through his dense jungles never really

scoring off him, on the contrary suffering daily casualties with the very remote chance if lucky of 'downing' a sniper. Always every moment of the 24 hours, whether in the camp or on the march, [they were] in danger of a shot from the surrounding jungle. Nothing to show for weeks and months of effort, no rest and no relaxation of mind or body, bad food and an entire absence of the amenities of life. These operations have no glamour for those engaged, far from it. They are thankless, disagreeable jobs which have to be got over and which involve a serious risk to life and health.[137]

The difficulty in dealing with Kuki warfare led him to recommend the operations as part of the First World War. Considering 'the strain physical and mental on officers and men', and the hard show given by them in the rugged mountains against what he called the 'crafty jungle fighters on their own chosen terrain', Ffrench-Mullen insisted that the government should recognise their efforts as part of the Great War: 'It is hoped by those who participated in them that they may be considered worth of recognition as a *humble part of the great war*'.[138] The GOI and British War Office later accepted this request. Accordingly, the two medals of the First World War – the British War Medal 1914–1919 and Victory Medal – were given to them, making it the 'humble part of the Great War'. Although this was not initially conceived, what makes the Kuki Operations part of the Great War was that the operations were funded from the War Fund and that large number of coolies were diverted from and paid the amount of those labourers going to France.

Seeing the performances of the Kukis in various encounters, Ffrench-Mullen provided some of his general estimations of Kuki fighters. He said that the Kukis 'are born snipers and can creep up to a camp at night without a sound'. They 'are certainly to be called brave as they take big risks in these efforts to shoot our people especially British Officers'. They 'have been known to stand the scorching fire of seven-pounder mountain guns and Lewis guns at close range and then pop up and snipe at our columns from the very place on which the scorching fire had been directed'.[139] This hard show, although brutally suppressed, had in fact gained them (or more appropriately, revived the lost martial status they once gained) a military signature of being 'fine soldierly material' in India. In the aftermath of the Anglo-Kuki War the name 'Kuki' became a military brand in recruitment, and hundreds of Kukis joined the colonial armies for this reason.

An overview of the Anglo-Kuki War 1917–1919 makes the event significant on some important grounds. First, the rising was directly connected to the world event, the Great War, partly, because the labour recruitment for France in the region the immediate cause of the rising, and partly, the operations were funded from the War Fund and the soldiers were granted medals. Its connection with the wider revolutionary ideas against colonialism was also established. The 'totality' of the Great War becomes significant when non-Europeans and the remote frontiers of the Empire are taken into consideration. Second, the counterinsurgency operations against the Kukis were different from the normal course of military operation in the region, one that was popularly known in the colonial world for its cruelty and 'barbarity'. A deeper insight could reveal the violent character of colonialism in the colonies, especially in the Empire's frontier, making the region a geography of violence. Third, it also signifies the failure of the colonial post-COIN programme of 'restoration' policy, which put them in contrast to the later developed idea of winning the 'hearts and minds' of the people affected by insurgency. Fourth, the tactics of 'guerilla warfare' adopted by the Kukis remained the *modus operandi* of all the insurgency movements in the region in postcolonial India. A similar motto of the Kuki rising *'lheppon bang kitho hite'* (let us stack like folded clothes) remains the guiding principle in all 'tribal' insurgency movements today in the region. Should the failure of the military solution of colonial COIN strategy to the Kuki rising also remain a viable lesson in the present as well?

Notes

1 British Library, London (BL), Asian and African Collections (formerly Oriental & India Office Collections) (hereafter AAC), Indian Office Records and Private Papers (hereafter IOR&PP), Mss Eur E325/13 (1920): 'Extract from the Proceedings of the Chief Commissioner of Assam in the Political Department', No. 8856-P, 27 September 1920 by A.W. Botham.
2 Assam State Archives, Guwahati (hereafter ASA), Political Deptt., File No. H – 281P of 1917, Political – A, December 1917, Nos. 39–80: 'Recruitment of Labour Corps from Assam for service in France', No. 39, Telegram from the Government of India (hereafter GOI), Army Department, 28 January 1917.
3 ASA, Assam Secretariat, File No. H – 1P of 1917, Political – B, April 1918, Nos. 316–499, k.w. 'Manipur coolie recruitment', Political Agent, Manipur (hereafter PA) to Chief Secretary to Chief Commissioner of Assam (hereafter (CS), telegram No. 267P, 5 February 1917.
4 For instance, the Tangkhuls headmen were against going to France even after several rounds of talks, but they eventually gave in when Higgins

threatened that he would go back to Imphal and bring the police to over-awe them. Manipur State Archives (hereafter MSA), R-2/231/S-4: *Tour Diary of J.C. Higgins, President Manipur State Darbar,* (hereafter *Higgins Tour Diary-I*) dated 6–9 April 1917

5 MSA, R-2/231/S-4: *Higgins Tour Diary-I*, 3 and 4 April 1917; *Documents of the Anglo-Kuki War 1917–1919*, edited by D.L.Haokip 2017, chapter 3: J.C. Higgins to CS Assam, 24 November 1917 (hereafter *Documents of Anglo-Kuki War*). See also BL, AAC, IOR&PP, IOR/L/PS/10/724: 1917–1920, 'Burma-Assam Frontier: Disturbances among Kuki Tribesmen in Manipur', File No. P-693/1919: J.E. Webster, CS Assam to Foreign Secy. GOI, 27 June 1919.

6 *Documents of Anglo-Kuki War,* Confidential D.O. No. 5.C. of H.W. Cole to B.C Allen, 17 March 1917.

7 Higgins also noted that Khutinthang and Pache killed mithun as far back as March and 'distributed portions of the flesh throughout the hills, thereby inducing other chiefs not to send their men'. The former also 'sent emissaries to the Haokips in the eastern hills and the tribes near the Chin and Lushai borders'. See *Documents of Anglo-Kuki War,* J.C. Higgins to CS Assam, 24 November 1917.

8 *Documents of Anglo-Kuki War,* J.C. Higgins to CS Assam, 24 November 1917.

9 BL, AAC, IOR&PP, IOR/L/PS/10/724: 1917–1920, File No. P-6933/1919: JE Webster, CS Assam to Foreign Secy. GOI, 27 June 1919.

10 BL, AAC, IOR&PP, IOR/L/PS/10/724: 1917–1920, File No. 383/1919: Webster to Foreign Secy. GOI, 7 November. 1917.

11 BL, AAC, IOR&PP, IOR/L/PS/10/724: 1917–1920, File No. 383/1919: Webster to Foreign Secy. GOI, 7 November. 1917; *Documents of Anglo-Kuki War,* J.C. Higgins to Chief Secretary, Assam, 24 November 1917.

12 BL, AAC, IOR&PP, IOR/L/PS/10/724: 1917–1920, File No. P-383/1918: Webster to Secy GOI, 7 November 1917.

13 MSA, R-2/230/S-4: *Tour Diary of JC Higgins, Officiating Political Agent in Manipur* (hereafter *Higgins Tour Diary-II*), dated 10 & 11 October 1917; See the 'Memorandum' of Kuki political prisoners to Commissioner, Surma Valley and Hill Districts', as appended in the letter of J.E. Webster to Foreign Secy. GOI, 27 June 1919, BL, AAC, IOR&PP, IOR/L/PS/10/724: 1917–1920, File No. P-6933/1919.

14 See MSA, R-2/230/S-4, *Higgins Tour Diary-II*, dated 13–18 October 1917.

15 National Archives of India (NAI), Foreign & Political Deptt. (hereafter FP), Secret-External, July 1918, Nos. 7–131: J.E. Webster, CS Assam to S.R. Hignell, Secy to GOI, FP, 7 November 1917. See also the same letter at BL, AAC, IOR&PP, IOR/L/PS/10/724 (1917–1920), File No. 383/1919: Webster to Foreign Secy. GOI, 7 November. 1917.

16 BL, AAC, IOR&PP, IOR/L/PS/10/724: 1917–1920, File No. 5115/1917: Foreign Secy. GOI to Webster, CS Assam, 26 November 1917.

17 See BL, AAC, IOR&PP, IOR/L/PS/10/724: 1917–1920, File No. P-6933/1919: Webster to Foreign Secy. GOI, 27 June 1919.

18 See their memo as enclose in the report of Webster to Foreign Secy., GOI, 27 June 1919, in BL, AAC, IOR&PP, IOR/L/PS/10/724: 1917–1920, File No. P-6933/1919.

19 BL, AAC, IOR&PP, IOR/L/PS/10/724: 1917–1920, File No. P-6933/1919: Webster to Foreign Secy. GOI, 27 June 1919.

20 He informed Pache that 'if an officer visit Mombi again, he will be shot and begging Pachei to adopt the same attitude'. *Documents of Anglo-Kuki War,* Higgins to CS Assam, 24 November 1917.

21 MSA, R-2/230/S-4: *Higgins Tour Diary-II,* 1 November and 1 December 1917.

22 Higgins reported that the forester of Kanbung hill produced to him 'a letter addressed by the chief of Ukha to Pachei chief of Chassad, enumerating certain chiefs who had assembled at his village and *sworn to resist* and inciting him to do the same'. MSA, R-2/230/S-4: *Higgins Tour Diary,* 8 November 1917.

23 It was reported that 'He threatened if they disobeyed him, to kill them before the fight, which was to take place in the cold weather between the Kuki and the *Sirkar'.* See *Documents of Anglo-Kuki War,* Higgins to CS Assam, 24 November 1917.

24 *Documents of Anglo-Kuki War,* Higgins to CS Assam, 24 November 1917.

25 BL, AAC, IOR&PP, IOR/L/PS/10/724: 1917–1920, IOR/L/PS/10/724: 1917–1919, File No. 2686/1919: 'Report on the Rebellion of the Kukis on the Upper Chindwin Frontier and the operations connected therewith' by J.B. Marshall, DC, Upper Chindwin District. Report from Manipur also shows that Ngulkhup and Khutinthang were also present in the Chassad conclave. *Documents of Anglo-Kuki War,* Higgins to CS Assam, 24 November 1917.

26 Literally, a 'strong wind', meaning a powerful enemy, the British.

27 *Nam cham khat* can only be translated as 'one free nation'.

28 *Documents of Anglo-Kuki War,* Higgins to CS Assam, 24 November 1917.

29 Higgins, for instance, reported that the Jampi and the northwestern Kukis 'are collecting large numbers of guns (estimated by my informant at 400 to 500), not only from the Kuki villages, but from the Kabuis and from villages in the North Cachar Hills'. MSA, R-2/230/S-4: *Higgins Tour Diary-II,* 10 December 1917.

30 The fact that Higgins did not encounter any opposition, no stockade (except one small one near the village) and no fortification when he visited Mombi in October 1917 was a telling case that no war preparation had been taken before the burning of Mombi. This was not the case when he returned in January 1918. See MSA, R-2/230/S-4: *Higgins Tour Diary-II,* 15–16 October 1917.

31 JH Hutton, DC Naga Hills, for instance, had intercepted the 'fiery-cross' sent by Chengjapao to the Khonoma of Naga Hills; daos were also sent to Maram village to cut the telegraph line; emissaries were also intercepted in North Cachar hills; and 'a bullet and a piece of charcoal' with a message 'to fight the Government' was also intercepted in Cachar frontier. See ASA, Political Dept. (PD), File No. 9C/M-61P of 1918, Political – A, March 1919, Nos. 1–255: 'Arrangements in connection with the operations against the Kuki rebels in Manipur': FM Clifford to WJ Reid (n.d).

32 MSA, R-2/230/S-4: *Higgins Tour Diary-II,* 22 December 1917.

33 MSA, R-2/230/S-4: *Higgins Tour Diary-II,* 1 November & 1 December 1917.

34 ASA, GSC, Sl. 260, File No. M/64-P of 1918, Political – B, March 1919, No. 135: 'Statement of Sugnu resthouse chaukidar (an Anal of Kareibung)'.

35 MSA, R-2/230/S-4: *Higgins Tour Diary-II,* 7 December 1917.

36 BL, AAC, IOR&PP, IOR/L/PS/10/724: 1917–1920, File No. 383/1919: Webster to Foreign Secy. GOI, 7 November 1917.

37 *Documents of Anglo-Kuki War,* Higgins to CS Assam, 24 November 1917. It was true that once a decision to fight the British was taken, the message of the 'unrest' spread like a wildfire on all sides. For Assam government view see BL, AAC, IOR&PP, IOR/L/PS/10/724: 1917–1920, File No. 383/1918: Webster to Foreign Secy. GOI, 3 December 1917.

38 BL, AAC, IOR&PP, IOR/L/PS/10/724: 1917–1920, Telegram from Foreign Secy. GOI to Chief Commissioner Assam, 11 December 1917.

39 See the translated 'parwana' as enclosure – II, of Webster letter to Foreign Secy. GOI, 27 December 1917, File No. 824/1918, IOR/L/PS/10/724: 1917–1920.

40 For instance, 'Mombi, Longya and Khengoi, Mangvum Haokip villages in the southeast had refused to accept the parwana ordering the chief to come and submit to punishment'. See MSA, R-2/230/S-4: *Higgins Tour Diary-II,* 22 December 1917.

41 See the 'Memorandum' of Kuki Political Prisoners to Commissioner'.

42 BL, AAC, IOR&PP, IOR/L/PS/10/724: 1917–1920, File No. P-6933/1919: Webster to Foreign Secy. GOI, 27 June 1919. See also MSA, R-2/230/S-4: *Higgins Tour Diary-II,* 20 December 1917.

43 Tintong was reported to go around the Kabui villages and ordered them to refrain from paying house taxes and join the rising. MSA, R-2/230/S-4: *Higgins Tour Diary-II,* 22 December 1917.

44 MSA, R-2/230/S-4: *Higgins Tour Diary-II,* 22 December 1917.

45 See MSA, R-2/230/S-4: *Higgins Tour Diary-II,* 23 December 1917.

46 MSA, R-2/230/S-4: *Higgins Tour Diary-II,* 23 & 24 December 1917.

47 MSA, R-2/230/S-4: *Higgins Tour Diary-II,* 20–31 December 1917.

48 ASA, GSC, Sl. 260, File No. M/64-P of 1918, Political – B, March 1919, No. 99: Higgins to Webster, 8 January 1918.

49 ASA, GSC, Sl. 260, File No. M/64-P of 1918, Political – B, March 1919, No. 99: Higgins to Webster 8 January 1918.

50 MSA, R-2/230/S-4: *Tour Diary of Political Agent, WA Cosgrave, 1916–1918* (hereafter *Cosgrave Tour Diary*) 4 January 1918.

51 *Documents of Anglo-Kuki War,* Higgins to CS Assam, 24 November 1917.

52 ASA, GSC, Sl. 260, File No. M/64-P of 1918, Political – B, March 1919, No. 99: Higgins to Webster, 8 January 1918.

53 ASA, GSC, Sl. 260, File No. M/64-P of 1918, Political – B, March 1919, No. 107: Cosgrave to Webster, 14 January 1918.

54 ASA, GSC, Sl. 260, File No. M/64-P of 1918, Political – B, March 1919, No. 134: *Tour Diary of JC Higgins* (hereafter, *Higgins Tour Diary-III*), 24 January 1918.

55 ASA, GSC, Sl. 260, File No. M/64-P of 1918, Political – B, March 1919, No. 132: Telegram from Imphal to CS, Assam, 2 February 1918; see also BL, AAC, IOR&PP, IOR/L/PS/10/724: 1917–1920, Telegram from CS, Burma to Foreign Secy. GOI, 4 February 1918; BL, AAC, IOR&PP, IOR/L/PS/10/724: 1917–1920, File No. P-2686/1919: Lt. Col. JLW Ffrench-Mullen, DIG, Burma Military Police to IGP Burma, 17 September 1918.

56 MSA, R-2/230/S-4: *Cosgrave Tour Diary-I,* 18 March 1918.

57 MSA, R-2/231/S-4: *Higgins Tour Diary-I,* 8 April 1918.

58 ASA, GSC, Sl. 260, File No. M/64-P of 1918, Political – B, March 1919, No. 107: Cosgrave to Webster, 14 January 1918.

59 ASA, GSC, Sl. 260, File No. M/64-P of 1918, Political – B, March 1919, No. 107: Cosgrave to Webster, 14 January 1918.

60 ASA, GSC, Sl. 260, File No. M/64-P of 1918, Political – B, March 1919, No. 130: 'Statement of Arubam Naimu Singh of Uripok, Imphal [Govt. Dakwalla from Palel to Tengnoupal]'.

61 ASA, GSC, Sl. 260, File No. M/64-P of 1918, Political – B, March 1919, No. 120: telegram from State office to Webster, 21 January 1918, and No. 121, Cosgrave to Webster, 23 January 1918.

62 ASA, GSC, Sl. 260, File No. M/64-P of 1918, Political – B, March 1919, No. 165: telegram to CS, 22 February 1918.

63 ASA, PD, File No. 9C/M-61P of 1918, Political – A, March 1919, Nos. 1–255: 'Arrangements', WL Scott to Reid, 21 February 1918.

64 ASA, GSC, Sl. 260, File No. M/64-P of 1918, Political – B, March 1919, 170: '[statement of] Kharga Singh Thapa, Chaukidar of the Tairelpokpi resthouse'.

65 See ASA, GSC, Sl. 260, File No. M/64-P of 1918, Political – B, March 1919, No. 134: *Higgins Tour Diary-III*, 22 January 1918.

66 ASA, GSC, Sl. 260, File No. M/64-P of 1918, Political – B, March 1919, No. 100: Cosgrave to Webster, 10 January 1918.

67 ASA, GSC, Sl. 260, File No. M/64-P of 1918, Political – B, March 1919, No. 141: *Diary of WA Cosgrave-II*, 23 January 1918.

68 ASA, GSC, Sl. 260, File No. M/64-P of 1918, Political – B, March 1919, No. 141: *Diary of WA Cosgrave-II*, 27 January 1918.

69 ASA, GSC, Sl. 260, File No. M/64-P of 1918, Political – B, March 1919, No. 121: Cosgrave to Webster, 23 January 1918; MSA, R-2/230/S-4: *Higgins Tour Diary-II*, 26 December 1917. See also ASA, PD, File No. 9C/M-61P of 1918, Political – A, March 1919, Nos. 1–255: 'Arrangements', WL Scott to Reid, 21 February 1918.

70 ASA, GSC, Sl. 260, File No. M/64-P of 1918, Political – B, March 1919, No. 121: Cosgrave to Webster, 23 January 1918.

71 ASA, GSC, Sl. 260, File No. M/64-P of 1918, Political – B, March 1919, No. 121: Cosgrave to Webster, 23 January 1918.

72 ASA, GSC, Sl. 260, File No. M/64-P of 1918, Political – B, March 1919, No. 141: *Cosgrave Tour Diary-II*, 24 January 1918.

73 BL, AAC, IOR&PP, IOR/L/PS/10/724: 1917–1920, File No. P-2686/1919: 'Report on the Rebellion of the Kukis on the Upper Chindwin frontier and the operations connected threwith' by JB Marshall, DC, Upper Chindwin District.

74 BL, AAC, IOR&PP, IOR/L/PS/10/724: 1917–1920, File No. P-2686/1919: Lt. Col. JLW Ffrench-Mullen, DIG, Burma Military Police to IGP Burma, 17 September 1918.

75 BL, AAC, IOR&PP, IOR/L/PS/10/724: 1917–1920, File No. P-2686/1919: 'Report on the rebellion of the Kukis on the Upper Chindwin Frontier and the operations connected therewith' by JB Marshall, DC, Upper Chindwin District.

76 'Civilised Barbarism and Savagery', *The Advocate of Peace (1894–1920)*, Vol. 63, No. 3 (MARCH 1901), pp. 51–53.

77 ASA, PD, File No. 9C/M-61P of 1918, Political – A, March 1919, Nos. 1–255: 'Arrangements', Cosgrave to Webster, 18 May 1918.

78 ASA, PD, File No. 9C/M-61P of 1918, Political – A, March 1919, Nos. 1–255: 'Arrangements', Cosgrave to Webster, 23 June 1918: '*Note on scheme of occupation of Manipur Hills*'.
79 BL, AAC, IOR&PP, IOR/L/PS/10/724: 1917–1920, File No. P-2686/1919: Lt. Col. JLW Ffrench-Mullen, DIG, Burma Military Police to IGP Burma, 17 September 1918.
80 ASA, PD, File No. 9C/M-61P of 1918, Political – A, March 1919, Nos. 1–255: 'Arrangements', *Conference at Government House*, Shillong 4 July 1918.
81 BL, AAC, IOR&PP, IOR/L/PS/10/724: 1917–1920, File No. P-2686/1919: Lt. Col. JLW Ffrench-Mullen, DIG, Burma Military Police to IGP Burma, 17 September 1918.
82 ASA, PD, File No. 9C/M-61P of 1918, Political – A, March 1919, Nos. 1–255: 'Arrangements': A. Vickers to JH Hutton, 4 June 1918.
83 See for instance, ASA, PD, File No. 9C/M-61P of 1918, Political – A, March 1919, Nos. 1–255: 'Arrangements', Cosgrave to Col. Banatvala, 13 June 1918.
84 ASA, PD, File No. M-33P of 1918, Political – A, December 1919, Nos. 1–144: 'Surrender and trial': 'Note made over to Mr. Higgins who is proceeding with Brig. Gen. Macquois to Tamu for a conference with Liet. Gen. Keary', by ND Beatson Bell, 25 March 1919.
85 ASA, PD, File No. 9C/M-61P of 1918, Political – A, March 1919, Nos. 1–255: 'Arrangements', Cosgrave to Webster, 13 May 1918: 'Statement of Waishon Kuki, Chief of Leirik, Lam No. 4'.
86 ASA, PD, File No. 9C/M-61P of 1918, Political – A, March 1919, Nos. 1–255: 'Arrangements', Cosgrave to Webster, 13 May 1918.
87 ASA, PD, File No. 9C/M-61P of 1918, Political – A, March 1919, Nos. 1–255: 'Arrangements', Cosgrave to Webster, 13 May 1918.
88 ASA, PD, File No. 9C/M-61P of 1918, Political – A, March 1919, Nos. 1–255: 'Arrangements', Cosgrave to Webster, 18 May 1918.
89 BL, AAC, IOR&PP, IOR/L/PS/10/724: 1917–1920, File No. 3505/1918: Webster to Foreign Secy. GOI,5 June 1918.
90 BL, AAC, IOR&PP, Mss. Eur E325/13 (1920): 'Extract from the Proceedings of the Chief Commissioner of Assam in the Political Department', No. 8856-P, 27 September 1920 by A.W. Botham.
91 BL, AAC, IOR&PP, IOR/L/PS/10/724: 1917–1920, File No. 3980/1918: Webster to Foreign Secy. GOI, 6 July 1918; see also ASA, Political Dept. (PD), File No. 9C/M-61P of 1918, Political – A, March 1919, Nos. 1–255: 'Arrangements', Cosgrave to Webster, 23 June 1918: '*Note on scheme of occupation of Manipur Hills*'.
92 BL, AAC, IOR&PP, IOR/L/PS/10/724: 1917–1920, File No. 3980/1918: Webster to Foreign Secy. GOI, 6 July 1918; see also ASA, Political Dept. (PD), File No. 9C/M-61P of 1918, Political – A, March 1919, Nos. 1–255: 'Arrangements', Cosgrave to Webster, 23 June 1918: '*Note on scheme of occupation of Manipur Hills*'.
93 ASA, PD, File No. M-33P of 1918, Political – A, December 1919, Nos. 1–144: 'Surrender and trial of the Kuki rebels in Manipur', No. 11: PA Manipur to CS Assam, 11 July 1918.

94 See, IOR, 3980/1918: Webster to Foreign Secy. GOI, 16 July 1918; ASA, PD, File No. M-33P of 1918, Political – A, December 1919, Nos. 1–144: 'Surrender and trial', No. 14: CS Assam to PA Manipur, 14 July 1918.
95 BL, AAC, IOR&PP, IOR/L/PS/10/724: 1917–1920, File No. 2829/1918: telegram from Viceroy 24 June 1918.
96 BL, AAC, IOR&PP, IOR/L/PS/10/724: 1917–1920, File No. 4316/1918: Webster to Foreign Secy. GOI, 2 August 1918.
97 BL, AAC, IOR&PP, IOR/L/PS/10/724: 1917–1920, File No. 5032/18: Webster, Assam to Foreign Secy. GOI, 12 September 1918.
98 BL, AAC, IOR&PP, IOR/L/PS/10/724: 1917–1920, Telegram from CC, Assam to Secy. GOI, FP, 19 September 1918. See also ASA, PD, File No. M-33P of 1918, Political – A, December 1919, Nos. 1–144: 'Surrender and trial', see No. 26 & 27.
99 ASA, PD, File No. M-33P of 1918, Political – A, December 1919, Nos. 1–144: 'Surrender and trial', No. 30: CS Assam to Secy. GOI, 25 September 1918.
100 ASA, PD, File No. M-33P of 1918, Political – A, December 1919, Nos. 1–144: 'Surrender and trial', Cosgrave to Webster, 26 September 1918.
101 ASA, PD, File No. M-33P of 1918, Political – A, December 1919, Nos. 1–144: 'Surrender and trial', Cosgrave to Webster, 26 September 1918.
102 ASA, PD, File No. M-33P of 1918, Political – A, December 1919, Nos. 1–144: 'Surrender and trial', Cosgrave to Webster, 2 October 1918.
103 ASA, PD, File No. M-33P of 1918, Political – A, December 1919, Nos. 1–144: 'Surrender and trial', Cosgrave to Webster, 26 September 1918.
104 Cosgrave also noted another event that tempered his negotiation with Tintong. He reported the attack on a small Kuki village – Natjang or Somekthangjaba (the people which belong to Tintong) – by the Kabui villagers of Akhui and Awang Khil. He said that he had received 'fairly reliable information that the Kabuis managed to kill everybody in this village except one man, and that in revenge for this raid, Kukis of Ukha and Hinglep burnt four villages, Lukhambi (Kabui Naga), Langkhong (Kabui Naga, Kukis and Koms), Maibum (Kuki) and Faileh (Kuki)'. ASA, PD, File No. M-33P of 1918, Political – A, December 1919, Nos. 1–144: 'Surrender and trial', Cosgrave to Webster, 12 October 1918.
105 ASA, PD, File No. M-33P of 1918, Political – A, December 1919, Nos. 1–144: 'Surrender and trial', No. 49: PA Manipur to CS Assam, 22 October 1918.
106 ASA, PD, File No. M-33P of 1918, Political – A, December 1919, Nos. 1–144: 'Surrender and trial', Cosgrave to Webster, 12 October 1918.
107 ASA, PD, File No. M-33P of 1918, Political – A, December 1919, Nos. 1–144: 'Surrender and trial', Cosgrave to Webster, 26 October 1918. 'Kept in jail' was later substituted with 'kept as a prisoner of war'. See ASA, PD, File No. M-33P of 1918, Political – A, December 1919, Nos. 1–144: 'Surrender and trial', Webster to Cosgrave, 8 November 1918.
108 ASA, PD, File No. M-33P of 1918, Political – A, December 1919, Nos. 1–144: 'Surrender and trial', Cosgrave to Webster, 26 October 1918. 'Kept in jail' was later substituted with 'kept as a prisoner of war'. ASA, PD, File No. M-33P of 1918, Political – A, December 1919, Nos. 1–144: 'Surrender and trial', Webster to Cosgrave, 8 November 1918.

109 BL, AAC, IOR&PP, IOR/L/PS/10/724: 1917–1920, File No. P-5728/1918, 'Plan of Operations Against the Kuki Rebels, September 1918', GOI, Burma Division to Chief of Army Staff, Army Hqtrs., 5 September 1918.
110 BL, AAC, IOR&PP, IOR/L/PS/10/724: 1917–1920, File No. P-5728/1918, 'Plan of Operations Against the Kuki Rebels, September 1918', GOI, Burma Division to Chief of Army Staff, Army Hqtrs., 5 September 1918.
111 BL, AAC, IOR&PP, IOR/L/MIL/17/19/42 (1919): 'Despatch on the Operations against the Kuki Tribes of Assam and Burman November 1917 to March 1919', Lt. Gen. HDU Keary to Chief of the General Staff, June 1919.
112 BL, AAC, IOR&PP, IOR/L/PS/10/724: 1917–1920, File No. 1008/1919: Webster to Foreign Secy. GOI, 7 January 1919.
113 BL, AAC, IOR&PP, IOR/L/MIL/17/19/42: 1919: 'Despatch on the Operations Against the Kuki Tribes' Macquoid to Keary, 27 April 1919, Appendix – II & III. See also Shakespear 1929: 236–37.
114 For detail of these cases, see Manipur Secretariat Library (MSL), Cabin No. 5, File No. 5: 'Kuki Rebellion – Cases (1917–18)'.
115 BL, AAC, IOR&PP, IOR/L/PS/10/724: 1917–1920, File No. 1783/1919: Webster to Foreign Secy, GOI, 13 February 1919.
116 BL, AAC, IOR&PP, IOR/L/PS/10/724: 1917–1920, File No. 1783/1919: telegram from CS Assam to Foreign Secy. GOI, 17 February 1919.
117 BL, AAC, IOR&PP, IOR/L/PS/10/724: 1917–1920, File No. 2268/1919: Webster to Foreign Secy. GOI, 8 March. 1919.
118 BL, AAC, IOR&PP, IOR/L/PS/10/724: 1917–1920, File No. 2661/1919: Webster to Foreign Secy. GOI, 9 April 1919.
119 ASA, PD, File No. M-33P of 1918, Political – A, December 1919, Nos. 1–144, 'Surrender and trial': 'Note of proceedings of a Conference about the operations against the Kukis held in Imphal on the 13th April 1918', by JE Webster, 14 April 1918, pp. 35–37.
120 ASA, PD, File No. M-33P of 1918, Political – A, December 1919, Nos. 1–144, 'Surrender and trial', No. 17, GOI, FD to CS, Assam, 19 July 1918.
121 See, The State Prisoners Regulation [Bengal Regulation III of 1818] in *www.myanmarconstitutionaltribunal.org.mm*
122 BL, AAC, IOR&PP, Mss. Eur E325/13 (1920): 'Extract from the Proceedings of the Chief Commissioner of Assam in the Political Department, No. 8856-P, 27 September 1920' by A.W. Botham.
123 BL, AAC, IOR&PP, Mss. Eur E325/13 (1920): 'Extract from the Proceedings of the Chief Commissioner of Assam in the Political Department, No. 8856-P, 27 September 1920' by A.W. Botham.
124 See the official *Notes* in ASA, Governor's Secretariat, Pol. B, August, 1921, Nos. 263–314.
125 This narrative and songs are taken from Haokip's *Tintong Haokip, Laijangpa* (Haokip 2013: 67–69).
126 Haokip (2013: 68).
127 The Guite chiefs and large number of other Kukis in southwestern hills of Manipur provided labour for France and abstained from fighting against the British. We have noted that their preoccupation was in paying-off their debts from the bamboo famine of 1912. They remained loyal to the British throughout the war period. For this reason, Kukis of southwestern

Manipur (including Guites, Haokips, Singsons, Vaipheis, Hmars, etc.) were seen as British 'friendlies'. For the song see Haokip (2013: 68)

128 This interesting narrative is taken from an unpublished paper by Luntinsat Kipgen, who had written a piece on the biography of Nohjang Kipgen, 'Anglo-Kuki Gaal Lai a Maapgam a Gallamkai: Pu Nohjang Kipgen, Saisempa Thusim', (in Kuki), presented in a seminar on the Anglo-Kuki War 1917–1919 at JNU.

129 This interesting narrative is taken from an unpublished paper by Luntinsat Kipgen, who had written a piece on the biography of Nohjang Kipgen, 'Anglo-Kuki Gaal Lai a Maapgam a Gallamkai: Pu Nohjang Kipgen, Saisempa Thusim', (in Kuki), presented in a seminar on the Anglo-Kuki War 1917–1919 at JNU.

130 ASA, Governor's Secretariat, Pol. B, August, 1921, No. 298, Pawsey to US, GoA, 22 January 1921.

131 ASA, Governor's Secretariat, Pol. B, August, 1921, No. 305: Foreign Secy to CS Assam, 21 May 1921.

132 MSL, Cabin No. 32: 'Khongjai Lal Result, 1919–1920'.

133 MSL, Cabin No. 32: 'Khongjai Lal Result, 1919–1920'.

134 BL, AAC, IOR&PP, IOR/L/MIL/17/19/42: 1919, 'Despatch on the Operations Against the Kuki Tribes of Assam and Burma, November 1917 to March 1919', Lieut.-Gen. Sir H.D.U.Keary, GOI, Burma Division to Chief of the General Staff, Army Hqtrs. June 1919.

135 BL, AAC, IOR&PP, IOR/L/MIL/17/19/42: 1919, 'Despatch on the Operations Against the Kuki Tribes of Assam and Burma, November 1917 to March 1919', Lieut.-Gen. Sir H.D.U.Keary, GOI, Burma Division to Chief of the General Staff, Army Hqtrs. June 1919.

136 BL, AAC, IOR&PP, IOR/L/MIL/17/19/42: 1919, 'Despatch on the Operations Against the Kuki Tribes of Assam and Burma, November 1917 to March 1919', Lieut.-Gen. Sir H.D.U.Keary, GOI, Burma Division to Chief of the General Staff, Army Hqtrs. June 1919.

137 BL, AAC, IOR&PP, IOR/L/PS/10/724: 1917–1920, File No. P-2686/1919: Lt. Col. JLW Ffrench-Mullen, DIG, Burma Military Police to IGP Burma, 17 September 1918.

138 BL, AAC, IOR&PP, IOR/L/PS/10/724: 1917–1920, File No. P-2686/1919: Lt. Col. JLW Ffrench-Mullen, DIG, Burma Military Police to IGP Burma, 17 September 1918.

139 BL, AAC, IOR&PP, IOR/L/PS/10/724: 1917–1920, File No. P-2686/1919: Lt. Col. JLW Ffrench-Mullen, DIG, Burma Military Police to IGP Burma, 17 September 1918.

References

Archival materials

Assam State Archives, Guwahati: Governor's Secretariat (confidential) Files and Political Department files, 1917–1921.
British Library, London: Indian Office Record & Private Papers, 1917–1920.
Manipur Secretariat Library, Imphal: Kuki Rebellion, 1917–1920.

Manipur States Archives, Imphal: Tour Diary of Political Agent in Manpur, 1916–1919.

National Archives of India, New Delhi: Foreign Political Department files, 1917–1921.

Books & articles

Brown, R. 1873. *Statistical Account of Manipur*. Calcutta.

Dun, E.W. 1886 [reprint 1992]. *Gazetteer of Manipur*. New Delhi: Manas Publications.

Haokip, D.L. 2017. *Documents of the Anglo-Kuki War 1917–1919*. Imphal: Reliable Publication.

Haokip, P.S. 2008. *Zale'n-gam: The Kuki Nation*. KNO Publication.

Haokip, V. 2013. *Tintong Haokip, Laijangpa: Unsung Hero of the Kuki Rising, 1917–1919*. Imphal: Private Circulation.

Kipgen, L. n.d. 'Anglo-Kuki Gaal Lai a Maapgam a Gallamkai: Pu Nohjang Kipgen, Saisempa Thusim' (in Kuki, received from the author in 2017).

Ray, A.K. 1990. *Authority and Legitimacy: A Study of the Thadou-Kuki*. New Delhi: Renaissance Publishing House.

Shakespear, L.W. 1929 (reprint 1980). *History of the Assam Rifles*. Guwahati: Spectrum Publications.

2

THE 'HAKA UPRISING' IN CHIN HILLS, 1917–1918

Pum Khan Pau

> *They [chief] said that their people absolutely refused to go to France; that they said they had no quarrel with Germany. . . . They said they would commit suicide rather than go.*
>
> *– Laura Carson (1927: 227).*

During the First World War, the British launched massive military operations not only in Europe, the epicentre of the war, but in the remote hill areas of the Indo-Burma frontier to suppress what is officially labelled an 'uprising' or 'rebellion' but locally known as *gal* (war) of the Kuki-Chin (Zo) people against their colonial masters. The military operations were carried out jointly by the Assam Rifles and the Burma Military Police. They happened at a time when Britain was fully engaged with the war in Europe and her military presence in India particularly in the Indo-Burma frontier was minimal. What triggered the 'Kuki uprising' and the 'Haka uprising', as the war in Manipur and the Chin Hills were officially referred to, was the recruitment for the Labour Corps for France.

A good number of works (Bhadra 1975; Chishti 2004; Dena 1991) have been produced on the 'Kuki uprising' in Manipur and one of these was Gautam Bhadra's piece in *Man in India* (1975) which unravelled the underlying causes of the war, of course from a Subaltern's perspective. There are others who view the 'uprising' from an indigenous perspective and called it a war, such as the *Thadou War* (*Thadou gal*)[1] or *Zou Gal*[2] or the 'first Kuki War of independence'.[3] In this chapter, however, I intend to focus on the less known and understudied 'Haka uprising' in the Chin Hills. Like the *Thadou Gal* or *Zou Gal* in Manipur, the 'Haka uprising' in the Chin Hills is also locally known as *Lai Ral*[4], where *gal* or *ral* imply war against an enemy. Although this war was often treated separately from 'Kuki uprising', fresh evidence shows the connection between the two in major ways, the point which has been discussed in much detail in the introductory chapter of this volume.

The paper seeks to pose the following questions: was the 'Haka uprising' or *Lai Ral* simply a direct response to the British labour recruitment, or a culmination of gathering discontents under colonial regime? Why did the 'Haka uprising' or *Lai Ral* only stay confined to the Haka subdivision, whereas the other two subdivisions in the Chin Hills, i.e. Falam and Tedim, remained calm and 'loyal' to colonial rulers. Lastly and more importantly, was it the chiefs' war or the peoples' war?

Colonial rule in the Chin Hills

To contextualise what I would call the Anglo-Zo[5] (Kuki-Chin) war, to generally refer to the 'Kuki uprising' and the 'Haka uprising', it is imperative to know, at least very briefly, how the British penetrated into the hill tracts inhabited by the Zo people in the Indo-Burma frontier and engaged with them. Though there are records of early Zo contact with the British since the eighteenth century, their relationship may be properly traced after the expansion of the latter into Assam and the Arakan frontier following the First Anglo-Burmese War (1824–1826). Following the expulsion of the Burmese from Northeast India, the process of systematic dissection of the Zo 'culture area', to borrow an anthropological term, had begun. Part of this large area was given to Manipur state, part of it to Tripura, part of it to British Chittagong Hill Tracts (1860), part of it to British Northern Arakan Hill Tracts (1866) and so on. The remaining part of this 'cultural area' (known as Lushai Hills and Chin Hills) also soon succumbed to British occupation after Upper Burma was conquered in 1886. The British began to see the strategic importance of the Chin-Lushai Hills, and hence from the late 1880s a series of military campaigns was launched against the Zo people. The most important military campaign, called the Chin-Lushai Expedition, was mounted from Burma, Assam and Bengal respectively during 1889–1891. It crumbled the last stronghold of Zo resistance and finally resulted in the division of the Chin-Lushai Hills into three administrative units, viz. Chin Hills, North Lushai Hills and South Lushai Hills, each under Burma, Assam and Bengal respectively. An attempt to amalgamate them into a single unit failed in 1892 (Pau 2007). The adoption of the Chin Hills Regulations in 1896, therefore, marked the formal establishment of British administration in the

Chin Hills, which became a district under the Chief Commissioner of Burma. It was divided into three subdivisions viz., Tedim, Falam and Haka. In 1898, North and South Lushai Hills also formed a district under Assam.

Since this chapter is concerned only with the events in the Chin Hills during the First World War, the following discussion will deal only with this part of the Zo inhabited areas. The early years of British administration in the Chin Hills saw a marked improvement in infrastructures that really improved Zo lifestyles and society as a whole. Roads and bridges were made and communications improved; markets were established at strategic locations while education introduced in collaboration with Christian missionaries enlightened the people. However, colonial rule also impinged on the traditional polity. The power and functions of the chiefs and headmen had been redefined by the Chin Hills Regulation of 1896. By regrouping villages, checking inter-village and intra-village raids and the practice of slave-raiding the British had heavily encroached upon the traditional rights and powers of the chiefs. Therefore, though the British had gained the 'loyalty' of some chiefs, not all chiefs or headmen had reconciled themselves to their rule. In the meantime, the progress of Christianity and introduction of education, which had also driven the people away from their traditional customs and practices, denigrated the influence of the chiefs. It was therefore the chiefs' obduracy to the progress of Christianity that an indigenous socio-religious reform movement spearheaded by Pau Cin Hau, also called *Laipianism*, got its popularity among the Zo people. Zo people were caught between two parallel movements, one for 'culture change' and the other for 'cultural adaptability' (Pau 2012).

Labour corps and local response

It was on this backdrop that recruitment for Labour Corps was made in the Chin Hills as part of the larger drive from the indigenous hill peoples of Assam and Burma after the outbreak of the First World War. The call was responded positively in the Naga Hills, Lushai Hills and also in the northern Chin Hills. With regard to the development in the Chin Hills, it began with E.O. Fowler, Assistant Superintendent of Tedim subdivision, who started enlistment in April 1917. On 1 May 1917, the Superintendent J.M. Wright also gathered all the chiefs, headmen and four elders from each village in the subdivision and made a speech in which he plainly told them 'recruitment was voluntary'.[6] He told the people to supply 1,000 men each from the three subdivisions of Haka, Falam and Tedim. Hau Cin Khup, the powerful Kamhau chief of northern Chin Hills, who had always been 'loyal' to the British since the Sukte-Sihzang rebellion (1892–1893) had collected more than 1,000coolies from Tedim subdivision. He was assisted by chiefs Pau Za Cin, Dong Tual and Pau Khaw Mang. The Superintendent of the Chin Hills had happily noted: 'This response by the Northern Chin is more remarkable when it is considered that there are only about 5,000 males between the ages of 20 and 40 in the subdivision'.[7] In Falam subdivision over 800 labourers had been enrolled. There was minor resistance from the Khuangli village, which spread to a certain number of villages in the Zahau tract. But it was soon overcomed.[8] Several chiefs had also shown their loyalty to the British by making donations to the War Relief Fund. Among these, the Zahau chief Van Ngul and Falam chief Van Hmung donated Rs.1000 and Rs.744 each.[9]

In 1917, B. Fisher, the Assistant Superintendent of Haka, met various chiefs of his subdivision and told them of the number of men each had to supply in proportion to the number of villages they held. In a village of 100 houses, Fisher, after deducting 10% for widows and cripples and from the remaining 90 houses, told the chiefs not to recruit more than 45 men, even if the village offered more. He further said 'no force was used and the Chiefs were not in any way threatened if they failed to obtain recruits'. Tan Nyer, brother-in-law of the chief of Sangte, had conveyed to Fisher that if the government was intending to recruit the Hakas they wanted to go at once, for if they went later when the hot weather was approaching they would catch fever in Burma. Similarly, the Sakta chief Shia Kaw also informed the British officer about the willingness of 90 Saktas to join the Labour Corps.[10] Though colonial records have us believe that the people of Haka subdivision were rather ready to go for Labour Corps in France, what remained unknown to officers can be gleaned from missionary account. Laura Carson, a missionary, recorded:

> word came that the Government was going to attempt to raise 'a coolie corps' from among our people, for service in France. This caused great excitement. One corps had already been raised among the Siyins in Tiddim and efforts were being made to raise another in the Falam subdivision. Haka would be next! All military British officers and sepoys who could be spared had been withdrawn from the Hills and had gone to France. Civil officers were sent to lower Burma for military training. Haka was therefore left without

a British officer and with only a handful of sepoys, most of whom were mere boys, no one dreaming that the Haka Chins would make any serious trouble. But there was an undercurrent of tense excitement. One could feel it in the air. There were only three English-speaking people in Haka at the time, two Anglo-Indian men and myself. There was a rumor of trouble and attempted revolt in Falam and our Haka civil officer was hastily recalled from lower Burma, and the sepoy guard for Haka was increased from twenty-six to fifty men.

(Carson 1927: 226)

The 'great excitement' noted above, Lian Sakhong explains, was due to fear that their *Khua-hrum* (traditional belief) would not be able to protect them in such a far away country as France (Sakhong 2003: 156). If both colonial record and missionary account were to be believed then there seems to be divergent views about the recruitment drive. At this stage while some chiefs were ready to help the British, others sought to oppose it. It appears that those who were in favour of joining the Labour Corps must have been converted Christians who had been free from the fear of the traditional belief 'Khua-hrum' as in the case of Shia Kaw, a converted Christian of the Sakta village. On the other hand, those who opposed the recruitment drive must have been conservative chiefs who strongly opposed Christianity because they thought that their 'Khua-hrum would not be able to protect them beyond its jurisdiction' (Sakhong 2003: 156).

In spite of all these expressions of readiness/willingness, Fisher later told the people of his subdivision in November that 'Hakas were not wanted at present'.[11] Why did the British stopping short of recruiting the people of the Haka subdivision when they were readily offering themselves to go overseas remain unexplained? Could it be that the people of Haka outwardly offered themselves while in the meantime secretly preparing for a major assault? Was that known to the British? Contrary to popular view, is it possible that the war in the Haka sub-division was because of exclusion from the Labour Corps rather than attempted inclusion?

The so-called 'Haka uprising'

A pioneer American Baptist missionary in the Chin Hills, Laura Hardin Carson, who had over the years established a close rapport with the Zo in the Haka tract received one of the earliest pieces of intelligence of impending trouble on the evening of November 1917 from a Christian convert named Shia Kaw:

> thirteen village had united, taking the sacred oath that they would attack Haka, kill the sepoys, take their guns and with them clear the Hills of the British and resume their own government . . . the men of Sakta had secreted their women and children in the jungle and carried out six months' provision for them, and they were spending their time day and night making ammunition, and wait for an opportunity to strike.
> (Carson 1927: 227–228)[12]

The Assistant Superintendent who had the matter investigated found Carson's fears unfounded. However, two days later, Tsan Dwe, a Christian young man who belonged to an important chief's family brought another warning that his brother had seen a large force congregated that evening only about three miles from Haka. Another investigation was conducted by the Assistant Superintendent which proved that whatever Shia Kaw said turned out to be true. On the morning of 23 November 1917, after he received another report of an advancing army of 5,000 strong Haka fighters towards Haka, Fisher ordered all his men to take shelter in the 'Police Lines' (Carson 1927: 227–230). This was reported to the Superintendent of Falam who, from Kalewa *enroute* to Rangoon, urgently wired Shillong for assistance (Shakespear 1929: 212).[13] The petty officials and the Mission workers, including Laura Carson, were ordered to take shelter in the Police Lines where they remained for the next 22 days.

The next morning a reconnoitring party of 15 mounted sepoys was ambushed by the Hakas near the station. They cut off the Falam-Haka road, felled huge trees across the road on the mountainsides, and made entanglements out of the telegraph wire and raised stockades from the materials taken from Pioneer Camp buildings. It was for the disturbances of the Hakas that only on 12 December did the Assistant Superintendent manage to clear the road for about 12 miles after 13 hours of hard work, to enable a Relief Column from Kalewa to come in (Johnson 1988: 416). On 16 December a 350 well-armed Relief Column under the command of Major L.E.L.Burne and four other British officers, accompanied by the Superintendent at Falam, reached Haka. Sporadic firing continued from a distance. In one of the event they rushed into the compound and killed the sergeant's wife and his daughter. Meanwhile fighting had been going on at Zokhua, Khuapi, Aitung, Surkhua, Hnaring and Sakta.

Contingents of the Assam Rifles from Aizawl and Kohima also arrived and in collaboration with two Burma Military columns mounted operations against the principal villages of Kapi, Aiton, Surkhua, Naring, Sakta and in the process there were many casualties reported, 30 to 40 in number.[14] Units from the Assam Rifles also began operations against villages northeast of Tao range, meeting stiff resistance from Buankhua, Buanlun and Thantlang. In February 1918, combined forces of Assam Rifles and Burma Military Police detachment moved to Lennakot (Sialmong) in the Northern Chin hills, and then to southern Manipur where there was more intense fighting between the Kukis and the Assam Rifles.[15] Elsewhere, the war was also felt in Zonghing in Mindat in the Pakokku Hill Tract and in the southern Lushai Hills, covering the upper Boinu and to Wantu, Laitet and Ngaphai resulting in extensive operations.[16]

In early 1919, the revolt of the Hakas was suppressed and leaders were brought to trial. 61 were sentenced under section 121 of the Indian Penal Code.[17] Two Haka Faron men, Za Nawl and Hreng Ol, were sentenced to death for killing Tum Hngel and her step-daughter Sui Zing, and Ral Chum of Hniarlawn for murdering Asing, a Chinese caretaker at the Pioneer Camp bungalow. The first two hanged themselves in the Haka lockup before the sentence could be carried out.[18] The other leaders were imprisoned in Haka, Falam, Tedim and Mingyan jails. 14 chiefs and others who were serving out their sentences in the Myingyan Jail were later deported to Taungyi and Lashio. Fines amounting to over Rs. 13,000 were levied on the villages participated in the uprising while punitive labour was imposed on some, to construct roads and an artificial lake near Haka, in lieu of imprisonment.[19] The 'Ralkap Tili' (Soldier's Lake), Falam Cinmual Football field and Falam Taungpat Road are still known, and commemorates, in the Chin Hills as the living testimony, and the legacy of, the Haka uprising and the First World War.[20]

Whose war was it, anyway?

The non-participation of the chiefs in the Falam and Tedim subdivisions poses the basic question: whose war was it? If it was the chiefs' war, as claimed by Wright, why had only a select few chiefs of the Chin Hills participated? On the other hand, if it was the people's war, again, why was it confined to Haka and not fought in Tedim and Falam? This is the official view, as expressed by J.M. Wright: 'this rebellion was a rebellion of Chiefs and elders and not a rising of the people'. Wright argued that the checking of slavery, freedom of migration granted to

84

villagers and intervention into the payment of dues were the general grievances that hurt the chiefs.[21] He further said, 'there was a deliberate misrepresentation [of the Labour corps recruitment] on the part of the disloyal chiefs who had grievances and were passively disloyal for some time past awaiting the favourable moment to rise'.[22] In the same tune Col. Leslie Shakespear, the Deputy Inspector General of the Assam Rifles who was heavily involved in the punitive measures against the Kukis in Manipur, said that the situation in Chin Hills was aggravated by attempts to check slavery, and that eventually led to the uprising. Counter argument to the official view is that the grievances cited above did not affect only the chiefs of the Haka subdivision; the chiefs in the Tedim and Falam subdivisions also bore the same brunt.

To label the war as the 'Chiefs' war' just because of the participation of some antagonistic chiefs is not convincing because many chiefs, who also suffered the same grievances remained 'loyal' to the British during the war. This is why colonial rulers made clear distinction between 'loyal' and 'rebel' chiefs. Missionary's account also slightly gives credit to the colonial argument by citing 'the perceived loss of power on the part of the Chiefs' being an important factor of the war. However, it made a division between Christian and non-Christian chiefs, where the latter were being charged as the sole culprit since they were upset because of their diminished prestige.[23] But the same missionary account admitted the chiefs' reluctance to storm the fort 'since these missionaries were under the protection of the British and were, in fact, within the garrison'.[24] In fact, the close rapport that Laura Carson had had with the Hakas, being the mission headquarters, is well recognised (Sakhong 2003: 158). What deterred the chiefs to storm the 'Police Lines'? If the missionary account was to be believed it may be that Christian chiefs also participated, either directly or indirectly, in the war. Otherwise, why should the non-Christian chiefs bother for the missionary presence in the garrison?

Furthermore, if it was only the 'Chiefs' war', why was the war confined to the Haka subdivision and not involve other Zo tribes of the north such as the Taisun, Sukte, Kamhau, Sihzang, etc. who were similarly circumstanced? In fact, the first ripples of the disturbances in Manipur in 1917 had been immediately felt in the Tedim area, but it was the Kamhau Chief Hau Cin Khup who kept 'a firm hands on his youngmen'. Likewise, in the Falam subdivision the Taisun chiefs Van Hmung, the Zahau chief Van Nul and his son Thang Tin Lian were all loyal to the British. Their contribution to the War Fund and assistance in obtaining labour recruits was well recorded in the annual Administrative Report.[25]

The explanation for the 'loyalty' of some of the most powerful chiefs' to assist the British during the war may be found in the nature of traditional chieftainship in the three subdivisions. Both the Tedim and Falam subdivisions had been under the rule of powerful chiefs, the former being 'autocratic' and the latter 'democratic' in their style of functioning (Stevenson 1986). Tedim subdivision was under the dominance of the Kamhau chief Hau Cin Khup, who initially fought against the British but later made an agreement with them in 1892 and remained loyal to the government since then.[26] He exerted remarkable influence on other subordinate chiefs under his realm. Similarly, the Falam tract was traditionally governed by the Council of Elders selected from the chiefs themselves. The Council had a 'democratic' style of functioning as opposed to the autocratic rule of Hau Cin Khup in Tedim.[27] Nevertheless, the Council acted as the supreme authority in all political matters. Chieftainship in the Haka subdivision was different. Each single chief was independent of its own, albeit there were some more powerful chiefs who had his own satellite villages but not the sort of paramount rulers found in the Tedim tract. The realm of influence and control over the people/villages in the case of the Haka chiefs was confined to the village itself, not beyond that. In such case even personal grievance against the British is enough to light a spark to the general grievances of the chiefs.

An added fillip to all these is widespread damage to crops by rodents and caterpillars in Haka in 1915. The damage, which also affected Falam, was particularly severe in Haka, where 340,000 rats were ultimately killed by the people. Shortage of food, and even starvation was reported from here, and that year the usual supply of food grain to the Military Police, which earned the people of Haka considerable profits, became almost impossible. The consequence of this was that the chiefs could not pay their dues to the government and in the following year they forfeited their commission. It was at this stage that orders came for the supply of men for the Labour Corps. Laura Carson thus records the reaction of the chiefs to the order:

> The Government orders were that no coercion was to be used; but the chief did not understand that. An order to bring in the men meant that *they must bring them*. Chief after chief came to me and asked what he should do. They said that their people absolutely refused to go to France; that they said they had no quarrel with Germany and why should they go and fight the Germans? They said they would commit suicide rather than go.
> (Carson 1927: 227)

Undoubtedly, the recruitment for the Labour Corps and reduction of British troops and officials from the hills which left the entire Chin hills insufficiently guarded were strong inducements.[28]

The months immediately following the suppression of the war were full of hardships for the Haka people. In the joint operations of the Burma Military Police and the Assam Rifles several villages had been burned with large quantities of grain. Punitive labour took the men away from the villages and the result was a terrible shortage of food, and almost famine conditions prevailed. 'One of the leading chiefs told me', Carson wrote, 'that for two months he had not had any food whatever except "banhtaw" which is the boiled sprouts of the banana tree. He said there were thousands in the same condition' (Carson 1927: 238).

Conclusion

We have seen that the Haka chiefs had initially agreed to supply labourers for France. However, there was a 'tense excitement' among the people. The unfolding events till the outbreak of the war suggest that the chiefs were very soon overawed by the people, putting them in between the devil and the deep blue sea. He knew that his people had 'absolutely refused to go to France' and vowed to 'commit suicide rather than go' to France. He also knew that if he do not supply men for the Labour Corps, the colonial state would be infuriated. Having been caught up in between, confused and indecisive, 'chief after chief' went to their trusted missionary Mrs. Laura Carson for advice. The fact that they eventually took up arms against the colonial state show that the chiefs eventually took the line of his people rather than his own commitment to the colonial state. In this sense, the Haka uprising was not the chiefs' war but the people's war against colonialism. As the paternal rulers, the chiefs merely provided the leadership based on the traditional social and political setting. Just as we could see multiple forms of domination and control under colonialism causing the war, the objective they spelt out was also clear. They came together, took a 'sacred oath' to 'attack Haka, kill the sepoys, take their guns and with them clear the [Chin] Hills of the British and resume their own government'. In other words, the aim of the war was to free their country from British and restore their own government. This was the same idea shared by their brethren Kukis of Manipur and Thangdut state. Overall the Anglo-Zo War in the Indo-Burma frontier was set on a well-founded aim and objective of freedom from colonialism than a mere outrage against colonial labour recruitment. Since the Zo society revolved largely around their traditional chieftainship institution, the chiefs provided the leadership and people the strength throughout. At any rate, the Anglo-Zo war during the First World War marked a significant milestone in the history of the Zo people.

Notes

1 See Kipgen (1976).
2 See Zou (2011).
3 See Haokip (1998).
4 See Sakhong (2003).
5 I use the generic term Zo to refer to both the Kuki of Manipur and the Chin of the Chin Hills. I think Zo is the only viable nomenclature under which the so-called Chin, Kuki and Lushai people can be brought together. Hence, the Anglo-Zo (Kuki-Chin) War in this paper.
6 British Library, London (BL), Asian and African Collections (formerly Oriental & India Office Collections) (hereafter AAC), Indian Office Records and Private Papers (hereafter IOR&PP), IOR/L/PS/10/724: 1917–1920, File No. P-2686/1919, 'Disturbance on Assam-Burma frontier 1917–1918': From J.M.Wright, Esq., I.C.S., Superintendent, Chin Hills, to the DIG, Military Police, Burma, 20 July 1918.
7 J.M. Wright, *Report on the Administration of the Chin Hills for the year 1916–17.*
8 Ibid., *1917–18.*
9 Ibid., *for the year ended 30 June 1915.*
10 BL, AAC, IOR&PP, IOR/L/PS/10/724: 1917–1920, File No. P-2686/1919, 'Disturbance on Assam-Burma frontier 1917–1918': From J.M.Wright, Esq., I.C.S., Superintendent, Chin Hills, to the DIG, Military Police, Burma, 20 July 1918.
11 Ibid.
12 Carson noted that the next afternoon Shia Kaw came in again saying that forces were collecting again, both north and south of us, and that Haka was to be attacked within the next three or four days. I told him that the Assistant Superintendent said he had investigated and found conditions in Sakta normal; that women and children had not been taken away; that the people were loyal and that at least 90 were ready to go to France, and that there would be no insurrection. He was greatly excited and distressed and begged us to heed the warning which he had risked his life to bring. That night the Christians asked permission to sleep in the Mission Hospital and Mr. Cope and the teachers patrolled the Mission property all night- but there was not disturbance.
13 In early December 1917 the DIG Assam Rifles received a wire from the Superintendent Chin Hills inquiring if he had any knowledge of likely trouble on the Chin Lushai border. The reply stated he had no such knowledge, the only minor trouble known of concerned Zongling in the Unadministered Area towards Arakan. 12 hours later came an urgent wire to Shillong from Falam, the headquarters station in the Chin hills, saying the southern Chins had risen, Haka station was surrounded, and begging for urgent assistance. Permission to act having been obtained, DIG sent orders

to Captain Falkland, Commandant 1st A R at Aijal, to march at once with 150 rifles for Haka, and in a few hours they were *en route* to cover the 16 marches as rapidly as possible. A few days later another urgent wire from Falam called for more help, and as active trouble had not as yet started in Manipur, Captain Montifore with 150 rifles of the 3rd A R at Kohima was ordered to the Chin hills, travelling as expeditiously as possible- by rail to Chittagong, river steamer to Rangamatti, country boats to Demagiri, whence onwards a fortnight's hard marching to Haka.

14 B. Fischer, the Superintendent of Pakokku Hill Tracts, reported that on 16 April 1918 a party consisting of Captain Alexander Assistant Commandant, a small escort and himself visited a group of villages known as Chan-im in order to calm the people who were very restless. They were attacked by the Chins, killing one Military Police Havildar and wounding Alexander and two others.

15 For details on the Kuki uprising in Manipur see Shakespear (1929: 209–232), Bhadra (1975), Kipgen (1976).

16 For an account of the "Kuki Punitive measures", in Manipur, see Shakespear (1929: 228), Reid (1997: 79–89).

17 *Report on the Administration of the Chin Hills for the year1918–1919.* Some of the most important Haka chiefs responsible for the trouble and sentenced under section 121 of the Indian Penal Code were: Lyen Mo son of Za Err, Van Mang son of Lyen Mo, Kin Hmon son of Lyen Mo, Tyer Non wife of Van Mang, KupHmin son of Lwe Sang, Tat Hmon son of YaKlwe, Ni Kwel son of KukHre, Tan Hnyer son of LyenKwe.

18 Ibid., 1919–1920.

19 Johnson, *Chin Mission*, pp. 423–424 also see *Report on the Administration of the Chin Hills for the year 1919–1920*

20 Salai Vang Cung Lian (UK) 'Chin involvement in World War I (The Great War)', *Burma News International*, 14 November 2014 (http://e-archive.bnionline.net/index.php/news/chinworld/17872-chin-involvement-in-world-war-1-the-great-war.html accessed on 20 January 2017)

21 BL, AAC, IOR&PP, IOR/L/PS/10/724: 1917–1920, File No. P-2686/1919, 'Disturbance on Assam-Burma frontier 1917–1918': From J.M.Wright, Esq., I.C.S., Superintendent, Chin Hills, to the DIG, Military Police, Burma, 20 July 1918.

22 Ibid.

23 Johnson, *Chin Mission,* pp. 409–410.

24 Ibid., p. 422.

25 J. M. Wright Report on the Administration of the Chin Hills for the year 1917–18.

26 Chief Hau Cin Khup won the following awards for his loyalty to the British: Silvermounted Da and a Certificate of Honour in 1901; KSM in 1917; a gun and a Certificate of Honour in 1918; a revolver and a Certificate of Honour in 1919. See Acts and Achievements of Hau Cin Khup, Chief of Kamhau Clan, Chin Hills, Tedim, Mandalay, Burma 1927.

27 See, Stevenson, Economic history.

28 E.O.Fowler commanded the 61st and 62nd Chin Labour Corps from the Tedim Subdivision to France. Altogether there were 1033 Chins from Tedim Subdivision consisting of 250 from Sukte tract, 700 from Kamhau

tract and 83 from Sihzang tract. They left Tedim on 27 May 1917 and returned to the Chin Hills in the middle of 1918 with 56 casualties. The Labour Corps from Falam composed a part of the 78th Labour Company. They were accompanied by the young Lumbang Chief Hlurr Hmung.

References

1927. *Acts and Achievements of Hau Cin Khup, Chief of Kamhau Clan, Chin Hills, Tedim*, Mandalay, Burma.

Bhadra, Gautam. 1975. 'The Kuki (?) Uprising (1917–1919): Its Causes and Nature', *Man in India*, 55: 1–14.

Carson, Laura S. 1927. *Pioneer Trails, Trials and Triumph*. New York: Baptist Board Publication.

Chishti, S.M.A.W. 2004. *Kuki Uprising in Manipur 1919–1920*. Guwahati: Spectrum Publications.

Dena, Lal. 1991. *History of Modern Manipur 1826–1949*. New Delhi: Orbit Publishers.

Haokip, P.S. 1998. *Zalen Gam: TheKuki nation*. KNO Publication.

Johnson, Robert G. 1988. *History of the American Baptist Mission*, Vol. 1. Valley Forge: Private Circulation.

Kipgen, Khaikhotinthang. 1976. *The Thadou War (1917–19): Kuki (?) Rebellion*. Imphal: Private Circulation.

Pau, Pum Khan. 2007. 'Administrative Rivalries on a Frontier: Problems of the Chin-Lushai Hills', *Indian Historical Review*, 34 (1): 187–209.

Pau, Pum Khan. 2012. 'Rethinking Religious Conversion: Missionary Endeavors and Indigenous Response Among the Zo (Chin) in the Indo-Burma Borderland', *Journal of Religion and Society*, 14: 1–17.

Reid, Robert. 1997 [1942]. *History of the Frontier Areas Bordering on Assam from 1883–1941*. Guwahati: Spectrum Publications.

Sakhong, Lian H. 2003. *In Search of Chin Identity: A Study in Religion, Politics and Ethnic Identity in Burma*. Copenhagen: NIAS Press.

Salai Vang Cung Lian. 2014. 'Chin Involvement in World War I (The Great War)', *Burma News International*, 14 November 2014, http://e-archive. bnionline.net/index.php/news/chinworld/17872-chin-involvement-in-world-war-1-the-great-war.html (accessed 20–01–2017).

Shakespear, L.W. 1977 [1929]. *History of the Assam Rifles*. Aizawl: Tribal Research Institute (TRI).

Stevenson, H.N.C. 1986 [1943]. *The Economic History of the Central Chins*. Aizawl: Tribal Research Institute (TRI).

Zou, David Vumlallian. 'A Commemorative Speech on ZOU GAL (Kuki Rising) 1917–1919', presented at the1st Zou Gal Day, 17 March 2011, MP's Club, South Avenue, New Delhi, http://zouwritersnetwork.blogspot. in/2011/04/zou-gal-kuki-rising-1917-1919.html (accessed 22–01–2017).

Part II

TACTICS, TECHNOLOGY AND SYMBOLS

3

BREAKING THE SPIRIT OF THE KUKIS

Launching the 'largest series of military operations' in the northeastern frontier of India

Thongkholal Haokip

During the winters of 1917–1918 and 1918–1919, the Assam Rifles and Burma Military Police launched operations at the imperial margin against the 'rapidly spreading rising amongst the Kuki clans', which 'was disconcerting and most difficult to deal with' for the Assam Military Police initially (Shakespear 1980: 224). With a combined force of Assam and Burma it was the 'largest series of military operations conducted on this side of India' (Shakespear 1980: 235). The Deputy Inspector General (DIG) of the Assam Military Police (now known as Assam Rifles) also lamented about the non-recognition of the military operations to which he was a part in the public which cost a whopping Rs. 28 lakhs during that time. He wrote: 'Very little was known to the public of these operations; one or two Calcutta papers only publish short and erroneous accounts of what they wrote of as 'outings of Political Officers and their escorts', and generally belittling a long, hard 'show' carried through eventually to a successful issue by the combined Military police forces of Assam and Burma'. The DIG of Assam Rifles with dismay cited the much publicised and comparatively less expensive expedition in Upper Assam: 'while of General Bower's force in the Abor Expedition, 1911–1912, which was greatly written up in the newspapers, 4 were killed, 7 wounded, and 54 died of disease' (Shakespear 1980: 237). The tribes of the Northeast frontier were constant trouble makers, and to keep them self-contained, different policies were framed specifically for these people.

One thing that is glaring than anything else about the tribes in the Northeastern frontier of British India was that subjugation, and particularly 'control', was fiercely resisted. As such 'indirect rule' and minimal interference on the custom and culture of the natives was largely followed by the British in their colonised territories since the Indian rebellion of 1857. Before the commencement of these operations against the Kukis,

> the general policy persued (sic) by the British was to refrain from any direct control over the tribe in the management of their internal affairs. . . . The hill areas and the hill people continued to enjoy independence and the villages were administered by the respective chiefs without any direct interference of the British authority.
>
> (Ray 1990: 63, 64)

The official colonial policy towards the tribes was explicitly mentioned by Woodthrope (1980: 6):

> The Government does not wish to exterminate these frontier tribes, but by converting them into our allies to raise a barrier between our frontier districts and other more distant races. Suppose a tribe to be utterly crushed or exterminated, we should find ourselves no better than before – probably much worse, having merely removed obstacles to the assaults of a fiercer and more formidable foe, whose very remoteness would render it for us to conciliate or punish him.

Until the second decade of the twentieth century the Kuki Hills 'surrounding the Manipur valley' and Somra Tract, as Shakespear (1980: xxx) and other colonial officers would call it, were largely unadministered territories as they were, so far, friendly to the British government (Reid 1942: 79). In such territories, 'Cases where hillmen are concerned and cases arising in the British reserve are excluded from the Darbar's civil and criminal jurisdiction' (Reid 1942: 78). Different neighbouring groups were also used against any who rose into revolt against the Raj. Thus, the policy of using one against another was followed to keep the frontier under their loose grip of control.

A resurgent 'Kuki Hills'

The Kukis were one of the dominant communities among the hill tribes of the British Northeast frontier. They were, to use Mackenzie's

(1884: 146) word, 'a hardworking', 'self-reliant race', and the only hillmen in their neighbourhood who can hold their own against the other powerful hill tribes. In 1917 labour corps was raised by the British Government for France amongst various clans of Nagas, Lushais, Meiteis and others, as Colonel L. W. Shakespear (1980: 209) mentioned, 'who willingly came in, having in many cases done this short of work for (British) Government before in border expeditions, and knew the work and good pay'. In 1917 more Labour Corps were needed, and to supply it the British Government felt that it was necessary to draw from other sources, 'viz the various Kuki clans inhabiting the hill regions of the native state of Manipur', who were described by Shakespear (1980: 210) as 'a people who had never left their hills and knew but little of us and our ways'. Due to this exigency the British, despite their well established principle of rule, had to interfere into the hitherto freedom enjoyed by the Kukis. Despite the Maharaja of Manipur obligation to prepare 2,000 labourers, he 'had no direct control over the hill mass which he had over his own Manipuri subjects in the matter of labour recruitment' (Ray 1990: 65). The sleepy Kuki hills woke up to this undue interference to their freedom and in their ways of life and self-rule, which they think was also against their traditional religious belief. Webster reported that: 'a good deal of unrest has been created among the Kuki tribes in the hills of the Manipur State by recruiting for the Labour Corps for France'.[1]

The meetings in March 1917 at Jampi among the various Kuki chiefs, 'have taken an oath after killing a mythan that none of them would go to France or send any of their people there'.[2] With the refusal by principal chiefs to send coolies Webster viewed that: 'It is essential to the administration of a country peopled with uncivilised tribes that they shall be made to understand that legitimate orders cannot be disobeyed with impunity and that defiance brings certain punishment'.[3] With the rising tide of rebellion in the Kuki hills the main policy of the British administration in Assam was that the 'recalcitrant Kukis' should be called to account and their guns surrendered, and those who refused to submit will have their villages burnt. Yet, the Kukis still kept room for negotiation and responded to the call of the Political Agent (P.A.) of Manipur for peaceful negotiation. The Kuki chiefs of the western hills invited the PA to meet them at Oktan. The P.A. met 'the chiefs and representatives of between 30 and 40 of the leading Kuki villages' on 10 October 1917. Sensing the general hostile attitude the P.A. reported:

But two hours of argument failed to move them and they proved obdurate against threats of punishment. They persisted that they feared to go so far from their homes and that if they had to die they preferred to die in their own country and would be prepared to meet force with force.[4]

The meetings ended with an informal agreement that another round-table conference will be convened by the PA in the near future. In spite of their informal agreement at Oktan to meet again for peaceful nego-tiation, the Political Agent, J.C. Higgins, took 50 riflemen to Mombi (Lonpi) after two days of the Oktan meeting and reached that village on 15 October. On 17 October 1917, he burnt down the village. This violent action did not only surprise the Kukis but also broke the trust on the part of the Political Agent. Since then passive resistance to the 'supply of labour' and 'surrender of guns' ended. Ngulkhup, chief of Mombi, closed down his country to the British and sent information to Pache that he had declared war against the Sahibs and if any officer came up he would have shot at them, and he requested Pache to do the same. Higgins reported that Ngulkhup 'has sent a message to Pachei chief of Chassad saying that if an officer visit Mombi again, he will be shot and begging Pachei to adopt the same attitude'.[5] Reporting on 24 November 1917, J.C. Higgins wrote about Khotinthang: 'He has recently been in communication with the chiefs of Mombi and Chas-sad with a view to concerted resistance to any attempt at coercion or arrest, and the latest information to hand indicates that Pachei chief of Chassad had called him to a council'.[6] Several meetings of the Kuki people in different parts of Kuki hills immediately followed the burn-ing of Mombi, after which the main resolution taken was to fight if the British attempt to arrest them or burn their villages. Despite the deci-sion by the Kuki chiefs to resist labour recruitment, the major resist-ance war began after the Chassad conclave, in which more than 150 Kuki chiefs gathered and unanimously decided to wage a war against the British Raj.

About the end of November or beginning of December in 1917, Pache, Chief of Chassad, summoned a 'big meeting' – a war conclave in which 150 Kuki chiefs of Assam and Burma participated includ-ing, Ngulkhup, chief of Mombi and Khotinthang, chief of Jampi. The Chassad meeting resolved 'not to obey any orders or summons from Government and to fight if Government tried to enforce orders'.[7] Higgins also reported about this meeting: 'Subsequently I learn from a good authority that he sent a bullet to the chiefs of Jampi, Ukha, Songphu, Henglep and Loibol with instruction to resist forcibly any attempt to impress coolies or to burn villages'.[8] However, despite being largely coordinated through the war communication system of *thingkho-le-malcha*,[9] threats by principal chiefs of dire consequences for not joining them in the fight with them, 'The Southwest of Manipur which had sent men to France remained loyal and the villages mostly belonged to non-Thado tribes' (Reid 1997: 80). There are also some chiefs among the so-called Thadou tribe who remained friendly and loyal to the Raj.[10] On the other hand, the British administration also decided that by 1 December 'the recalcitrant Kukis should be called to account without delay and that those who refused to submit should have their villages burnt'.[11] The British policy thereof is clearly evident during this time when J.C. Higgins said:

> if the chiefs surrendered themselves and their guns submitted to the punishment imposed on them, they would still save their villages from being burnt, & that if they used force and kill any one, they would certainly lose men, both in the fighting and by execution after they had been suppressed.[12]

In this compelling circumstance, the Political Agent of Manipur was authorised to summon the Kuki chiefs to Imphal in which the President of the Durbar was to 'decide what punishment shall be inflicted on them and their villages for their organised resistance to the demands of the State' so as 'to restore the authority of the Manipur State over the tribes under its control'.[13] The summons were accompanied by a promise to the chiefs that, apart from not requiring to provide coolies,

> if they submit to the Durbar's jurisdiction and if the orders for the punishment of the villages are carried out promptly and completely, no villages will be burnt. At the same time they will be warned that further contumacy and defiance assuredly will result in their villages being burnt and in more severe punishment being inflicted eventually.

Webster was also doubtful of the positive response from the Kukis when he said: 'No other form of punishment is practicable, as the offending chiefs are almost certain to abscond on the approach of the punitive force and cannot be arrested in such a vast area of wild, mountainous and sparsely populated country'.[14] Living in trepidation between the two dominant forces, there were also many who were neutral to both the sides to escape their wrath.

The Kuki 'rebellion', according to the British, started in December 1917 and lasted for one and a half years (Shakespear 1980: 136). Two decades after the end of the war Robert Reid (1942: 82) made a succinct observation: 'if there had been no recruiting for the Labour Corps there would have been no rebellion'. Freedom is central to the existence of the Kukis. For the Kuki men, fighting the superior British military force would be hard, but having the thought of losing their 'freedom' was harder. The passive resistance against recruitment for labour corps turned into an active armed resistance after the burning of Lonpi on 17 October 1917 by an intemperate British officer. The Kuki rebellion, as the official colonial version so regarded and recorded the uprising as in the words of Robert Reid, the Governor of Assam 1937–1941: 'The most serious incident in the history of Manipur and its relations with its Hill subjects'; 'commencing in the closing days of 1917, it cost 28 lakhs of rupees to quell, and in the course of it many lives were lost' (Reid 1997: 79). As the largest series of military operations conducted in the Northeast frontier, different colonial strategies were adopted in two stages at a stretch of three years to suppress the uprising. This chapter will show that the uprising was brutally suppressed after a well-thought-out scheme to break the spirit of the Kukis.

The small war: British counter-guerrilla strategy

During imperial expansion of western powers, small wars were closely associated with such colonial expansion. In small wars, which are basically 'operations of regular armies against irregular, or comparatively speaking irregular, forces' (Callwell 1906: 21), 'unconventional tactics are the soul of this war' (quoted in Porch 2013: 20). The operations of the regular armies against irregular forces were often laden with brazen categorisation and delegitimisation of indigenous resistors as 'thugs, bandits, criminal tribes, bitter-enders, or fanatics' (Porch 2013: 2). The so-called 'civilising ministration' was conducted with inherent brutality by western imperial powers that were 'functioning democracies', that concerns were often raised about the brutality of the tactics and operations of the regular armies.

To counter a guerilla warfare, 'which is a war of the masses, a war of the people' (Guevara 1961: 15), and largely carried out by a 'relative diminutive groups of fighters utilised surprise as a force multiplier to carry out ambushes, sabotage and raids to harass and forage on the margins of large clashes of armies' (Porch 2013: 4), Lazare Hoche laid down tactical principles during the late sixteenth century for a successful counter-guerilla operation. He 'divided the theatre into sections, each with its network of posts linked by mobile patrols, informed by an active intelligence service. The fittest soldiers were organized into fast-moving mobile columns that hunted down and surprised hardcore bands of insurgents' (Porch 2013: 5). Depriving peasants of their food and livelihood while seizing the hostages, combined with scorched-earth campaign, 'smashed and demoralized the insurgent base' (Porch 2013: 8). Marshall de Castellane explains the rationale of the scorched-earth campaign:

> how do you act against a population whose only link with the land is the pegs of their tents? . . . The only way is to take the grain which feeds them, the flocks which clothe them. For this reason, we make war on silos, war on cattle, the *razzia*.
>
> (quoted in Porch 2013: 21–22)

In such operations,

> Civilized standards of warfare, even basic human rights and judicial procedures, were considered superfluous by Europeans in non-Western settings against an enemy viewed as culturally, racially and morally inferior, and whose subjugation was approached in the spirit of total war.
>
> (Porch 2013: 76)

In order to deprive the rebels of foods and new recruits, populations were moved to concentration camps run by the military.

The first 'Punitive Measures' 1917–1918

After it was clear following the 'big meeting' at Chassad that the Kukis decided to wage war against the British Raj, the war cry spread so fast and so wide in the whole Kuki hills. During the first operations, military columns were sent to identified rebel areas and the Political Agents toured the hills and were actively engaged in suppressing the uprising by using coercive diplomacy or forceful persuasion in which 'recalcitrant Kukis' were 'called to account' through the threat to burn their villages.

The colonial administration immediately dispatched columns of the 3rd Assam Rifles station at Kohima and the 4th Assam Rifles station at Imphal against the rebels. These two columns were 'aided by operations directed from Burma, acted vigorously and continuously against the rebels with varying measures of success' (Reid 1997: 80). The initial policy of the British was a prompt action against the rebel chiefs by isolating and eliminating them from the hills, thinking that the war was instigated by few chiefs and leaders and people are not with them. As it was, disarmament was the chief object of the first operations.[15] Before the close of the first operations against Kukis Cosgrave wrote on 23 March 1918:

> I think that disarmament should be the first aim of our policy and before the rains set in I want to make a start disarming as well as to detach rebel villages from adherence to such leaders as the chiefs of Ukha and Mombi who should be isolated and proceeded against with exemplary severity.[16]

For instance, on 23 January 1918 Cosgrave sent a message to the chief of Saibom Machet saying: 'if he came and surrendered to me today with his licenced gun I would not punish him as severely as other villages'.[17] However, such initial policy of selective elimination did not work out, not only because the Kukis did not confront the British in a battleground but choose guerilla warfare to prolong the rising but also because the Kuki masses were behind their leaders, hiding them, supply them with food and other materials. Webster, Secretary to the Chief Commissioner of Assam, reported:

> The general impression founded on experience on other part of the Frontier was that when the Kukis realised their inability to withstand the column sent against them and found their villages and property destroyed and themselves harried from pillar to post, opposition would collapse and their submission would be only a question of days.[18]

So the tactics of the British colonial state, despite claiming to be the most civilised and advanced society of the time, was to indulge the most 'barbaric' and inhuman forms of warfare, which today are prohibited by the Protocols of the 1977 Geneva Conventions. Such warfare included indiscriminate burning of recalcitrant villages, their properties, foodstuffs, livestock and driving the hapless women, children and aged into the jungle under chilling winter and hunting them down from pillar to post to capture them, and to use those captured, particularly the women and children, to break the spirit of the Kuki fighters.

As several military columns of the British moved from one place to another in the Kuki hills to punish the rebel villages, the policy of 'scorched earth' was becoming more evident. For instance, the P.A. of Manipur Mr. Cosgrave toured the Southwestern hills during the months of February and March and every rebel village was punished in similar fashion. Here is his report about Henglep: 'We halted at Hinglep and punished the village severely by shooting more than 20 metnas and collecting a large quantity of paddy . . . and destroyed about 100 maunds of paddy'. When inadequate amount of paddy and other livestock were found the military column will not rest until 'hidden stores' in the jungle are found and destroyed. Cosgrave also reported about Songphu village:

> As the search parties which we sent out could not find any metnas and very little paddy while I had information that this is a well off village we decided to halt here for another day so as to search for and destroy the enemies' property.[19]

In the first operations the military 'greatly underestimated' the Kukis, of the number of firearms and other warfare techniques. In the words of Shakespear (1980: 216): 'The Civil authorities were inclined to treat the idea of the Kukis having many fire arms as absurd, giving as their view that perhaps 100 or so were at most scattered about the hills'. While underestimating the rebel forces Webster stated:

> In proceeding to the disaffected villages the Political Agent proposes to take escort of 150 rifles, which will be more than sufficient to overcome any possible opposition, and the Chief Commissioner is satisfied that the force on the spot will be amply sufficient to punish the tribes without incurring the very slightest risk of military aid having to be requisitioned.[20]

However, the total number of guns obtained by the end of the war stood at 1,158. This initial failure leads the British to shift their policy from selective elimination of 'rebel' leaders to 'a definite plan of campaign against the Kuki rebels'. The Kukis adopted jungle or guerilla warfare, one of the unique warfare during those times, to fight the stronger conventional military columns. Under such circumstances, it was impossible to capture the 'rebels'; voluntary submission was even more difficult. The mobility of the Kukis was one of the factors that worked to their advantage in jungle warfare. Shakespear (1980: 215) commented: 'The Kukis, being a people of nomadic habits, constantly change their village sites, consequently their homes'. Robert Reid (1997: 80) claimed that

> large number of villages had been destroyed but, owing to the nomadic habits of the tribe and the flimsy nature of their

house, the loss sustained was small. . . . But owing to their methods of fighting, in ambushes and stockades, which they quickly abandoned, as soon as outflanked, the Kukis had sustained very few casualties, fewer in fact, than they inflicted.

The first operation was called off towards the end of May 1918 as 'further operations in the hills became impossible, owing to the climate' and 'the state of the rivers'. As Robert Reid (1997: 80) reported:

> They (the Kukis) were still far from being subdued. . . . They were able to supplement their supplies from their Naga neighbours who, though friendly to the forces of law and order, were afraid to refuse the demands of the more ruthless Kukis, better armed than themselves and living in their midst.

Another report also stated: 'the Kukis of the Manipur Hills themselves show no signs of intending to submit' (Ibid., p. 623). According to the colonial military officer Macquoid, these operations were 'incomplete and unsatisfactory owing to lack of co-ordination'. The failure in this operation was largely attributed to the absence of 'previous experience' by the British officers and recruits 'of jungle warfare'.

Plan of operations against the Kukis

Having largely failed in their previous operations against the Kuki rebels with a huge loss of men due to their underestimation of the firepower and effective jungle warfare techniques, 'the local officers had realised the seriousness of the situation', and even during the peak of the first operations, the idea of having a well though-out scheme of operation was envisaged by the first week of March 1918. H.D.U. Keary, the Commanding Officer of the second phase of Kuki operations, reported:

> The sudden blaze of rebellion, which spread simultaneously throughout the length and breadth of the hills from Kohima in the north to the Pakokku Hill tracts of Burma in the south, made it impossible last year to formulate put into force any complete and thought out plan before operations started.[21]

The General Officer Commanding the Burma Division of the first Kuki Punitive Measures wrote on 5 September 1918:

> One thing remains clear, viz., that the operations should in any event proceed and the entire rebel country be overrun and effectively occupied, roads made and our troops should penetrate to every corner of every area. Only in this way, i.e., by actual demonstration will we prove to the Kukis our mastery and that resistance is futile.[22]

Thus, the operations evidently intended to overcome 'the difficulties of transportation, the state of military technology, and, above all, demographic realities [that] placed sharp limits on the reach of even the most ambitious states' (Scott 2009: 4).

Objectives of the operations

The main objectives of this 'Plan of Operations' was 'the subjugation of the rebel Kukis of Assam and of N.E. Thaungdut and Somra in Upper Burma', and as in the case of the first operations, the 'complete disarmament of the tribes inhabiting them'. It specifically intended 'To break the spirit of the Kukis to such an extent that they will become completely weary and demoralised and be ready to surrender themselves, their guns and property', and to inflict pains and penalties as may decided.[23] In order to achieve this, 15 rebel principal chiefs were identified and they were placed under a 'Special List', and they were declared 'guilty of notorious crimes, whose capture and punishment was especially desired by the Government'.[24]

After these principal chiefs were caught or surrendered' penalties in the form of fines and other punishments would be imposed and enforced upon them and their people. The rebel Kukis would be forced to construct bridle paths fit for transport throughout the rebel Kuki areas so as to open the whole Kuki hills for administration. With these necessary outposts would have to be established in the whole Kuki country after the troops withdraw. With all these openings, it also aimed to establish necessary posts to hold the Kuki country. Construction of roads as a pacific agent, disarmament of the country and finally imposition of a new administration were also the objectives of the operations.

Scheme of operations

In July 1918, Colonel C.E.K. Macquoid, the General Officer Commanding of the Kuki Punitive Measures, and General H.D.U. Keary, the Commanding Officer of Burma Division of the Kuki Punitive Measures, along with the D.I.G. of Assam Rifles Colonel L.W. Shakespear met at Shillong, in which they 'decided that military operations would be necessary in the cold weather of 1918/19' (Reid 1997: 81), and they 'examined the scheme of operations, generally approving and only altering certain minor details' (Shakespear 1980: 231). The new scheme for the second phase of counter-guerrilla warfare operations, which originated from Major A. Vickers of the 3rd Assam Rifles and largely carried through with slight alterations,

> was to divide the rebel hills into areas, appointing detachments for each, in which lines of posts were to be established sufficiently strong to enable them to combine in a number of small handy Columns with which to harry the rebels till they gave in; movable Columns also in each area were to drive the Kukis on the line of posts.
>
> (Shakespear 1980: 230)

Even in the middle of the first operations, the D.I.G. of Burma Military Police sought information on the 'policy of the Assam Administration in putting down the present rebellion', in which Cosgrave reported about the suggestion by Captain Patrick for the deployment of 'half a dozen aeroplane' to put down the rebellion in a very short time.[25] It was pointed out that 'in the absence of landing places probably they could not be used in the hills',[26] the suggestion to use aeroplanes was disapproved. However, better modern weapons were sanctioned for use by the military forces in the second operations to overcome the difficulties of geography and jungle warfare techniques. In the first phase of operations, the dominant weapons used by the British military were Martini Henry rifles and a few 7 lb. mountain guns. In the second phase, the military forces were to be better equipped with .303 rifles, Lewis guns, stokes mortar and rifle grenades. These cutting edge weapons to be inducted newly in the second operations were largely as a result of the experience of the previous operations and mitigate the loss on the part of the military.

Cutting the food supply short of the Kuki fighters was one of the main objectives of the British, so that they surrender due to shortage of food supply. During the first operations, the Kuki fighters were also able to acquire necessary food items from their Naga neighbours. The British learnt that:

> They (Kukis) were able to supplement their supplies from their Naga neighbours who, though friendly to the forces of law and order, were afraid to refuse the demands of the more ruthless Kukis, better armed than themselves and living in their midst.
>
> (Reid 1997: 80)

Different strategies were put forward to achieve this objective. Cosgrave suggested:

> Another point which I think deserves consideration is the inducement of the friendly Anal Langang and cognate people of Sibong to settle in the plains so that the Kukis who with the present military operations will probably find it difficult to cultivate their own Jhums may not have a supply store ready at hand.[27]

Having lost heavily in the first operation due to unfavourable jungles and the techniques of guerilla warfare adopted by the Kukis, the 'plan of action' was to neutralise the Kukis through superior modern weapons and 'to put an end to the Kuki revolt by force of arms, break the Kuki spirit, disarm the Kukis, exact reparation and pave the way for effective administration of their country'.[28] To possibly do that a special training was needed for the troops and the 'experience gained in the last season's operations' were a good resource to better prepare and train soldiers for the next operations, and every possible profiting has to be made from the experience gained in the previous operations. Henry Keary suggested: 'Up to that time the troops detailed for the operations will be under special training under their officers and all preparations as to equipment, supplies, transport and medical arrangements will be made'.[29] Brigadier General C.E.K. Macquoid also revealed that: 'The operation of the previous year had disclosed the tactics of the enemy. From this experience officers and men had benefited in that they had been thoroughly trained and pracitsed to overcome them'.[30] As Robert Raid succinctly described:

> The scheme of operations consisted in dividing the hostile territory into areas, each with one or more well-equipped bases

and chains of outposts, from which small and mobile detachments could operate against the rebels and keep them on the run. In the southeastern hills, friendly Chins, and in the southwest Lushai and friendly Kukis, were armed and employed as scouts and irregulars.

(Reid 1997: 81)

Cosgrave wrote on 7 February 1918 about the policy of the Assam Administration in putting down the present rebellion:

The question of policy is not an easy one and I think that in addition to complete disarmament of certain areas and tribes it will be necessary to have out during the next rains a considerable number of Military Police in outposts while some new briddlepaths notable one from Shugnu to Lenacot must be made.[31]

Thus the method invented in the second phase of operation in practice amounts to military occupation of the Kuki hills.

However, as Richard O'Connor rightly said the 'mobility allowed farmers to escape the impositions of states and their wars' (cited Scott 2009: 4). On the other hand, living within the state meant, virtually by definition, taxes, conscription, corvee labour and, for most, a condition of servitude; these conditions were at the core of the state's strategic and military advantages (Scott Scott 2009: 7).

Area of operations

An extract from the proceeding of the Chief Commissioner of Assam was, for instance, lucid in this respect. It described the 'Kuki rising of 1917–1919' as 'the most formidable with which Assam has been faced for at least a generation', covering an area of 'over some 6,000 square miles of rugged hills surrounding the Manipur Valley and extending to the Somra Tract and the Thaungdut State in Burma'.[32] The area of operation, as described by Webster, is 'a vast area of wild, mountainous and sparsely populated country'.[33] For the purpose of operations the whole 7000 square miles of Kuki hills was divided into six areas (see Figure 3.1):

1 Northwest: Jampi area – between the Barak and the cart road – with its Supply Bases at Bishenpur, Henema and Tapoo,

2   Southwest: Henglep area with supply base at Moirang,
3   South: Manlun and Lenacot area based on Imphal and Chin Hills main bases,
4   Southeast: Mombi (Lonpi) area with its supply base at Suganu,
5   East: Burma road area with supply base at Imphal/Palel and Tamu,
6   Northeast: The Northeast or Aishan area based on Kohima and Homalin main bases.

Shakespear (1980: 231) further divided the Northeast area into three sub-areas: Chassad area, east of the valley, with a supply base at Yaingangpokpi; North Tangkhul area, northeast of the valley with its supply base at Tadapa and the North Somra and Tuzu river area, southeast of Kohima with a supply base at Melomi. These areas were to assigned military commanders:

1   Northwestern Hills (Jampi Area): Major Marshall, Lt. Walker, Capt. C.E. Montefiore, Lt. Needham.
2   Southwestern Hills (Henglep Area): Capt. Goodal, Capt. Fox, Lt. Carter.
3   Southeast (Lonpi Area): Capt. Coote and Lt. Askwith
4   Eastern Hills (Chassad Area): Capt. Parry and Black
5   Northeastern hills (Tangkhul and Somra Area): Lt. Mawson, Capt. Prior and Lt. Rees.

With the demarcation of the whole Kuki hills into areas with their main bases, each area was enclosed by a chain of military out-posts and was provided with substantial numbers of flying columns whose duty was to expeditiously hunt the Kukis from pillar to post, burnt down their villages, destroy their properties, foods and live-stock and to frustrate cultivation and any attempt to rebuild their villages.

The second 'Punitive Measures' 1918–1919

In order to pacify the Kukis once and for all, military operations were launched as previously planned on 15 November 1918 by the Assam Rifles. The Burma Military Police could only join the operations in the beginning of December due to outbreak of epidemic. Incursions were made into the Kuki Hills and stockades, and villages and properties were destroyed. During the operations in Burma the knowledge and

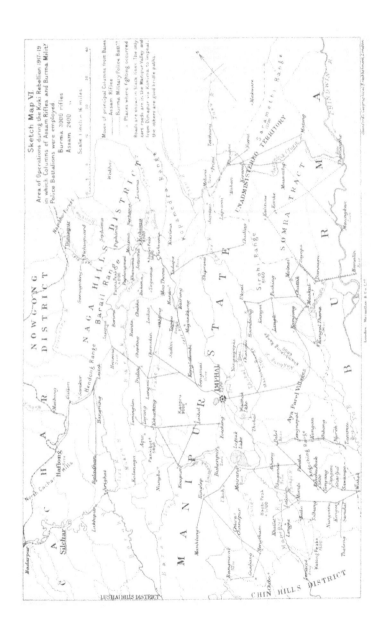

Figure 3.1 Area of Operations during the Kuki Rebellion

Source: L.W. Shakespear. *History of the Assam Rifles.*

previous experience of Ffrench-Mullen was much utilised by the GOI, Burma, and Mr. Henry Keary. In the words of Wright:

> His knowledge of the country, of the history and events of last year's operations, of tactical points, of the characters of the senior officers and troops at my disposal, as well as the character of the opposing tribes, was most valuable asset to me throughout, enabling me to make plans and dispositions with absolute confidence in their correctness.[34]

In these operations, coordination among various columns was emphasised. The strength of British forces in the second phase of operations was 6234 combatants, 696 non-combatants – from Assam Rifles and Burma Military Police.[35]

Concentration camps

One of the most difficult tasks before the military police officers was the distinction between rebel villages and so-called 'friendlies' who are cohabiting the hills at not so distant locations; more so, the friendlies in rebel villages. Colonel L.W. Shakespear (1980: 230) described this situation:

> A difficulty existed in the numbers of friendly villages in amongst the rebel localities, and it was often not easy to distinguish these people from those to be dealt with. This was to a certain extent overcome during the hot weather by the Political Agent arranging for concentration camps in the Manipur valley to which all these friendlies were advised to repair in order to avoid the wrath to come.

In order to hard-press the rebels, the Area Commander 'collect men, women and children in certain concentration camps, where they were fed and maintained till the guns were surrendered'.[36] The concentration camps not only served the purpose of confining the women, children and the aged in an appalling living conditions; it also served as a temporary camp for the interrogation and torture of rebels caught or surrendered. The concentration camps during the first phase of 'punitive measures' were mainly for the British 'friendlies'. However, in the second phase of operations in 1918–1919, it was mainly for the Kuki 'rebels'.

Counter-guerilla operations

During the first phase of operations the advantage the Kukis had was carefully taken into account, 'who know their hills and forests, carry no packs, do not bother themselves over supplies, who are rarely seen in their forests, and who are adepts at guerilla and jungle warfare' (Shakespear 1980: 236). The rearmed Assam Rifles and Burma Military Police were not only trained in Stokes mortars, Lewis guns and rifle bombs, but also in counter-guerilla warfare. From the experience during the first operations itself, it was felt 'the wisdom of having a large number of small columns operating at one time is clearly proved'.[37] Thus, in the whole Kuki hills, 'a series of separate operations carried on simultaneously'.[38] The mobility and coordination of the Kuki fighters, which was to their advantage in the first operations, was noted carefully, and to limit their movement several bases were established and the opening of outposts and flying columns between bases limited the movement of the Kuki fighters by the ubiquitous presence. In the South, Southeast and Northeastern areas, in order to limit the movement and also prevent the escape of the Kuki fighters the Chin and Lushai borders were secured and guarded, and they escaped into the Somra tracts.

In order to illustrate such coordinated and brutal operations, the Northwest area is taken into account. This area, which is about 640 square miles in extent, was subdivided into two political areas: Jampi and North Silchar Road Area. It was penetrated from four directions by four military columns – Captain Montefiore from the north, Major Marshall from the east, Lieutenant Walker from the south and Captain Copeland from the west. These four columns advanced towards this area from their respective advanced bases, i.e. Bishenpur, Henema and Tapoo, on the pre-arranged date of 15 November 1918. The concentration of rebel Kukis were identified through informants and troops quickly moved towards such villages and gave a surprise attack. In the Jampi sub-area Macquid reported:

> The Chanachin garrison under the command of Subedar Hari Ram, 3rd Assam Rifles, surprised Laiyang with a loss to the Kukis of 28 killed and many wounded. The whole live and dead stock of the village fell our hands and the village was burnt.[39]

After rebel villages were overthrown and burnt, permanent posts were formed in strategic villages. If rebel Kuki chiefs fled their village, they had to be chased until caught, killed or surrendered. In the North Silchar Road sub-area, the 'main objective was the death, capture or surrender of the two rebel chiefs, Tinthong and Enjakhup', and three columns under Major Marshall, Captain Montefiore and Copeland respectively marched towards a strongly built and well placed Kolkang, and the concentration village was attacked. Unable to withstand the modern weapons, Tintong and Enjakhup, with a large following of men, women and children, dispersed and fled. Lieutenant Walker and Captain Copeland were in pursuit of the two principal rebel chiefs. Finding themselves hard pressed, both Tintong and Enjakhup dropped their followers and moved towards the south. With information that the two rebel chiefs would be heading towards Ukha territory, orders were sent to immediately block the passes. Completely exhausted and hungry, Tintong demanded aid and food from Ngullen, chief of Khongyang, whom the British friendly chief made him prisoner. Enjakhup, on the other hand, headed back towards Kolkang, who was ambushed by Captain Copeland and was captured. With the capture of these two rebel chiefs all active opposition in the Northwest area ceased and this area was by February reported as 'thoroughly subjugated'.

Forbidding cultivation

After having put the Kuki civilian population in concentration camps and a proclamation was made 'forbidding cultivation', an order was passed enforcing a blockade to food supply from the neighbours. And, 'had they not surrendered by the end of March, they would have been too late to prepare the ground for the next harvest, and would in consequence have been faced with a famine'.[40] After having a disruption of two agriculture seasons, most of their food-grains destroyed and their movements restricted by the ubiquitous presence of the British troops in the Kuki hills and cutting off access to neighbouring villages, it was difficult to continuously supplement their dietary needs from the forest produce. Reid (1997: 80) reported: 'More serious was the destruction of considerable quantities of grain and livestock and the interference with cultivation'. As 'The rebels, who by this time were beginning to feel the pinch of hunger were impressed by the ubiquity of the forces opposed to them, and the first of the leading rebel chiefs surrendered in December' (Reid 1997: 81).

Using 'friendlies'

The policy of 'divide and rule', as a mechanism to maintain colonial rule by identifying and manipulating various divisions in order to prevent unified resistance to rule, was also used in the Kuki Punitive Measure. The policy attempts to prevent unity ever dividing the peoples of India one against the other (Stewart 1951: 53, 57). As in the case of the Lushai expedition 1850 where Colonel Lister recommended the formation of a Kookie levy to be employed as scouts in the southern jungles, to collect information concerning the Lushais, and the events which were occurring on the other side of our frontier, as well as to keep a watch over the Kookies in our own territory and Manipur (Woodthrope 1980: 15.), the Lushai and Chin friendlies were used as spies and fighters in the Kuki operations. Reid (1997: 81) wrote: 'In the south eastern hills, friendly Chins, and in the southwest Lushai and friendly Kukis, were armed and employed as scouts and irregulars'. Keary reported that the Chin friendlies in Burma

> rendered useful service. They prevented an influx of rebel refugees into Burma territory on any scale, and, when pitted against an approximately equal force of Kukis led by two prominent chiefs, they routed it with loss and pursued relentlessly, killing one chief and driving the other to submission.[41]

Macquoid also reported: 'Lieutenant Rundle and his Chin Friendlies, in a running fight in pursuit of a rebel gang, killed Ngulbul, chief of Longya, on the Special List, who, together with Ngulkhup, Chief of Mombi, were the leading chiefs of these areas'.[42] Hard pressed on all sides, Ngulkhup also soon gave up resistance.

Whereas the opposition started from the month of March 1917, an active warfare and counter-operations went on for more than one year (December 1917 to May 1919), suspending two agriculture seasons, and with systematic destruction of villages, properties and all sources of livelihood. The counter-operations, carried out with 'continuous active service in mountainous country', was carried out by the combined forces of Assam and Burma Military Police – 6234 combatants, 696 non-combatants, 7650 transport carriers, etc.[43] It was the 'largest series of military operations' in the eastern frontier of India, eclipsed only by the Second World War in the region in 1944 (Shakespear 1980: 235–236). Robert Reid (1997: 80) also reported that: More than 6,000 combatants, about 8,000 transport coolies and non-combatants, two provincial governments (Assam and Burma) and one princely state (Manipur), all under the supreme direction of the Government of India, took active parts in suppressing the Rising. Besides the Assam Rifles and Burma Military Police, some regular troops such as Sappers and Miners and the Manipur State Military Police also gave their cooperation.

In the second operations, the Kuki fighters put up a much stronger resistance than the previous winter. Despite this stronger force of resistance, the losses on the part of the British troops were minimal due to their previous training before the operations, and the use of stockade mortars was very much feared by the Kuki fighters, though only few were used in the operations. The organised resistance against the British ended with the surrender of Pache, Chief of Chassad, on 5 March 1919. By the beginning of April, troops gradually withdrew and the war came to an end.

Conclusion

The military tactics largely followed in the Kuki Punitive Measures can be broadly termed as scorched-earth, counter-guerilla warfare. In this operation against the Kuki rebels, 'scorched-earth policy' was largely deployed to crush the morale of the Kukis. In other words, the new strategy was a 'morale warfare' in which indiscriminate destruction of the 'rebel' villages, granaries and jhum fields was carried out. It also involved the capturing of any 'rebel' Kukis and incarcerated them in 'concentration camps', 'regrouping' of the 'friendly' hill populations in the valley or around the military outposts in the hills. For this purpose, the whole 'rebel areas' were divided into six areas under different commands, and each area was provided with a base camp in the valleys. A series of military outposts were created across the sector area, each equipped with a 'flying scout' whose duty was to pursue the 'rebels', to carry out the 'scorched earth' policy being projected to deprive the 'rebels' a home and food supply. The whole idea was to break the spirit of Kukis and to 'crush his morale' so that they surrender and submit themselves to the British. Various forms and techniques of threats and intimidations were also served to the whole Kuki populace. It was also a sort of coercive diplomacy or forceful persuasion, besides practicing the usual divide and rule policy followed not only between various communities cohabiting this 7,000 square miles of hilly area, but also within the various Kuki clans.

As the 'most serious incident in the history of Manipur' and the 'largest series of military operations conducted' in the Northeast frontier, brutal punitive measures were adopted and inhuman treatment and torture were meted out ot the Kukis for their defiance of authority. The uprising was suppressed by 'force of arms' to crush the 'morale' of the Kukis by identifying them as 'enemy' and harass them so as to force them to submission. After the brutal suppression of the uprising, 'the Kukis were now made to open up their country by constructing fair bridle paths through their hills connecting with points in the Manipur and the Chindwyn valleys, and also connecting the various posts with each others' (Shakespear 1980: 237). Elsewhere I had written that:

> The war could have still continued had not the British went rampaging the Kuki villages by destroying houses and paddy stocks, finding the weaknesses of a Kuki man who has great love and responsibility to his family. The Kuki chiefs and warriors fearing an impending outbreak of famine surrendered to the British and this marked the end of the war.
>
> (Haokip 2006)

What is glaringly intriguing is 'the degree to which concern over the acquisition and control of population was at the very centre of early statecraft' (Scott 2017: Chapter 5). Today guerilla warfare has become the only technique deployed to fight the indomitable state and its forces. This warfare system is adopted by the liberation fighters in Northeast India into impenetrable jungles, and despite military technological advancement, the state forces still cannot fully overcome the barriers of terrain and guerilla warfare techniques. It was indeed the Kuki fighters who employed this art of warfare as a way of organised resistance to repressive forces of the state.

Notes

1 British Library, London (BL), Asian and African Collections (formerly Oriental & India Office Collections) (hereafter AAC), Indian Office Records and Private Papers (hereafter IOR&PP), IOR/L/PS/10/724: 1917–1920, File No. 383/1919: J.E. Webster, Chief Secretary to the Chief Commissioner of Assam, to The Secretary to the Government of India in the Foreign and Political Department, Shillong, 7 November 1917.
2 Documents of the Anglo-Kuki War 1917–1919, edited by D.L.Haokip, 2017, H.W. Cole to B.C. Allen, 17 March 1917 (hereafter Documents of Anglo-Kuki War).
3 BL, AAC, IOR&PP, IOR/L/PS/10/724: 1917–1920, File No. 383/1919: J.E. Webster to the Secretary to the Government of India, Shillong, 7 November 1917.

4 BL, AAC, IOR&PP, IOR/L/PS/10/724: 1917–1920, File No. 383/1919: J.E. Webster to the Secretary to the Government of India, Shillong, 7 November 1917.
5 Documents of Anglo-Kuki War, 705 M.S. J.C. Higgins to Chief Secretary to the Chief Commissioner of Assam, 24 November, 1917.
6 Documents of Anglo-Kuki War, No. 705 M.S. J.C. Higgins to Chief Secretary to the Chief Commissioner of Assam, 24 November, 1917.
7 BL, AAC, IOR&PP, IOR/L/PS/10/724: 1917–1920, IOR/L/PS/10/724: 1917–1919, File No. 2686/1919: 'Report on the Rebellion of the Kukis on the Upper Chindwin Fronteir and the operations connected therewith' by J.B. Marshall, DC, Upper Chindwin District, Indian Office Record, British Library, London.
8 Documents of Anglo-Kuki War, No. 705 M.S. J.C. Higgins to Chief Secretary to the Chief Commissioner of Assam, 24 November, 1917.
9 *Thingkho le malchapom* is a small bunch of wooden sticks and king chilli bind together. It is sent to different villages as a message to inform an emergency situation that requires an urgent need for a united fight against an enemy. It is dispatched as a relay from one village to the next adjoining village and so on until the last remaining village is reached.
10 For instance, the chief of Songpi village, Mr. Semthong Kuki, was friendly to the British throughout the 'rebellion'. Due to his loyalty and friendliness Songpi became the headquarters of one of the three subdivisions set up in the hills, which today is the headquarters of Churachandpur district.
11 Manipur State Archives (hereafter MSA), R-2/230/S-4: Higgins Tour Diary, December 1, 1917.
12 MSA), R-2/230/S-4: Higgins Tour Diary, December 24, 1917.
13 BL, AAC, IOR&PP, IOR/L/PS/10/724: 1917–1920, File No. 383/1918: J.E. Webster, Chief Secretary to the Chief Commissioner of Assam, to the Secretary to the Government of India in the Foreign and Political Department, Shillong, 3 December 1917.
14 BL, AAC, IOR&PP, IOR/L/PS/10/724: 1917–1920, File No. 383/1918: J.E. Webster to the Secretary to the Govt. of India, Shillong, 3 December 1917.
15 MSA, R-1/S-A/12: Tour Diary of W.A. Cosgrave, Political Agent in Manipur, for the month of February 1918
16 MSA, R-1/S-A/12: Tour Diary of W.A. Cosgrave for the month of March 1918.
17 MSA, R-1/S-A/12: Tour Diary of W.A. Cosgrave, Political Agent in Manipur, for the month of January 1918.
18 BL, AAC, IOR&PP, IOR/L/PS/10/724: 1917–1920, Report of Webster, Secretary to the Chief Commissioner of Assam, to the Secretary to the Government of India, Foreign and Political Department, 27 June and 8 July, 1919.
19 MSA, R-1/S-A/12: Tour Diary of W.A. Cosgrave, Political Agent in Manipur, for the month of March 1918.
20 BL, AAC, IOR&PP, IOR/L/PS/10/724: 1917–1920, File No. 383/1918: Letter from J. E. Webster 3 December 2017.
21 BL, AAC, IOR&PP, IOR/L/MIL/17/19/42 (1919): Henry Keary to Chief of the General Staff, Shimla, June 1919, 'Despatch on the Operations against the Kuki tribes of Assam and Burma', November 1917 to March 1919.

22 BL, AAC, IOR&PP, IOR/L/MIL/17/19/42: 1919: C.E.K. Macquoid, General Officer Commanding, Kuki Punitive Measures letter to Lieutenant General Sir Henry DU. Keary, Commanding Burman Division, Controlling Kuki Punitive Measures, Imphal, Burma dated 5 September 1918.

23 BL, AAC, IOR&PP, IOR/L/MIL/17/19/42 (1919): From the Henry Keary, General Officer Commanding, Burma Division to the Chief of the General Staff, Army Headquarters, Simla, No. N.E.F.O.P.B. – 69, dated 5 September 1918.

24 The wanted rebels on the list were: Semchung of Ukha, Pakang of Henglep, Ngulbul of Longya, Ngulkhup of Lonpi, Leothang of Goboh, Pache of Chassad, Ngulkhokhai of Chassad, Tintong of Laijang, Enjakhup of Thenjang, Heljason of Loibol, Mangkho-on of Tingkai, Khotinthang of Jampi, Chengjapao of Aisan and Lunkholal of Chongjang.

25 Tour Diary of W.A. Cosgrave, Political Agent in Manipur, for the month of February 1918, Manipur State Archives, R-1/S-A/12.

26 BL, AAC, IOR&PP, IOR/L/PS/10/724: 1917–1920, Telegram from the Chief Secretary to the Govt. of Burma, Rangoon to the Secretary to the Govt. of India in the Foreign & Political Department, Delhi 5 January 1918.

27 MSA, R-1/S-A/12: Tour Diary of W.A. Cosgrave, Political Agent in Manipur, for the month of February 1918.

28 BL, AAC, IOR&PP, IOR/L/MIL/17/19/42 (1919): Henry Keary to the Chief of the General Staff, Army Headquarters, Simla, June 1919.

29 BL, AAC, IOR&PP, IOR/L/MIL/17/19/42 (1919): From Henry Keary, General Officer Commanding, Burma Division to the Chief of the General Staff, Army Headquarters, Simla, No. N.E.F.O.P.B. – 69, dated 5 September 1918.

30 BL, AAC, IOR&PP, IOR/L/MIL/17/19/42: 1919: Brigadier General C.E.K. Macquoid, D.S.O., General Officer Commanding, Kuki Punitive Measures letter to Lieutenant General Sir Henry DU. Keary, Commanding Burman Division, Controlling Kuki Punitive Measures, Imphal, Burma dated 5 September 1918.

31 MSA, R-1/S-A/12: Tour Diary of W.A. Cosgrave for the months of January & February 1918.

32 BL, AAC, IOR&PP, IOR/L/PS/10/724: 1917–1920,Mss. Eur E 325/13: 1920, 'Extract from the proceeding of the Chief Commissioner of Assam in Political Department' by A.W. Botham, 27 September 1920.

33 BL, AAC, IOR&PP, IOR/L/PS/10/724: 1917–1920, File No. 383/1918: Letter from J. E. Webster, Chief Secretary to the Chief Commissioner of Assam, to the Secretary to the Government of India in the Foreign and Political Department, dated 3 December 2017.

34 BL, AAC, IOR&PP, IOR/L/MIL/17/19/42 (1919): Henry Keary to the Chief of the General Staff, Army Headquarters, Simla, June 1919.

35 BL, AAC, IOR&PP, IOR/L/MIL/17/19/42: 1919, 'Despatch on the Operations Against the Kuki Tribes' Macquoid to Keary, 27 April 1919, Appendix – III.

36 BL, AAC, IOR&PP, IOR/L/MIL/17/19/42: 1919: Macquid to Henry D'U Keary, 27 April 1919, Despatch on the Operations against the Kuki tribes of Assam and Burma, November 1917 to March 1919.

37 MSA, R-1/S-A/12: Tour Diary of W.A. Cosgrave, Political Agent in Manipur, for the month of February 1918.

38 BL, AAC, IOR&PP, IOR/L/MIL/17/19/42: 1919: Macquoid to Henry Keary, GOI, Kuki Punitive Measures, Imphal, 27 April 1919.
39 BL, AAC, IOR&PP, IOR/L/MIL/17/19/42: 1919: Macquid to Henry D'U Keary, 27 April 1919, Despatch on the Operations against the Kuki tribes of Assam and Burma, November 1917 to March 1919.
40 BL, AAC, IOR&PP, IOR/L/MIL/17/19/42 (1919): Henry Keary, GOI, Burma Division, to Chief of General Staff, Army Headquarters, India, Shimla in June 1919.
41 BL, AAC, IOR&PP, IOR/L/MIL/17/19/42 (1919): Henry Keary, GOI, Burma Division, to Chief of General Staff, Army Headquarters, India, Shimla in June 1919.
42 BL, AAC, IOR&PP, IOR/L/MIL/17/19/42: 1919: Macquoid to Henry Keary, GOI, Kuki Punitive Measures, Imphal, 27 April 1919.
43 BL, AAC, IOR&PP, IOR/L/MIL/17/19/42: 1919: 'Despatch on the Operations Against the Kuki Tribes of Assam and Burma, November 1917 to March 1919', Brig-Gen. CEK Macquoid, General Officer Commanding Kuki Punitive Measures to Lieut-Gen. Sir Henry D.U. Keary, Commanding Burma Division, Controlling Kuki Punitive Measures, 27 April 1919, Appendix – I.

References

Callwell, C.E. 1906. *Small Wars: Their Principles and Practice.* London: Harrison & Sons.
Guevara, Che. 1961. *Guerrilla Warfare.* London: Penguin Books.
Haokip, Thongkholal. 2006. 'The British Northeast Frontier Policy and the Kukis', *Ahsijolneng Annual Magazine*, https://ssrn.com/abstract=1621818
Mackenzie, Alexander. 1884. *History of the Government with the Hill Tribes of the North-East Frontier of Bengal.* Calcutta.
Porch, Douglas. 2013. *Counterinsurgency: Exposing the Myths of the New Way of War.* Cambridge: Cambridge University Press.
Ray, Asok Kumar. 1990. *Authority and Legitimacy: A Study of the Thadou-Kukis in Manipur.* New Delhi: Renaissance Publishing House.
Reid, Robert. 1997. *History of the Frontier Areas Bordering on Assam from 1883–1941.* [originally published in 1942]. Guwahati: Spectrum Publications.
Scott, J.C. 2009. *The Art of Not Being Governed: An Anarchist History of Upland Southeast Asia.* New Haven: Yale University Press.
Scott, J.C. 2017. *Against the Grain: A Deep History of the Earliest States.* New Haven: Yale University Press.
Shakespear, L.W. 1980. *History of the Assam Rifles.* [originally published in 1929]. Guwahati: Spectrum Publications.
Stewart, Neil. 1951. 'Divide and Rule: British Policy in Indian History', *Science & Society*, 15 (1): 49–57.
Woodthrope, R.G. 1980. *The Lushai Expedition 1871072* [originally published in 1873]. Guwahati: Spectrum Publications.

4

'THESE CRAFTY JUNGLE FIGHTERS'

Tactics, technology and symbols of Kuki war

D. Letkhojam Haokip

They [Kukis] are most skilful in devising fortifications and defences and traps.

Their woodcraft is superb. Their tactics are 'shoot and run'.
– Lt. Col. J.L.W. Ffrench-Mullen

The official historian of Assam Rifles, Col. J.W. Shakespear, who took an active part in the operations against the Kukis, has noted about the Kuki war of 1917–1919:

> The rapidly spreading war amongst the Kuki clans was disconcerting and most difficult to deal with. . . . It grew therefore into the largest series of military operations conducted on this side of India eclipsing them all in casualties and arduousness of active service.
>
> (Shakespear 1977: 224, 235–236)

Scholars hardly had given any serious thought on such commendations given by field officers, who witnessed the military encounter not only of the state military forces but also of the Kuki fighters. The war was 'disconcerting' and 'most difficult' to deal not only because of the harsh terrain, to which scholars have given undue emphasis, but also due to the tactics and technology of warfare employed by the Kukis. It was described to be 'hit and run' or 'guerilla' warfare. Although the term may not completely capture the reality of Kuki tactics of warfare, the fact that such 'guerilla' warfare was the most efficient way in dealing regular forces in a rugged geography was also visible in the case of the Anglo-Kuki War 1917–1919. British counterinsurgency operations against the Kukis went on for two consecutive seasons (years) and was said to be most 'ardous'. Lieut. Col. J.L.W. Ffrench-Mullen, for instance, commented on the Kuki tactics of 'guerilla' warfare as not only enervating but also most 'demoralising' to trained troops. There was, he said, 'nothing to show for weeks and months of effort, no rest and no relaxation of mind or body'. The operations have 'no glamour' and it was a 'thankless, disagreeable jobs . . . which involve a serious risk to life and health'.[1] This chapter concerns the Kuki strategy and tactics of warfare and the different weapons and war symbols used by them during the war with British forces.

Understanding 'guerilla war'

There was rich literature on war in history, which made a clear distinction on war (conventional, between states), small war (counterinsurgency operation, by regulars against 'irregular') and guerilla war (armed resistance against the state, following 'hit and run' tactics). This distinction was based purely on the tactics adopted and the legitimacy of the war fought. Otherwise, war remains war in all respects, which means a state of conflict and open hostility involving war equipments, tactics and strategies. The famous military historian Carl von Clausewitz sees war as unlimited violence and an act of force to compel an enemy to one's will (Cited in Roxborough 1994: 623). What is central to war are tactics and strategy. In her recent work, Beatrice Heuser evoked the way in which 'Strategy' in war was understood in time ('evolution'). With an overview of different ideas on war strategy, largely from 1500 C.E., she shows, unlike the common view notion of separation, how military strategy cannot be separated from political goals of the state (the grand tactic), and that both political goals and military strategy are in turn closely linked to contemporary economic, social and cultural affairs. In this way, the division of labour in war starting and war fighting is not intrinsic, but rather a cultural phenomenon associated with the emergence of the modern state, the bureaucratisation of war and the rise of militarism in late-nineteenth-century Europe (Heuser 2016). In this sense, the dichotomy between the grand or political strategy and military strategy becomes invisible and inseparable. This applies to conventional war as to the 'small wars' or 'asymmetric wars' and also to the insurgency 'guerilla war'.

Yet, there was a larger issue at the distinction between 'war', 'small war' and 'insurgency' or guerilla war. In the first, there were at least two belligerents in war; in the second and third there were a belligerent versus non-belligerent. The worst is 'insurgency' which in civilisational category is 'rebellion'. In the last, we can see that the terminology is not just about tactical differences but based on the larger issue of race and culture. Thus, when the tribes fought against an established authority or of the intruders of their sphere of autonomy, it was invariably dubbed as 'rebellion', 'insurgency', 'savagery', 'crime' and so on, and never as 'war'. This racial and civilisational overtone has been slowly deconstructed, only to see itself in the old bottle. Jeffrey B. White, for instance, defines the phenomenon of 'irregular war' as the oldest form of warfare that goes by many names – tribal warfare, primitive warfare, 'little wars', and low-intensity conflict – and opines that the term that captures the wide variety of these is 'little war'.[2] What constituted 'little war' is yet to be spelt out clearly. What was close to 'little war' has been what we popularly known today as 'insurgency', 'irregular war' and 'guerilla war'. It tends to merge the gap between 'guerilla war' and the so-called primitive warfare. Truly, this cannot be done. For instance, one cannot equate the so-called 'surprise tactic' of the hill tribes of Northeast in the past with that of 'guerilla war' tactic of the twentieth-century Anglo-Kuki War 1917–1919.

What constituted 'guerilla war' tactics then? To treat 'guerilla warfare' as 'primitive' and 'uncivilised' warfare is to commit a serious error in history. The term 'guerrilla', derived from Spanish *Guerrilleros*, referred to 'irregulars' operating against regular armies.[3] What is unique to the 'guerilla' warfare according to Ian F.W. Beckett is that they operated in difficult terrain, such as mountains or deserts, had local knowledge denied to their opponents, availed the support of people from inaccessible regions and could prolong war due to their mobility and 'hit-and-run' tactics, which easily evade larger forces (Beckett 2004: 2). To Davis, 'jungle warfare is the nature of fighting determined by terrain and weather that limits the movement of foot troops or track (small combats), and often fight in the blazing sun and rainstorm using arms that can be carried on back' (Davis 1944: 211–212). The objective of guerrilla tactics, according to Pahazos, is not to occupy and consolidate certain areas but to make swift strikes, to achieve results and then withdraw rapidly to distance themselves from enemy's stronghold. Normally, it follows two methods of operations: attack by arms and propaganda (Pahazos 1952: 221).

In *The Insurgent Archipelago*, John Mackinlay puts forward the concept of an evolution of insurgency from the Maoist paradigm of the golden age of insurgency to the global insurgency of the start of the twenty-first century. He defines this distinction as 'Maoist' and 'post-Maoist' insurgency (Mackinlay 2009). Yet, most insurgency and counterinsurgency (COIN) theorists agreed that the strength of insurgents who invariably adopted the guerilla tactic was largely due to the popular support. Surely, most guerilla warfare or insurgency was driven on the aphorism of Mao Zedong famous line: 'The guerrilla must swim in the people as the fish swims in the sea' (Zedong 1937). So long as the insurgency enjoyed mass support, it will retain the strategic advantages of mobility, invisibility and legitimacy, and hence it would be difficult to defeat and can even hold on indefinitely.

The classic example of this is the failure of French occupation of Spain during the Napoleonic wars when the Spanish forces, enjoying popular support, dispersed and took to guerilla tactics, proving decisive against the superiority of the French army. Hence, all COIN theorists and strategists recommended different strategies over the ages, ranging from being brutal to humane, over the supporting population. If the 'population' was crucial in insurgency, some theorists suggested that the use of 'force of arms' should also be extended to the civilian population to end insurgency. This theory which came in the forms of the infamous 'scorched earth', 'butcher & bolt', the 'razzia', 'blockhouse', 'cordon & raking' and so on, was popular form of colonial COIN strategy. The unpopularity of the same principle slowly gave way to principle of winning the 'hearts and minds' of the supporting population. In both the cases, 'population' was central to the defeat or survival of insurgency, and hence the insurgency movement has become people's war.

What is evident from the above discussion is that 'guerilla warfare' is one of the most popular tactics of war popular among not only non- or anti-state insurgents, but also among state forces when confronted with the superior enemy regulars. In this sense, guerilla war is a modern form of war tactics and perhaps the most decisive method against the regular armies. This chapter concerns the Kuki war strategy during the Anglo-Kuki War 1917–1919. Instead of being 'primitive' and 'savage', the Kuki tactics of war, described to be 'guerilla warfare', was an amalgam of traditional warfare and modern tactics against the colonial armies. It will be seen that the Kukis had adopted guerilla or 'hit and run' tactics with western-made firearms (flintlocks, muskets, etc.) as the dominant strategy to repel the superior invading forces of the British. Besides, they made use of large numbers of stockades and breastworks at different strategic points along the routes leading to the villages and around the village precincts. In many big villages, they also fortified in their traditional way, the art they had stopped for quite sometimes. While gunpowder was largely their own manufacture, many other traditional forms and technology of war were also used by them. For instance, they used their traditional stone trap *panjies* (small and sharp bamboo stakes planted on the narrow path), and bow and poisonous arrow, complemented with their modern forms of stockade. Besides, they also used traditional symbols of war such as *sajam* (pieces of meat), *thinkho-le-malchapom* (chilli bound with burnt wood), bullet, charcoal, beads and swords for mobilising and communication purposes.

Formation of Kuki forces

It was often argued in most military reports that the enemy Kuki forces were lacking organisation and discipline. It was described as fluid, disorganised and scattered forces under the leadership of their village chiefs. In light of this, the combination of forces was unthinkable and cooperation of the enemy was unexpected. However, once the operation began, it was found that Kukis from different areas cooperated in the war efforts and in many cases joined together to fight the British troops. Besides, it was found that there was similarity in their tactics, technology and symbols of war across the Kuki hills. How this unity was possible puzzled the officers. The first thing in this respect was the role of traditional war council in forging unity among different areas of Kuki hills. Every Kuki village had the chief council to decide and traditional *som-in* to train the youth in the art of warfare who would go to war under the leadership of the chief. This village force was also part of the larger forces of the clan under the leadership of the clan *pipa* (head), who also head the clan war council. Thus, we have the larger forces of the clan army who were under the direct control of the clan head and normally formed the operative part of the Kuki war. The grand councils of these clan heads constituted the Kuki war council, which takes the final decision for war and peace that concerns the tribes. It was these clan councils which decided not to send coolies to France for the Great War in March 1917. The same councils decided to go for a war against British government after Mombi was burned down on 17 October 1917. Based on the consensus reached at most of the clan war councils, the grand Kuki war council was held at Chassad at the end of November 1917, where the decision was finally taken to wage war against the British. 150 chiefs participated in the council and took a vow to fight in their respective areas and took the sacred war ritual called *sathin-salung-neh* (feasting on the liver and heart of animal). In this council all the necessary war strategies and tactics were also taken up. It was the grand war council that provided unity and strength among them while each of the clan army fought from their respective areas, occasionally circulating their clan warriors to help others.

Each village of the clan head forming the tactical headquarters, all the warriors of that area fought the British troops. There were at least five such tactical headquarters or area of operations. In the Manipur western and northwestern hills, including North Cachar Hills, the war was commanded by five chiefs: Khotinthang (Jampi), Tintong (Laijang), Lunkholal (Chongjang), Khupkho (Langkhong) and Heljashon (Loibol). In the Southwestern hills, Pakang (Henglep), Semchung (Ukha), Haoneh (Nabil) and Paosum (Songphu) led the war. In the southern hills, it was commanded by Ngulbul (Longya), Ngulkhup (Lonpi) and Tongjang of Mualtam. In eastern hills, including upper Burma, Lhukhomang Pache (Chassad), Paokholen (Bongbal) and Paboi (Sita) commanded the war. In the northeastern hills, including some parts of the Naga Hills, it was commanded by Chengjapao (Aisan).[4] This was how Kuki forces organised under their respective clan heads for the war.

The effectiveness of Kuki traditional administration was widely noted by the colonial administrator. The recruitment and involvement of non-Chiefs such as Enjakhup (Thenjol) and Ngulkhokhai (Chassad) to mentor and lead the war was a new development in the military formations. The number of arms in each tactical headquarters cannot be ascertained. However, it is discussed under firearms in the following section. The tactical headquarters issued field orders and were also responsible for construction of fortifications, stockades, *panjies*, manufacturing and acquisition of arms, supplying ammunitions, food and others. They also enforced discipline, maintained correspondence with other areas, acquiring information on the position of the enemy through spies and so on. With this formation, one can have a glimpse of unity in diversity in the Kuki war. In the following section, an attempt is made to discuss on their war tactics, technology and symbols during the Anglo-Kuki War.

'Hit and run': Kuki war tactics

Rapidity is the essence of War

– Sun Tzu

The Kuki tactics was mostly confined to 'hit and run' or 'shoot and run' tactics popularly known as 'guerilla warfare'. Sniping against the marching military column from their dispersive[5] and difficult ground and then withdrawing rapidly to a safer hideout or stockade only to reload their muzzle-loader rifles, and ambushing the same party again was common throughout the battleground. For this, the Kukis heavily depended on their previous and strategically built stockades, instead of marching out to attack them in an open or pre-specified battleground, sometimes going for hours of exchange of fire. They sometimes attacked the night camps of military columns as well as some of their outposts. However, such attacks were also not in the form of 'rushing' over the camp but largely firing blank from a certain distance or at times sneaking close to the camp and sniping the sentry and then withdrawing rapidly. In this context, the objective of their warfare was not to kill as many sepoys as they could, but to harass them with incessant sniping and make the march most unpredictable, uncomfortable and demoralising to the troops. For this, they make maximum use of the rugged topography and locally available military materials such as rampant use of hidden stockade, *panjies* (sharp bamboo spike planted on the narrow path), stones or log chutes/traps over the narrow path along the acclivities, poisoning of arrow and hill streams.

Evidences of a deliberate target on the British officers of the military columns can be seen from statement of Ngulkhup and a colonial officer. The former stated that the rifle and ammunition he had seized at Karong will not be 'wasted' against the sepoys but reserved 'to kill the Bara Sahib with it, even if it cost him his own life'.[6] Harassing the military columns in general and targeting the British officers (the Sahibs) was the general policy adopted by the Kukis during the war. J.B. Marshall, for instance, reported: 'There can be no doubt it was part of the settled policy [of the Kukis] to try always to shoot the British Officers'.[7] Targeting the Officers or commander indeed was not a new or modern tactic (Lionel Giles 1910:145). The Kuki tactics centred on breaking their enemy's resistance or operations. All the field reports are loaded with the methods adopted by the Kukis against the military forces. The five-week military campaign of Captain Coote from 28 January 1918 from Imphal and Lieut. Stedman from Chin Hills against the southeastern Kukis was a revelation of guerrilla warfare tactics. A telegram in relation to the 'repulse' of Lieut. Stedman column on 29 January 1918 reported:

> On twenty ninth, an attack on, repulsed with the loss of five killed nine wounded including myself. On approaching village, my left flankers were fired on from top of the steep bank. Thinking it was usual fire and run away tactics, I fire one round from gun and charged. To my surprise, we were

met by a steady well aimed and continued fire which I judge
to be from at least fine Martini rifles by their sound. Before
reaching the top having been hit four times I rolled down the
Khund. . . . Howchinkhup informed me that unless I took the
coolies straight back to Lenacot they would desert. At Lenacot, subedar major again places casualties at four killed and
13 wounded.[8]

Steadman was 'mortally' injured, and 11 of his riflemen were killed
and many more wounded (Palit 1984: 70). The Kukis open fire only
from the stockades, forts or from a certain naturally protected site.
For instance, they ambushed Coote's column at the foothills at Chakpi
(Lonpi frontier or border) from their stockade, inflicting fatal injuries to
three riflemen and immediately retreating before their opponent could
see them. At night, they sniped the British camp at close range and
wounded one sepoy who died the next morning. The column was also
ambushed near Nampho Kuno (Naphou Khunou) village and wounded
other riflemen and two carriers (Shakespear 1977: 217). A little away
from Nungoinu the column met another ambush where the leader of
left flank was killed. The skirmishes took at the stockade (40 to 50
yards in size), and the fight took three quarters of an hour and resulted
in the death of two advance guards (a gun havildar and a gun layer)
besides inflicting injuries to many sepoys (Shakespear 1977: 78–79).
Deception and forage as the basis of military tactics came to light
during the war. Ambushing the British suppliers or rations again remind
us of their skill in surprise, forage and deception. 1) The skirmishes
near Suampo between Herbert's column and the Kukis inflicted heavy
injuries to Cloete's column at Loibol; 2) the attack to the Vickers and
Sanderson column in the northwestern hills at Chonjang and Khoupum,
killing and wounding the British riflemen and carriers; 3) ambuscading
Hooper's column, who escorts a ration for Government military outposts by Loibol and Manlun villages; and 4). to Parker, S.D.O of Upper
Burma by the Kukis of Somra tract, resulting in heavy causalities to the
British without injuries on their part and taking away all the rations
from the enemy, was indeed a combined effort, taking a 'surprising' tactic to overawe the enemy.[9] The Kukis from Henglep and Ukah (Ukha)
attacked Goodall and Carter, who marched with 120 rifles to destroy
them by late February 1918, inflicting many casualties (Shakespear
1977: 222). The Kukis also killed two British riflemen at Bamkushan
village and many casualties were inflicted (Shakespear 1977: 225–226).
In the Chassad area (northeastern hills), the Kuki snipers deployed
the same tactics to counter the combined forces of the Assam Rifles

column (under Coote and Higgins) and Burma Military column and killed Molesworth (lieutenant rank). There were also an open confrontation at the stockades of Chatrick and Maokot where Coote lost a rifleman and six of them were seriously wounded. The severity and intensity of Kuki warfare in the Chassad area necessitated reinforcement and rations. R.H. Henderson, the President of the Darbar, had to lament for the delayed return of Cosgrave column to Imphal: 'it is very unfortunate that Cosgrave has now had to postpone his date of return'.[10] The Kukis evade the superior strength of the British when the latter secure their position but sniped or ambushed them when they are unprepared, and busy chasing evaders. On their failure to get Kuki sniper, the British forces damaged or burnt down the deserted villages to the ground, shot mithuns and cattle and punished unarmed women and children. For instance, Coote's column, after suffering from the elusive Kuki snipers in the jungle, poured down their anger over the helpless villagers (mostly women and children) of Changpol, Gnarjal and Pantha with some inhuman atrocities.

The Kukis blocked the Silchar and Moreh road, the lifeline in those days, destroying Rest houses, outposts and cut-off telegraph lines, thereby inflicting damage and keeping the enemy in constant engagement within 7000 sq. miles. This was nothing but a deliberate attempt to reduce the British forces. Moving out and encamping into the forest, making their position unassailable sending out spies, tribute collections and attacking enemy when their position would favour them was a clear indication of their expertise in the art of warfare. Thus, foraging, deceiving and attacking from the front, rear and from the sides or at night to the weary British soldiers could be seen. Their success would not be possible without collecting foreknowledge on the British strategies and tactics carried out by spies.

Similar tactics were employed by the Kukis during the second phase of operations and indeed inflicted many casualties on the military columns. For instance, in November 1918 Tintong and Enjakhup ambuscaded Marshal and Walker at three places: Loibol, Kebuching and Laijang. The severity and intensity of Kuki warfare in the area compelled Montifiore and Needham to cooperate with Marshal (Shakespear 1977: 234). Evasion as a bait to entice the enemy came to light. Coote and Rundall drove Ngulkhup from pillar to post and he surrendered at Tamu. British columns that chase Pache and Chengjapao meted sniping and ambushed on the way. Ngulbul, Chief of Longya was shot dead while fighting from the stockade, holding his little son in his arms (Palit 1984: 77). Despite their hard show, the changing strategy of the military forces in the second phase of operations, and unlike the previous operations, they were rounded up in the areas and had been hunted from pillar to post without rest. Civilians were also now not spared; they were killed and captured in their jungle hideouts and put in the 'concentration camps'. Granaries destroyed in totality and cultivation and reoccupation of village was prevented. The Kukis did their best by their 'hit and run' tactics wherever they could, but they had to eventually give in when there was no place to move on and no food to sustain their war. The capture of Tintong and Enjakhup and surrender of Pache in March 1919 at Imphal marked the end of active warfare. In April 1919, the Anglo-Kuki War eventually came to an end (Shakespear 1977: 235).

Yet, the crucial point is that the Kuki method of warfare was one that was most difficult to deal with in the rugged jungles and mountainous country. It best suited the topographical feature of the region and it could only be conquered with special counterinsurgency strategy prevailing in other parts of the world known as 'blockhouse' or 'area' system. What is interesting about the Kuki method of warfare is that with their incessant sniping and attack they inflicted many casualties on the troops (whom they keep them on their guard 24 x 7 while in the hills) without themselves being killed or captured. Except learning some jungle warfare from the Kukis and committing some 'tragic inhumanity' in the hills, the Government troops had nothing to show for their hard efforts. Shakespear rightly noted that 'Coote had retreated to Imphal after upgrading his skilled in the jungle warfare'. The difficulty in dealing with the Kuki method of warfare is best described by Lieut. Col. J.L.W. Ffrench-Mullen:

> There is nothing more disheartening to troops than chasing the elusive savage through his dense jungles never really scoring off him, on the contrary suffering daily casualties with the very remote chance if lucky of 'downing' a sniper. Always every moment of the 24 hours, whether in the camp or on the march, they were in danger of a shot from the surrounding jungle. Nothing to show for weeks and months of effort, no rest and no relaxation of mind or body, bad food and an entire absence of the amenities of life.[11]

The war technology

In the fight against the military troops, the Kukis mainly used old muzzle-loader guns, muskets and leather cannons (*pumpi*) fueled by their own produced gunpowder. In certain areas, they used bow and poisonous arrow or sometimes poisoned the stream used by the military forces. Besides, they largely used their traditional defence system such as the village fortification (wooden palisades), stockades, *panjies*, stone/log/bamboo traps or chutes and so on. All these weapons of war and defensive systems, mostly derived from local materials (except guns) show their craftsmanship and skills. We also have an account of Kuki artisans making guns from condemned gun barrels purchased from the Burma or Bengal. It is, therefore, important to draw our attention on this aspect of war technology the Kukis had used against the government troops during the rising.

Firearms (meipum, meithal)

The most potent weapon of the Kukis during the war was indeed the muzzle-loader rifles, old tower muskets and flintlocks. References of Kukis using martini rifles came to light in the southern Manipur. They had fascination for firearms since they started using them from the later part of the eighteenth century. By the dawn of the nineteenth century, a good number of guns found their way into the Kuki hills from Burma and the Chittagong markets (Guite 2011a). The use of guns for hunting, raiding and burial ceremonies was a testimony to the use and value of guns among the Chin-Kuki ethnic groups (Parry 1976: 148, 203, 255). By the second half of the nineteenth century, firearms had already replaced their traditional weapons, like bow and arrow.[12] As guns became priceless possessions of every Kuki man, they also did anything to get one for themselves. This was made possible by purchasing from valley traders. Singh (1992: 289) noted that Kukis living in the Manipur (1877–1878) had a large number of muskets and ammunitions and some of them served as irregulars in the Manipur Army.

The colonial administrators had withdrawn about 6,000 guns, including 123 from the Kukis of Manipur south during the 'Chin-Lushai Expedition 1889–1895' (Carey and Tuck 1932: 22 & 112–113) and about 1195 guns between 1907 and 1917 exclusively from Manipur.[13] Kim Vaiphei argued that most of the guns confiscated belonged to the Kukis because they had acquired the art of manufacturing, and nearly every house possessed a gun for the purpose of hunting (Vaiphei 1995: 13). Official reports claim 1,158 guns were confiscated after the war. However, the account of unsurrendered arms is not available. This shows that they had procured arms long before the war from Chin Hills (Burma) and Chittagong from traders. According to Carey and Tuck, obsolete weapons sold out, as old iron in England was shipped out to Rangoon and Chittagong ports and transited to the 'native' people (Carey and Tuck 1932: 213). The old barrel guns were purchased from these two ports and the Kuki blacksmiths made them into guns.

The Kuki used three types of guns locally – *songchep*, *jangvoh* and *thihnang*.[14] Among these three, *Songchep* is the most primitive form of gun, *Jangvoh* is a modified or modernised form of *Songchep* and *thihnang* is a licenced gun. The skilful Kuki blacksmiths were able to repair and even make some rough firearms from the gun scrap. A spot of the upper part of a *Jangvoh* (local made) barrel is perforated on which a cap is pasted and is to be hit or struck by a flattened piece of iron. *Thihnang* (muzzle-loader) is procured from traders. The Kuki musket could inflict a mortar wound at any distance up to 400 yards.[15]

We have some scattered information during the war that Tintong got hold of some Kuki smiths for making firearms, and the question of surrendering unlicensed and licence guns came in the communications between the Kuki Chiefs and the British Officers. Unlicensed guns could be locally made or purchased through smugglers. Thus, there was a large number of unlicensed guns in the possession of the Kukis during the war.[16] Besides, the Kukis also received some firearms from other tribes during the war.[17] It is difficult to give exact numbers of guns possessed by the Kukis during this time. One estimate for the Kukis of the northern area put it that they had 3,000 fighting men with 1,000 muskets, mostly muzzle-loaders.[18] Similar estimates also came from different Kuki areas but which is difficult to confirm. For instance, in the Somra Tract, Street estimated that the Kukis possessed about 300 guns, Gen. Keary demanded 500 guns from them and 450 guns were finally confiscated. At the end of the war, the total numbers of guns confiscated from the Kukis was officially put at 1,158 guns.[19] The Kukis were expert users of these old flintlock or percussion muzzles-loaders, which was shown during the war. They made efficient use of them for their jungle-fighting and guerilla tactics. (Shakespear 1929: 217).

Leather cannon (pumpi)

Another curious weapon of the Kukis during the war was the use of locally made 'cannon' called *pumpi*, which was officially known as 'leather cannon'. To D.K. Palit, it is a rough missile. This is purely a Kuki invention for the war, although the use of it for hunting was also known among them previously. Buffalo's hide is rolled into a compact tube of size 2 inches or more and two and a half or more feet in length is tightly bound with strips of leathers to form the barrel of cannon. The bamboo tube is also tightly bound with animal leather as above. Then they bored a hole into the right place, as in some muskets or cannons, and filled it with their locally made gunpowder, along with stone or slugs. The *pumpi* is fastened to a tree facing towards where the enemy would be approaching. There are two methods of exploding or firing. One is by hand when the enemy is approaching the target position. Another is by a 'trip cord' that the advance party touches off. The string when touched drops a stone on the percussion cap attached to the barrel. Yet their *pumpi* is only one shot, and at the most they refill the gunpowder, slugs or stones or iron pieces to re-use it (Shakespear 1929: 215).

During the war, this powerful weapon was used in large numbers among the Kukis of southern, eastern and northeastern hills. The British captured some leather cannons with 4-inch bores and about 5 feet long from the possession of the Manipur eastern Kukis.[20] Leather cannons found in the Manipur northeastern (Aisan areas) showed that at least 40 bullets and 1/4 lb. gunpowder were loaded with it. More than three leather cannons were discovered from different stockades. It is good for two discharges. Leather cannons were sometimes carried and fired upon the British camp. One such instance came at Helkukhai, a village in Naga Hills where the British forces encamped.[21] The British operations against Ukha during December 1917 perhaps revealed the opening of leather cannons against the British forces. The Kuki opened stone-shoots against the British on 29 December.[22]

Gunpowder (meilou)

The art of manufacturing gunpowder was known to the Kukis for a long time. In the 1890s the Chin Hills officers learnt that the Kuki-Chin people knew the art of making gunpowder from their own local materials. Carey and Tuck believed that the idea of gunpowder making might have come from the Chinese through the Burmans (Carey and Tuck 1932: 225). Gunpowder making processes found in the Lushai Hills, Manipur and the Chin hills were the same. A.S. Reid remarked that each Kuki village 'manufactures its own gun powder' (Reid 1893: 232). He felt that the Kuki-Chins are untutored as remotest races in Central Africa yet endowed with intelligence, which enables them to discover for themselves the manufacturing of gunpowder (Reid 1893: 2). Sanajaoba (1988: 11) opines that the Kuki-Chin, Meitei and Burmese perhaps learnt the knowledge of gunpowder making from Chinese traders who came to Manipur, until about 1813 A.D.

The Kukis used nitrates obtained from excrement to manufacture gunpowder. The excrement and the urine-impugned deposit on the upper layer of the soil is then towelled up and placed in a basket. In south Manipur, the excrement of bat found in the natural caves especially Senlung cave is the source for it. To extract nitrates, water is poured repeatedly until it is clear. The reddish water was boiled until most of it has evaporated and then it is poured into a wooden plate (Carey and Tuck 1932: 225–226). The nitrates obtained is mixed with equal amount of charcoal and grounded together into gunpowder. Thus, seven parts of saltpetre mixed with five parts each of charcoal and sulphur makes gunpowder. They extract two classes of gunpowder – the coarse ingredient is used in the barrel and the fine dust used in priming the pan (Carey and Tuck 1932: 225–226). Every Kuki village knew the art of making gunpowder. To quote F.M. Clifford during the Anglo-Kuki War: 'they are making their own gunpowder, and for caps, many of them used paper caps that are sold in the bazaars with toy pistols'.[23] Manufacturing gunpowder required intensive labour with involvement of the village community for producing the required amount for the war. With this art, there is no wonder that the Kukis could withstand the imperial forces for almost two years.

Village fortification

Since after the prohibition of fortification under colonial government, the Kukis had stopped the tradition they had held for long. However, they still possessed the knowledge of making fortification. Once the war broke out, some of the big villages took up fortification of their villages as defensive structure. For instance, the big villages of Chassad and Mombi (Lonpi) were fortified once the war broke out. In both the villages, we can see that the fortification was made of strong timbers or sharp wooden palisade and at certain points with thick wooden planks with loopholes to discharge arrows and bullets. The narrow gate was made of swinging wooden plank, not at the main road approaching the village, but at different points where the approach was most difficult. While the wall of the fortification was covered with sharp bamboo spikes so that climbing is difficult, the whole area around the village fortification was surrounded by pitch filled with *panjies*. In all the cases, the areas surrounding the village was filled with *panjies* so that approach to the village was difficult without cleaning up these sharp spikes concealed under dry leaves and small pits. In many cases, line of stockades was also constructed around the village as the first defensive line, connected with the village through a deep pitch for retreat. Many of these stockades were found to be well built, bullet proof with the help of thick wooden planks with loopholes and at the outer layer with stone boulders so that the stockade was also impregnable from mountain guns. Only the village people knew where to move about to avoid the ordeal of such defensive measures. The following two pictures of fortification will show the level of preparation taken by the Kukis during the war.

The construction of fortification indeed would require huge amounts of labour, as it is evident from Mombi (Lonpi) and Chassad forts (see Figure 4.1). The description of the two village fortifications can give the general idea of how fortification was made during the war. Big trees from forests were felled and cut into equal length and size, approximately 3 to 3.5 inches in diameter and 7.5 to 8 foot from the ground level, and about 4 to 4.5 inches in the case of rough planks having the same length as above. Generally, a village has one footpath passing through and an exit, but sometimes it happens that the footpath stretched to the village only. Thus, apparently, a village stockade would have one or two gates. The entrance at Mombi stockades has a proper wooden door frame and plank of approximately 2 to 2.5 feet in breadth and 6 to 7 feet high; like a normal house, the opening is from the inside (Shakespear 1929: 217). Mombi and many villages burnt down during the early phase of the war were rebuilt along with its fortification. Stockades were also built on the same principle, yet slight variations can be seen. The gateway of Chassad was made of swinging timbers. About five timbers each, possibly 3 inches in diameter and 7.5 foot in length,

Figure 4.1 Inside Mombi Fort and swinging gate of Chassad Fort
Source: L.W. Shakespear. History of the Assam Rifles.

are perforated and bound with a round log fixed with two perforated posts – about 7 feet from the ground. The swinging gate if closed cannot be identified as a gate. Perhaps the idea behind is to hide the stockade gate publicly (Shakespear 1929: 225–226). The timber used in the construction of forts and stockades is locally called '*palpeh*' (plank use in fence). The upper parts of the timbers are sharpened. The nature of fortification indeed involved a large number of people. In certain cases, the Kukis took the help of their neighbouring tribes to construct their forts and stockades.[24]

Yet, it is interesting to note that the Kukis hardly defended their village, including the fortified village, against British troops. This instance gives some possible explanations. One explanation often given was due to the superior weapons used by the military column in which the fortification became useless. This was especially so with the famed use of seven-pounder mountain guns, one of the most dreaded weapons of the time. In the second phase of operations, the British substituted the mountain guns with a more powerful gun – Stokes Mortars – which had produced a 'devilish' fear among the hill tribes. The Kukis knew that they could not withstand the mountain guns at all costs, and defending their village against such guns was suicidal. Therefore, they normally withdrew into the jungles before the approaching column reached their village. Then, the crucial point is why would they invest so much energy when it is not going to give them any defence against the enemy? Here, some informed and knowledgeable persons said that such fortification was not meant to withstand the military forces but to protect them from any surprise attack. In case of any surprise, these forts gave them time to evacuate their villages through secret passages. This explanation makes sense if read together with other defensive postures such as the series of stockades along the route to the villages where the advance parties would be posted. The advance party would give warning to the next and so on until information of the invading party reached the village in short time, giving them ample time to evacuate the village to the jungle hideouts prepared in advance.

Stockade or breastwork

Evidences from various military field reports also show that large numbers of stockades, big and small, were erected by the Kukis at different strategic points along the routes leading to their villages. The construction of stockade was a big public affair. The Kukis took the assistance of other tribes. Few examples from the description of field reports will suffice our understanding of Kuki stockades. At least five strong stockades deserve mention here: one at Chakpi, one each near Khailet, Nungoinu, Haika and an unnamed stockade on the rock surface near Nungoinu. Among these the stockade that lies a little away from Nungoinu village (about one mile before reaching Khengjoi) are instructive of their method of construction. The length of this stockade was 40 to 50 yards. Many trees were felled to obstruct enemies. The two rows of heavy timber bore multiple loopholes for discharging bullets and arrows. The position of it was by nature already strong but had been rendered stronger by piling up more rocks and timber breastworks at weak spots, while the passage through the stockade was with a double row of heavy, loopholed timber posts. Coote's column estimated about 300 Kuki rebels waited for the British soldiers to come, after examining the number of sitting places for firing, the trampled state of the ground and foodstuffs and drums left there (Shakespear 1977: 220). At Kaichin village, 21 separate stockades were built more or less in echelon with 60 to 100 loopholes.[25]

The Chakpi stockade was located on the Chakpi River crossing point, which is beyond Sugunu and one mile away from Lonpi with the object of repelling British force (Nehkhothang et.al, 2005: 9). Higgins description of what he called the 'Kuki stockade' near Maokot is sufficient to give the importance of stockades as part of the Kuki war:

> The stockade was a very strong affair. It consisted of a barricade of timber, about 1½ foot in thickness, backed by two foot of earth, which was backed again by a thin timber partition. Behind the stockade was a deep trench and 42 loopholes were pierced in the stockade a little above the ground level. It was thus absolutely bulletproof. It was 75 yards in length, with each flank rosting on a mass of rocks, in the right of which was a small enfilading post capable of holding two or three men. Leading away from the position were two communication trenches, covered by bridges on the ground level. A considerable field of fire had been cleared in the front of the position.[26]

We have similar descriptions from various parts of the Kuki hills where we see more or less in the same form. For instance, we have descriptions of stockades by Captain Montefiore in southern Manipur, Captain Patrick in Chassad and Major Hackett in Thaungdut and Somra Tract. Similar finding in Chin Hills by Falkland also shows the art of making stockade this way had a wider knowledge. Falkland, for instance, noted:

> An inspection of the Kwarang stockades was a revelation. I did not think the Chin had so much energy in him. The palisades about eight feet high and of various lengths excluded from the top of Kwarang peak to the bottom of the village distance quarter mile being broken only by slips in the hillsides. Below the posts was a solid stone parapet 3 feet thick and 4 feet high. Below this again a trench 5 feet deep; the trench presumably to protect men reloading guns for the firers. Besides this, there were sniping places for single men and pairs. Bow traps, *panji* pits and other Hunnish devices for sweeping one off the road into a bed of stout stakes below.[27]

Shakespear also observes that 'the position by nature strong had been rendered still more so by pilling of more rocks and timber breastworks at weak spots, while the passage through was stockade with a double row of heavy timber posts loopholed'.[28] During the war, the Kuki fighters encamp in the jungle normally near their stockades or man them once information of the approaching troops was received. Foods were normally supplied from the nearby villages. Normally certain camps for the fighters would also be constructed near the stockades in the interest of refraining the fighters from normal social life, discipline and so on. It was also said that the Kukis had a strong belief in fighting away from the civilian population to avoid terrorising them.

Although it would be out of place to discuss how the Kukis had defended their stockades during the war, the comments given by certain officers demand some attention here. For instance, Bertram Carey felt that the

> Kukis built strong stockades and failed to defend them, and their resistance cannot be regarded as sturdy. As usual their losses are unknown: they were certainly small owing to their methods of fighting which consist in firing from ambush and then running away.[29]

Such a conclusion made by a person who had not witnessed the various encounters in Kuki stockades only demeans the hard show given by both the contending parties. We have several evidences to show that in many of the Kuki stockades fierce fighting took place and sometimes for several hours. The engagement at, for instances, Khailet, Khengjoi, Hengtam, Gobok, Maokot etc. show a heavy exchange of fire between the two parties with substantial numbers of casualties on both sides. The Kukis normally had fewer casualties due to their strong defensive system of stockades. Based on the field reports, Lieut. Col. Ffrench-Mullen had concluded that the Kukis 'have been known to stand the scorching fire of seven-pounder mountain guns and Lewis guns at close range and then pop up and snipe at our columns from the very place on which the scorching fire had been directed'.[30] It is impossible to expect the Kukis to withstand the scorching fire of seven-pounder mountain guns and Lewis guns with their old tower muskets and muzzle-loaders, but on many occasions they did it was a fact evident from various military reports.

Stone trap (songkhai)

Construction of stockades was not the only technique used by the Kukis to fight their enemy. Associated with these stockades were their famous stone traps/chutes, *panjies*, *pumpis* (leather cannon) traps and so on. Stone boulders, both regular and irregular shapes, or logs cut at certain lengths, that could easily roll down the slope were heaped and bound together with an animal skin or rough bamboo basket. They are put up a little distance above the road hanging on the slope of the hills and fastened with a rope that has to be cut down when the enemy passes on the road. Sometimes they were hung on the branch of the tree above the road if they could be concealed and fastened with a rope, taken to a certain distance away from the road where it could be cut when the enemy pass on that path (Haokip 2013: 40).[31] Normally, stone traps were hung near the stockades, and a combination of the two along with *panjies* (planted on the narrow roadsides) worked extremely well against the enemy. When the enemy approached along the road, the Kuki snipers would first pour down bullets at them from their secured stockade, leading to sudden disarray among the troops who would be inflicted by *panjies* when they took positions on the side of the road. When many of them were lamed by *panjies* and became immobile, then stone chutes would be released from above the acclivities.

In certain cases, the Kukis also added the famous leather cannon (*pumpi*), sometimes planted as trap and sometimes with human agency. The cannon trap was triggered by a rope across the path of pit connected to the cannon's trigger and percussion cap. Sometimes a bend bamboo or trees (locally call *pelpeh*, having the capacity to throw upward to the enemy at a height of 8 to 9 feet) was laid to injure those who escape stone traps. The whole concept was to harass and disorganise the invading party from further movement or to slow down their momentum so that the Kukis could buy sufficient time to evacuate their village.[32] Evidence has shown that on many occasions the efficient deployment of these combination caused major confusion, sometimes with several casualties on the invading party. Captain Coote and J.C. Higgins's column, for instance, encountered this combination of defences during their invasion of Ukha Kukis in December 1917–January 1918.[33] The columns in different parts of the hills faced similar cases during the first and second phases of operations.

Panjies (soutul)

Panjies locally called *soutul* is perhaps one of the most common weapons used in defence. In the words of R.G. Woodthorpe, it is a

> small pointed stakes of hardened bamboo are in time of war attached to the bag . . . stuck in the ground along the path in escaping from a pursuer, or in the approached to a village are capable of inflicting very nasty wounds in bare foot and will even penetrate thick leathers.
>
> (Woodthorpe 1978: 74)

They used to strengthen village stockades by fastening or position like modern iron barbed wires, planted nearby ridge, beneath a log-trap and on footpath (Carey and Tuck 1932: 230; Haokip 2013: 43). Big *panjies* size range could be 2 to 2.5 feet, and tiny *panjies* (porcupine quill shaped with sizes of 5 to 6 inches) were hidden among the grass or fallen leaves. Like bamboo arrows, *panjies* are smeared with a poisonous substance to increase effectiveness. *Panjies* were stuck in places where the enemy was expected to approach.[34] *Panjie* pits (concealed holes in which pointed stakes are embedded ready to impale the persons who falls in) as a technique came to light during the Anglo-Kuki War. Reports revealed that British trained dogs were killed by *panjies* in the Aisan area. The poisonous substance locally called *gu* is extracted from va tree; it is a dark blue colour and extracted from a tree grown on the border of Manipur and Lushai hills. It is grounded with capsicum (King Chilly) seeds and tobacco juice (Shakespear 1988: 195). J. Shakespear had done experiments by pricking a cock with *panjies* without poison and another cock with smeared *panjies* and to his surprise the latter cock died immediately. Thus, smeared *pan-jies* might have played the role of a 'silent spring'. In the Chin Hills, *panjies* inflicted a deep wound to the British forces.[35] Two British soldiers were wounded by them and another one was injured with slugs.[36] *Panjies* were seen effectively employed in the Naga Hills as well. One sepoy was killed. Intoxication of spring water or streams with the seed of wild beans called '*ga*' or creeper called *gucho* (another poisonous substance) during dry seasons heavily reduce one's stamina.[37] Though not popular, it was identified by the British as one measure employed by the Kukis against their enemy during the war.[38]

Signs and symbols of the war

The amount of coordination, cooperation and uniformity in war efforts among the Kukis during the war surprised the local officers. Instead of being a mere village or local level warfare, the Kukis from all over their inhabited areas fought from their own chosen location and stood together like one whole army under one command. Several meetings of the chiefs-in-councils in different *gamkai* or *lhang* (areas or regions) were held, their agreements communicated to each *gamkai* and also to the people. Orders were also issued for war preparations, mobilisation was carried out across the hills and progress of the war was regularly communicated from one area to another. All these required a swift circulation of information with definite terms and in absolute secrecy. In the absence of a writing tradition and modern means of communication such as road, telephone, telegraph and postal services, it draws our attention to how the Kukis managed to communicate important information across the 7,000 square miles of rugged highland. Government police, the intelligence department and spies were able to intercept a series of items used by the Kukis to communicate to each other. Based on these few discoveries, one can actually enter into the secret world of the Kukis intelligence agency, which had been surprisingly well established. Traditionally, the Kukis had well-defined items for communication. In fact, every item had certain embedded meanings, and the use of them for communication was known to all. It is interesting to note that the Kukis had used some of these in great numbers during the war that have been intercepted by colonial surveillance system. Besides others, items such as the curious piece of meat (*sajam*), charred wood with chilli (*thingkho-le-malcha-pom*), bullet, gunpowder, bead and sword were intercepted on several occasions. Besides, Kukis also used lighting, smoke and acoustic signals like whistle by mouth, drum, horn, gong etc. as means to communicate. Some of these are described below.

Sajam *(piece of meat)*

Among the Kukis, in all war and peace councils, resolutions were affirmed with a sacred oath *Sathin-salung-neh* (sathin – *liver*, salung – heart, neh – to eat, discussed under war ritual) to symbolise the faith one must keep with the decision and of forging bonds, unity and cooperation among the partakers of the ceremony. The meat is sliced out into pieces for all the members present and also for the absentees. The absentees' shares were sent out to them conveying the decisions taken binding and final on them as well. The pieces of meat are called *sajam* and the process by which it was communicated is called *sajamlhah* or sending off a piece of meat (Haokip 2005). The Kukis have performed at least four such Chiefs' Councils during March 1917, which has direct bearing on military formations discussed above.[39] In every War Council, pieces of meat and other items were sent off around the hills to communicate the decision taken. J.C. Higgins, for instance, reported about Chengjapao, Chief of Aisan:

> In the spring, before orders to commence recruiting labour for France had been received, he killed a mithun and sent round pieces of flesh to all the leading chiefs in the state, begging them to resist efforts to recruit by all means in their power.[40]

Similarly, he also informed that Khotinthang, Chief of Jampi, also 'killed a mithun as far back as March last and distributed portions of the flesh throughout the hills, thereby inducing other chiefs not to send their men'. During the same time, Pache, Chief of Chassad, and Ngullen, Chief of Khongjang, were also reported to have 'killed a mithun and sent the flesh to other chiefs, urging them to refuse to recruit men for the labor corps'.[41] When Higgins was fighting against the Kukis of Ukha areas, he received information that the Chassad chief sent pieces of meat to Ukha Kukis not to disperse, but to stand against the British column, and he was sending reenforcements of 1,000 men.

Thus, *sajam* was used not only for communication but also for rallying the people to fight the British. It was used not only to inform the people to oppose labour recruitment but also to take on the warpath against the British forces. Several meetings were held and resolutions taken in different parts of the hills, and it is observed that sending the flesh of animals killed on the occasion definitely played a role in the communication and mobilisation of the Kuki troops for the war effort. The effect of *sajam* had also affected other tribes as well, among whom the pieces of meat were sent. For instance, the Tangkhuls of Hundung village also killed a pig to oppose labour recruitment.[42] Higgins reported that 'The efforts of Kuki have been successful in deterring many villages from sending their men and the number obtain will not exceed 250 at the most'.[43] The Anals, Lamkangs and Kabuis also refused to send labour, stating they were warned by the Kuki not to accept *parwana* circulated by Government and remain neutral or faced dire consequences (Laldena 2012: 126).[44]

Thingkho-le-malchapom *(charred wood tied with chilli)*

A red king chilli *(malchapom)* fastened with a burnt firewood *(thingkho)* is a unique symbol of the Kukis related to war. While burnt firewood and chilli had different meanings on different occasions for the Kukis, the combining of the two, sometimes with other items, was typically a war symbol.[45] Tarun Goswami asserted that half-burnt pieces of wood tied with chilli was a pre-arranged secret code sign agreed upon by the Kuki to inform the people about the commencement of war/fighting with the British and on receiving this one has to remain alert and ready for the battle. It was passed on from one man to another and from one village to another village (Goswami: 401). J.H. Hutton, the Deputy Commissioner of Naga Hills, intercepted one of these circulated by Chengjapao, chief of Aishan, among the Nagas of Naga Hills. He trekked the route through which *thingkho-le-malcha* passed such as from the areas of Sakhabama, Kekrima, Khizobama and Losama, between 3 April and 8 May 1918. Following is an extract:

> Chengjapao gave it to Jessami with instructions to take it to Lozaphehomi and sent it through to Khonoma avoiding the villages of Viswemi and Kohima and secreting its receipt and dispatch. It consisted of burnt wood, a bit of a pine torch, a chilli, a bullet, gunpowder and a Kuki ear bead, the latter signifying 'hear and obey'. The rest of the message described the trouble suffered by the Kuki (the chillies, which perhaps signified the smarting they would inflict on their enemies); the simultaneity of their rising in which they wished Khonoma to join (the burnt stick); and the treatment they would give to their enemies (the torch, powder and bullet).[46]

In another instance, the northwestern Kukis sent out a piece of char-coal and a bullet to the Kuki of Ente Punji Assam and told them to fight the British.[47] The chief of Chongjang village also sent out the half-burnt firewood and a chilli to the neighbouring Kuki villages (Goswami 1985: 401).

The significance of burnt wood fastened with chilli has been noted by some colonial observers besides what we have noted from Hutton's account. T.H. Lewin ascribed the different items associated with war and others of the Lushais who were close kin of the Kukis. He remarked:

> If the tips of the cross-pieces [Phuroi] be broken, a demand for black mail is indicated; a rupee to be levied for each break. If the end of one of the cross-pieces is charred, it implies an urgency and that the people are to come even by torch-light. If a capsicum is fixed on to the 'Phuroi', it signifies that diso-bedience to the order will meet punishment as severe as the capsicum is hot.
>
> (Lewin 1870: 133)

Truly, the burnt wood not only signify the burning situation the Kukis are facing against the enemy, but also of the seriousness their decision to fight them back and to those who did not join them in the effort. Their villages would be burnt down, and punishment would be as hot as king-size chilli. It was in short the Kukis 'fiery cross'.

Burnt wood tied with chilli symbolised the severity of the situation in which people were informed about the war but also ordered them to prepare for the war. Like *sajam*, it was normally issued after an important resolution was taken where a declaration of war was made. We have several 'war councils' held among the Kukis after the burn-ing of Lonpi; the largest and final decision being taken was at Chassad War Council in the end of November or beginning of December 1917, where 150 Kuki chiefs from India and Burma participated and took a vow to fight the British. After all such war councils, *thingkho-le-malchapom* was sent out across the hills, not only among the Kukis but also among other tribes. As we have seen in the case of one that was sent across the Naga Hills, this Kuki 'fiery cross' was circulated across the hills like a wildfire, passing off from one vil-lage to another rapidly. Perhaps this is the fastest means of com-munication regarding the declaration of the war, where no meeting at every village was necessary and no words were demanded from the torchbearers as it went on in speed from one hand to another.

The very arrival of this signal and everything related to the decision of the war and all have to start preparation in earnest. In this way, we can see that the war broke out simultaneously across the several thousand square miles of roadless rugged mountain. H.D.U. Keary, the Commanding Officer of the second phase of Kuki operations, for instance, reported:

> The sudden blaze of rebellion, which spread simultaneously throughout the length and breadth of the hills from Kohima in the north to the Pakokku Hill tracts of Burma in the south, made it impossible last year to formulate put into force any complete and thought out plan before operations started.

Meichang *(bullet)*

We also have evidence to show that bullets were used by the Kukis during the war as a means of communication. We have already noted that a bullet was sent along with burnt wood and chilli. Scott also reported from Cachar that 'Hawbamang Kuki headmen of Turning-cham, Manipuri Kuki *punjis*, came to Bara Malang about a week ago and gave bullet to two women, threatening that if they did not give every assistance there would be trouble'.[48] It was also reported that after the famous Chassad War Council, the Chassad chief Pache sent out bullets to the chiefs of Jampi, Ukha, Songphu, Henglep and Loibol with instructions to resist forcibly any attempt to impress coolies or to burn villages.[49] In the context noted above, circulation of bullets during the war signifies an order to shoot the enemy British forces. In this way, bullets and gunpowder had also become important symbols of war.

Khichang *(beads)*

Beads are some of the most valued items the Kuki have irrespective of sex. Both boys' and girls' ears are perforated to hang beads so as to induce his or her obedience. The Kukis believed that if a person is let off without earrings he/she will remain disobedient. Sending off beads to others perhaps carried a message to obey the order to fight the British. Besides, the gift of beads to daughters symbolised love and affection; to maternal families, it is a sign of respect and seeking blessings. When Ngulkhup sent bead to Pache chief of Chassad, J.C.

Higgins felt that it was a means to incite him to resist the British.[50] J.H. Hutton interpreted beads as part of the Kuki 'fiery cross' as 'hear and obey'. Ngulkhup sent to W.A. Cosgrave a cornelian bead as a message that expressed his willingness to surrender through a messenger, Bion Anal.[51] We can have three different meanings to the use of beads by the Kukis here. However, during war, it urges the receiver to fall in line with the sender. Ngulkhup was a junior clan member to Pache and it was impossible to the former serving any such command over the latter according to Kuki tradition. Instead, when Ngulkhup sent beads to Pache it would only mean seeking help and goodwill on his declared war against the British. In the second case, the use of beads by Chengjapao to the Nagas of Naga Hills could be taken as 'hear and obey', although this may also be more closely associated with a request to take part in the war. In the third case, the bead represents goodwill from a more powerful British government. Thus, in the absence of written script, beads also served the purpose of communication in a big way.

Chem *(sword)*

The sword was also a very significant symbol of communication among the Kukis having different meanings. T.H. Lewin noted that sending out of the chief spear (often carved and ornamented) symbolises a general meeting or Assembly, a fighting dao tied or attached with a piece of red cloth signified hostility and war (Lewin 1870: 133). Thus, the Political Agent in Manipur McCulloch informed that whenever he wanted to assemble the Kuki chiefs he used to send out a sword as a 'fiery cross'. We also have many cases of *dao* being sent out to different villages with specific message. Chingakhamba Sanachaoba Singh had distributed a dao each to Tintong, Khotinthang, Ngulbul, Ngulkhup and Pache. It was interpreted to stir up the Anglo-Kuki War and to cut telegraph lines.[52] Kuki chiefs also sent out swords among the villages of the western hills sometimes to summon them for assembly, sometimes to supply provisions, mend roads and so on. In the northern hills, a sword was sent to certain villages with an order to cut down the telegraph line. In certain cases, a sword was sent among the Kuki chiefs. For instance, the Chassad chief sent a sword to the Jampi chief as a warning to punish them for not keeping their promise to close down the Dimapur road. Therefore, *dao* was used for different purposes, but in most cases it was in the form of giving a warning or threat.

Dah *(gong) and ivory*

The Kukis also used good numbers of gongs and drums during the war, especially in the battleground as a signal. Montefiore, for instance, reported that the Kukis used gongs during their encounters with the British forces. He felt that it was a 'signal to retire to their second line'.[53] The Naring villagers set up a howl of defiance from the village. They used the noise as a signal to stand and fight when the British attacked.[54] Sounding of gongs signified retirement to the second line of defence.[55] Besides, Kukis also used gongs on other occasions in dealing with the government. Traditionally, a gift of a gong and *mithun* symbolised a plea for mercy, favour and peace. Thus, the Kuki chiefs who met Mr. Higgins at Oktan brought with them Rs. 1500, three gongs and one mithun as *salam* and requested that he will not call coolie from them.[56] We have already noted that Ngulkhup sent a gun and cornelian beads to Cosgrave as a peace overture. When the chiefs of Chassad and Jampi made an overture for peace, they also offered to pay their house-tax, licenced guns, two elephant tasks and Rs. 3,000.[57] Similarly, when Chengjapao, chief of Aisan, surrendered he came with a piece of elephant tusk. In the context noted above, items like gongs, beads, elephant tusks or *mithun* represented a symbol of peace and friendship normally used by the Kukis. The colonial understanding of the meaning attached to them as *salam* (presents) and tax in other circumstances connoted a sign of submission. But the true meaning lies in the Kuki traditional notion of the same. Giving of a gong is, for instance, a great affair in Kuki society. Being one of the priceless items the Kukis had in their homes as heirlooms, the presentation of a gong represents the highest form of gift to the receiver. Thus, a gong was normally given in marriage to signify the willingness of the giver to have a lasting relationship as *tucha-nupa*. Exchange of gongs was also made between two persons or chiefs for a lasting friendship – similar with elephant tusks, beads or *mithun*. Therefore, when the Kuki chiefs offered gong, bead, elephant tusk or mithun to the British they symbolised the intention of peace and friendly settlement of the tangled question, not a sign of submission/surrender as it was usually conceived by the British officers.

War rituals

Another aspect of the Kuki war against the British was their strong belief in the traditional *pathen* (god) who will put them into victory. Traditional Kukis never took to war unless they were assured of their victory. Here, the role of the priest (*thempu*) becomes significant. In a war council, the *thempu* would administer three connected war rituals: *phun-san* (omen), *galmi-lhim* (hypnotise enemy) and *sathin-salung neh* on the advice of the gathering chiefs. *Phun-san* is done by examining healthiness of liver of either pig, *mithun*, cow or buffalo (Carey and Tuck 1932: 228). *Aisan* (*Ai*, wild turmeric black or blue in colour; *san*, divination), *Nang-san* (*Nang*, a piece of bamboo fibre) and interpretation of dreams, etc. are other forms of *phun-san*. On behalf of the leader who is intended to led the war, the priest salutes (narrating how the animal's ancestor was taken home, feed and cared by his [priest] ancestors with love and care) to the spirit of the chosen animal for the rite and pleads to forecast the future state of warriors or the intended: 'May your liver show sign of disease; for losing war and healthy signs for victory'. Cutting a piece of *Ai* into two, representing he and his enemy, and he threw on the ground after chanting his spells to lay in *khup* (downward) and *thel* (upward), one variant of *khup*, is to overcome. Then he slices in round an end of the fibred (made of bamboo, 2 feet long) in about 2.5 inches and pulled apart at least twice after invoking the bamboo for him and the enemy. Too many nodes and zigzag at the breaking point are interpreted to be unfavourable. Interpretation of dream(s), particularly of the chief or intended warrior, letting two cocks fight, putting two eggs or rice in a bowl of water, etc., constitute other forms of omens studied before the war or game.

Based on these *phun-san* rituals, the priest would interpret whether the warrior should go for the war or not. The fact that Kukis had finally decided to go for the war with the government shows that their *phun-san* or their priests have approved for it. One interesting account during the rising testifies to this. The 'statement of Waishon Kuki, Chief of Leirik', noted:

> The enemy Kukis is all talking that they have got their God and the said God has been helping them in the present Kuki War. The British Government never be able to bring them in submission and at the end they (Kukis) would be victorious.[58]

The fact that their God was with them and helping them or that they were invincible to government troops and will win the war are the attributes of their firm belief in their *phun-san* and their *thempu*. Tintong, one of the war leader in the western hills, was said to visit Twiluong dil (a river lake) and asked for a mythological 'living sword' from the spirit of the lake, the sword making him invincible to the troops (Haokip 2013: 27).

Once war was declared, the Kuki priests also performed another ritual to hypnotise the enemy. Some priests were gifted with this black art and become helpful during the war. This ritual was performed near the war theatre or enemy's path by chanting *Gallou-thu* (magical potions and spells). The priest accompanied the warrior(s) to the spot and invoked the spirits of *Ai-lhim* to dismantle the spirits of his opponent; putting his magical materials (herbs) in a tube, he fixed into the ground (*theikhetkhum*). *Ai-lhim* is normally buried on the path of the enemy, its pungent smell acting as sleeping pills to them.[59] It is a completely different matter whether such ritual worked or not; the point is that the Kuki warriors were assured of its effectiveness, which gave them courage and agility to their power to fight and attain victory. Thus, when the *thempu* pronounced, 'my job is done, the sign is good, it's the right time . . . victory in your hand', then all fears of the enemy were taken away by magic, which gave them strength.

Another source of strength and unity among the Kukis was the ritual of *sathin-salung-neh* (ritual feasting on the liver and heart of animal sacrificed). This is another war ritual that solemnised the agreement taken among people present as sacred and not to be broken in the future, a ceremony resorted to in war and peace. It symbolised the faith one must keep with the decision and of the forging bonds, unity and cooperation among the partakers of the ceremony. Summing up the resolutions, the senior most clan member would pronounce: 'He who defy or betray today's resolution and oath should die immature, meet unnatural death and may he die soon as the liver of animal got rotten fast'. It is followed by cutting the tail off of the animal by the youngest clan member, symbolising their unity (Haokip 2005). It is a mandatory sacred oath before any war is taken to put all of them together firmly until the war is over. It is an oath that one gave up their life for the community even to the cost of death; only victory can bring them back home.

Conclusion

The Kukis fought the British with their traditional method of warfare known by different names such as guerrilla warfare, little war or irregular war. Their main weapons included muzzle-loader rifles such as old tower muskets and flintlocks. In certain cases, we have reference of Martini rifles being used by Kukis. These guns were fueled with their own local production of gunpowder. In many cases, guns were accompanied by their own made leather cannons, locally known as *pumpi*. Besides guns, the Kukis also sometimes used other traditional weapons like bow and arrow. They also relied on their traditional methods and technology of defence such as the fortification of villages, construction of a series of small stockades along the route in the strategic points of the jungle and laying of different sizes of *panjies* and stone traps where the enemy was expected. While the 'hit and run' method of warfare was mainly deployed to face the imperial forces, they also sometimes met the enemy in direct exchange of fire from some of their strong stockades. Overall, the strength of the Kukis was in their method of guerilla warfare. For organising purposes, the Kukis also resorted to their traditional method of transmitting information by using secret codes in the form of pieces of meat (*sajam*), firebrands (*thingkho-le-malchapom*), bullets, gunpowder, sword, beads etc. With such methods of communication, they could inform each other of the progress of the war and were able to fight the government troops in unison. Overall, we can see that despite the lack of central command for all the areas, each area coordinated and cooperated with each other to make them one, fighting the same enemy.

Although the Kukis had succeeded in killing many British soldiers, their main objective was to kill the British officers who led the military columns while harassing the soldiers with maximum casualties on the one hand and sparing their own lives from direct encounters with military forces on the other. The idea was to harass the invading party as much as possible so that they might withdraw from the hills and leave them alone. Considering the terrain they were fighting, the guerrilla tactics they employed and the various defensive measures the Kukis had deployed were perhaps the best strategies that found its echo even today in the war tactics adopted by various insurgent outfits in the region and beyond. However, to say that this is a simple adaptation to the topography, or was purely 'primitive' warfare, is to deny the modernity of guerilla warfare across the globe, and more importantly, to the various innovations the Kukis had made in the war defending themselves from the modern army of the mighty British Empire. If the war tactics and technology were quite effective in defending against outside forces in the hills, the same did not work well when the colonial government decided to stay in the hills permanently with large military forces. The military occupation of the hills and the commission of untold tragedies and inhumanity on the Kuki population in the second phase of operations eventually brought the Kukis to the ground. Thus ending the Anglo-Kuki War 1917–1919 by 'force of arms'.

Notes

1 British Library, London (BL), Asian and African Collections (formerly Oriental & India Office Collections) (hereafter AAC), Indian Office Records and Private Papers (hereafter IOR&PP), IOR/L/PS/10/724: 1917–1920, File No. P-2686/1919: Lt. Col. JLW Ffrench-Mullen, DIG, Burma Military Police to IGP Burma, 17 September 1918.
2 See, White, Jeffrey B. 'A Different Kind of Threat, Some Thoughts on Irregular Warfare', www.cia.gov/library/center-for-the-study-of-intelligence/kent-csi. (Accessed 12/5/2017).
3 See, Kalyanaraman, S. 'Conceptualisations of Guerrilla Warfare', www.idsa.in/system/ files/strategicanalysis_skalyanaraman_0603.pdf, (Accessed 13–05–2017).
4 Documents of the Anglo-Kuki War 1917–1919, edited by D.L.Haokip, Reliable Book Centre, Imphal, 2017, chapter 2: J.C. Higgins to CS Assam, 24 November 1917;& Cole to Allen 17 March 1917.
5 Dispersive would means here the soil of the Chiefs from where they were fighting the British.
6 Assam State Archives (ASA), Dispur, Governor Secretariat (Confidential), Sl. 260, File No. M/64-P of 1918, Political – B, March 1919, Nos. 134 & 135: Tour Diary of JC Higgins, January–February 1918 and 'Statement of Sugnu resthouse chaukidar (an Anal of Kareibung)'
7 BL, AAC, IOR&PP, IOR/L/PS/10/724: 1917–1920, File No. P-2686/1919: 'Report on the Rebellion of the Kukis on the Upper Chindwin frontier and the operations connected threwith' by JB Marshall, DC, Upper Chindwin District.
8 ASA, File No. 9C/M-61P of 1918, Appointment and Political Department, Political – A, March 1919, Nos. 1–255, Telegram No. 406P., from Secretary to Government of Burma to Chief Secretary to the Chief Commissioner of Assam dated Rangoon, the 31 January 1918.
9 Manipur State Archives, R-/230/S-4: Tour Diary of J.C Higgins, dated 20–31 December 1917.
10 ASA, File No.9C/M-61P of 1918, Appointment and Political Department, Political,- A, March 1919, Nos. 1–255: 'Memorandum' from R.H. Henderson to J.E. Webster 30 January 1918.
11 BL, AAC, IOR&PP, IOR/L/PS/10/724: 1917–1920, File No. P-2686/1919: Lt. Col. JLW Ffrench-Mullen, DIG, Burma Military Police to IGP Burma, 17 September 1918.
12 The Kuki who fought Cotton farmers of British subjects in favour of one Chakma chief did not use firearms in 1777. Carey does not notice gun usage until 1835. (Carey and Tuck1932: 45). In January 1850, Lushai Kuki opened fire towards Lister's camp while the latter was camping into Lushai Hills. The formation of Kuki Levy in June 1850, and subsequently a supply of arms to them, was indeed an instance of the Kuki using arms. In May 1860 the Manipuri Rajas had issued 200 muskets, some spears, daos and royal swords to the Kuki (Khongsai) at Moirang (Singh1995: 162–163). The Colonial administrators had withdrawn about 6,000 guns during the 'Chin-Lushai Expedition 1889–1895 (Carey and Tuck 1932: 22).
13 Manipur State Archives (MSA), Manipur Administrative Reports 1918–1919, p. 2.

14 Interview with Tongkhohen Haokip (85), Lajangphai Churachandpur on 23/06/2003 and Jamkhoson Haokip (80) T.Boljang Churachandpur on 10 October 2013. The latter is a blacksmith who used to make guns and repair licenced guns when asked.

15 BL, AAC, IOR&PP, IOR/L/PS/10/724 (1917–1920), File No. P -2686/1919 No.901P.-2C,-2 Government of Burma Political Department; from J.L. Ffrench-Mullen to H. DesVceux, IGP Burma dated 17 September 1918, p. 40.

16 ASA, File No. M-33P. of 1919, Appointment and Political Department, Political – A, December, 1919, Nos.1–144: 'Report of Thangkhong Lambu from Anal Khul', 11 October 1918, p. 17.

17 ASA, File No. M-33P of 1919, Appointment and Political Department, Political – A, December 1919, Nos. 1–144: 'Surrender and trial of the Kuki rebels in Manipur': J.H.Hutton to Deputy Commissioner dated 5 November 1918, p. 27.

18 ASA, File No. 9C/M-61P of 1918, Appointment and Political Department, Political,- A, March 1919, Nos. 1–255, pp. 44–45: N.D. Beatson Bell Notes, 9 June 1918.

19 BL, AAC, IOR&PP, IOR/L/MIL/17/19/42: 1919: 'Despatch on the Operations Against the Kuki Tribes' Macquoid to Keary, 27 April 1919, Appendix – III.

20 BL, AAC, IOR&PP, IOR/L/PS/10/724 (1917–1920) File No. E-2686/1919; letter from J.L. Ffrench- Mullen to H. DesVceux, IGP Burma dated 17 September 1918, p. 40.

21 BL, AAC, IOR&PP, IOR/L/PS/10/724 (1917–1920) File No.P-6933/1919, "From J.H. Hutton D.C., Naga Hills to Commissioner, Surma Valley and Hill Districts, Silchar 13 May, 1918, p. 3–8.

22 BL, AAC, IOR&PP, IOR/L/PS/10/724 (1917–1920), File No.P-6933/1919, Telegram No. 367 P: from the Chief Secretary to the Government of Burma to the Secretary to the Government of India in the Foreign and Political Department Delhi, dated 18 January 1918, pp. 2-

23 ASA, Dispur, File No. File No. 9C/M-61P of 1918, Appointment and Political Department, Political – A, March 1919, Nos. 1–255, p. 17, letter from F.M. Clifford to Reid.

24 ASA, File No. File No. 9C/M-61P of 1918, Appointment and Political Department, Political – A, March 1919, Nos. 1–255: 'Memorandum of additional discussion at Government House' from J.E Webster to Henry Keary, L.W. Shakespear, J.C Higgins and Chief Secretary dated 31 July 1918, p. 64.

25 BL, AAC, IOR&PP, I0R/L/PS/10/724 (1917–1920) File No: E- 2686/1919, Captain Montefiore's report on operations of No. 4 Column against the Kukis from 18–28 February 1918 in Report on the Rising in the Haka Subdivision, Chin Hills, during 1917–1918 from J.M.Wright to DIG, 20 July 1918, Annexure J, p. 43.

26 MSA, R-2/231/S-4: Tour diary of JC Higgins. No. 1, column, chassad, 8 April 1918.

27 BL, AAC, IOR&PP, I0R/L/PS/10/724 (1917–1920), File No. E-2686/1919: 'Reports on the Rising in Haka Subdivision, Chin Hills, during 1917–1918', Annexure F. from H.L.Falkland, Officiating Commandant Ist Lushai Hills Bn. to Commandant Chin Hills dated Aizawl, 7 May 1918, p. 31.

28 Construction of fortifications, stockades or wooden palisades remind us of the Mauryan Architecture of Patliputra City girded with wooden war and pierced with loopholes to discharged arrows. For detail see Gupta (1980: 231–235).

29 BL, AAC, IOR&PP, I0R/L/PS/10/724 (1917–1920) File No: E- 2686/1919 from Bertram Carry to Chief Secretary to the Government of Burma dated 2 July 1918, p. 4

30 BL, AAC, IOR&PP, IOR/L/PS/10/724: 1917–1920, File No. P-2686/1919: Lt. Col. JLW Ffrench-Mullen, DIG, Burma Military Police to IGP Burma, 17 September 1918.

31 BL, AAC, IOR&PP, IOR/L/PS/10/724 (1917–1920) File No.P-6933/1919; Telegram No. 367 P: from the Chief Secretary to the Government of Burma to the Secretary to the Government of India in the Foreign and Political Department Delhi, dated 18 January 1918, p. 2.

32 BL, AAC, IOR&PP, IOR/L/PS/10/724 (1917–1920) File No. E-2686/1919; Annexure H. Reports on the operations of No. 4 Column from 18–28 February 1918 by Captain Montefiore; in J.M. Wright, Letter to the Deputy Inspector- General of Military Police, Burma dated Camp Rangoon 20 July 1918, p. 40.

33 BL, AAC, IOR&PP, IOR/L/PS/10/724 (1917–1920) File No.P-6933/1919; Telegram No. 367 P: from the Chief Secretary to the Government of Burma to the Secretary to the Government of India in the Foreign and Political Department Delhi, dated 18 January 1918, p. 2.

34 BL, AAC, IOR&PP, IOR/L/PS/10/724 (1917–1920), File No. P-2686/1919 from J.M. Wright, Superintendent Chin Hills to the Deputy Inspector-General of Millitary Police, Burma dated Camp Rangoon 20 July 1918, Annexure-J p. 44.

35 Ibid., p. 44.

36 J.H. Hutton Letter to Commissioner Surma Valley, No. 380G.,dated Kohima, the 13 May 1918, 2.

37 Interview with Hemkhojang Haokip (90) Kholmun Village Churachandpur,10 October, 2013. He was born at Monglham Sadar Hills, brought up there and later migrated to Churachandpur.

38 BL, AAC, IOR&PP, IOR/L/PS/10/724 (1917–1920) File No. P-2686/1919. No.901P.-2C,-2. Government of Burma Political Department, from J.L. Ffrench-Mullen to H. DesVceux, IGP Burma dated 17 September 1918, p. 40.

39 Documents of the Anglo-Kuki War 1917–1919, chapter 2: Cole to Allen dated 17 March 1917.

40 Documents of the Anglo-Kuki War 1917–1919, pp. 70

41 Documents of Anglo-Kuki War, J.C. Higgins to CS Assam, 24 November 1917;& Cole to Allen 17 March 1917.

42 Documents of the Ango-Kuki War, pp. 21–22.

43 Documents of Anglo-Kuki War, p. 73.

44 ASA, File No. 9C/M-61P of 1918, Appointment and Political Department, Political – A, March 1919, Nos. 1–255: 'Arrangement' pp. 17–18: Telegram No. 251T, from Chief Secretary to Chief Commissioner of Assam to Commissioner, Surma Valley and Hill District dated 6 February 1918.

45 Traditionally, chilli is burnt on the day of sending off the bride. The groom's party were locked up in a house and chilli is burnt as a part of

rigging them. Burnt wood was sometime used in administering the oath. The accused had to declare 'If I lie let fire burnt me as I bite this half-burnt firewood' to prove his innocence.

46 BL, AAC, IOR&PP, IOR/L/PS/10/724 (1917–1920), File No. 4895, 'Despatch on Operations Against the Kuki Tribes of Assam and Burma', November 1917 to March 1919, p. 3: Letter No. 380G, from J.H. Hutton, Deputy Commissioner, Naga Hills, to Commissioner Surma Valley and Hill district Silchar dated Kohima, dated Kohima the 13 May 1918, p. 3.

47 ASA, File No. File No. 9C/M-61P of 1918, Appointment and Political Department, Political – A, March 1919, Nos. 1–255, p. 17, from F.M. Clifford to Reid, 25 February 1918.

48 ASA, File No. File No. 9C/M-61P of 1918, Appointment and Political Department, Political – A, March 1919, Nos. 1–255, p. 32.

49 Documents of the Anglo-Kuki War, pp. 65–74.

50 ASA, File No. M-33P. of 1919, Appointment & Political Department, December 1919, Nos. 1–144, p. 10: 'Statement given by Bion Anal Chingsanglakpa of Anal Village, Lam No. 3' from C.S Gunning to Chief Secretary dated 13 August 1918.

51 ASA, File No. M-33P. of 1919, Appointment & Political Department, December, 1919, Nos. 1–144 p. 9, from W.A. Cosgrave to Webster, 9 August 1918.

52 BL, AAC, IOR&PP, IOR/L/PS/10/724 (1917–1920) File No. P 6993, 1919, No. 6310P, Political Department, Political Branch: J.E. Webster to the Secretary to the Government of India, Foreign and Political Department, Shillong, the 27 June 1919, p. 8.

53 BL, AAC, IOR&PP, IOR/L/PS/10/724 (1917–1920) File No. P-2686/1919: J.L. Ffrench- Mullen to H. DesVceux, IGP Burma dated 17 September 1918, p. 27.

54 BL, AAC, IOR&PP, IOR/L/PS/10/724 (1917–1920), File No. P-2686/1919: 'Report on the Rising in the Haka Subdivision, Chin Hills During 1917–1918' from J.M. Wright Superintendent, Chin Hills to DIG of Millitary Police Burma No. 20–1 dated Camp Rangoon 20 July 1918.

55 Ibid,. p. 43.

56 Memorandum submitted to the Commissioner, Surma Valley and Hill Districts, by 12 Kuki Political Prisoners dated Kohima, May 18, 1919, see Documents of the Anglo-Kuki War, pp. 117–119.

57 ASA, File No. M-33P of 1918, Political – A, December 1919, Nos. 1–144: 'Surrender and trial of the Kuki rebels in Manipur', No. 11: PA Manipur to CS Assam, 11 July 1918.

58 ASA, File No. File No. 9C/M-61P of 1918, Appointment and Political Department, Political – A, March 1919, Nos. 1–255, p. 39: 'Statement of Waishon Kuki, Chief of Leirik, Lam No. 4', 8 May1918 enclosed in W.A Cosgrave telegraph to Webster dated 13 May 1918 dated 13 May 1918.

59 Interview Hemkhojang(90), Kholmun village, Tongkhohen(85), Laynagphai and Thongjang(60) of K. Salbung on 15 October 2015 at K. Salbung village. They originated from Sadar Hills Monglham, but migrated to their present place during the 1990s due to the ethnic cleansing programme of the NSCN (I.M.) on this aspect. The first and second person were practitioner of charms and magic before they were converted to Christians, and the third one witnessed such acts during his boyhood days.

References

Assam Secretariat, *Appointment and Political Department, Political – A*, December 1919. Assam State Archives.

Assam State Archives (ASA), Assam Secretariat, *Appointment and Political Department, Political – A*, March 1919. Assam State Archives.

Beckett, Ian F.W. 2001 [2004]. *Modern Insurgencies and Counter-Insurgen cies, Guerrillas and Their Opponents Since 1750*. London and New York: Routledge and Taylor & Francis Library (accessed 13-5-2017).

Carey, S. Bertram and H.N. Tuck. 1932. *The Chin Hills*, Vol. I. Culcutta: FIRMA KLM Pvt. Ltd.

Clausewitz, Carl von. 1940. *On War*, Translated by J.J. Graham. BK-11, Sep. 2, Vol. I.

Davis, Watson, ed. 1944. 'Jungle Warfare', *The Science News Letter*, 46 (14) (September 30): 2111–2112, *Society for Science and Public*, www.jstor.org/stable/3921293

Giles Lionel. 1910. *Sun Tzu On The Art of War*, The Oldest Millitary Treatise in the World, Translated from the Chinese by Lionel Giles. London: LUZAC & Co.

Goswami, Tarun. 1985. *Kuki Life and Lore*. Halflong, Assam: NC Hills District Council.

Guite, Jangkhomang. 2011. 'Civilisation and Its Malcontent: The Politics of Kuki Raid in Nineteenth Century Northeast India', *The Indian Economic and Social History Review*, 48 (3): 339–376.

Gupta, S.P. 1980. *The Roots of India Art*. New Delhi: B.R. Publishing Corporation.

Haokip, Nehkhothang, et al. 2005. *Untold History of Manipur*. Imphal: Anglo-Kuki War Memorial Foundation.

Haokip, Vumkhoneh. 2013. *Pu Tintong Haokip: Unsung Hero of the Kuki Uprising 1917–1919*. Imphal: Private Circulation.

Heuser, Beatrice. 2016. 'Theory and Practice, Art and Science in Warfare: An Etymological Note', in Marston Daniel and Leahy Tamara (eds.), *War, Strategy and History: Essays in Honour of Professor Robert O'Neill*, pp. 179–196. Acton, Australia: ANU Press.

Kalyanaraman, S. 'Conceptualisations of Guerrilla Warfare', www.idsa.in/system/files/strategicanalysis_skalyanaraman_0603.pdf (accessed 13-05-2017).

Laldena. 1990 [2012]. *History of Modern Manipur*. Imphal: Reliable Book Centre.

Lewin, T.H. 1870 [1978]. *Wild Races of the South-Eastern India*. Calcutta: FIRMA KLM Pvt. Ltd.

Mackinlay, John. 2009. *The Insurgent Archipelago*. London: Hurst.

Pahazos, Alexander. 1952. 'Guerrilla Warfare', *Foreign Affairs*, 30 (2): 215–230.

Palit, D.K. 1919 [1984]. *Sentinels of North East India: The Assam Rifles*. New Delhi: Hans Raj Gupta & Sons.

Parry, N.E. 1932 [1976]. *The Lakhers*. Culcutta: FIRMA KLM Pvt. Ltd.

Reid, A.S. 1893 [2008]. *Chin Lushai Land*. Aizawl: Tribal Research Institute (TRI).

Roxborough, Ian. 1994. 'Clausewitz and the Sociology of War', *The British Journal of Sociology*, 45 (4): 619–636. doi:10.2307/591886 (accessed 10-04-2017).

Sanajaoba, Naorem (ed.), 1988. *Manipur Past and Present*, Vol. I. , Delhi: Mittal Publications.

Shakespear, J. 1912 [1988]. *The Lushai Kuki Clans*. Aizawl: Tribal Research Institute (TRI).

Shakespear, L.W. 1929 [1977]. *The Assam Rifles*. Calcutta: FIRMA KLM Pvt. Ltd.

Singh, L. Joychandra. 1995. *The Lost Kingdom*. Imphal: Prajatantra Publishing House.

Singh, R.K. Jhalajit, 1992 [1965]. *A short History of Manipur (From A.D. 33 to the present time)*, Imphal: Author.

Vaiphei, Kim. 1995. *The Coming of Christianity in Manipur with Special Reference to the Kukis*. New Delhi: The Joint Womens Programme.

White, Jeffrey B. 'A Different Kind of Threat, Some Thoughts on Irregular Warfare', www.cia.gov/library/center-for-the-study-of-intelligence/kent-csi (accessed 12-05-2017).

Woothorpe, R.G. 1873 [1978]. *The Lushai Expedition, 1871–1872*. Calcutta: FIRMA KLM Pvt. Ltd.

Zedong, Mao. 1937. *On Guerilla Warfare*, chap. 6.

Part III

IDEAS, IDEOLOGY AND INSTITUTIONS

5

PATRIOTS AND UTILITARIANS IN THE ANGLO-KUKI WAR

The case of southern Manipur, 1917–1919

David Vumlallian Zou

'Tis the land of my birth, I shall not part with it! . . . I shall yet fight the wild Boar, injured.

– *Zougal song*

Tribal and peasant uprisings occurred frequently even before British rule; but since the late nineteenth century, such events were drawn into the political struggle of anti-colonial nationalism. Nationalist historiography has successfully linked up tribal protests with the narrative of the Nation. In the nationalist version, tribal unrest is one of the many struggles that contributed to India's freedom struggle to realise a nation-state of its own in 1947. In the 1960s, the vogue for history from below[1] expressed dissatisfaction with grand nationalist history because it neglected the agency of the tribal people themselves. In India, the same concern for the underdog animated the Subaltern Studies project that was initiated in 1982. The subaltern manifesto assumed that there was 'an autonomous domain' of popular politics that was independent of 'the domain of elite politics' (Guha 1999: 4). After decades of independence, the subaltern collective felt disillusioned with conventional historiography (including Congress-style nationalism) for its alleged elitist politics. Therefore, the subaltern collective declared the 'historic failure of the nation to come to its own' in failing to win 'a decisive victory against colonialism' (Guha 1999: 7). In other words, India's anti-colonial struggle is still incomplete and we can still keep blaming British colonialism for our present failures.

In the first volume of the subaltern project, David Arnold (1999) wrote about the 'rebellious hillmen' of the Eastern Ghats, Andhra

Pradesh. These hillmen qualified as subalterns because of their 'restricted territoriality' and their xenophobia for outsiders who came from the valley. The hillmen of the Eastern Ghats had a long tradition of protest (*fituri*) – Congress-style nationalist resistance against the British as well as Naxal communist resistance against the Indian nation-state (Arnold 1999: 141). The hillmen of the Eastern Ghats participated in the 'war of nationalist liberation against the British' (Arnold 1999: 141). When they waited in vain for the Indian version of 'bourgeois-democratic revolution' (Guha 1999: 7), they launched another *fituri* in the 1960s.

Internal factors in the Kuki rising

While I have problems with the subalternist narrative, it is possible to see some parallels of the *fituri* in the Kuki protests of the hill areas of Manipur. Like Arnold's 'rebellious hillmen', the Kuki 'rebels' of 1917–1919 had restricted sense of territoriality, xenophobia and post-Independence militancy against the Indian state. Gautam Bhadra, who became a member of the Subaltern Studies, had independently studied the Kuki uprising and published it as a research article in 1975 (Bhadra 1975). He emphasised the importance of understanding internal factors of tribal organisation in explaining the Kuki uprising. Bhadra said, 'External pressure can operate only through internal organization' (Bhadra 1975: 10–11).

Bhadra noted how the British adopted the policy of grouping together all Kuki villages in 1913. Villages numbering less than ten households were merged. This policy led to convulsion in the political organisation of Kuki chiefdom. Bhadra argues that the merging of small territorial chiefs with clan chiefs of the big villages changed the internal structure of Kuki polity. The colonial policy of sedentary settlement is a project of modernisation that conflicted with the anarchist tendency of Kuki chiefdom. Bhadra explains why this sedentarisation project happened to be so disruptive to traditional Kuki chiefship:

> The opportunity to form a new village was a way to protest against the chief, a kind of escape from the control of the unpopular chief. . . . It was a political safety valve through which a custom left a scope for own expression of grievances and thus stabilized its own institution of chieftainship. Migration among the Kukis inhabited a thorough going protest movement against the office of chieftainship.
>
> (Bhadra 1975: 27)

If the Kuki rising was directed against the modern (though colonial) policy of sedentarisation, then it would appear that the protest was a romantic reaction to preserve a decaying institution. While there is much to admire in the sheer courage to stand up to the then super-power, the revolt smacks of a refusal to adapt to new global forces of European imperialism and modern commerce. To a point, the Kuki rising was a resistance to the project of colonial modernity; it required the exchange of the nomad mode of life for sedentary agriculture or terrace cultivation. Although the colonial policy of indirect rule rested on the preservation of chiefly institutions, the thrust for grouping of chiefs unintentionally disrupted this traditional institution.

While giving primacy to internal factors, Bhadra noted the role of external factors that caused the Kuki revolt – increased house-tax, crop failure from 1911 to 1915, demand for coolie labour (*pothang*), forced labour recruitment for the First World War, etc. In this paper, the focus is on another internal factor of the Kuki rising – land dispute among rival chiefly houses.

Land claims and the triangular contest

Unlike the subaltern point of view, the nationalist perspective is ill-suited to capture the complexities of internal factors behind the Kuki rising. However limiting this framework is, the anti-colonial element of the Anglo-Kuki conflict appears to fit into the grand narrative of Congress nationalism. But closer examination will reveal that chiefs of southern Manipur were divided during the course of the Kuki rising from 1917 to 1919. Whereas some chiefs of southern Manipur decided to resist, some opted to collaborate with the Raj. To suppress uprising in these parts of Manipur, the Lushai Hills Battalion encamped at Bungmual at the tri-junction of the Lushai Hills, Chin Hills and Manipur State. The existence of a few sources in the Mizoram State Archives will be able to shed some light on the resistance as well as collaboration of chiefs in southern Manipur on the borders of present-day Mizoram.

In the context of southern Manipur, this anti-colonial uprising happened at the backdrop of a triangular contest between three dialectal groups – the Zou (led by Manlun chiefs), the Paite (led by Guite chiefs) and the Thadou (led by Haokip chiefs). In colonial records, all the three groups were known as 'new Kukis' because of their linguistic and cultural affinities. Various hill tracts of southern Manipur were under the influence of the Thadou, Zou and Guite chiefs. Rivalry within the chiefly houses of the Zou and the Guite is visible in their land disputes over the possession of Chivu salt springs of the Tonzang village on the east bank of the Tuivai river.[2] During the Anglo-Kuki War, the Zou chiefs were in close alliance with the Thadou chief of the Ukha village.

The Ango-Kuki war did not start as a triangular feud of chiefly lineages over land claims. It kicked off as a raid against the Nepali cattle herders of the Khuga [Tuitha] valley of present-day Churachandpur town. The British policy of settling Nepali ex-servicemen in the Khuga valley displeased a section of the Thadou as well as Zou chiefs. Of all the valley of southern Manipur, the Khuga valley has the best available land for wet-rice cultivation. The raid against the Nepalis (British loyalists) took place on 28 December 1917.[3] Both the Zou and the Thadou groups were allegedly involved in this incident. In this regard, a military intelligence (dated 31 December 1917) mentioned the Manlun villages (the Manlun is a chiefly lineage of the Zou people):

He [Mr. Thongjalet] informed me that the looting of the Nepali graziers in the Khuga valley was entirely the work of the Manhlun villages of the southern border and the hills between the Khuga and Manipur rivers. He says that there were some 200 of them, but cannot say how many guns they had. When they heard of our arrival, the ones with guns joined Ukha, and the rest went home.[4]

In this triangle, the alliance between the Zou chiefs and the Thadou chief of Ukha is confirmed by a military report dated 1 January 1918:

There are about 700 Manhlun Manchung [Zou] Kukis now at Buksao Henthang and Thingat Somthong. Henthang has killed a mithun and they have decided to make war on the sirkar, help Ukha and kill the sahibs. They have many guns with them . . . 15 [men] above reached Ukha, but when we prevented their friends from coming, they came back and joined them by a roundabout way.[5]

Chief Thangtual (a Paite chief) saw the Kuki uprising as an opportunity to win British favour for his land claim in southern Manipur. Chief Thangtual advanced his claim for Chivu land on the basis of his collaboration with the Pangmual Column of the British army under the command of Subedar Bhawan Singh.[6] Apart from his own Paite dialect, Chief Thangtual spoke a smattering of Hindustani, Zou and

Thadou. He was able to act as scouts and interpreter for the Subedar at Pangmual. On 23 May 1918, Thangtual sent in his claim petition to the Superintendent of the Lushai Hills:

> I did my best to help Pangmual Column. . . . I did my best in this way to help the Government; and I do not ask for money for my help; but I beseech that your honour will kindly grant me the valley of Chivu for terrace cultivation, which is one day's march from my village and which is within Manipur territory. . . . I therefore earnestly beg the favour of your kindly granting me a small piece of land that I might help the Government in any case in future.[7]

The Lushai Superintendent supported Thangtual's claim petition for Chivu land and he immediately forwarded it to the Political Agent of Manipur. He wrote, 'This locality is . . . held by Gaothanga a Zo chief who has joined the insurrection. I recommend that . . . claim for favourable consideration when affair are settled'.[8]

W.A. Cosgrave, Political Agent in Manipur, replied within a month and he confirmed that 'the Chibu [Chivu] salt-wells are situated on the land of the rebel Kuki village. . . . Tunzan (Somlun Chief) which was occupied and burned by me in last March'.[9] To burn down the village of Tonzang (misspelt as Tunzan by Cosgrave), the British army found a collaborator in Pumjakham[10] (chief of Thanlon). The Political Agent of Manipur was in favour of granting the salt springs of Chivu to Pumjakham. Therefore, Cosgrave remarked:

> if the lands of Tunzan are confiscated they will be given to him [Pumjakham] as a reward for the valuable service he rendered to me in March. Under the circumstances I cannot hold out any house of Thangtuala getting these lands.[11]

Although Cosgrave refused to consider Thangtual's land claim, he granted the latter the right of use in obtaining salt from the Chivu salt spring. He informed the Superintendent of the Lushai Hills: 'I have no objection to the villages in the Lushai Hills near Bungmual obtaining salt from the Chibu salt wells in the same way as I have allowed the loyal Kamhows to do'.[12]

Throughout history, salt springs were scare and highly valued pieces of landed property. And all the salt wells (such as Ningel, Waikhong, Chandrakhong, etc.) close to the Kangla Palace in the Imphal valley had been royal monopolies since the dawn of recorded history. Even

161

under British colonial rule, taxes from salt wells remained a lucrative (though declining) source of revenue for princely Manipur. Because Chivu was too far from the Kangla Palace, the Chivu salt springs remained beyond the control of valley-based Meitei princes who ruled at Imphal and Moirang. Since 1872 or thereabouts, the British authorities at Imphal gave the Kamhows of the Chin Hills access to the Chivu salt wells to reciprocate the loyalty of the Kamhows. This right of use was British reward to the Kamhows for their assistance against the Lushai (Mizo) chiefs during the Lushai Expedition of 1871–1872. The expedition took place at a time when the Lushai chiefs had a series of local rivalry with the Kamhow chiefs. On this occasion, Chivu was used as the camp site for the Manipur column commanded by General Nuthall and Maharaja Chandra Kirti Singh (Carey and Tuck 1896). The Maharaja of Manipur erected memorial stones at Chivu camp for himself and for the British official General Nuthall to 'commemorate the part which the Manipuries played in the Lushai expedition' (Carey and Tuck 1896: 123).[13]

During the course of the Kuki uprising, the Superintendent of the Lushai Hills and the Political Agent of Manipur became entangled in land claims and disputes of rival houses of the Zou and Guite chiefs. The two British officials had their own candidate for a prospective confiscation and land grant. To a point, the decision to collaborate or resist the British during the Anglo-Kuki conflict was determined by considerations about claims to the salt springs of the Chivu valley in southern Manipur.

When the colonial authorities denied Thangtual his claim over the Chivu salt spring of Tonzang village, he made another claim to land that belonged to the rebel chief of Behiang village. The tiny valley of Behiang was on the western bank of the Tuivai River opposite the eastern bank of the Chivu salt springs. Both Chivu springs (within Tonzang village) and Behiang valley belonged to the clan of Manlun chiefs of the Zou community. Taking advantage of the disturbances, these Zou chiefs of Manipur threatened to raid neighbouring Paite villages under the jurisdiction of the Lushai Hills District. A telegram (dated 19 September 1918) reads: 'Information received that Joh [Zou] men threaten to raid Chingbunga and Luanbunga in our territory directly'.[14] Because the political institution of chiefship was (as still is) a hereditary office, the politics of land claims became closely connected to competition among chiefly lineages under colonial rule. Thangtual was an adept player of the political game under the rules set by the British administrators. Using the Lushai (Mizo) language,

Thangtual petitioned again the colonial authorities for a land grant at an alternative site in Behiang valley:

Ni kum a Chivuphai ka dil kha Manipur sap in mi kape a ti kha. Tun a Behiang ram hi leileh tur shawmnga 50 lai ti thei tur awm a, mikhaw ngai a he mi Behiang ram hi miti shak thei ka beishei a ni. Leileh tur Chivu aiin a lo tamzawka ni.[15]

(Translation: The Manipur *sahib* has allocated the Chivu vale that I requested last year. Now there is cultivable land in Behiang enough for about 50 [households]. I beg you to kindly let me do this in the land of Behiang where cultivable land exceeds that of Chivu).

When the Anglo-Kuki hostilities came to an end, the land claims over the Chivu salt springs and Behiang valley was finally resolved in favour of maintaining the status quo by refusing to confiscate landed property that belonged to the rebel chiefs. When the chief of Behiang decided to end his fight with the British, his village came to be treated as 'friendly'.[16] In November 1918, W.A. Cosgrave wrote to the Superintendent of the Lushai Hills: 'the chief Langzachin of Behiang has surrendered with his guns and revenue and that I have informed the Commandant, Aijal, that this village should be regarded as friendly'.[17] Here, war did not provide an excuse to deprive the property rights of the rebels; and this historical precedent established a degree of sanctity of property rights at a critical moment in the history of southern Manipur. This appears to be the beginning of a new political vocabulary of '*daai*' (right) in the vernacular language of Kuki chiefs. In early 1919, the Political Agent of Manipur wrote:

Manipur State Darbar and I are all opposed to the confiscation of lands of chiefs who were previously in rebellion, on the ground that this will cause bad feeling for years, the land of Behiang cannot be given to Thangtuala.[18]

Unlike forest clearing for shifting cultivation, saltwells and terrace cultivations were distinct categories of land that incentivised more sedentary type of settlement. These settled plots of wet-rice fields in small vales were only tiny islands in a sea of villages based on *jhum* cultivation. With or without state protection, security of land tenure was called for gradually both for terraced and irrigated fields that

Thangtual was proposing to start at Behiang valley in 1919. Not far from this agricultural reclamation, more settled type of agriculture was already developing in the Champhai valley of the Lushai Hills and among the Tashons and Zahaus of the Chin Hills with greater security of land tenures. On the whole, colonial rule had the effect of strengthening social forces that promoted the development of rights of private property in land, especially in irrigated fields. When H.N.C. Stevenson conducted a study of the land tenure of the Chin Hills during the 1930s, he confirmed the existence of the private rights in landed property called *bul ram*:

> clearing of virgin jungle establishes a perpetual right to cultivate . . . it is the sanction for hereditary cultivation titles which in themselves form the only inducement to the villager to improve his land holdings by permanent works such as terrace.
>
> (Stevenson 1943: 87)

The norms of private alienable land title (*bul ram*) emerged alongside the older Commons type of land tenure. And *bul ram* is reported to have originated among the democratic communities of the Tashon (Falam) of central Chin Hills, which was geographically contiguous to southern Manipur (Stevenson 1943: 92). *Bul ram* is the equivalent to *patta* (private land title) in British India. Among the autocratic chiefs of Kamhows (northern Chin Hills) and the Kukis (southern Manipur), land tenure did not evolve in the direction of *bul ram*, but as a form of Commons where the chief was theoretically the trustee who kept land on behalf of the village community. However, in practice, the tragedy of the Commons made hill lands the private property of the Kuki chief who could arbitrarily sell land in the market or evict members of his community at will. Even irrigated wet-rice paddy fields (let alone terraced fields) were not safe from confiscation by the Kuki chief, especially when villagers decided to migrate to a new place. With this type of insecure land tenure, no enlightened individual can be expected to make permanent improvements to his or her land. Nevertheless, during the late colonial period, agricultural lands enjoyed more security of land tenure first in the valley of Imphal. In decades after the Anglo-Kuki War, this tendency spread to the valley portions of the hill areas such as the Khuga (Tuitha) valley that witnessed the creation of a new colonial headquarters at present-day Churachandpur, a town in southern Manipur.

Land as romantic home or real property

In times of peace, rational consideration of land tenure mattered a lot; but in times of war, strong passions seized the imagination of anti-colonial patriots who fought against the British. During the Anglo-Kuki War, the community lands of the Kukis were romanticised even by ordinary villagers who declared, "Tis the land of my birth'. At such moments in history, patriotic passions took over. While the Guite or Paite chiefs were guided by utilitarian reason, the Zou and Thadou chiefs exhibited a romantic sense of patriotism to some degree. A song of the Zou gal, composed by Pu Mangzathang Dopmul, confirms the hurt sense of honour felt by the heroes of the anti-colonial protest:

> *Tuizum Maangkang kiil bang hing khang*
> *Zota kual zil bang liing e,*
> *Pianna ka gamlei hi e, phal sing e!*
> *Ka naamtem hiam a i Zogam lei laal kanoh*
> *San si.n zeel e,*
> *Ngal liam vontawi ka zau lo lai e.* (Pau 1985: 1)

Free translation:

> The seafaring White Imperialist coils like the *kiil* plant
> Tremors of earthquake do quiver the Zo world,
> 'Tis the land of my birth, I shall not part with it!
> Stain'd with blood is my sword
> That has routed the raiders of Zo land
> I shall yet fight the wild Boar, injured.

Even 100 years after the Anglo-Kuki War, a rational debate has not begun on the question of land ownership. Who owns the land – the Kuki chiefs or ordinary citizens? Can the ordinary citizen of the Kuki community claim to own a piece of 'the land of my birth' in secure title? The answer is 'No'. For the ordinary Kuki, land is merely a romantic home of his or her ancestors, but not a piece of real property that can be validated in law. This type of land tenure had its great days; but even the best norms can become out of joints with times. In the Khuga valley of what is today Churachandpur (then settled by Nepali graziers and raided by the Thadou and Zou rebels in 1917), land *patta* developed by stealth rather than by open legislation as elsewhere in many towns of northeast India. Here agricultural lands transformed into *patta* land with secure land titles.[19] And this new land tenure provided a firm foundation for the emergence of the second largest town of Manipur – that too in a supposedly rural area.

Notes

1 This school of history writing can be traced back to 1963 when E.P. Thompson published The Making of the English Working Class. Thompson sought to rescue the English working class 'from the enormous condescension of posterity' and he rejected conventional historiographies that 'tend to obscure the agency of working people' (p. 12).

2 Mizoram State Archives, Aizawl, (hereafter MZSA), CB-9, Political Department, File No. 85, 1918.

3 MZSA, Correspondence to J.E. Webster (Chief Secretary to the Chief Commissioner of Assam) dated Camp Kangwai [Kangvai] steam, dated 28 December 1917.

4 MZSA, Correspondence to J.E. Webster (Chief Secretary to the Chief Commissioner of Assam) dated Camp Lanva stream, dated 31 December 1917.

5 MZSA, Correspondence to J.E. Webster (Chief Secretary to the Chief Commissioner of Assam) dated Camp Tuila stream 1 January 1918.

6 MZSA, CB-9, Political Department, File no. 85, 1918 – Handwritten petition of Thangtuala to Superintendent of Lushai Hills, dated 25 May 1918.

7 MZSA, CB-9, Political Department, File no. 85, 1918 – Handwritten petition of Thangtuala to Superintendent of Lushai Hills, dated 25 May 1918.

8 MZSA, CB-9, Political Department, File no. 85, 1918 – Note by the Superintendent of the Lushai Hills to Political Agent of Manipur, Aijal dated 28 May 1918.

9 MZSA, CB-9, Political Department, File no. 85, 1918 – Correspondence from W.A. Cosgrave (Political Agent in Manipur) to the Superintendent, Lushai Hills, Aijal, dated Imphal 20 June 1918.

10 Pumjakham appears to be a Paite chief, if not of the Guite clan. He was the cousin of the renown Hauchinkhup of the Chin Hills.

11 MZSA, CB-9, Political Department, File no. 85, 1918 – Correspondence from W.A. Cosgrave (Political Agent in Manipur) to the Superintendent, Lushai Hills, Aijal, dated Imphal 20 June 1918.

12 MZSA, CB-9, Political Department, File no. 85, 1918 – Correspondence from W.A. Cosgrave (Political Agent in Manipur) to the Superintendent, Lushai Hills, Aijal, dated Imphal 20 June 1918.

13 The Maharaja's stone represented British victory in the Lushai Expedition (1871–72) as if it were Manipur's own doing; and it claimed to have defeated the Lushais and even the Kamhows who allied with the British in this war against the Lushais. Amused with the claims on the Maharaja's stone inscription, Carey and Tuck remarked, 'It will be noticed that the Manipuris claim to have done more conquering, than our records credit them with' (Carey & Tuck 1896: 123).

14 MZSA, CB-9, Political Department, File no. 85, 1918 – Telegram to Commissioner, Silchar, from Superintendent, Lushai Hills, dated 19 September 1918.

15 MZSA, CB-9, Political Department, File no. 86 – Thangtuala's petition to the Superintendent, Lushai Hills, dated Tawnzang 12 January 1919.
16 The surrender took place near Bungmual on 22 October 1918. See MZSA, CB-9, Political, File no. 85, Copy of telegram no. 416 P dated 22 October 1918 from the Political Agent, Imphal, to the Commandant 1st Lushai Hills Battalion, p. 32.
17 MZSA, CB-9, Political, File no. 85, Correspondence dated 4 November 1918 from W.A. Cosgrave, ICS, the Political Agent in Manipur to the Superintendent, Lushai Hills, Aijal, p. 34.
18 MZSA, CB-9, Political Department, File no. 86 – Correspondence from W.A. Cosgrave to the Superintendent, Lushai Hills, dated 22 February 1919.
19 Technically, the patta lands in Manipur are called *dak chitha* or *jamabandi*.

References

Arnold, David. 1982/1999. 'Rebellious Hillmen: The Gudem-Rampa Risings, 1839–1924', in Ranajit Guha (ed.), *Subaltern Studies I*, pp. 88–142. New Delhi: Oxford University Press.

Bhadra, Gautam. 1975. 'The Kuki (?) Uprising (1917–1919): Its Causes and Nature', *Man in India*, 55 (1): 10–56.

Carey, Bertram S. and H.N. Tuck. 1896. *The Chin Hills: A History of the People, Our Dealings with Them, Their Customs and Manners and a Gazetteer of Their Country*, Vol. I. Rangoon: Superintendent, Government Printing.

Guha, Ranajit. 1982/1999. 'On Some Aspects of the Historiography of Colonial India', in Ranajit Guha (ed.), *Subaltern Studies I*, pp. 1–8. New Delhi: Oxford University Press.

Pau, Gouza and Kai Kho Hau, eds. 1985. *Zola.sanneem la (An Anthology of Zou folksongs)*. Churachandpur, Manipur: Co-operative Press.

Thompson, E.P. 1991. *The Making of the English Working Class*. London: Penguin Books.

Stevenson, H.N.C. 1943. *The Economics of the Central Chin Hills*. Bombay: The Times of India Press.

6

'AS MEN OF ONE COUNTRY'
Rethinking the history of the Anglo-Kuki War

Ningmuanching

> *These Kukis all hang together and in the fighting against*
> *the Assam column and ourselves, southern Kukis*
> *undoubtedly marched north-east to help their relatives.*
> – *Lieut. Col. J.L.W. Ffrench-Mullen*

During the First World War, a confederation of Kuki chiefs in the hills
of Manipur persistently refused to obey the orders of the colonial state
and supply coolies for France. Demonstrating a spirit of defiance against
British authority, they avoided meetings with the British officers. After
an unsuccessful negotiation with the Political Agent who went to the
hills to meet them, the Kukis rose in armed resistance against the colonial state. A pervasive reluctance to provide coolie labour for France
developed into an armed resistance against colonial rule by some Kukis,
as they called for united resistance against colonial rule. The people of
the hill shared grievances against colonial control, especially on the
issue of going to France as coolies during the First World War. What
were the motivations and the contexts which shaped such a response to
colonial rule? For the answers, it is necessary to study the Kuki rising of
1917–1919 in the context of the establishment of colonial administration and its intervention in the lives of the hill people.

In her study of the Tana Bhagat Movement, Sangeeta Dasgupta has
moved beyond the conventional interpretation of tribal movements as
an opposition between tribal and non-tribal, the less-civilised against
more-civilised, or insiders versus outsiders. She refutes the general perception that tribal communities were united in their resistance against
non-tribal because of the presumed 'inherently antagonistic' economic
interests of the two broad groups (Dasgupta 1999; Sarkar 1985). Dasgupta argues that, though Tanas opposition to the Zamindars, banias

and the British was significant, the movement must also be seen as a conflict that arose out of the internal hierarchy within the Oraon community, which she claimed was further intensified by the British with their administrative arrangements and agrarian legislations. As a marginalised group within Oraon society, the Tanas challenged both tribal and non-tribal elements that were responsible for their dependent and subordinate status. The Tana Bhagat Movement was therefore, an attempt of a marginal group of the Oraon society to reorder their world (Dasgupta 1999: 1–2). Although the operations of marginalised section of Kuki population against the dominant chiefs is difficult to excavate from our evidences, the Kuki rising definitely show popular participation in a effort to fight against the increasing colonial intrusion into their livelihood and hence comes within the orbit of people's war.

This paper argues that the Anglo-Kuki War 1917–1919 was a war of not only the dominant sections of Kuki society but was also a popular war against domination and control from the outside. The people of the hill rose to renounce British sovereignty in the hills in an attempt to reclaim their hitherto existing freedom, authority and alliances that were gradually breaking down with colonial intervention in their lives. The Kuki rising was, therefore, an assertion of the 'tribal' chiefs, representing multiple leadership figures, and their people for self-determination in the face of subordination under colonialism. This paper will locate the Kuki unrest in the context of increasing colonial intervention in their everyday lives, and the popular resistance against such interventions. Therefore, the rising was related to livelihood struggles of common people against outside disruption. For instance, the colonial mediation in internal conflicts and their various lifeways directly or indirectly infringed upon their traditional social, cultural and economic relationship and networks, causing much resistance. Their refusal to go to France was for instance related to the Kukis' cultural notion of death and afterlife. Therefore, the collective consciousness exhibited by the Kukis was not limited to a specific group (e.g. chiefs) or villages, it was inextricably linked to one's belonging to the land and cultural landscape. Instead of being a mere chief's war or a particular tribe (say Thadou), the war was a much larger conglomeration of the Kuki population across the hills.

Colonial discourse on the Anglo-Kuki War

Reading official documents like administrative reports, telegrams and letters sent by British officers engaged in Kuki 'punitive' operations revealed the dominant colonial discourse on the Kuki rising of

1917–1919. In an attempt to make sense of the Kuki's courage to fight with arms, different views were posited which eventually fall in line with its dominant civilisational notion on the 'tribe'. First, some officers were of the opinion that the uprising was caused by British procrastination in not dealing at once and fully with it when the trouble first showed up (Shakespear 1977: 209–212). The 'rebellion', according to them, could have been prevented if it was dealt with strongly at once. The inadequate attention given to the hill tribes or the forbearance of the British rulers was, therefore, seen to have been misinterpreted by the Kukis as fear and hence their armed resistance (Shakespear 1977: 209–212). For Shakespear, the 'rebellion' was caused by inefficient control of the Kukis in the Manipur state (Shakespear 1977: 209–212). Robert Reid felt that the President of the Durbar failed to give enough attention to the hills, by not undertaking the usual tours into the hills (Reid 1997: 79).

Some officers also felt that Kuki rising was an expression of Kuki savagery. The political officer of the Sugnu punitive column, for instance, described how the corpse of one sepoy killed by the Kukis has been found headless.[1] Shaw depicted the 'rebellion' as an event that unfolded the practice of head-hunting by Thadou Kukis, evident in the way they handled the enemies they killed. He wrote:

> The Thadou considered themselves great headhunters and have not given up the practice as was seen so recently as the Kuki rebellion in 1918–1919. They place great value on a head because each head means an additional slave for the soul.
>
> (Shaw 1928: 78–79)

He went on saying that due to lack of contact with the outer world 'ancient thoughts and traditions carry more weight among' the Kukis who 'still think they own the country they inhabit and regard the other tribes as their underlings' (Shaw 1928: 50).

With this idea, the colonial argument went on saying that the hill tribes were shown to be easily duped by outsiders such as the people from the plains. This amounts to looking at the rising as, to use Ajay Skaria apt terms, 'childlike' and 'boisterous school-boys' who could easily be instigated by mischief-makers when the teacher's attention was diverted (Skaria 1997: 739). Thus, the Kukis were thought to have lost their senses and were seen to be easily cheated by a Manipuri pretender from the plain who instigated them to fight against the British.[2] The appeal of the instigator was assumed to be the basis of the armed resistance. It was reported that a Manipuri named Chingakhamba Sana Chaoba Singh, who claimed to have possessed 'supernatural powers', had instigated the Kukis to fight against the colonial state.[3] In him, the British found a reasonable explanation as to why the 'savage' hill tribes would dare to fight against the British. This is a deliberate attempt not only to criminalise the armed resistance but also to demonise the hill people as 'savage' and 'primitive' people who had no sense of war but being incited to commit 'savagery' against civilisation. Thus, the term 'rebellion', 'outrages' and so on were used to describe the event.

In this line of thinking, the Kukis opposition to labour recruitment was also explained. Although all agreed that such recruitment drive incited the Kuki rising, the event was explained in terms of their refusal or their fear to leave their hills due to isolation and ignorance.[4] It was reported that the Kukis were 'ignorant hill men' who refused to work in an unfamiliar environment away from their homes.[5] They were understood as 'a people who had never left their hills', whereas other tribals such as the Nagas, Lushais and others had (Shakespear 1977: 209–212). Such explanation was not really to deny the fact that the Kukis were few of the hill tribes who had a good connection with the outside world such as Assam, Bengal, Burma and Manipur for which most colonial accounts were testimony to it. But it was a deliberate attempt on the part of the colonial state to drive a dominant discourse that the Kukis had fought the British merely to evaporate their savage instinct of 'head hunting' and so on. In short, it was an attempt to reduce the 'war' (*gal* in Kuki version) as a mere act of savagery, a criminal act in the colonial court of law.

This dominant colonial discourse on 'rebellion' as a 'child-like' act of 'ignorance' and savagery has been challenged by most 'native' historians who wrote on the Anglo-Kuki War. The dominant literature on the rising focussed on its political aspects, which are of course important but neither the sole or the most important cause of the rising. Very few studies noted on the important role of economics, and even less focussed on cultural aspects of the rising. An analysis of the socio-economic and political contexts reveals interesting aspects of the Kuki rising. All these aspects can be located within the cultural notion of things which colonial interventions had greatly disrupted over time. Thus, if labour recruitment and the fear of death were important factors, they were not per se the primary cause. The Kukis had a different worldview on labour and death, which was central to their opposition to labour overseas. The cultural significance of labour and death explains their resistance to labour recruitment. Similarly, while it is a fact that the Thadou chieftains provided the leadership in the rising, it is significant to note why they had provided the leadership and what objective they wanted to gain at the end of the war. Besides, the dominance of chiefs (Thadou chiefs) during the war generated the idea that the war was the chiefs' war and it was mainly fought by the Thadou chiefs. Evidence, however, shows that the war was the people's war and it was fought not only by and for the chiefs but by and for all sections of the Kuki population who took part in the war as 'men of one country'.

The story of the unrest

In 1917, the prolongation of the First World War and the need for an 'ample and well regulated influx of men' for combatant and non-combatant services from every part of the colonial Empire imposed an increasing strain on labour demands. India was, therefore, asked to increase her monthly supply of recruits to all services.[6] The Chief Commissioner of Assam undertook the recruitment of 'the many hardy races suitable for work in cold climates' available in the hills of Assam for non-combatant service. Accordingly, by June 1917, eight Corps of men for service in France were formed from the different hill districts of Assam. A group of Nagas and Kukis of the Manipur State constituted one of the corps dispatched to France.[7] A second request for labour corps was made in the following month and a durbar was arranged by the British officers in Manipur for the Kuki chiefs to attend in order to explain to them the reasons why their men were wanted, the nature of the work required of them, the pay to be received etc. The Kuki chiefs however refused to attend the durbar.

The Kuki chiefs like Ngulkhup of Mombi and Ngulbul of Longya in the hills south of Manipur valley denounced state authority and were not reluctant to use force (Shakespear 1977: 210). Moreover, it appeared that the attempt to recruit coolies was not successful because of the influence of Khutinthang, chief of Jampi, and Pache, the Chief of Chassad and hereditary head of the Haokip clan. If these two chiefs brought in their men, the British believed that the 'smaller chiefs' would do the same. While negotiation was going on in October 1917, J.C. Higgins, the officiating Political Agent in Manipur, took 50 rifles to Mombi and arrested Ngulkhup, chief of Mombi, bacause he had, it was reported, threatened to attack and kill the women and children of those who supplied coolies to the British.[8] Failing to arrest the chief, Higgins burnt down Mombi on 17 October 1917 while the sepoys fed on the village livestock.[9] Higgins was ordered to return to Imphal and take no further action against the Kukis without prior approval from the government. On the other hand, the Kukis took this intemperate behaviour of the local officer as a direct insult to their pride and thus called off all furhter negotiations with the government. This was followed by war preparation and the eventual outbreak of armed resistance against the British government.

All efforts to bring in the Kukis after the Mombi event failed.[10] Reports arrived about the gathering of Kuki chiefs at Ukha: 'They were said to have sworn an oath to resist by force of arms any attempt to impress coolies by force, to arrest them or to burn their villages'. Licenced guns were demanded from Naga villages that were to be used in armed resistance against any British officer.[11] The chiefs of Mombi and Longya, identified as the principal 'rebel' chiefs, now sent in messages to the Political Agent that their country was closed to the British (Shakespear 1977: 211). It was clear that the authoritarian and paternalistic notices of the British rulers had failed to induce the chiefs to come in.[12] In December 1917, the British officials decided to call the recalcitrant chiefs for explanation; they would burn the villages of those who refused to do so.[13] The Kukis retaliated by raiding the police stations and destroying rest houses. The Kukis also killed chowkidars, damaged telegraph lines and blocked the road to Burma (Shakespear 1977: 213). Rumours about the Kukis marching on to Imphal valley caused much panic and trouble in the valley during the uprising.[14] On another occasion, 'There was a panic in sadar bajaar at Imphal and a stampede amongst the bajaar people mostly women'.[15] Signs of British presence like bungalow, hill rest houses, outposts or *thanas* as well as all who work for the British, like *chaukidars, chaprassis, lambus* and *dakwallas*, were victims of the uprising as shown by information about Kuki outrage.[16] Other *chaukidars* if not killed were threatened; a bungalow chaukidar at Waikhong was found drunken than usual 'having been drowning his sorrows consequent on being told by the Kukis of Aihang that the bungalow and himself would suffer the same fate as the Tengnoupal bungalow and chaukidar'.[17] The Kukis singled out Government servants in order to 'intimidate people from working for Government or the State authorities'.[18] The opposition between those who worked for the government and the 'rebels' was clearly visible. For instance, the Kukis sent a *dao* to the big village Maram and ordered the villagers to cut the Telegraph line, but the state *lambu* warned that they would be imprisoned if they did it.[19] Explicit in the behaviour of the Kukis was their utter dislike for the British and their rule and sympathy shown to their fellow hillmen.

The colonial state responded by initiating operations against the Kukis in the hills surrounding the valley of Manipur. The weather, the difficult terrains of rivers and forests and the possibility of disease were some of the problems they encountered. Besides, the 'active scantily-clad Kukis', who, though using inferior arms, 'know their hills and forests, carry no packs, do not bother themselves over supplies, who are rarely seen in their forests, and who are adapted to guerilla and jungle warfare' were formidable opponents (Shakespear 1977: 236). As the punitive columns of the colonial state and the Kukis engaged in armed conflict, and the burning of villages continued for almost two years, the colonial rulers envisaged military operations. Negotiations were opened with the leading Kuki chiefs. They were promised a fair trial and were assured that no further recruitment of coolies would take place if the Kukis surrendered with their guns (Reid 1997: 81). But most Kuki chiefs remain recalcitrant and military occupation finally quelled the Kuki rising. Everywhere the food storage were destroyed, their village burnt down, and regular agricultural operation were harassed. Therefore, wants of food was acute everywhere in the rebel areas. Eventually the Kukis have to give in when the suffering of the mass become increasing by the days due to colonial scourge earth policy against them. The civil authorities resumed political authority in April 1919 (Reid 1997: 81–82).

How might we understand this important historical event of resistance against colonialism during the high noon of the First World War then? The dominant historiography make us understand that the Anglo-Kuki War 1917–1919 was a 'rebellion' against labour recruitment for the First World War and it was the war mainly fought at the behest of the Thadou-Kuki chieftains. It is true that labour recruitment for the war was one important factor but it was not the only cause of the rising. Besides, it is also true that the Thadou-Kuki chiefs provided the leadership but it is also true that the war was fought not only by the Thadou chiefs but all sections of the Kuki population. The study of the Anglo-Kuki War needs to look into factors other than labour recruitment. In fact, labour recruitment itself needs a relook, say for instance, why they opposed it. The cultural aspects of their opposition to labour recruitment for the war had never been taken seriously. Further, one needs to investigate why the Kuki chiefs were opposed to colonialism and what they expected from gaining freedom. In the following sections, an attempt is made to understand these deeper meanings of the rising.

Contextualising the 'rebellion'

No single factor can explain the outbreak of Kuki uprising in 1917. The gathering discontentment, accumulated over a period of time, eventually led to the rising in 1917. Colonial official historians were quick to blame the native state of Manipur – the inefficiency of local administration, its *pothang* (porterage) system, foul play of the *lambus* and so on. All agree that Kukis opposition to the labour corps was the immediate cause. But none of them have tried to explain why the Kukis opposed labour corps in the first place when they were used as 'best' porters previously. Scholars working on the Anglo-Kuki War have therefore looked into other aspects of the rising such as the dislocated social and economic processes under colonialism. Gautam Bhadra, for instance, explains that the colonial policy of sedentarisation was central to the dislocation of Kuki polity, economy and social structures which largely depended on their freedom of migration. Migration not only provided them fresh soil for the *jhum* economy but had also been 'the political safety-valve' through which a custom left a scope for own expression of grievances and thus stabilised its own institution of chieftainship. Whenever the chief become unpopular, people freely choose to migrate to other villages or set up a village of their own so that such migration immediately evaporated their sense of protestion against the office. Thus, the bar against migration and formation of the new villages not only 'hampered' the Kukis' mode of production but it also 'destroyed' the 'safety valve' for the functioning of their political organisation (Bhadra 1975: 10–56). But few have looked into how colonial policy had also directly affected the economic livelihood patterns of the Kukis and to their political organisation. An attempt is made in the following sections to explain these aspects.

General economic grievances

Constrained economic livelihood in the hills was central to understand the gathering discontentment among the hill people of Manipur, which culminated in the Kuki uprising in 1917. Tribes were generally seen as homogenous self-subsisting cultivators. The different activities for subsistence, in addition to growing rice in *jhum* and terraces, were subsumed under the common term 'simple cultivators' (Corbridge 1988: 6). In the hill tracts of Manipur, equally important for subsistence was the sale of plaintains [leaves of a tropical plant] that grew in the region. Depending on favourable soil and climate, pan leaves, which did not grow well in the Imphal valley, grew well in the 'valley that intersect the hills' and formed an 'extraordinarily profitable crop' for villages in the valley of the Irang and the Barak (Allen 1980: 78). The 'hill people' were also suppliers of raw cotton essential for weaving, the most important industry in Manipur (Allen 1980: 86). Grown extensively in the hills, cotton was a cash-producing crop generally sown in *jhum* fields which had yielded a crop of rice the previous year. However, heavy rains tended to injure the crop and hailstorms sometimes destroyed the crop altogether (Allen 1980: 77). The livelihood activities of the 'hill people' dependent on land and agriculture which are subject to the depredation of nature and constrained by the ecosystem. Seen in this light, there is room for questioning the validity of the perception that often attributed the backwardness of the economy of the tribals to the lack of 'profit maximizing mentality of the commercial farmer' (Corbridge 1988: 9).

Apart from the constraints of nature, another source of conflict regarding livelihood was the influx of Gurkhalis with their cattles into the hills. The conflict between Nepali graziers and hill people over space and livelihood was one important factor to the discontent of hill people against colonial state. We have several reports of the destruction of hill crops by the cattle of Nepali graziers who were settled by the colonial state among the hill people.[20] The colonial policy to create 'reserves' and confine Gurkhalis within a demarcated areas in the hills was clearly spelt out by one government official: 'all these Nepalis should be given a large area of land on which to settle and not to be permitted to live outside these area'.[21] This policy safeguarded the Gurkhalis' right to continue living within the hills, while the hill people's plight at the destruction of their crops by the cattle of the Gurkhalis continued unabated. This policy was provocative as some villages were ordered to move and make room for the Nepali graziers. A Kuki village was, for instance, ordered to move when the Gurkhali colony was formed in 1906. Two years later, in 1908, W.A. Cosgrave, the Vice President of the Manipur State Durbar, found that the village had not moved according to orders. The village was regarded as 'a nest of bad mashes and determined to disobey orders' that deserved to be burnt.[22] Conflict over resources heightened as boundaries were not easily accepted. Disputes over boundaries became a constant problem. As Cosgrave pointed out, 'new waste areas cannot be given to Nepali graziers without the hillmen suffering'.[23] Creating the Gurkhali reserve from 'waste land' was a source of distress for the hill people as Nepali graziers generally overflowed out of the reserved area.[24]

Despite the conflict, Nepali graziers were encouraged to live in the hills because they were a source of state income as they paid foreigners tax and grazing fees annually.[25] Ghee produced by Gurkali graziers were bought in bulk by contractors who supplied rations to battalions of Assam Rifles employed in the hills.[26] Sometimes, cultivated lands were made over to the Nepalis and compensation was paid to the former cultivators.[27] In 1916, Nepali graziers were found moving with their herds of cattle to settle in a valley within the hills.[28] The Kukis around this area were active participants during the Kuki rising that forced the Gurkhalis to move from the Kuga valley.[29] A human head sent by one of the rebel chiefs to another changed hands from village to village and was shown to Nepali settlers near the River Irong. The buffaloes of many of the Nepalis were killed by some bands of Kukis on their way to settle in the unadministered territory east of the State.[30] As Cosgrave pointed out,

> much of the bad feeling of the Kukis round Ukha . . . against Government was in my opinion due to Nepalis being allowed to settle two or three years ago in the Kuge valley, as the Nepali graziers buffaloes always damage the hillmen's crops.[31]

Another source of discontentment was the project of a silk rearing and spinning industry, which was undertaken during the first decade of the twentieth century (Dena 2008: 64–65). For Kuki villages, rich in cattle, the experiment with the silk industry resulted in the loss of grazing land for their prized cattle called *metna*. The Kuki chief of Ukha, said to be 'richer in metnas than any other Kuki village', for instance, voiced his distress to the Political Agent during his tour in the hills:

> The Chief tells me that he will be ruined if the Silk Company gets the Kuga Valley where his metnas graze, so I have told him to come with me to Moirang to meet Mr. Malcolm. I fancy that unless the silk company put a fencing round their portion of the Kuga Valley metnas from the Kuki villages will join the Company's cattle.[32]

Declining authority of the chiefs

In addition to livelihood struggles caused by nature and the aggravation by people under colonial rule, the experiences of the colonial justice and imposition of law and order was far from pleasant. The state's role of arbitration infringed into the everyday lives of the hill people in different ways. Once the 'overlords' were disarmed and the tributary system dismantled, colonial arbitration became an important space of interaction between the colonial rulers and the ruled. Kukis were identified as the 'most persistent litigants' in this respect.[33] *Lambus*, the hill peons who had become a symbol of state power in the hills, became the new figure of authority in the hills contesting the traditional authority of the chiefs. Complaints under colonial administration were very often directed against *lambus*, who abused their power by extorting money from the people with a promise of preventing punishments that followed disobedience of State orders.[34] Naturally sympathetic towards their local collaborators than ordinary hill people, complaints against *lambus* by disarmed Kukis were dismissed as an expression of dissatisfaction with the *lambus* for their role in confiscating guns from the village. Half the criminal and civil cases were pending for years that overwhelmed the work of the colonial administrators.[35] This highly demanding and crucial role of an arbitrator in the affairs of the hill people entailed greater intervention of the Political Officer into the everyday lives of the hill people.

Boundary cases were settled by making villagers swear to the boundaries of the land given to them years ago.[36] The Political Agent found oath taking as a valuable system of solving disputes over resources.[37] In such cases, the defendant and plaintiff took an oath on the lives of their respective villagers. The case was decided based on the acceptance of the oath by rest of the villagers.[38] However, in disputes which were difficult to settle according to the custom of oath, the greater problem lay in the way relevance or irrelevance was overlooked in the search for a less troublesome and easier justice system. In dealing with inter-village boundary disputes and conflicts over resources, which were common cases, sticking to 'customary' law was found useful. This was done without reforming the laws regarded as 'customs'. The prudence of this with respect to the changing contexts is questionable. In a dispute between two villages over a small patch of land at the boundary of the villages, the system of oath taking was found to be ineffective as a solution. The problem was that the two villages 'wanted to swear the land was theirs' and neither party would accept the other's oath. Shakespear's account about how he settled this case revealed the nature of colonial justice.

> I prohibited both from cultivating the land, under the penalty of Rs. 100 till they have come to some conclusion. The patch in dispute is hardly 50 yards square, and it is far better uncultivated as it forms a boundary between the khets of the two villages at this point.[39]

In this way, problems that called for a long process of careful considerations and discussions were solved rather quickly. Thus, the colonial authority enforced order based on colonial reasoning. In the process, the people were denied their rights to justice, which they normally received through their traditional justice system.

A notable feature of the justice system in hills was an arbitrary invocation of 'customs' in settling any disputes. The role of arbitration also infringed on the everyday lives of the Kukis. It was especially intrusive to the chiefs, who found his authority being demeaned by the day under colonial interventions. In many cases, the chiefs have been sued by his villagers and in most cases loss the case. The following domestic case involving the Kuki chief of the village *Mombi* and his choice for a wife best illustrated one such invocation of 'custom' in favour of the villagers against their chief:

> I halted today and made some enquiries. These Mangvung Chiefs rule mixed lot of people of many different families. I was called on to settle a domestic quarrel. The Chief sometimes back became ensnared by a women of low degree, marriage with whom, the villagers say, is against their customs and would bring harm on the village, so they sent the lady away and provided the chief with a suitable bride, who is by no means uncomely, but he still hankers after the forbidden fruit. I advised him to be satisfied with his bride.[40]

The passage clearly indicates that the power of the chief was diminishing against the 'custom' said to be empowered under colonial rule. However, Colonial officers could reform 'custom' in the name of proper administration. The example of colonial rulers' interference in customary migration fee that added to the grievances of the Kuki chiefs was suggestive of the point. In 1908, an officer of the Chin Hills, Lushai Hills and Manipur state passed an order 'not to realise for the chiefs migration fee of Rs.10 for people who go across the border into another district'. With this order, the ordinary Kukis who had their property detained by the chief before they left the village began to show their discontent. The 'unnatural action on the part of the chief' in detaining paddy or the property of his fugitive became an issue of dispute between Kuki villagers and their chiefs.[41] Thus, the legitimacy of privileges enjoyed by the Kuki chiefs came to be questioned by ordinary villagers under colonial rule. Chiefs of villages in the hill tracts surrounding Manipur were found to exercise different degrees of influence over their people. While the existing domination exercised by influential chiefs could serve as a useful tool in controlling a large number of people, colonial administrators at the same time transformed chieftainship. In the colonial system of indirect rule, chiefs were allowed to exercise control only in ways the colonial ruler deemed appropriate. In the process, the chief was transformed into a figure of controlled authority. The increasing decline of chief's authority and the mounting disputes in the society was seen by many Kukis, including the chiefs, as a problem and desired to put an end to it if possible.

Colonial arbitration was a source of discontentment in other way round. Take, for example, the case of a village which was made to pay compensation to another village for the destruction of crops by their cattle. To avoid confrontation with colonial power such compensations were normally paid but with disgruntle. For instance, a Kuki village of Samu Kom was made to pay Rs. 15/- as compensation to Khude Khulen village under the colonial hand of justice. But the fact that such payment was not made willingly was shown in subsequent periods. Cosgrave wrote in his diary about this later development:

> The Marring of Khude Khulen village complained to me that last year the Kukis of Samu Kom (offshoot of the leading hostile village SITA) had paid them Rs. 15/- as compensation for damage done to their crops by metna, but that this year as the Kukis are at war with the Sarkar the Kukis came and forcibly took away from them Rs.30/- i.e. the amount which the Kukis had willingly paid last year plus a similar amount as interest. The outrage, if it may be called an outrage, is a trifling one but it shows how the Kukis are trying to show that the Sahibs' reign is at an end.[42]

It was not only to show that the Sahibs' reign is ending but also to challenge the authority which make them subservient. Cases such as this became a source of division amongst the hill populaces, and it was seen with exasperation by most hillmen. What came to be understood as 'paying off old scores' were instead the internal conflicts generated by the experiences of colonial rule and its role as an arbitrator (Bower 1986: 44). The chiefs as an active agent during the rising should be located within this declining sphere of their traditional authority under colonialism.

Pothang *or forced labour system*

Pothang system in Manipur was another important source of grievances to the hill people in general and to the Kukis in particular. While the system was abolished in the valley in 1913 due to opposition from the valley people, the same continue in the hills despite similar opposition. It is important to note the significance of coolie labour for the functioning of the colonial state and the native government of Manipur as a subsistence livelihood activity in the lives of the hill people. The hill people figured in the treaties between the colonial state and the Manipur Raja as an important labour resource essential for the expansion and consolidation of British rule. Coolie labour was a prerequisite in any undertaking of the colonial rulers in their administration of the region.[43] By the 1890s Tangkhuls and Kabuis, in particular, formed the bulk of paid coolie recruits for expeditions.[44] In 1911, the Abor expedition was accompanied by hundreds of Tangkhul coolies.[45] The Kukis too were utilised by the colonial state as hill porters. Respected by people such as the Angamis, the Kukis were seen as the best coolies amongst the hill people: 'The Kookies . . . have done admirable service as hill porters on dangerous expeditions, and they are the only tribe able to defend themselves against the Angamis who have, as numerous reports show, a real respect for them' (Mackenzie (1979: 148). In 1882, Lieutenant Dun wrote the following about the potential of the groups who had played a prominent part in the Kuki rising:

> In appearance, they exactly resemble the Lushai Kukis, who have settled this year in Cachar, but they are slightly superior in physique. . . . They are the best carriers in the state and for military transport possess the great advantage of being able to protect themselves to a great extent. They are apt to give way to fits of childish rage and passion if hurried or annoyed on the march. They drink a good deal of liquor: but I never saw one intoxicated . . . they are keen hunters, pay their chiefs a religious devotion, and are delighted at any opportunity of a fight.
>
> (Dun 1975: 132)

Their usefulness measured as such by the colonial rulers was not always compatible with the preference of the Kukis in livelihood activities. Choosing coolie labour as a way of earning was not a uniform attitude, much less an essential racial inclination. The employment of Kukis as hill porters was marked by resistance which was represented as 'fits of childish rage'. Bolting was another form of resistance to labour recruitment. This was met with violent punishment. T.C. Hodson, an officer on tour, shot a Kuki who tried to run away in 1901.[46] Hodson's explanation for shooting the Kuki was that he had fired the gun in the air to frighten the bolting man, as his example would have inspired others to set off too.[47] As he further explained: 'My coolies were already short, I feared that if one man ran off, others would follow, and I should be left stranded'.[48] Maxwell defended Hodson and said that Hodson's aim was 'to get away from the village as soon as possible for fear the Kukis who are the most savage and uncivilised of our hill tribes should attack him'.[49] Violent acts of the colonial officials were thus justified on the grounds of the 'uncertain temper' of the 'savage' and 'uncivilised' Kukis. People who resisted by bolting were labelled 'unlovable creatures'. In 1900, Maxwell wrote about his contempt for the trouble-making coolies: 'the Kuki coolies commenced to give trouble by making a bolt of it, but were recaptured only just in time, and placed under guard. Of all our hill tribes, the Kuki is certainly the most unlovable creature'.[50] Thus, the access of the colonial state to the labour required from the hill people was made difficult by Kukis resistance to coolie labour.

Understood by colonial officials as the 'most necessary people', coolies were without proper accommodation.[51] They were exposed to diseases like cholera.[52] The deplorable condition of manual workers from the hills and their complaints indicated the struggles of the hill people. And yet, dependence on this form of earning seemed to increase. One British officer was surprised 'to find in the middle of Mayangkhang a single Kuki house in which a Kuki lives who works as a coolie for contractors on the road'.[53] Coolie work disrupted agricultural pursuits as men were sometimes retained long beyond cultivation season.[54]

Coolie labour and manual work formed a necessary way of earning money or daily food for many of the poor hill people. They would only do such coolie works under compulsion by state law or by poverty. By 1905, a Naga could earn four annas a day by working as a coolie (Allen 1980: 97). In the trade routes that connected Manipur to Cachar and Lakhipur, Naga coolies were employed by traders to carry loads of fish and betel-nut across the hills. Cachar-Manipur trade in betel-nut and fish was especially brisk.[55] For instance, the Nagas were reported to be happy for the food they got to eat during expeditions. They 'got more pigs, dogs and fowls than they could eat'.[56] This indicates the poverty or destitution of some hill people within the hills who were compelled to take up coolie work under harsh conditions for survival. The hill people who were engaged in manual work in the valley were, irrespective of ethnicity, a class in themselves. Kukis who were said to be better off economically due to their efficient agriculture system hardly chose to work as coolies unless they were compelled to do so by state authorities.

Bamboo famine and indebtedness

In 1911, rice crop in the southern portion of the state (inhabited mainly by the Kukis) suffered severely due to the sudden invasion of rats and caused great distress to the people. Previously, in such times of scarcity, rather than mere dependence on jungle products, the hill people planted crops other than rice, such as *chail, tebi* (a large sulphurous bean) and maize that rats would not usually destroy. Thus, they avoided the risks associated with reliance on rice alone. Before the subsidiary crops ripened for consumption, the villages depended mainly on jungle roots such as *mun, kachu*, bamboo seeds[shoots], *hakai* a jungle bark, *har* a jungle tuber, *sag* a kind of spinach, *kachu* leaves and jungle *kachu*. Thus total starvation and large-scale loss of life was avoided.[57] Later on, the state stepped in to alleviate the food crisis. Shopkeepers were arranged to sell rice at a rate higher than the market price to the needy on credit, to be paid within two years.[58] The relief measures from the government, by way of arranging rice on credit at a higher price than usual, became a source of oppression for the hill people. Larger villages that could pay cash for the rice arranged for them initially ended up buying rice at a high price.[59] The hill people who had no money had to pay for the rice they obtained, on credit or from the state, eventually by working as coolies.

Deaths due to starvation were reported during this scarcity before the end of the year (in 1912) as ravages by rats and the subsequent scarcity of food continued for another year.[60] However, by November 1912, Higgins attempted to recruit the indebted hill people as coolies in order to recover the rice loan.[61] Those who refused to work as coolies found their petition for more rice rejected. In response to this injustice, they approached the higher authority by sending complaints, through telegraph, about their plight and how the officers in the state treated them.[62] Indeed, poor economic conditions rendered realisation of famine loan difficult. The administration, however, refused 'to sanction the remission of the irrecoverable balance', which had eventually reduced the hill people to bonded labourers of the state. The statement made by the Vice President of Manipur State Durbar reflected the hardship that the hill people had to endure. He reported:

> the recovery of so large an amount must be gradual. Pressure is being constantly brought to bear on the recipients to repay their advances and many of them have been turned out to work as coolies under the State Engineer and their earnings impounded.[63]

As remission would bring loss to the state's budget, the political officers H.W.G. Cole and J.C. Higgins agreed that the cost of rice supplied to the Kukis should be recovered regardless of how long it took in recovering the same to avoid 'losing large sums of money which it is entitled to recover and is capable of recovering'.[64] As officials persisted with the attempt to recover the famine loan from the 'poor and helpless' hill people, some people even migrated to the unadministered territory.[65]

Repayment of famine debt went on for some time. Many of them have their debt cleared or remission by enrolling themselves in the labour corps for the First World War. The Kukis, especially from the southwestern area of the hills, who went to France were those indebted to the state and traders for rice supplied to them during the food scarcity of 1912.[66] Thus, the British Raj continue to demand coolie labourers during the war, although officials in Manipur stressed that condition was not favourable for further recruitment in Manipur. This shows how the colonial state took advantage of the poor economic conditions of the hill people. Based on the assumption that the hill people could be 'induced' to do certain things, Higgins made a suggestion to employ measures that would persuade the hill people to give in and ensure successful recruitment in the future. He wrote that 'the safe return of some of the original labourers, with full pockets and a satisfactory account of the conditions of service may induce recruits to come forward later on'.[67] Thus, Higgins narrowed down the main causes of the hill peoples' reluctance to two issues: lack of safety and comfort. He believed that economic compulsion would motivate them to enrol as coolies for France if they were given the assurance of safety and comfort in conditions of service, not knowing the fact that labour has different meanings to the hill people.

Cultural resistance to labour recruitment

We have seen that their refusal to enrol for the labour corps was often described as due to their long isolation and 'home loving' spirit. They were shown as 'shy' and unwilling not only due to the self-sufficient economy of the hills with no desire for money but also because of their strong fear of the plain:

> The circumstances of the hill districts of Assam differ completely from the plains of India in which labourers ordinarily are recruited. The hillmen generally are home loving, with a great fear and dislike of the plains. They nearly all have their

own cultivation or business and are reasonably well off and contented at home and while some classes of them are in the habit of going down to the plains for short spells in the dry season to earn a little cash, no ordinary wages would induce them to leave their homes and cultivation for long periods.[68]

Indeed, all hill people as 'tribals' have been seen as a geographically isolated, homogenous group of cultivators who supplemented their cultivation with hunting and food gathering (Corbridge 1988). Based on such an understanding of the hill people, officers of the hill districts cited the perceived dislike of the hill people of the plains, reluctance to leave their comfort in the hills, contentment as cultivators and lack of keenness to earn wages in difficult and unfamiliar conditions as reasons for the difficulty to obtain recruits for labour corps in France.

Such argument fail to take into account the reality faced by the hill people in the hills. We have seen that life in the hills was far from comfortable; their livelihood patterns had been disrupted with the interventions of colonialism. The uncomfortable conditions of life in the hills and in the state labour services were hardly the reasons for reluctance to labour in general and to France in particular. With much irritation, the Kukis gave porterage under *pothang* system of Manipur state and in different military expeditions in the region. But participation in the labour corps 'for France' (as it was locally known) has different cultural meaning to the Kukis. Understanding this cultural meaning would explain well into why the Kukis had opposed labour recruitment in the first place and why some of them had to go for it out of economic compulsion due to their indebtedness during the bamboo famine. In this cultural perspective, the conditions of service matter in completely different forms. To most hillmen, serving as labourers in the 'unhealthy' plains and particularly to the 'unknown' land 'beyond-the-sea' (*tuitogal*) had different meanings. In this, the cultural idea of death was central.

The service condition of labour corps for France required them to wait for entrainment in the plains, a long journey across the plain of India and then months of journey over the seas, and then in different war theatres in Europe. Such toiling over the plain was generally known to the hill people as 'detrimental to the health and spirits'.[69] Diseases like cholera, pneumonia, colitis, dysentery, heart failure, and sunstroke, proved fatal to their bodies as to their imagination. They were quite aware of the consequences of such exposure from their earlier experiences as to the cases of those who enrolled themselves in the Labour Corps. Many of them died even before embarkation.[70] Webster, Secretary to the Chief Commissioner of Assam, for instance, noted that all these deaths were 'due to the special hardships and risks to which they were exposed in connection with the mobilisation of the corps'. Deaths from sunstroke and pneumonia that occurred prior to entrainment were, he said, due to 'the inevitable hardships which men accustomed to the hills suffer when they are taken down to the plains in the hot weather'. He described how coolie recruits were taken down in batches along the road on the way to embarkation who after having 'suffered a good deal from the long marches in the heat', were detained in places infected with cholera, without suitable halting camp, while waiting for their train journey. An unhealthy halting place in temporary shelters erected for them led to the 'outbreak of cholera while on the train journey'. Exposure in temporary shelters, indirectly or directly, led to deaths due to pneumonia and heart failure. Thus, it is clear that the coolies were exposed to various hardships and diseases along the 'journey they had to undertake across India' even before they were shipped off to France.[71] Adding to this hardship was the problem of gratuity which was not extended to those who died before embarkation.[72] Thus, the reluctance of the hill people to go to France as coolies was not without any substance, even if we see from the point of service conditions that they were all quite aware of.

However, to see their refusal to join the labour corps based on such service conditions only is to miss an important point. Higgins, for instance, felt that the hill people's misunderstanding of the cause of deaths was central to their opposition to labour recruitment: 'I find they are convinced that the men who were reported as having died of sickness were really killed in fighting'.[73] Fear of death being a universal phenomenon, would the Kukis in this context be so illogical to take up arms and fight the British, who were much more superior to them because they were afraid to die 'fighting'? It was not death per se that concerned the Kukis (although death was nonetheless important to their opposition) but how and where people died while going to the labour corps. Kukis had a very strong concept of death that was central to their cultural worldview, having important meaning in their lifetime. People who died in certain ways are seen as 'unlucky'. For example, it is unlucky if the cause of death is due to an attack from evil spirit or animals or unnatural death like death in war, in flood, falling from trees, etc. There was separate burial rituals for them. The discrimination shown towards such special cases of death is explicit in Hodson's anthropological account about the death ceremonies of the Kukis:

> Special rules exist for the burial of special cases of death. Women who die in . . . childbirth, those who are slain by an enemy . . . killed by a wild beast . . . who die far from their home, of cholera, or some disease or who chance to fall from a tree and are killed, are regarded as peculiarly *unfortunate in their deaths* as the manner of their deaths betoken that they owe their fate to the hostility of some powerful and malignant spirit. The graves of the dead who die in the ways I have enumerated, are dug by a special class of people, sometimes only by the oldest men and women, and in some cases only by the near male relatives. Their graves, too, are nearly always apart and away from the graves of the ordinary dead.
>
> (Hodson 1901: 305–306)

William Shaw also added to the list of unlucky deaths – accident, cholera, yaws, leprosy, small pox, or in battle or child-birth – in which no death ritual was performed (Shaw 1928: 56). The deaths that they heard from, and witnessed to, those who joined the labour corps came under these categories of 'unfortunate' deaths or 'bad death' (*thise*).

To the Kukis, death ritual was very significant for ensuring comfort in the afterlife. In a normal death, the burial ritual was normally elaborate with provisions. The degree of elaborateness in burial ceremonies differed for men and women, common man and chiefs, as well as rich and poor (Hodson 1901: 305–306). But for this to happen, the body of the dead is a must. All rituals revolved around the corpse without which no ceremony can take place. This is clearly visible from the memorandum of the imprisoned Kuki chiefs to the Chief Commissioner (Surma Valley and Hill Districts) who claimed:

> Manipur Lambus . . . told us that all men who went to France are dying . . . the Political Agent came there and we gave Rs.1,500/-, 3 gongs and one mithun . . . requested him not to call coolies from us as it is the custom of the Kukis to bring the head of the dead man wherever he died.[74]

The Kukis believed that a person who died under the category of 'unfortunate' deaths is deprived of a comfortable life in the next world. Their soul wanders around the world subject to all hard-ships. They could not reach *mithikho* (dead-men's village) to join back their family there or have become slave to others who killed them. Therefore, not to die a normal death and the non-performance of any death ritual was something the Kuki feared most in their life-time. In other words, to die a normal death was not only an impor-tant life project to every Kuki, but it was also a project for future life in *mithi-kho*.

Therefore, to the Kukis the idea that 'all men who went to France are dying' was not only the question of fearing death away from home (the unlucky death) but also the question of life after death (depriving comfortable life in the next world). In other words, going to France (to the unknown world 'beyond-the-sea') and exposing their bodies to categories of 'bad death' (*thise*) was a serious cultural question. Rather than the fear of death caused by fighting in a war (as we are make to believe), being exposed to the causes of death categorised as 'unfor-tunate' or 'bad death' was central to the Kukis' opposition to labour recruitment. What were known as customs or sets of rules governing a 'homogenous' people and relevant only in their isolated hills was but a way of being, and beliefs intertwined with people as social/cultural beings. The hesitation to go to France was not because of the simple fear of death from fighting; it was rooted in their cultural notion of death and afterlife.

What we can see from the various causes of the Kuki rising testifies to the multiplicity of factors ranging from social, economic, politi-cal and even cultural. It reminded us of what Corbridge has shown on how the formulation of tribal policies was based on the 'ideology of tribal economy and society'. According to this idea, tribes were depicted as living in an exotic world marked by the love for pleasure over hard labour, egalitarianism and a lack of hierarchical structure. In this scheme of things, cultural matters prevailed in importance over economic issues (Corbridge 1988). Similarly, what becomes significant in the case of Kukis in their fight against colonialism was the predomi-nance of cultural reasoning of things so central to their worldview. In this sense, what appeared to be 'ignorant', 'child-like' and 'primitive' in colonial eyes was not really so in the eyes of the Kukis. The Kukis felt themselves as patriots and freedom fighters who make logical deci-sions and act accordingly. Their decisions were motivated by their eco-nomic and cultural reasoning, keeping in mind their social, economic, political and cultural values of things rather than being 'apt to give way to fits of childish rage and passion'.

Concluding remarks: a people's war against colonialism

If Kuki war against colonial authority was based on the deep-seated grievances over colonial control and domination down to their every-day lifesyles and cultural practices, then how might we characterise such a war? This can be seen broadly in two ways. On the one hand, the war cannot remain as the war of the chiefs but can only be seen in terms of the people's war. On the other hand, a people's war is always with certain clearly defined objective and in the context of the Kuki rising it was a war against colonial regime of domination and control. Binay Bhushan Chaudhuri, for instance, understood the radical movements of tribes/*adivasis*, unlike those with limited aims against specific grievances, an opposition directed against the State. The aim was, according to him, to tear apart the 'structure of domination' and replace it with an 'independent *adivasi* polity' (Chaudhuri 2009). The Kuki resistance to colonialism also shows this overarching aim against domination very clearly. Once a mere opposition to labour recruitment for France began to give way to a radical armed resistance or a 'War' (*gal* in local parlance) for freedom, it was difficult to distinguish, as Prathama Banerjee's study of the Santal rebellion shows, between the rebellious and the non-rebellious (Banerjee 1999: 214). The Kukis from different parts of the hills were now 'joining up' to fight the colonial regime together.[75] The 'young braves' of deserted villages gathered together in a specific hostile village, along with their guns, to resist the armed columns.[76] Groups of men with guns made their way to a village 'to help as the Sahibs were coming'. Three Anal villages, for instance, joined with their guns and requested other Anal villages to also show their support and unity as 'men of one country'. Guns were to be the main weapon of resistance.[77]

In the presence of multiple hill polities, it is not surprising that mobilisation was not carried out through the appeal of any particular leadership figure. Rather than the appeal of a leader, influential village or 'overlordship' that characterised the hill polity, mobilisation of villages within the hills during the rising against the *Sirkar* or British Raj was carried out on the ideology of people's belongingness as 'men of one country' or being people of the same territory. In this case, it was the hills beyond the limitation of one's village. While the colonial state held the chiefs solely responsible for the 'rebellion', the resistance was not the whim of some dictatorial chiefs. The people in one village opposed their chief, who had collected eggs and fowl as the precedence before meeting the Political Officer.[78] This was suggestive of a new world order. The role of an authoritarian chief became defunct during the rising and people's wills came at the forefront.

Ones belongingness to the hills entailed participation in the rising in some way or another. This was because hill villages that refused to move to the valley had to supply rations for the men gathered to fight the punitive columns.[79] Rice was demanded from villages that had not sent men or had refrained from joining in the fight against the Sahib.[80] Rather than their desire or dislike of the rising, it was their connection with or their being of the hill territory that, to a certain extent, determined their participation in the movement. In other words, the mere location of the villages within the hills legitimised and enabled the Kukis to coerce and make demands of rations and food from them. The only way one can distance themselves from the rising was to move out of the hills. Interestingly, all the Kuki villages choose to remain in the hills or refused to move in the valleys when the government asks them to do so. This shows their tacit support to the rising.

With a desire to deprive the Kuki 'rebels' of their 'convenient sources of food supply', the British insisted that those whom they called 'friendly' villages should be removed either to the Manipur or Kubo valley. The idea was not to comfort the 'wretched' hill villages but to deprive the rebel Kukis of food supply. Cosgrave spelt out the objective clearly as follows:

> If we can induce all the friendly . . . villages to settle temporarily in either the Manipur or Kubo valleys and not to cultivate any *jhum*s this year in the hills we ought to find it easier to reduce the rebel Kuki villages to subjection next cold weather if the work cannot be completed before the rains.[81]

Desperate to deplete the food supply of rebels and to encourage the 'friendly' villages to move to the valley, Cosgrave suggested that land should be given temporarily at half rate, or that the women and children be put in concentration camps while the men served as coolies.[82] Interestingly, in their strategy to evade government scheme to dismantle the rising by cutting off their food supplies, the so-called 'friendly' villages came up with all excuses for why they should not be taken down to the valley. For instance, they pointed out specific sites in the valley where they should be settled, their reason being that the 'climate there is cooler' and they could not live in the hot plain.[83] The claim for a particular site or climate tolerable to their bodies and minds was not only to claim for the impossible and their cultural hostility to the plain filled with deadly diseases, but a means to dismantle official policy of transplanting them in the valley. They succeeded in making their point. As such, demands were not acceptable to the government; the so-called 'friendly' villages refused to move in the valley and hence could clandestinely help the 'rebels'. In this way, many of the hill villages who did not directly take part in the fighting had actually joined the war by supplying food and other supplies to the 'rebels'. In the sense noted above, we can see that the War was fought not only by the chiefs and their followers but the whole Kuki population of the hills. They all participated, in one way or the other, in the rising as 'men of one country'.

Besides, the popular participation also dispels the idea that Kuki rising was mainly a Thadou-Kuki's war. The truth is that all the Kuki tribes had joined the war in a different capacity. We have already noted how the Anal villages grouped them together to fight the British forces. The Zous of southern Manipur hills also joined the war in large numbers. Many other Kuki tribes living among the Thadous or in villages mixed up with the Thadou villages also actively participated in the rising. Therefore, to say that the Kuki rising was the chiefs' war against colonialism, or that it was mainly the Thadou chiefs, would miss many points in this respect. Rather, one can say that it was the war fought by all sections of the Kuki population in which the great Thadou chiefs provided the leadership.

People's urge for freedom from authoritarian regime can be seen from the actions of the 'rebels' and from their various expressions they made during the war. It was particularly clear from their actions that the Kukis were fighting against the 'Sahibs' and 'Sarkaris'. Cosgrave, for instance, remarked:

> The Kukis are not out against Manipuris but *only* against the Sahebs and their Subordinates. The Kukis are clever enough to understand that the administration of the Hill tracts of Manipur is not in the hands of the Manipuris but of the Sahibs whom they regard as responsible for all their troubles about the recruitment for the Labour Corps.[84]

Surely the 'troubles' of the Kukis was not only with labour recruitment but it was more to do with the broad forms of domination and control. Their aim therefore was, in Chaudhuri's apt term, 'to tear apart' the 'structure of domination' and replace it with an 'independent *adivasi* polity'. Thus, the Kukis unleashed their power, instead of a mindless attack on anyone, by attacking the signs and symbols of colonial authority – police stations, rest houses, telegraph lines, roadways, chowkidars, postmen, peons, sepoys and so on (Shakespear 1977: 213). Hence, the rising was clearly an expression of discontentment against the domination of the British colonial regime.

From their expressions, one can similarly surmise that Kuki rising was a political movement to free their hill country free from colonial domination. The vision was an independent world where subordination, aggression and exploitation from outside would be absent. They wished that their everyday lives within the hills should not to be disrupted. This is best reflected in a popular song sung among the Zous. They knew the rising as '*Zou Gal*' (Zou War). The English rendition of the *Zou gal* song is instructive:

> The seafaring White Imperialist coils like the 'kiil' plant,
> Tremors of earthquake do quiver the Zo world,
> 'Tis the land of my birth! I shall not part with it!
> Stain'd with blood is my Sword
> That has routed the adversaries of Zoland,
> I shall yet fight with the wild Boar, injured. (as quoted in Zou 2005: 89)

This song reflects two forms of struggle they were daily engaged with in their 'motherland' (the 'land of my birth', generally expressed as 'fatherland' or *pupa-gam* in daily usage). On the one hand, it testified their daily struggle against the '*Kiil*' (a wild creeper that hinder movement in the forest or competed the crops in the field) and the wild-boar (that attacked on their standing crops) – both symbolised their everyday conflict with nature. On the other hand, it depicted their daily struggle against colonialism ('the seafaring white imperialist') who had disrupted their lifeways just like the *kiil* and wild-boar. Just as they struggled hard to get away from the latter, they desired to fight, with their 'stained' sword, the former who had 'routed' their world like the tremors of an earthquake. Thus, instead of being child-like, their notion of the 'War' was rooted in their political vision of their 'motherland', which they refused to 'part with' but aspired to free from all 'adversaries'.

Therefore, the message of the war was put straight forward – the 'white imperialist' should not undermine the political status of the Kukis. They should not treat them as the oppressed subordinates who lacked any political desire for self-determination and freedom. Such political vision of a freed 'fatherland' was also later clearly expressed before William Shaw, the official ethnographer of the Thadou-Kukis. Shaw recorded that the Kukis strongly felt 'they are destined to be rulers of their earth and not to be submissive to any one' (Shaw 1928: 50). He has also noted that even after their defeat in the 'Kuki rebellion' and their prestige among other hill tribes has been much shaken with the establishment of three hill subdivisions, they continued to aspire for their 'Raj' or an 'independent *adivasi* polity' in Chaudhuri's apt term. He said: 'Their tails are not down and I have heard said that they hope to become a "Raj" some day' (Shaw 1928: 23). He went on noting that 'they do not consider themselves beaten yet and still brood over the future ahead of them which to their sorrow, is not developing as fast as they would like' (Shaw 1928: 50). This 'future' appeared during the Second World War when the Indian National Army (INA) and the Japanese Army opened up the 'Eastern Gate' but ended again in disarray when the two global forces were defeated in the battles of Imphal and Kohima in 1944. Thus ended another hope to become a 'Raj'.

Acknowledgements: This paper is a revised version of a chapter in my Ph.D. dissertation. I would like to thank my supervisor, Dr. Sangeeta Dasgupta, for her helpful comments.

Notes

1 Manipur State Archives (hereafter MSA), Imphal, Acc. No. R-1/S-A/74: 'Progress of Operation Against Kukis, 1918'.
2 MSA, Acc. No., R-1/S-C/191: 'Progress of Events in Manipur in Connection With the Kuki Disturbances- 1919, Telegram dated 18/1/1918.
3 MSA, Acc. No. 39, R-N-2/S-A, Administration Report of the Manipur State, 1917–1918.
4 See MSA, Acc. No., R-1/S-C/191: 'Progress of the Events in Manipur in Connection with the Kuki Disturbances, 1919; Acc. No.R-1/S-A/74, 'Progress of Operations against Kukis-1918'.
5 MSA, Acc. No. 38, R-N-2/S-A, Administration Report of the Manipur State 1916–1917, p. 1.
6 Manipur Secretariat Library (hereafter MSL), Imphal, Cabin No. 28: A.H. Bingley, Secretary to the GOI, Army Department to the Chief Commissioner of Assam, 11 June 1917, Secret File.
7 MSL, Cabin No. 28, 'Proceedings of a Conference held at Government House, Shillong on the 22 June 1917 in Files about the raising of 2nd Manipur Labour Corps'.
8 National Archives of India (hereafter NAI), New Delhi, Foreign and Political Department, Secret-External Proceedings, July 1918, Nos. 7–131: 'Rebellion of the Kuki tribes in Manipur and in the Upper Chindwin's District in Burma and of the Chins in the Southern Chin Hills. Reports on the Operations Against Them', (hereafter, Rebellion of Kuki Tribes . . . Operations Against Them), Webster's letter, 7 November 1917.
9 MSA, Acc. No. 12, R-1/S-A: Tour Diary of J.C. Higgins, Esq, I.C.S, Political Officer, Southern Kuki (Sugnu, Mombi), Column No.1, (hereafter Tour Diary of J.C. Higgins), for January-February 1918.

10 MSA, Acc. No. 232, R-1/S-D: 'Kuki Rebellion, 1920', Foreign and Political Department Secret E Proceedings, November 1920, Nos.105–107 (hereafter, Kuki Rebellion 1920).

11 MSA, Tour Diary of J.C Higgins, for Jan-Feb 1918.

12 MSA, Kuki Rebellion, 1920.

13 MSA, Tour Diary of J.C.Higgins, for October 1917.

14 MSA, Acc,No.74,R-1/S-A, 'Progress of the Operations Against Kukis, 1919'.

15 MSA, Acc,No.74,R-1/S-A, 'Progress of the Operations Against Kukis, 1919'.

16 MSA, Tour Diary of J.C Higgins, for Jan-Feb 1918. See also MSA, Webster's Letter Dated 5.1.1918 Camp, Vaselui; NAI, Webster's Letter dated 25 January, 1918, in 'Rebellion of the Kuki tribes . . . Operations Against Them'.

17 NAI, Webster's Letter dated 25 January, 1918, in 'Rebellion of the Kuki tribes . . . Operations Against Them'.

18 MSA, Office Copies of the Tour Diary of W.A. Cosgrave, Esquire I.C.S Political Agent in Manipur from January to March 1918, (hereafter Tour Diary of Cosgrave 1918), dated 22 January,1918.

19 MSA, Tour Diary of Cosgrave 1918, dated 14 January 1918; MSA, R-1/S-A/74 Letter from W.A. Cosgrave to J.E. Webster.

20 See for instance, MSA, Acc. No.R-1/S-1–8: Tour Dairy of Maxwell, the Political Agent of Manipur [hereafter Maxwell Diary], December, 1904.

21 Maxwell Diary, December, 1904.

22 MSA, R-1/S-A/20, Diary of Cosgrave, 9 April 1908.

23 MSL, Cabin No 1: Diary of W.A Cosgrave Political Agent in Manipur for the Month of December 1918.

24 MSA, Acc. No.R-1/S-A/12, Higgins Diary, 31 March, 1917.

25 MSL, Cabin No, 1. Cosgrave Diary, 28 March, 1919.

26 MSL, Cabin No, 1. Cosgrave Diary, 18 March, 1919.

27 MSA, Accession No.R-1/S-A/12, Higgins Diary, 9 July, 1916.

28 MSA, Acc. No. R-1/S-A/12: Higgins Diary, 18 April 1916. A British officer reports about a ' party of Nepali herdsmen from the Kabow valley with over 250 buffaloes, going to settle at Khuga'.

29 MSL, Cabin No, 1. Cosgrave Diary, May 1918.

30 MSL, Cabin No, 1. Cosgrave Diary, April 1918.

31 MSL, Cabin No, 1. Cosgrave Diary, 8 August, 1919.

32 MSA, Acc. No. R-1/S-A/20: Diary of W.A. Cosgrave, 8 March 1908.

33 MSA, Administration Report of the Manipur Political Agency, 1893.

34 MSA, Acc. No. R-1/S-A/20: Cosgrave Diary, 21 December 1908.

35 MSL, Cabin No.1, Sl. No. 8, Shakespear Diary, 2 May 1905.

36 MSL, Cabin No.1, Sl. No. 8, Shakespear Diary, 12 April 1905.

37 For the Naga custom of 'Oath' taking in solving disputes see Hodson (1974: 109–113).

38 MSL, Cabin No.1, Sl. No. 8, Shakespear Diary, 2 May 1905.

39 MSL, Cabin No.1, Sl. No. 8, Shakespear Diary, 2 May 1905.

40 MSL, Cabin No.1, Sl. No. 9, Political Agent's diary for 1912–1913, 16 January 1913.

41 MSA, Acc. No.R-1/S-A/20, Cosgrave Diary, 25 February, 1908.

42 MSA, Cosgrave Diary, 10 February, 1918.

43 According to the treaty of 1833 signed between the British Government and the Manipur Valley State, the Raja had agreed to furnish a number of Nagas to assist in the construction of the road between the territories of the British government and Manipur, to provide hill porters to assist in transporting the ammunition and baggage of British troops in case of war with Burma. See Mackenzie (1979: 151).

44 MSA, Administration Report of the Manipur Political Agency for 1892–93.

45 MSL, Cabin No. 16: Summary of events in Manipur, 1911–1912.

46 MSL, Cabin 24, Call. No. 25 XXV: Maxwell Reports 1901.

47 Ibid.

48 Ibid.

49 Ibid.

50 MSA, Acc. No. R-1/S-1–8, Maxwell Diary, 17 February 1900.

51 MSL, Cabin No. 1, Woods Diary, 20 March 1904 [emphasis added].

52 MSA, Higgins Diary, 10 August 1916.

53 MSA, Acc. No. R-1/S-A-20, Diary of W.A.Cosgrave, 9 April, 1908.

54 For instance the 'impressed hillmen' who were detained for six months during the operation against Kuki rebels, began to grumble as they wanted to get back to their villages and cultivation. MSL, Cabin No. 1, Diary of W.A Cosgrave Political Agent in Manipur for the Month of March 1919.

55 Woods Diary, 15 March 1904, Cabin No.1, MSL.

56 MSA, Acc. No. R-1/S-B/32, Summary of Events in Manipur 1908–1911, 24 February 1911.

57 MSL, Cabin No. 38, File No.156, Extract from Mr. Higgins's diary for May and June 1912 in 'Supply of rice to Hillmen'.

58 MSL, Cabin No. 38, File No.156: J.C. Higgins to J. Shakespear, 9 April 1912.

59 MSL, Cabin No. 38, File No.156: J. Shakespear to Chief Secretary, Assam, 11 May 1912.

60 MSL, Cabin No. 38, File No.156: Short Summary of Tipaimukh Mohurrir's report dated 26.9.12.

61 MSL, Cabin No. 1. Diary of Major J. Shakespear, Political Agent of Manipur for 1912–1913 [hereafter Shakespear Diary], November 1912.

62 MSL, Cabin No. 1. Shakespear Diary, 1 December 1912 to 5 January 1913.

63 MSL, Cabin No. 38, File No.156: Vice President Manipur State Darbar to the Comptroller, Assam, 11 March 1915.

64 MSL, Cabin No. 38, File No.156: Cole to the Comptroller of Assam, 24 March 1915.

65 MSL, Cabin No. 38, File No.156: Higgins to the Political Agent in Manipur, 19 January 1915.

66 MSL, Special File No. 239: Note by W.A. Cosgrave, Political Agent in Manipur, dated 30 June 1918 in Office of the Political Agent in Manipur.

67 MSL, Cabin No. 28, File No. xxxiv: JC Higgins, Officiating Political Agent in Manipur to the Chief Secretary, Assam, 2 November 1917.

68 MSL, Cabin No. 28, File No. xxxiv: J.E. Webster to Secretary to the Central Recruiting Board, Shimla, 30 August 1917.

69 MSL, Cabin No. 28, File No. xxxiv: J.C. Higgins to Chief Secretary, Assam, 2 November 1917.

70 This is evidence in the list of labourers who died after enrolment but before embarkation. See MSL, Cabin No. 28, File No. xxxiv: Chief Secretary, Assam to the Adjutant General in India, Shimla, 22 August 1917.

71 Ibid.

72 A request for considering the cases of some families in Manipur reads: 'Certain men of the Manipuri labour corps died previous to embarkation, and their relatives do not understand . . . invidious distinction which deprives them of their gratuity'. See MSL, Cabin No. 28, File No. xxxiv: J.C. Higgins to Chief Secretary, Assam, 2 November 1917.

73 MSL, Cabin No. 28, File No. xxxiv: JC Higgins to J.E. Webster, 24 September, 1917.

74 NAI, Office of the Political Agent, Special file No. 385, 1919, as quoted in Chishti, The Kuki Uprising in Manipur, pp. 45–46.

75 Cosgrave was informed that Kukis of Chassad areas from the East had joined Kukis of Mombi area. MSA, Cosgrave Diary, 5 January 1918.

76 MSA, Cosgrave Diary, 31 January 1918.

77 MSA, Acc. No. R-1/S-A/74, 'Information from Sugnu Resthouse Chaukidar', 24 January 1918, 'Progress of Operations against Kukis'.

78 MSA, Cosgrave Diary, 23 January, 1918.

79 MSA, Cosgrave Diary, 4 February, 1918.

80 MSA, Cosgrave Diary, 3 February, 1918.

81 Ibid.

82 MSA, Cosgrave Diary, 7 February, 1918.

83 MSA, Cosgrave Diary, 4 February, 1918.

84 MSA, Cosgrave Diary, 24 January 1918.

References

Allen, B.C. 1980 [1905]. *Naga Hills and Manipur: Socio-Economic History.* New Delhi: Mittal Publications.

Banerjee, Prathama. 1999. 'Historic Acts? Santal Rebellion and the Temporality of Practices', *Studies in History*, 15 (2): 209–244.

Bhadra, Gautam. 1975. 'The Kuki (?) Uprising (1917–1919): Its Causes and Nature', *Man in India*, 55 (1): 10–56.

Bower, Ursula Graham. 1986 [1950]. *Naga Path: Adventure to Naga Inhabited Areas.* London: Murray.

Chaudhuri, Binay Bhushan. 2009. 'Revaluation of Tradition in the Ideology of the Radical Adivasi Resistance in Colonial Eastern India, 1855–1932 Part I', *Indian Historical Review*, 36 (2): 273–305.

Corbridge, Stuart. 1988. 'The Ideology of Tribal Economy and Society: Politics in the Jharkhand, 1950–1980', *Modern Asian Studies*, 22 (1): 1–42.

Dasgupta, Sangeeta. 1999. 'Reordering a World: The Tana Bhagat Movement, 1914–1919', *Studies in History*, 15 (1): 1–41.

Dena, Lal. 2008. *British Policy Towards Manipur, 1762–1947.* Imphal: Nongeen Publications.

Dun, E.W. 1975 [1886]. *Gazetteer of Manipur.* New Delhi: Vivek Publishing House.

Hodson, T.C. 1901. 'The Native Tribes of Manipur', *The Journal of the Anthropological Institute of Great Britain and Ireland*, 31: 305–306.

Hodson, T.C. 1974 [1911]. *The Naga Tribes of Manipur*. New Delhi: Low Price Publication.

Mackenzie, Alexander. 1979 [1884]. *The North-East Frontier of India*. New Delhi: Mittal Publications.

Reid, Robert. 1997 [1942]. *History of the Frontier Areas Bordering on Assam from 1883–1941*. Guwahati: Spectrum Publications.

Sarkar, Tanika. 1985. 'Jitu Santal's Movement in Malda: A Study in Tribal Protest', in Ranajit Guha (ed.), *Subaltern Studies IV: Writings on South Asian History and Society*, pp. 136–164. New Delhi: Oxford University Press.

Shakespear, J.W. 1977 [1929]. *History of the Assam Rifles*. Aizawl: Tribal Research Institute (TRI).

Shaw, William. 1928. 'Notes on the Thadou Kukis', edited with introduction, notes, appendices, illustrations and index by J.H. Hutton. *Journal of the Asiatic Society of Bengal* (n.s.), XXIV: 78–79.

Skaria, Ajay. 1997. 'Shades of Wildness, Tribes, Caste and Gender in Western India', *The Journal of Asian Studies*, 56 (3) (August): 726–745.

Zou, David Vumlallian. 2005. 'Raiding the Dreaded Past: Representations of Headhunting and Human Sacrifice in North-East India', *Contributions to Indian Sociology* (n.s), 39 (1): 75–105.

7

'SPEAK AS ONE FREE NATION'

Significance of the Kuki war council

Sonthang Haokip

Lheppon bang kitho tin, nam cham khat in vabang pao tadite.

(Let us stand together like folded clothes; like birds, let us speak as one free nation)

– *Anglo-Kuki War song*

Historians often view that tribal people had no clear notion of 'war' and whatever wars they fought were often reduced to a civilisational category like 'raids', 'outrages' or worst, 'savagery' and 'barbaric'. This civilisational category has its own historical juncture as to its categorical discourse, both of which relates to the coming of 'state' and 'civilisation'. It was thought, and perhaps it is still, that any society lacking 'state' is lacking 'civilisation' and any society lacking both lacks all the notions that the two have. Hence, such society was often seen as 'savage', 'barbarian' and 'primitive'. Under such category, the non-state tribal hill people were also invariably fitted. It was within this dichotomous reconstruction of society into state and non-state, civilised and uncivilised that the idea of warfare also been trapped in and subjectivised. Thus, the war fought by the tribal people can never come under the popular civilisational category of 'war'. Instead, it was categorised as 'raid', 'savage warfare' or 'barbaric'. If some modification is made on these old civilisational categories, the term 'little war' still carries the stigma. Unlike the 'civilised warfare' called 'war', which was fought between two states or societies with the specific aim of tangible or untangible, and with certain morality, the war fought by the tribal people was thought to be savage because it was indiscriminate, brutal and lacking any objective.[1]

This chapter argues that such civilisational categorisation has no place in reality and was largely artificial and a myth. The truth is that no war fought by any society in history is lacking any aim or morality, and every war, from a pacifist approach, is savage and barbaric. Besides, the very dichotomy that the war fought by the state is 'civilised' and the tribe is 'savage' can often reverse in the battleground when the two meet. The case of the Anglo-Kuki War is one significant point to address on this aspect of warfare. Here, the British colonial state that claimed to be the most advanced and civilised society of the time indulged in all sorts of 'barbaric' and 'inhuman' acts of warfare, like indiscriminate and systematic burning of 'rebel' villages, properties, foodstuffs, livestock and driving the hapless women, children and aged into the jungle under chilling winter and hunting them down from pillar to post to capture them. Whosoever they caught was incarcerated in the 'concentration camps', where they were asked to do all odd jobs. On the other hand, the so-called tribal Kuki hillmen maintained a good sense of what is often regarded as 'civilised warfare', such as having a clear definition of their enemy targets such as the British government or the 'sahibs' and 'sarkaris', avoiding indiscriminate attack on people, of the war aims of freeing their country, protecting their reputation and so on. The Kuki war showed a clear idea of their notion of war in general and how they started this war in particular, which evaded the dominant notion of 'raid' carried out by some hot-headed brigands for a particular local aim or grudge. The Anglo-Kuki War shows clearly how the Kukis took decisions to go for the war in their traditional War Council (*Sathin-salung-neh* or *Hansa-neh*), usually taken up by their highest political body, the grand chiefs-in-council (the *Haosa Inpi*). In this chapter, the significance of this Kuki War Council during the Anglo-Kuki War 1917–1919 will be discussed.

Understanding the Kuki war and its war council

Like in every society, war is a grand public affair among the Kukis. As a rule, war (*gal*) is an important public affair in which the whole village is involved. In a war between two or more villages, a village war council was usually held in the chief's house and a ceremonial war rite was performed by feasting on the *sathin-salung-neh* (feasting on the liver and heart of animal killed for the purpose), also called *hansaneh*. Under the leadership of the chief or a chosen leader, all the able men in the village set out for the war. Before the party leaves, the village priest (*thempu*) make a mixture from the *ai* plant and then anointing each warrior on the forehead and says: 'May your enemies become stupefied so that you may kill them easily and may Pathen bring you safely back with many heads on your count'. This is called *Gal-lhim*. The whole village will then send them off with food and other items until a certain distance from the village. If the party return with success, the village turns out in full strength with drums and horns and the party will then sing the song called *Hanla*. They then enter the village in procession. Soon after they arrive in the village, a victory celebration is done where *Minlo* or *kiminlo* is done by reciting the genealogical tree of the warrior who had taken head. Special headdress called *thu'pa* is worn on the knot of the successful warrior as a mark of great deed. For three days, they are fed on food separately cooked and eaten off banana leaves. This food is called *Gal-an*.[2]

The word '*shim*' is used to mean 'surprise raid'. When a Kuki go to a war, he would use the term '*shim*' in which they attacked the enemy village when they are least prepared, usually at the wee hour and after killing as much they could they would rapidly withdraw. *Shim* signifies an aggression to enemy village. *Veng* is another term which means 'defend', connoting a defensive policy. If the village is big, it is divided into *veng* for defensive purpose, each having one or more *som* (bachelor's house). In pre-colonial period, village fortification was usually maintained for defensive purpose. When there was imminent danger from enemy, certain *chang* (stockades) would be put up on the warpaths and guarded by the warriors against an approaching enemy. The tactics of warfare changed from case to case depending upon the type of enemy one confronted. Sniping and guerilla warfare was usually employed against the large state forces when stockades will become quite elaborate and the war fought on a much larger conglomeration of villages. This happened in the past against the army of the surrounding kingdoms like Manipur, Tripura, Cachar and Burma.

To fight against the state aggressive policy applied only to the colonial sense of 'raid' on its frontier villages and defensive by sniping and attacking to its forces once it climbed out the hills. Since a much larger force is needed to fight against them, the cooperation of either certain cognate villages or the whole tribal community is necessary. For each of this, the Kukis also have a peculiar traditional council to deliberate and decide upon the matter. If the choice amounts to group of villages, the chiefs of these villages would sit in council and decide, and plan for the war. If it is based on tribal community, the grand tribal war council was convened for the same purpose. Although many non-chief or representatives may participate in this war council, it was invariably the 'assembly of chiefs' or chiefs-in-council (*haosa inpi*). This war council was the focal point of unity during the war. It was this body which decided whether they should go to war or not; if so, how should they go about it and what would be their objectives? It was decided clearly on this line and then only mobilisation and preparation for the war could begin.

There are some important features of the Kuki War Council. If a war council is held based on clan, then seniority accordingly on genealogical tree is invariably invoked but in the deliberation of the matter expertise and age becomes influential. If war council is held based on community and of conglomeration of different clan groups, then it was purely based on egalitarian or democratic lines, where all the participating chiefs from different villages expressed freely and decisions were taken on majority opinion. Those who are not inclined to go with majority opinion could not be compelled to go for the war, although they would be naturally insisted to do so. If the war council was based on clan, the *pipa* (head) of that clan invariably convened the assembly of chiefs of that clan. If the war council was based on community or tribal, anyone of the clan heads (*pipa*) may convene based on the place of convenience or of his political stature.

Once a decision is arrived at in the war council, the resolution was solemnised with a sacred ceremony called *sathin-salung-neh*. This is the feasting together of all the participants in the council on the liver and heart of the animal killed to commemorate the grand council. The Kukis believed that the strength of a person lies in the size of liver and heart.[3] Thus, a cowardly person was usually called *thinkhaneo* (small liver) and *lungneo* (small heart). Therefore, feasting on the heart and liver was very significant on that count. It gives the partaker of the feast not only the courage, but it was also believed that it gave a person more strength and audacity. Liver especially strengthened the heart and gave courage. Since *sathin-salung-neh* is related to power, strength and courage, it was also sometimes called *hansaneh* (lit. courage meat eating, meaning the feast of bravery). *Sathin-salung-neh* is also performed when an important decision is taken between two or more people. The idea is that apart from giving them strength and courage, it was a sacred ritual that binds all the partakers to stick with the resolution. In other words, it signified the unbreakable vow taken among the members. As the resolution was taken in a group, no one could break it unilaterally. In short, it was a vow that could not be broken.

Another interesting feature of the Kuki war council was that while all the participants will feast on *sathin-salung* and the meat of animal killed, part of the meat will be split into pieces for distribution. These pieces of flesh called *sajam* were then circulated around the hills among those villages who could not attend the war council so that they should also symbolically consume the meat as a sign of acceptance of the decision to go to war and then join the war. This process of mobilising the people for the war was called *sajam-lhah* (passing off meat). While *sajam* was normally sent to particular chiefs and villages to perform or be part of the same oath taken in the war council, there was also another practice to inform the masses about the decision to go to war called *thinkho-le-malchapom*. It is a smouldering firewood bound with red chilli. Sometimes other items like gunpowder, bullet, beads, etc. could go along with this. It was analogous to the 'fiery cross' to inform the people that war has been declared and preparation should start in earnest. It was also a warning to those who would like to abstain from the war that any disobedience to the proclamation will be met with punishment. While *sajam-lhah* may be performed for other important decisions taken by the chiefs-in-council, *thingkho-le-malchapom* is directly related to the war. These set of Kuki war symbols are discussed in detail in other chapters in this volume. I just want to show here their connection with the Kuki war conclave as a method to communicate to the public about the important decisions taken.

It is customary and established practice among the Kukis that no war, how small it would have been, can be fought unless a war council was convened and a ceremonial *sathin-salung-neh* was performed. This is a peculiar custom that marked out the Kukis from among the numbers of tribes in the region. This is a highly cultured practice whose analogous comparison was found in the King's war council of the state or of similar war councils in democratic societies. The strong sense of the war conclave excluded the dominant civilisational notion that the tribal people have no established concept of war and all the wars they fought were but savagery and raid. As war council is not regularly formed unless war becomes eminent, it escaped the eyes of most colonial ethnographers. Otherwise, it was a well-established practice among the Kuki-Chin people, which have been invoked whenever needed.

Kuki war councils during the Anglo-Kuki War

Scholars have often misunderstood the distinction between war councils and other councils organised by the chiefs-in-council during the Anglo-Kuki War. We have information from colonial archives and local sources that several number of chiefs-in-councils were convened since March 1917 in different parts of the Kuki hills such as in Aisan, Chassad, Jampi, Taloulong, Laijang, Henglep, Ukha, Lonpi, Longya, Sangnao etc. Not only one council was held in each place, but in certain places councils were held again and again as the situation demanded.

But it is very difficult to say for sure which of these councils was actually the war council and which of them was the chiefs-in-council for other matters. However, it is necessary to maintain differentiation between those chiefs conclaves held before October 1917 and those held after this date. Although the chiefs-in-councils held in the former are important and decisive, it is doubtful whether we can call them war councils. But certainly those councils held after the burning of Mombi (Lonpi) on 17 October 1917 were all in the nature of war councils. It should be remembered that the 'assembly of chiefs' before October 1917 were mainly to decide on the question of labour recruitment where it was resolved that no man should be sent for France. Although some utter the use of force, peaceful resolution was the general opinion maintained until Lonpi was burned. Detail discussion on this aspect is given in chapter 1 of this volume. The councils convened after the burning of Lonpi in October 1917 were not only more prominent than those of the previous ones were, but they were directly concerned with war and strategy to fight against British colonialism. Before we come to the details of these chiefs-in-councils, let us see how they have been recorded in colonial archives.

J.C. Higgins reported that Chengjapao, chief of Aishan, was the first to kill a mithun in his village and 'send round the flesh to other Kukis, inciting them to swear an oath, sealed by eating the flesh, not to go to France'.[4] Aishan's announcement was followed by a series of councils held in different parts of Kuki hills – Chassad, Jampi, Taloulong, Mombi, Ukha, Henglep, etc. For instance, H.W. Cole, the Political Agent in Manipur, reported that Chengjapao (chief of Aishan), Khutinthang (chief of Jampi), Pache (chief of Chassad), and Ngullen (chief of Khongjang), 'have taken an oath after killing a mythan (mithun) that none of them would go to France or send any of their people there'.[5] Higgins also reported that Khutinthang 'killed a mithun as far back as March last and distributed portions of the flesh throughout the hills, thereby inducing other chiefs not to send their men'. He also 'sent emissaries to the Haokips in the eastern hills and the tribes near the Chin and Lushai borders'. Similarly, Pache also, in March, before he was called on to send coolies, 'killed a mithun and sent the flesh to other chiefs, urging them to refuse to recruit men for the labor corps'.[6]

We also have another round of series of council held in different parts of Kuki hills after the burning of Lonpi on 17 October 1917. Indication from the official reports show that war councils were held in different parts of the hills after the burning of Lonpi. It was reported that Lonpi people went back to their village and its chief Ngulkhup declared his country 'closed' to the Sahibs and Sarkaris and sent a bead to Pache, chief of Chassad, to inform his decision and ask him to take a similar attitude.[7] On 31 October 1917, Higgins also reported that 22 chiefs of the Haokip villages round Moirang had met at Ukha with 40 guns and decided not to send coolies to France and *to resist forcibly* any attempt to arrest them or burn their villages'.[8] They also informed their decision to Chassad.[9] He also reported that Tintong, chief of Laijang, also went to Henglep during the same time to attend the war council there.[10] On the other hand, indication was also made that there was another war council held at Jampi. Higgins reported that Khutinthang 'has recently been in communication with the chiefs of Mombi and Chassad with a view to concerted resistance to any attempt at coercion or arrest'.[11] Once all these regional war councils were formed and all have asked the Chassad chief to convene the grand chiefs-in-council, Pache eventually invited them all in his village for the War Council. Higgins reported that 'the latest information to hand indicates that Pachei chief of Chassad had called him [Khutinthang] to a council [at Chassad]'.[12]

The Chassad War Council was reported by the Burma authority which took place somewhere at 'the end of November or beginning of December' 1917. J.B. Marshall, DC Upper Chindwin District, reported:

> About the end of November or beginning of December [1917] also a big meeting of the Kuki Chiefs was held at Chassad. About 150 chiefs are said to have been present including Pase [Pache], chief of Chassad, Ngulkhup chief of Mombi, Ngulbul, another south Manipur chief, and Shempu, chief of south Somra. At this meeting, it was *resolved not to obey any orders or summons* from Government and *to fight* if Government tried to enforce orders.[13]
>
> (Emphasis added)

Reports from Manipur also confirm the participation of Ngulkhup (Chief of Lonpi) and Khutinthang (chief of Jampi). After the Chassad war council, Higgins also reported that Pache 'sent a bullet to the chiefs of Jampi, Ukha, Songphu, Henglep and Loibol with instruction to resist forcibly any attempt to impress coolies or to burn villages'.[14]

In the southern hills, among the 'Manhlun Manchung Kukis' [Zous], it was also reported that Henthang chief of Buksao killed a *mithun* and convened a war council at Buksao where 'they have decided to make war on the sirkar, help Ukha and kill the sahibs'.[15] Such war councils were also occasionally held in different places during the war when

204

the need arose. For instance, after the withdrawal of military troops from the hills in order to refit during the rain, it was reported that there was a gathering of Kukis at Tingai Mangol (Tingkai Mangkho-on). It was also reported that a large gathering of 'the Haokips and Manhlun Manchong Kuki association' was held at Tuidam to decide on the 'stringent measures' to be taken 'to breakdown the stockades of the British Government at Kaupum, Tengnoupal, Moirang, Shugnu, Ukhrul, Dulin, Kangchupkhul' and to decide the case of punishment to 'people of the friendly villages of Government'.[16] Once the question of clemency was floated by the government, we also see a series of councils held in different places to decide whether they should surrender or not. For instance, Thangkhong Kuki interpreter had reported that he met 17 Kuki chiefs at Lonpi who were willing to surrender if 'they are not sent to jail', and the Lonpi chief had told him that he is afraid to surrender alone and hence called a big gathering of Kukis on 25 October 1918 to decide on the question of surrender.[17]

The above councils are what the colonial archives had recorded. There were many more such chiefs councils held in different places which are not recorded. What is significant from the above recorded grand chiefs' councils are two major and different resolutions taken. The councils before October 1917 resolved not to send any men for the labour corps to France and were followed by *sajam-lhah*. However, the councils that followed the burning of Lonpi in October mainly talk about war and resolution 'to fight' and 'resist forcibly' against the government. They were generally followed, not by *sajamlhah*, but mostly by symbols of war like bullets, *thingkho-le-malchapom*, gunpowders, beads, swords, etc. as their 'fiery-cross'. The differences are significant in that while the former chiefs-in-councils were generally meant to take a major decision on contribution of labour, whereas the former councils were purely of war councils. It would be interesting to discuss on few of these councils so that we can have better insight into the significance of the Kuki 'assembly of chiefs'.

The Jampi war conclave, November 1917

Historians had created so much of confusion over the Jampi conclaves that it is quite difficult to reconstruct properly. It was assumed that there was only one such conclave at Jampi, which is not true. As the political centre of the northwestern Kukis, there were at least two major conclaves at Jampi, as noted above. The first chiefs-in-council (*haosa inpi*) at Jampi was held in March 1917 and another conclave was held after the burning of Lonpi. There was much discussion on the role of Tintong Haokip, chief of Laijang, whenever the Jampi meeting is discussed. But Tintong had recorded before the Advisory Committee at Kohima in May 1919 that he was not present at the Jampi conclave in March 1917. It was also recorded that the Jampi meeting in March was 'a council of the Shitlo [Shitlhou] chiefs'.[18] However, Tintong was said to be at the chiefs' meeting at Taloulong, which was a much larger chiefs-in-council. Besides, the much talked Jampi meeting mostly talked about 'war', whereas the March meeting was concerned mainly with 'not sending labourers to France'. Therefore, most of the narratives collected from oral sources on the Jampi conclave could have been related to the war conclave convened by the same chief at Jampi after the burning of Lonpi. We have seen that chief Khotinthang had informed others of the decision taken in his area to Pache of Chassad and Ngulkhup of Lonpi. In the sense noted above, the Jampi war conclave of October/November 1917 may be explained here, mainly by shifting the available narrative.

The chiefs who attended the Jampi War Council were, apart from Khotinthang who convened the council, Tintong Haokip (chief of Laijang), Songchung Sitlhou (Sangnao), Lunkholal Sitlhou (Chongjang), Letkhothang Haokip (Loikhai), Vumngul Kipgen and his son Lhunjangul (Tujang), Enjakhup Kholhou (Thenjang), Leothang Haokip (Goboh), Mangkho-on Haokip (Tingkai), Heljason Haokip (Loibol), Onpilen Haokip (Joupi), Onpilal Haokip (Santing), Jamkhokhup (Boljang) and Nguljahen Haokip (Boljang) (Doungel 1986: 27–28; Haokip 1988: 89; Haokip 2008: 154). The meeting was marked by heated exchanges of words among the chiefs. Songchung talked about the might of the British government and felt that declaring war against them would be disastrous to the Kukis (Kipgen 1982: 42). Lhunjangul expressed his unwillingness to wage war at such a critical juncture when the number of arms and ammunitions was inadequate (Haokip 1984: 24).

However, all the other chiefs were in favour of not surrendering to the government and to go to war if the government insisted on enforcing their orders. Of the most vocal chiefs in this meeting was Tintong Haokip, chief of Laijang, after taking the names of his ancestors, and firing his gun at point blank, he retorted: 'Even if I am alone, I will fight the "white men" until my last bullet and gunpowder' (*Kachangseh hijongleng kameichang le kameilou abei masangsea mikangte kakap ding ahi*) (Haokip 1984: 25; Kipgen 1982: 42). He also said that, 'If ever there was a time to fight the "white-men", now is the opportune time' (Haokip 1984: 25). Tintong also cut down the tail of *Mithun* meant for the council (Haokip 1984: 24). He was eventually chosen to

be the 'General' for the war in the area (Kipgen 1982: 42). It was probably on this occasion that the chief of Jampi, Khotinthang Sitlhou,
assumed the title 'Raja' and Tintong as the 'Bara Sahib'. Mithun was
killed to commemorate the occasion and *sathin-salung-neh* ceremony
was performed by all those present in the war council. Thus, a powerful confederacy of the Kuki Chiefs in this area was eventually formed
(Kipgen 1982: 42).

The Chassad war conclave, November/ December 1917

Much confusion was also created by historians on Chassad conclaves.
We have seen that there were also at least two major chiefs' conclaves
at Chassad. The first was held in the month of March 1917 and the
second was reported to be at the end of November or beginning of
December 1917. We have also noted that while the former conclave
concerned mainly 'to refuse to recruit men for the labour corps', the
later was purely a war council, where a decision was taken 'not to
obey any orders or summons' and 'to fight' if the government tried to
enforce orders. The importance of the Chassad War Council lies not
only in the fact that the final resolution to go to war was taken, but it
was also the largest and most significant council where a decision was
taken on 'national' lines and where 150 Kuki chiefs from India and
Burma participated. The Chassad chief Pache (Lhukhomang) killed
mithuns to commemorate the grand occasion. The chiefs present also
performed the sacred war rite *sathin-salung-neh* and vowed to stand
together until the last leg. The importance of this war conclave at
Chassad is also shown by the song composed by Pache to commemorate the 'Assembly of Chiefs' (as quoted in Haokip 2008: 151–152):

Phai chungnung kol kimvel'e;
Kolmang tolkon;
Ikal lhangphai thin eisem gom me;
Phai thin sem gome;
Lheppon bang kitho tin;
Nam cham khat in vabang pao tadite

Translation:

From all around the valley of Manipur;
From beyond the horizon of Burma;
The valley storm brought us together;

The valley storm had brought us together;
Let us stack together (stand together) like the folded clothes;
Like the birds, let us speak (fight) as one free nation.

This connotes the political significance of the Chassad War Conclave in which all the gathering chiefs vowed to stand together like 'folded clothes' against the great storm, the British empire, and also promised to speak in one voice like 'the birds'. It reiterated that they were 'one free nation'.

Apart from these two large 'Assembly of Chiefs', the war councils, we also have many other chiefs-in-councils held at different places since March 1917. We already noted some of them, which have been recorded. Besides them, there were also meetings at Sangnao in March, Khonjang, Laijang, Ukha, Henglep, Mombi, Joujang, Phailenjang, Haflong and Mechangbung.[19]

Conclusion: the significance of the Kuki war council

The significance of Kuki war conclaves or councils lies not only in shaping the character of the Kuki war but also the dimensions in which the Kuki war should be understood. It characterised the Kuki war as a 'national' war fought against an established 'enemy', not merely as a 'raid' and 'savagery', and the Kukis were patriots and freedom fighters, not merely raiders and brigands. Invoking the most sacred traditional war council, therefore, evades the very idea of criminal intent and acts of barbarism. War based on war council resolutions demand conformity to war decorum; an attack directed only to the enemy, the nature of such attack and the particular method to be followed were engrained within predefined norms at the war council. In this context, the Kuki war, to the scale it was fought against imperial forces, and that too for almost two years of active engagement, can never be seen as an act of savage warfare and marauding raid. Besides, the invocation of the sacred war council also means that it was neither an individual's war nor the chief's war. It was people's war against a powerful enemy, in this case the colonial government. Since the enemy to be fought was a very powerful force, it was necessary that it had to be a 'national' war, and for such major decisions to be taken it needed a war council like we see during the Anglo-Kuki War 1917–1919. Overall, this war could not have happened and been sustained unless it was taken first in the traditional war conclave, which the Kukis held in the highest order.

Notes

1 For an enlightening discussion on tangible/intangible or positive/negative war aims, see Fried 2014. While tangible war aims include, for instance, acquisition of territory or economic, military or other benefits, intangible includes accumulation of credibility or reputation. Similarly, positive war aims may cover tangible outcomes and negative war aims forestall or prevent undesired outcomes.
2 Shaw 1983: 79–81.
3 The same concept is also visible among the Lusheis, their close brethren in Lushai Hills. See Lewin 2004: 140.
4 MSA, R-2/231/S-4: Tour Diary of J.C. Higgins, President Manipur State Darbar, dated 3 and 4 April 1917. See also Documents of the Anglo-Kuki War 1917–1919, edited by D.L.Haokip, 2017, chapter 3: J.C. Higgins to CS Assam, 24 November 1917 (hereafter Documents of Anglo-Kuki War).
5 Documents of Anglo-Kuki War, Confidential D.O. No. 5.C. of H.W. Cole to B.C Allen, 17 March 1917.
6 Documents of Anglo-Kuki War, J.C. Higgins to CS Assam, 24 November 1917.
7 Documents of Anglo-Kuki War, Higgins to CS Assam, 24 November 1917.
8 MSA, R-2/230/S-4: Higgins Tour Diary, 1 November and 1 December 1917.
9 MSA, R-2/230/S-4: Higgins Tour Diary, 8 November 1917.
10 Documents of Anglo-Kuki War, Higgins to CS Assam, 24 November 1917.
11 Documents of Anglo-Kuki War, Higgins to CS Assam, 24 November 1917.
12 Documents of Anglo-Kuki War, Higgins to CS Assam, 24 November 1917.
13 British Library, London (BL), African and Asian collections (AAC), Indian Office Records and Private Papers (IOR&PP), IOR/L/PS/10/724: 1917–1920, File No. 2686/1919: 'Report on the Rebellion of the Kukis on the Upper Chindwin Frontier and the operations connected therewith' by J.B. Marshall, DC, Upper Chindwin District.
14 Documents of Anglo-Kuki War, Higgins to CS Assam, 24 November 1917.
15 Mizoram State Archives (MZSA), Correspondence to J.E. Webster (Chief Secretary to the Chief Commissioner of Assam) dated Camp Tuila stream 1 January 1918.
16 Assam State Archives (ASA), Political Deptt. (PD), File No. 9C/M-61P of 1918, Political – A, March 1919, Nos. 1–255: 'Arrangements', Cosgrave to Webster, 13 May 1918: 'Statement of Waishon Kuki, Chief of Leirik, Lam No. 4'.
17 ASA, PD, File No. M-33P of 1918, Political – A, December 1919, Nos. 1–144: 'Surrender and trial', Cosgrave to Webster, 26 October 1918. 'Kept in jail' was later substituted with 'kept as a prisoner of war'. See ASA, PD, File No. M-33P of 1918, Political – A, December 1919, Nos. 1–144: 'Surrender and trial', Webster to Cosgrave, 8 November 1918.
18 BL, AAC, IOR&PP, IOR/L/PS/10/724: 1917–1920, 'Burma-Assam Frontier: Disturbances among Kuki Tribesmen in Manipur', File No. P-693/1919: J.E. Webster, CS Assam to Foreign Secy. GOI, 27 June 1919.
19 Documents of Anglo-Kuki War, Higgins to CS Assam, 24 November 1917.

References

Doungel, L. 1986. 'Aisanpa Pu: Chengjapao Doungel Hinkho Thusim' (History of ChengjapaoDoungel, Chief of Aisan), Dimapur.

Fried, M.B. 2014. *Austro-Hungarian War Aims in the Balkans During World War I*. Palgrave Macmillan.

Haokip, J. 1984. *Chin-Kuki Ho Thusim' (Manipur & Burma) History of the Chin-Kukis of Manipur and Burma)*. Imphal: Private Circulation.

Haokip, P.S. 1988. *Zalengam – The Kuki Nation*. KNO Publication.

Haokip, P.S. 2008. *Zalengam – The Kuki Nation*. KNO Publication.

Kipgen, K. 1982. *The Thadou-Kukis – A Brief Account of History and Culture*. Imphal: Private Circulation.

Lewin, T.H. 2004 [1869]. *The Hill Tracts of the Chittagong and the Dwellers Therein*. Aizawl: Tribal Research Institute (TRI).

Shakespear, L.W. 1980. *History of the Assam Rifles*. New Delhi: Spectrum Publications.

Shaw, William. 1983. *Notes on the Thadou-Kukis, With an Introduction by J.H Hutton*. New Delhi: Cultural Publishing House.

8

REVISITING THE 'MILITARY'

Role of *som* institution in the Anglo-Kuki War

Ngamjahao Kipgen

They [Kukis] are born snipers. . . . They are certainly to
be called brave. . .

They have been known to stand the scorching fire of seven-
pounder mountain guns and Lewis guns at close range.
            – Lt. Col. J.L.W. Ffrench-Mullen

Common stereotypes plague indigenous or tribal people and continue
to hold onto imageries of headhunters, raiders and savage warriors.
It is true that tribal people did not live a completely peaceful existence and intertribal warfare existed. However, unlike the colonial-
ist, the aims of such warfare tended to be for sustenance, prestige,
or revenge rather than total warfare designed to conquer territory or
political subjugation (Zou 2005; Guite 2011) or defend their territory. As one Kuki elder eloquently states, 'Our forefathers were dedicated to defend our country [ancestral land]'. The idea of territory
or *Zalengam*[1] meant something different to the Kukis as they defend
their 'nation', the land of their ancestors. The spirit of nationalism
and sense of a common identity have existed among the Kukis prior
to their colonial encounters.[2] During the Anglo-Kuki War 1917–1919,
we also see a strong sense of commitment to defend their land, culture
and for the preservation of their independence.

The indigenous Kukis carried on age-old warrior traditions of
defending their people and ancestral homeland. Historically, there
has been a strong sense of honour placed on being a 'warrior'. The
existing literatures on the Kukis have given little or no attention on
the formation and shaping of the military or warriors despite their

immense contribution in the Anglo-Kuki War 1917–1919. This paper
is intended to revisit the 'military' in traditional Kuki society and the
Anglo-Kuki War by discussing the significance of the *som* or *som-
in* (youth dormitory) institution in imparting the warrior-tradition.[3]
It relies on ethnohistorical and oral accounts and attempts to examine the socio-cultural and political significance of the *som* institution,
which forms an integral part of traditional Kuki society.

An examination of *som* organisation has become central if one has
to look for the warrior-tradition of the Kukis. Traditionally, the *som*
played the roles of policing and supervising hunting and warfare,
teaching the youngsters ethics and values – respect for the elders and
caring the helpless. Much of the existing records such as the colonial accounts during the Anglo-Kuki War pertains to the 'war operations', 'punitive measures against Chiefs', 'warfare and tactics' and so
on. Scholars have also made little or no effort to incorporate the well
organised military organisation or warrior-tradition while deliberating
on such subject. Therefore, it is pertinent to underline the fabric and
mechanism fostering unity and vigor in the erstwhile Kuki society by
revisiting the *som* institution.

From a functionalist perspective, the necessary purpose delivered by
the *som* concerning norms and institutions was that it acted as 'organ'
that works towards the proper functioning of the entire 'body' of the
traditional Kuki society.[4] The strong values and sense of sacrifice among
the Kuki youths ingrained from their training at *som* acted as an important agent in bringing solidarity, strength and audacity. Such values and
tough military training built on the edifice of *som* institution have been
instrumental in their warfare such as in the Anglo-Kuki War 1917–1919.

The Kuki military formation in the Anglo-Kuki War

There is no specific account to show how the military formation of
the Kukis was during the Anglo-Kuki War. But this should not imply
that there was no specific military culture. It is true that the Kukis did
not have any standing and paid army like the colonial state. It is also
true that there was no paid general to lead the soldiers to war against
enemies. Yet, this should not lead us to assume that the Kukis lacked
any trained fighting men and trained leaders to lead them in the war.
There are ample evidences to show that the Kukis had fought gallantly
and skillfully against the trained military forces during the War, a point
recognised in colonial field reports. There are also evidences to show
that large numbers of Kuki fighters were involved in the war under the
able leadership. There was no specific training given to Kuki soldiers,

no special recruitment drive taken, before and during the war. All able-bodied men turned up and took up their weapon to defend their country. Therefore, it is pertinent to ponder on some of these facts before we consider the role of *som* institution in all these Kuki military affairs.

During the Anglo-Kuki War one of the main weapons used by the Kukis was firearms, mostly old flintlock and muzzle-loaders muskets. Only in one stray case bow and arrow was used, whereas the use of spear and sword was completely blank. Firearms were assisted slightly by their tradition leather cannon (*pumpi*), stone trap (*song-khai*) and *panjies* (*sou*). The dominant use of firearms amounts to special training and sophistication. Official figure of the number of guns confiscated after the War was 1,158 guns.[5] A much larger number of them were confiscated before the war: between 1907 and 1917, when the British had collected from the Kukis 1,195 guns as precautionary measure.[6] But interestingly there is no account of special training given on this count. Enjakhup had trained some in the northwestern hills and that is it; in all other areas there is no training given to the Kuki fighters. Instead there is an account which says that an attempt is made by the Kukis to save as much gunpowder as possible and efforts were also made to produce more so that they did not run short of it when they face the military forces.

Besides, it is difficult to provide the exact numbers of Kuki fighters during the war. There are some scattered colonial sources which give roundabout figures of the Kuki fighters. In his final report to Government of India, General Keary, who commanded the British forces in the second phase of operations, puts the strength of Kukis as 8 to 1 of the British forces, which was 6,234 combatants and 696 non-combatants – from Assam Rifles and Burma Military Police. This give a rough figure of the whole Kuki population of the time, fighting against the British (i.e. 7000 × 8 = 56,000).[7] While giving a rough estimate of the strength of Kuki warriors in the northern part of Manipur, the Chief Commissioner of Assam put it at 4,000 houses, and 3,000 fighting men, having about 1,000 muskets. He said:

> It is estimated that in the northern area alone there are about 4,000 hostile houses, that about 3,000 fighting men are out against us, armed with something less than 1000 muskets, mostly muzzle loaders. Altogether, the enemy may be placed at 3000–4000 men, with 1000–1500 muskets. This is probably an outside estimate, but it is better to be on the safe side.[8]

It was also reported that the Kukis collected at Jampi was said to number 2,000 to 3,000 and have nearly 1,000 guns.[9] The Anal informant who came from Mombi also told Higgins, whose column was proceeding to Mombi, that there were a large number of Kukis between Sugnu and Mombi which he put it at 2000 fighters with five stockades.[10] The Deputy Commissioner of Upper Chindwin was also informed that the sellers from Sandin Chin was told by Kinki Chins that he should keep 8,000 baskets of paddy ready as about 8,000 Kukis with arms and equipments are coming shortly.[11] The attack on Nepali *gots* in Khuga valley was said to be done by 200 strong Manlun-Manchong fighters. The attack on Nepali farms near Karong was said to be done by 100 strong Kukis with guns. When J.C. Higgins was attacking the Ukha Kukis, he got information that the Chassad Chief Pache had sent 1,000 Kuki fighters to help them.[12] Similarly, when four military columns were sent against the southeastern (Mombi) hills Kukis, it was reported that 200 Haokips from the Ukha area, and 300 from Chassad came for help.[13] The Burma officers estimated the strength of Mombi fighting forces at 700 men armed with guns.

On the tactics of the Kuki war, sufficient evidences show that they behave as if they are well-trained soldiers. The Kuki method of warfare was said to be 'hit and run' tactic in which the fighters would give 'incessant sniping' and ambush from a hideout spot and then vanish nowhere. Sometimes they met the invading forces in their stockades. Higgins felt that the Kukis 'incessant sniping and attack' was the most difficult to deal with. He said: 'The Kukis method of warfare and the nature of the country, in which we have to operate, make it certain that we shall suffer casualties continuously'.[14] Lt. Col. Ffrench-Mullen also reported that

'there is nothing more disheartening to troops than chasing the elusive savage through his dense jungles never really scoring off him, on the contrary suffering daily casualties with the very remote chance if lucky of "downing" a sniper . . . They are thankless, disagreeable jobs.

He called the Kuki fighters as the 'crafty jungle fighters on their own chosen terrain'.[15] Brig.-Gen. C.E.K. Macquoid also reported:

The enemy to be dealt with were, in their own way and manner of fighting, by no means lacking in courage. In the art of lying concealed and laying ambushes they could not be excelled. They scarcely ever showed themselves, yet their presence could always be felt.[16]

Lt. Gen. Keary also said that Kuki fighter 'were not lacking in courage or skill'.[17]

The Kukis also occasionally met the British columns at their stockades. Lt. Col. Ffrench-Mullen, for instance, reported on the battle at Khailet that the left flank was 'held by dropping fire' and as the flankers push up the hills, 'the fire become very heavy from several directions at once. Mountain guns were fired upon them but they did not retreat. The column finally retreated when Lieutenant Stedman was hit and 8 of them were killed and 8 wounded'.[18] Similar was at the battle of Hengtam, when the Kuki fighters 'kept up a brisk and well directed fire from the stockade', and they were 'not dislodged from the big stockade' until several shells of 7 lb. mountain gun were fired at close range and 'had deluged it with bullets from magazine rifles'. Altogether some 1,300 rounds of .303 [rifles] and Martini Henry ammunition were fired. They withdrew after taking away the dead.[19] This is also the case at Maokot 'Kuki Stockade' defended by about 100 Kukis with 50 guns from the villages of Maokot Chingsang, Maokot, Lakhan Khaihol, Langja, Mattiyang and Khulen Bongbal. The fight went on for more than three hours.[20]

There was a strong sense of *esprit de corps* among the Kuki fighters. They hung together until it was difficult to hang-on. J.B. Marshall, for instance, reported that 'these Kukis hang together' in their fighting against the Assam and Burma columns.[21] With such cooperation, courage and skills the Kukis could withstand the colonial military forces for almost two years. After the first phase of operations, W.A. Cosgrave, the Political Agent in Manipur, for instance, reported: 'Personally, I am now inclined to think that the suppression of the Kuki rebellion is too big a matter for our Assam Rifles and that the operations next cold weather should be made over to the Military Department'.[22] He also said that in spite of their inferior armament, the Kukis 'managed to kill more of our poor sepoys than we know we have killed on the other side' and the Kukis are therefore 'master of the situation'.[23] Lt. Col. Ffrench-Mullen also felt that although the Kukis were certainly punished severely, their morale was not broken yet.[24] Col. Shakespear also similarly felt that fighting against the Kukis was 'disconcerting and most difficult to deal with' (Shakespear 1977: 224).

It is interesting to provide here some of the important estimations given by Lt. Col. Ffrench-Mullen to the Kuki fighters.

1   They are most skilful in devising fortifications and defences [stockades] and traps.
2   They are certainly to be called brave as they take big risks in these efforts to shoot our people especially British Officers.

3   Their woodcraft is superb and they are rarely miss so their marks-
    manship is considering their weapons of high quality.
4   They are born snipers and can creep up to a camp at night without
    a sound.
5   They have been known to stand the scorching fire of seven-
    pounder mountain guns and Lewis guns at close range and then
    pop up and snipe at our columns from the very place on which the
    scorching fire had been directed.
6   Their tactics are 'shoot and run' from carefully devised jungle
    observation post built for one or two men with an easy line for
    retreat.[25]

For all these military qualities of fighting and skilfulness, Gen. Keary
saw what he called a 'fine soldierly material' in the Kukis and hence
recommended them for the future recruits of colonial army. For the
same reason, Lt. Col. Ffrench-Mullen even asked for World War
medals for the British troops who had a hard show against the Kuki
fighters.

The pertinent point is from where this 'fine soldierly material' the
Kukis came from? It would be simplistic to assume that this was what
Kukis had been born with. Nothing of this sort was naturally born
with any person. We have noted that they were not given any special
training before the war. Then how come the Kukis were so expert in
the use of their guns, fought like born snipers, skilful in devising fortifications, stockades and traps. Where did they get their bravery so as
to withstand without fear of the shelling of mountain guns and rifles?
From where did they learn their tactics of 'shoot and run' or what is
popularly known as 'guerrilla warfare'? Here, the role of their traditional *som* (bachelor's dormitory) become significant. In fact, one may
say that a good hunter is a good soldier. But even hunters need some
kind of training. In both cases, it was their traditional multi-purpose
institution called *som* which provided the training ground for all these
manly jobs. In this context, *som* institution played tremendous role in
organising and sustaining the Kuki war during the Anglo-Kuki War.
In the following sections we will discuss the role of *som* in traditional
Kuki society, especially how it groomed young boys as readymade
'soldierly material' for the community and beyond.

Kuki society and its village segment

Each Kuki village is by nature a distinct political and administrative
unit. Its population in the village is a closely knit families and clans,

promoting common sentiment and under a single chieftain.[26] It is theoretically a 'separate state', ruled by its own *Haosa* or Chief on hereditary line (Shakespear 1983 [1912]: 42). The village territory, having a clearly demarcated boundary with other villages, also theoretically belonged to the chief. He was the political and administrative head of the village and the final arbiter in all matters. He was supreme head of the village within the limits of his territory, and the villagers were bound by custom to obey him (Chatterjee 1975: 14). However, the Chief's position in the village was not that of an autocrat but the benefactor and a benevolent ruler. If his subject disliked him or his system of administration, they could easily move to another village or Chief (Hunter 1908: 217). This greatly circumscribed the powers of the Chief. Besides, the well laid out customary law guided both the Chief and the people that the chief could neither misuse his power nor oppress his people.

Similarly, the same customs guided the village administration. The mode of village government may be best understood as democratic by arrangement. In the discharge of his duty as the political and administrative head of the village, the chief was assisted by his council of elders or *semang-pachong* who are appointed by him with the concurrence of the people. Both the Chief and *semang-pachong* were assisted by very vibrant institution called *som*, headed by *som-upa* or or *tollaipao* whose role in the village administration we will come shortly. Besides, there are other village officers such as *lhangsam* (village crier), *thih-pu* (blacksmith), and *thiempu* (village priest). In this administrative set up the chief and his council (*semang-pachong*) decided where the *som* was implemented. Virtually, *som* has become the implementing agency of the village administration either in terms of political, economic, cultural or military policy of the village council.

While the village as a whole is politically and administratively an independent unit, it is not completely independent from other Kuki villages. Each Kuki village is in some ways closely connected and related to each other. Their connection is best manifested by clan and kinship networks and relationships. Kukis are all connected to each other by clan and kinship relationships, in which each clan had the clan head (*pipa*) who was in turn connected to other clan heads through a more senior clan head in the lineage which went up the ladder of seniority and ultimately ended with the grand clan head, also known as *pipa* or *phung-upa* or *inpipa*. Thus, each village is by nature headed by a chief who is invariably the head of his clan in the village. He is similarly connected to another chief of his senior clan member in other villages on the one hand, and possibly to other chief(s) of his junior clan members also in other villages. Through this customary connection, he is bound to regularly pay his customary *sating*,[27] to his senior brother/chief and also received from his junior brother(s), if there is any. Non-payment of *sating* is a serious matter in clan relationship among the Kukis. It is also the responsibility of each village to assist the village belonging to his clan members, either his senior or junior, when they are in need of help. This clan relationship becomes most visible in practice especially in times of war, where each clan is supposed to join hands against the enemy. In principle, the enemy of one of the clan members or villages would ultimately become the enemy of all the clan members. It was under such a situation that the political power of the clan *pipa* becomes most explicit, and his orders are supposed to be binding to all the junior clan members.

Networks of common language, customs and marriage relationships also facilitate connections between two or more villages among the Kukis. They are equally forceful as the clan factor. While marriage relationship between two villages was undoubtedly a very strong factor for war and peace, the common language and customs shared by different villages could be a binding factors when it comes to dealing with other linguistic groups. Therefore, although every Kuki village is practically independent from other villages in their internal matter, it was interrelated and connected with all the other Kuki villages through clan, custom, language and even marriage relationships. These networks make the Kukis one of the closely-knit tribal communities in the region and become a binding force behind their unity and strength over the centuries. Conceptually, this social and political relationship among the Kukis through village, clan and others may be best understood in term of segments, and hence of its segmentary character similar to the African Nuer (Evans-Pritchard 1940: 143).[28] Like the African Nuer, the Kukis also maintained close relationships between territorial segments (village) and lineage segments (clan) and habitually expressed social obligations in a kinship idiom. The strength of the community lies in the strength of each segment (village) and the strength of each segment depends on the strength of its implementing institution, *som*. It was mainly through this segmented clan network and relationship, and the strength of each segment, that one can best observe the unity and strength among the Kukis during the Anglo-Kuki War 1917–1919. It was from this line of argument that a deeper insight into the workings of *som* becomes pertinent, the point we shall now show.

Som: origin and evolution

Som is a very old institution among the Kukis. It is very difficult to say when it started and how it evolved over time. However, from the various oral sources this important institution play pivotal role when the Kukis came into contact with other hostile communities. The need to have regular, trained and disciplined fighting men could have therefore evolved this important institution. Hence, from its beginning the military character of *som* is well known although more activities were eventually given to them in time of peace in the subsequent period. The migration history of the Kukis shows that they started fighting against their enemy since the time they settle down in and around Chungkhopi, established by Pu Chongthu, which is said to be in upper Burma in the confluence of Chindwin and Irrawaddy rivers. The powerful enemy eventually destroyed Chungkhopi and Kukis also lost their script written on the parchment (*savunjol*) during this attack; the enemy having littered it and dogs had eaten up. It was possible that *som* institution evolved and become prominent during this period.

It is said that Kukis used to have a separate *som-inn* (dormitory) for the young boys of the village in the past as one can also observe among its kindred group Lushai tribe in the nineteenth century, which they called *zawlbuk*. However, in the nineteenth and twentieth centuries, *som-inn* was shifted and scattered in smaller groups of young men to the chief's house and in certain respectable houses of the village where maiden lady/ies serve them as *som-nu*. The reason given was that putting the warriors of the village in one location at the *som-inn* was often an easy prey to a powerful enemy during a surprise attack. The capture and killing of the whole fighting force will eventually lead to the destruction of the whole village. To circumvent such tragedy, it was therefore decided to scatter the warriors in different locations in the village and inside the normal houses. Hence, the enemy would find it difficult to identify the house where the warriors sleep and on their attack of the first house the whole warriors could raise up from different houses and hence repulsed the enemy and save further tragedy. Despite this, the young boys in the village were under a single command of *som-upa* or *tollaipao* for purposes of war and also in certain other common village affairs. This scatter state of Kuki *som* was one reason why it escaped the eyes of most colonial specialists on the Kukis. But this should not demean the importance of *som* as one of the central institutions of the Kuki village. Therefore, in the following sections I will discuss the role and functions of *som* and its connection with the Anglo-Kuki War at the end.

Som as rites de passage

Every Kuki boy in the village, after attaining certain age, had to enter the *som-inn*. This was the mandate of customs and practice. By entering the *som*, a boy gains admittance to the circle of men. All members of a *som-inn* have obligations and rights determined by age and the time of initiation into the *som* community. *Som* is linked with an elaborate system of age groups. Each age group discharges prescribed duties and enjoys definite privileges, and in the course of his life, a man passes automatically from one age group to the other. The members of the Kuki *som* are divided into two groups according to age – seniors and juniors. The head or elder of the dormitory called *tollaipao* is selected from the senior group. It is his obligation to take care of all the members of the dormitory and maintain discipline among them. The juniors follow the commands of the *tollaipao* and receive different types of apprenticeship from them. The overall control of the scattered *soms* in the village is under the hand of *som-upa*.

Respect for elders and parents was held to be a sacred duty in the Kuki society.[29] Being a society based on gerontocracy, age among the Kukis had both prestige and power because it was the older people who knew and passed on to the younger generations the ways of society to which they were expected to conform. Strict discipline was maintained in every *som* and the *som-upas* were empowered to punish and fine offenders against the *som* code of conduct. Leadership in traditional Kuki society rested largely upon age and seniority. The leaders appointed amongst them were vested with the authority to discipline the members. *Som* is an institution where all leadership qualities can be cultivated with the help and guidance of the senior members and elders of the village. It was a place where the boys were physically and mentally trained up.

Over time, this institution could produce brilliant students who would attain the status of an influential person in the Chief's village court (Goswami 1985: 97). The Chief of the village was the main guide of the *som* organisations by virtue of his position, but he did not directly interfere in its day-to-day administration. However, the leader of the *som* often consulted the Chief and his *semang-pachong* of the village on all important matters. The *rite of passage* of the young boys in the *som* was a continuous and long process of training and testing until they got married and accepted family responsibility. The young men became self-reliant, obedient and disciplined. Their loyalty and sense of service to the corporate body was well developed in the *som*. Sociologically speaking, *som* was the key institution of the Kuki society, as it played a centrifugal role in the Kuki village. The entire fabric of the village – social, cultural, political and religious life – revolved around the *som* organisation. It was an important and holistic learning centre, where the youth learnt crucial lessons of life, livelihood and the life-world. It serves as the nerve centre of traditional Kuki village life. It is, therefore, pertinent to begin with how *som* had assisted the village administration over time.

Principles and values imparted in the *Som*

There are certain principles and values imparted in Kuki *som-inn*, which are crucial in understanding the military character of the Kuki social set up. These principles are what had governed the life of Kuki fighters during the Anglo-Kuki War and made them 'fine soldierly material' to the British as they always were for their community. It was these principles that governed the military setting of the Kuki fighters during the war and the source of their strength, courage and skillfulness. Apart from many other values and principles, the idea of equality, *esprit de corps*, selflessness, skills and morality were something *som* had imparted to the Kuki people. How these values had been imparted in the *som* will be discussed below.

Communitarianism and esprit de corps

The traditional Kuki society was largely characterised by the principles of cooperation and communitarianism rather than individual interest and individualism. The spirit of egalitarianism was a common feature of the Kuki community life, inculcated most forcefully in the *som* itself. Except on the ground of age, all the members of the *som* – rich and poor, strong and weak, and regardless of clan – all were treated equally. Discrimination on these lines was not permitted in the *som* disciplinary rules which are strictly enforced. This institution taught them to value the importance of every individual in the community. It promoted the principle of cooperation and discouraged individualism. Thus, all the inmates of *som* should abide by this rule and in the process become part of their social behaviour and relationship. In a sense, the main feature of the *som* atmosphere was to eliminate jealousy and possessiveness and to inculcate the sense of communitarianism based on the dogma of 'everyone belongs to everyone else'. This value instructs them to think and behave as a compact social unit. It resulted into a sense of cooperation and commonality rather than individual interests.

As cooperation and coordination among members required leadership and loyalty towards him, the *som* also inculcated this value. Here, age played an important role. The boys who entered the *som* from an early age were trained to respect their elders and do things without protest and with respect and sincerity. The *som* leader and elders were also required to enforce this rule strictly. These set of disciplines, cooperation and respect to elders/leaders eventually developed what is known as *esprit de corps* among the *som* members. A Kuki octogenarian asserted: 'The fear of outside aggression, latent in any warrior society, strengthens the feeling of mutual dependence of the *som* members and adds to its vital role in Kuki society'.[30] These principles of cooperation, discipline and *esprit de corps* were deeply entrenched among the Kukis.[31]

Khut-them *(skill and dignity of labour)*

An equally important part of the training imparted in *som* was *khut-them*, or skills and industry. The *som* boys were taught the art of not only fighting and hunting, which are the primary concern of the *som*, but also the skills necessary for war, of daily use, of economic process, cultural artefacts and others. As fighting and hunting were the primary concern of the *som*, the boys from the first day he entered the *som* were trained in the art of fighting and hunting under the guidance of the elders. They were also taught how to make bow and arrow, how to use, maintain and repair the guns, how to manufacture gunpowder, how to make palisade, stockade, *panjies* (*sou*) etc. The art of making basket, woodcraft, blacksmith etc. was also equally imparted at the *som*. They were also taught the art of agriculture, culture (from singing to dancing) and traditions (history, customs, etc.). In all ways, the *som* had become the traditional educational and training institute of the Kukis. All these arts and activities required sincerity, commitment and handwork. The *som* took special training to impart the value of industry and discourage laziness and idle life. Thus, the boys from the day he entered the *som* was subjected to the *som* disciplinary system that required each member to be industrious in every way. For instance, the boys would be engaged with activities until they were asked to sleep at night. Idleness was something the *som* discipline deplored.

Tomngaina *(selflessness and patriotism)*

Tomngaina, as a moral code of conduct, was also imparted in the *som*. It is the moral principle of self-sacrifice or selflessness, devotion to the community and love for country. It was the responsibility of the *som-inn* to look after the welfare of the village community, especially those who needed help and the weaker section of the village community such as orphans, widows and the poor. For example, if the widow needs her house to be built or repaired, her *jhum* field cut, weed, harvest etc., the *som* is morally obligated to help her out. Similarly, if an orphan or poor people need food, clothing, etc. the *som* will look after their needs. If a person is ill and needs treatment or there is death in the village, it was the *som* who had to look after all the needful. If the village road or water-pent, etc., need repair, it was the *som* to look after. Their activities will go on indefinitely for the welfare of the village. Of these, perhaps, the original and most important one is the village defence. They are to protect the village from enemies all the time or go for war against the enemy. All these responsibilities were taken up by the *som* with duty, responsibility and discipline without expecting anything in return. This is the spirit of selflessness and patriotism called *tomngaina*. Thus, *som* members were guided by the principle of *tomngaina*, which became part of their behaviour and growth. A sense of brotherhood and duty towards other members of the society was one of the highest moral values every Kuki was expected to adhere to. Thus, a good Kuki should be courteous, selfless, dauntless and diligent. 'Tomngaina permeated all spheres of life by extending help to the fellow members of the society in carrying out different tasks during any ritual events, ceremonies and calamities', said an elderly Kuki man.[32] This was the guiding principle in the everyday life of a Kuki. *Tomngaina* owes its allegiance to the *som* institution.

Khankho *(morality and good behaviour)*

Khankho is another ethical principle of Kukis. It is a behaviour by which a person is identified as a dignified individual. It is also the social behaviour and ways by which groups organise themselves in day-to-day life guided by customs and practices. A Kuki individual is bound with societal obligations and customary laws that evolved around the system of *khankho*. This ethical value was developed not only in the family, but also in the village *som*. The boys were taught by the elders what he ought to do or not to do, what is customary and what is not. In short, they were taught what is defined to be good and what not in the society. Respect to parents, to elders, to aged persons, to the chief or kindness to others including the poor, needy, orphans, widows etc., are few examples of *khankho* which the *som* imparted among the boys. The Chief rules under the system of *khankho*, and he is the custodian of the *khankho* system and punishes a villager who violates the system according to the customary law of the Kukis (Chongloi 2009: 16). Thus, all the fundamental practices of healthy social living which can be put under the principle of *khankho* were inculcated in the *som*.

Role of *som* in the village society

The traditional Kuki society was a patriarchal society with a strong warrior-tradition. Military force or warrior is an important instrument amongst the Kuki society, as it served the purpose of maintaining and establishing a socio-politcal order. The military was used against other village or tribes in order to maintain the balance of power or to create a new centre of political power.[33] The military, therefore, was an essential aspect of the organisation in traditional societies. *Som* constituted an important pillar of Kuki village administration and effective instrument to assist the Chief in his day-to-day administration. The competency of the Chief was doubly strengthened by the *som* institution. The *som* members were the source of strength for the Chief as they provided the much needed help in the times of crisis. The Chief derived power and strength from them. *Som* members rendered free and compulsory services to the village community with the Chief himself as the supreme commander. The Chief therefore paid personal attention towards the *som* military set up and led them in times of war (Carey and Tuck 1987 [1895]: 3).

A Kuki Chief enjoyed a great deal of political as well as military power. Being a supreme commander of the village force, the success or failure of the war with other tribes depended solely on the Chief's ability to control the *som*. The Chief led the people in war, and it was expected of him to be the first to attack and the last to retreat (Lewin 1870: 243; Hunter 1908: 60). For instance, the Chassad Chief become quite famous across the eastern hills because he successfully maintained a class of warriors in his village and over the villages under him to carry out his order and to protect the land and its people.[34] All the brave Haokip youths of Chassad village served in the Chief's army (warriors group); they were well-trained and equipped with arms and ammunition (Haokip 2008: 45). The role of *som* in creating such strong forces in the village is well acknowledged. Overall, the *som* acted as the implementing or enforcement agency of the chief and his village administration in times of war and peace. It produced the much needed military or warrior class in the village. It also acted as the cementing factor in the village community. Thus, *som* organisation formed an important institution around which the village social, economic and political life of the Kukis revolved.

The *som* also organised games, sports and festivals in the village. Annually they would call *som-kivah* celebration where the young one will enjoy with full jubilation. During festival, the *som* members collected *ju-bel* (rice wine in a clay pitcher) and invite the Chief and his *semang-pachong* to offer the *ju* (wine). On this occasion, the *som-upa* addresses the gathering in the following manner:[35]

> *Jaumtah Haosa pu le Semang Pachong ho*
> *Nacha teu keiho Som hung kivah ding katiu vin,*
> *Nei phal peh thei diu ham ole kho sunga nohphah na umding*
> *ham?*
> *A umlou ding le lunggel nei pha leu chun katiu ahi.*

(Free English translation)

> Respected *Haosa* (Chief) and *Semang-Pachong* (council of ministers)! We, the members of this *som* who are like your children have intended to perform the ritual of *som-kivah*. We would like to seek your kind permission to arrange for the same provided that such observance does not disturb the daily activities in the village.

Role of *som* in village defence and warfare

Perhaps the most important role of the *som* in the village was concerning the village defence and warfare. In the days when war and raids from neighbouring tribes and villages were frequent, an institution of *som* played a vital role. It was the inmates of *som* who make the village fortification and stockade, dig trench around the village, guard the village (day and night), guarded the cultivators when they are working the field, and went out to attack enemy village in war. Thus, the duties and functions of the *som* members were directly related to the safety and security of the whole village community. A Kuki cultural expert asserts:

> The armed force of a Kuki village consisted of all able-bodied men and represented a combination of all established age groups. There was no formal organisation or training, experience in handling their weapons being gained through games

of skill, the hunt, and actual fighting. Their entire boyhood having been spent outdoor – on the farming and tending cattle, turned them into the robust and vigorous warrior that they were.[36]

A common adage in the past among Kuki says: '*som umlouna a, khosung alhasam'e*' (a village without *som* is weak and volatile). The Chief of Gelnel village said,

> The absence of this youth organisation in any village, therefore, led to serious drawbacks because the young people who served as the most potent force for the existence of Chief's power could not easily be brought together in times of crisis.[37]

Som played a vital role in coordinating the activities of all male members of the community and gained particular importance in those warlike societies. *Som* continued to remain a vibrant institution among the Kukis till about the Anglo-Kuki War. For instance, an elderly man in Molsang village recalls: 'The *som* members assist in building up fortified gates and in digging the necessary rifle trenches outside village fence during the Anglo-Kuki War'.[38]

As far as their traditional method of warfare is concerned it is best understood with the term '*shim*' (attack), which involved the method of approaching the village to be attacked silently and wait till the wee hours in the morning when they make a surprise attack on the village. As soon as the enemies are killed, the party would immediately return. Colonial ethnographers like Carey and Tuck (1987 [1895]: 227) noted that the Chins, Lushais and Kukis are noted for the secrecy of their plans, the suddenness of their raids, and their extraordinary speed in retreating to their fastness. The essence in their tactics was surprise, and no disgrace to a party of warriors which, on finding the enemy attack on the alert, quickly returned home without attempting any attack. J.H. Hutton also said that 'frightfulness' is a normal policy of Thado warfare' (in Shaw 1929: 143). He also said:

> In war the Thado, when he gets the chance, often carries out massacres on a fairly large scale, partly because he enjoys killing, partly, at any rate, from deliberate 'frightfullness', adopting that method of cowing the other side.
>
> (Shaw 1929: 23, fn. 1)

This is the technique they developed from hunting in which they are most expert. Shakespear (1983 [1912]: 196), for instance, noted that:

> The Kookies are great hunters, and are passionately fond of the sport, looking upon it, next to war, as the noblest exercise for man. . . . In this the Kookis excel, being able to prowl about the jungle noiselessly as tiger-cats, and being equal to North American Indian in distinguishing tracks.

The Kukis believed that to be a good warrior one must be first a good hunter. Hunting is, for them, a training ground for a good fighter. He is an expert tracker and has an intimate knowledge of the ways and habits of all game, and he shoots at everything that comes to the gun (Carey and Tuck 1987 [1895]: 215). Nothing pleases him [Kuki] so much as to be out after a game with his muzzle-loading gun or arranging and setting traps to snare wild animals. He is a good tracker and has an uncanny knack of knowledge where the game is likely to be (Shaw 1929: 86). Hutton also said: 'Little game survives where the Thado settles' (in Shaw 1929: 23, fn. 1).[39]

Before going to a war, every Kuki fighters had to take an oath before the chief council. The following pledge is recited in this ritual:

> *Tunin hikom dohkhang jupholmun a hin*
> *Haosa upa, semang pachong ho angsunga kakitep ahi*
> *Nungthu akhoh le nung-ah pang ingting*
> *Mathu akhoh le ma-ah pang ingting*
> *Hiche kalval a jongchu akijolou nahlaileh*
> *Kanei kagou jouse toh, kasum kasel to jong pantha ing'e*
> *Gaal masang ahe kiti a kanung chontahleh*
> *Hiche kadohkhang juchep hi kalol khahheh!* (excerpts from Doungel 2007)

Translation:

> Herein this platform (where wine is served) on this propitious day
> In presence of the Chief and council of ministers
> To partake in the background of any circumstances or difficulties
> To partake in the forefront in any impending eventualities
> Even in such cases I happen to remain unsuccessful
> I shall sacrifice all my possessions (wealth)
> If I happen to forfeit in the events of any war
> I hereby took an oath on this cup of wine to perish!

In defending their village, they developed the technique of 'ambush' or 'hit and run' to the approaching enemy on the way. Ambuscades in thick jungles are laid for an approaching enemy whence the Kuki warrior will fire and disappear, to lie up again further on if a suitable opportunity is afforded. They also made *songkhai* and *songphel thaang* (a form of trap, using stones). The Kukis were highly trained and skilful in jungle-fighting and guerrilla warfare such as stone traps called *song-khai/song-thang*.[40] They also used *panjies* (sharp bamboo spike planted upside-down) on the paths where enemies are expected. If the enemy forces could not be beaten back this way, they would immediately return to the village and evacuate the women and children in the jungle, and the fighting men would defend the village as long as they could withstand it. If the enemy is stronger, then they would eventually vacate the village and hide in the jungles. This method was especially popular during the Anglo-Kuki War when the Kukis put up their fortifications, stockades, stone traps and *panjies* and indulged on 'guerilla' or 'tip and run' tactics. Keith reported that:

> The Kukis had as usual made a determined stand anywhere, but had been unremitting in their sniping, their principal aim being obviously to kill British officers. . . . The snipers would lie very close in the thick jungle, let the flankers and the advance guard pass them, and wait for the British officers. These latter had naturally a narrow escapes.[41]

In both offensive and defensive warfare, the Kuki warriors, if they won the war, would be highly celebrated. Being trained and disciplined for years at the *som*, war is for them like a game. Just as they enjoyed hunting, they were also in a position to enjoy warfare. A Kuki veteran hunter said: 'With mind so alert and physique so robust there was no room for idleness and idle thought amongst the *som* members. They were mentally prepared to sacrifice their lives for the defence of their village'.[42] A Kuki *thiempu* (priest) narrated their role during the war and peace:

> They performed rituals and ceremonies on agricultural practices, hunting and war rites. Rites and ceremonies remain an important part of the tradition and culture of warrior societies. For instance, ceremonies before war protect and prepare the warrior for combat. Ceremonies after the war honour his service and the songs reintegrate him into the community and

out of the unnatural state of war – to return to a normal and balanced spiritual and mental state afterward.[43]

Successful hunting and warfare were also the most celebrated activities in Kuki society. With the return of successful warriors, there would be three days victory celebration in the village and it a taboo to cross the village boundary on those days. The warriors were decorated with special headdresses called *thu'pa* (Shaw 1983: 79–81). They were held high in the village community. This point to the presence of a strong warrior-tradition among the Kukis in which the aim of all men from their childhood was to become the famous warrior in the village community, the most prestigious profession so to say of the age. It was from this cultural background that one could only locate the strength, courage and skills of the Kukis in the Anglo-Kuki War 1917–1919.

Conclusion

An extract from the Assam Government report says:

> The Kuki rising, 1917–1919, which is the most formidable with which Assam has been faced for at least a generation . . . the rebel villages held nearly 40,000 men, women and children interspersed . . . over some 6,000 square miles of rugged hills surrounding the Manipur valley and extending to the Somra Tract and the Thaungdut State in Burma'.[44]

We have already noted the techniques, forms and character of the Kuki war against the British and the various estimations given by the Btitish military officers on their fighting styles, skills and courage. We also noted that the Kukis had no regular army nor was there any specific military training. Then one wonders how could they withstand the might of well-trained and well-equipped British military forces almost two years of continuous engagement. It is the conclusion of this paper that it was possible due to the well established institution of *Som* (bachelor's dormitory) in every Kuki villages. We have also noted that each Kuki village was closely connected to each other by clan and kinship networks and relationships. Hence, once war was declared by the clan *pipas*. all the villages belonging to his clan members rose up against the British in unison and all their warriors in their respective village *som* who have been adapted to warfare as their cultural practice in the *som* were then fielded in the battle. Thus, like a wildfire

229

the whole Kuki hills rose up in arms with speed and dimension. In no time, they collected their guns, pounded gunpowder, fortified their villages, erected stockades and raised stone traps and panjies across the hills. As fighting was part of their cultural practice, their spirit was not easily broken, even if they were fighting against the army of the most powerful empire of the world. They did not lack skill and courage, but it was the sheer military might and superior weapons of the British forces vis-à-vis the barbaric ways they were dealt with by the latter that they finally gave in. William Shaw have found them later: 'Their tails are not down and I have heard said that they hope to become a "Raj" someday' (Shaw 1929: 23). That is the warrior spirit which remained unbroken even after their defeat, and the spirit the Kuki *som* had imparted over the ages.

Notes

1 'Zale'n-gam' which means 'freedom of the people in their land' (Haokip 2008).
2 P.S. Haokip asserts that the Kuki rising of 1917–1919 serves as a foundation of Kuki nationalism (see Haokip 2008).
3 Almost all trans-border tribes such as the Chins, Mizos, Kukis and the Nagas have a traditional institution of bachelor dormitory where the entire young group in the village spends the night. Mizos call it *zawlbuk* (Shakespear, Lushei-Kuki 1983 [1912]), the Nagas refer to it as Morung (Mills, Ao Nagas 1926), and the Kukis call it the *Som* (Shaw, Notes on the Thadou Kukis 1929).
4 Within functionalist theory, the different parts of society are primarily composed of social institutions, each of which is designed to fill different needs, and each of which has particular consequences for the form and shape of society. For further details, see Turner and Maryanski 1979.
5 British Library (BL), African and Asian Collections (AAC), Indian Office Record & Private Papers (IOR&PP), IOR/L/MIL/17/19/42: 1919: 'Despatch on the Operations Against the Kuki Tribes of Assam and Burma, November 1917 to March 1919', Brig. Gen. C.E.K. Macquoid to Lieut.-Gen. Sir H.D.U. Keary, 27 April 1919.
6 Manipur Administration Report, 1918–1919, p. 2
7 BL, AAC, IOR&PP, IOR/L/MIL/17/19/42: 1919, 'Despatch on the Operations Against the Kuki Tribes' Macquoid to Keary, 27 April 1919, Appendix – III.
8 Assam State Archives, Dispur, File No. 9C/M-61P of 1918, Appointment and Political Department, Political – A, March 1919, Nos. 1–255: 'Arrangement in connection with Operations against the Kuki Rebels in Manipur', p. 44: 'N.D. Beatson Bell Notes', 9 June 1918.
9 ASA, Governor's Secretariat (Confidential), (hereafter GSC), Sl. 260, File No. M/64-P of 1918, Political – B, March 1919, Nos. 1–397 (Part-II), 'Progress of events in Manipur in connection with the Kuki Disturbances', No. 108: Hutton to Higgins, 11 January 1918.

10 ASA, GSC, Sl. 260, File No. M/64-P of 1918, Political – B, March 1919, Nos. 1–397, 'Progress of events', No. 134: Tour Diary of JC Higgins, Pol. Officer Southern Kuki (Shugun-Mombi) column No. I, 23, January.

11 BL, AAC, IOR&PP, IOR/L/PS/10/724: 1917–1920, Telegram No. 57-T, 8 December 1917: Chief Secy. Assam to Secy. GOI, Foreign Dept.

12 Manipur State Archives (MSA), R-2/230/S-4: Higgins Tour Diary, 1 January 1918.

13 ASA, GSC, Sl. 260, File No. M/64-P of 1918, Political – B, March 1919, No. 134: Tour Diary of JC Higgins, 24 January 1918.

14 ASA, GSC, Sl. 260, File No. M/64-P of 1918, Political – B, March 1919, No. 99: Higgins to Webster 8 January 1918.

15 BL, AAC, IOR&PP, IOR/L/PS/10/724: 1917–1920, File No. P-2686/1919: Lt. Col. JLW Ffrench-Mullen, DIG, Burma Military Police to IGP Burma, 17 September 1918.

16 BL, AAC, IOR&PP, IOR/L/MIL/17/19/42: 1919, 'Despatch on the Operations Against the Kuki Tribes of Assam and Burma, November 1917 to March 1919', Brig. Gen. C.E.K. Macquoid to Lieut.-Gen. Sir H.D'U. Keary, 27 April 1919.

17 BL, AAC, IOR&PP, IOR/L/MIL/17/19/42: 1919, 'Despatch on the Operations Against the Kuki Tribes of Assam and Burma, November 1917 to March 1919', Lieut.-Gen. Sir H.D.U.. Keary, GOI, Burma Division to Chief of the General Staff, Army Hqtrs. June 1919.

18 BL, AAC, IOR&PP, IOR/L/PS/10/724: 1917–1920, File No. P-2686/1919: Lt. Col. JLW Ffrench-Mullen, DIG, Burma Military Police to IGP Burma, 17 September 1918.

19 MSA, R-2/230/S-4: Cosgrave Tour Diary, 18 March 1918.

20 MSA, R-2/231/S-4: Tour diary of JC Higgins. No. 1, Column, Chassad, 8 April 1918.

21 BL, AAC, IOR&PP, IOR/L/PS/10/724: 1917–1920, File No. P-2686/1919: 'Report on the Rebellion of the Kukis on the Upper Chindwin frontier and the operations connected threwith' by JB Marshall, DC, Upper Chindwin District.

22 ASA, PD, File No. 9C/M-61P of 1918, Political – A, March 1919, Nos. 1–255: 'Arrangements', Cosgrave to Webster, 18 May 1918.

23 ASA, PD, File No. 9C/M-61P of 1918, Political – A, March 1919, Nos. 1–255: 'Arrangements', Cosgrave to Webster, 23 June 1918: "Note on scheme of occupation of Manipur Hills"

24 BL, AAC, IOR&PP, IOR/L/PS/10/724: 1917–1920, File No. P-2686/1919: Lt. Col. JLW Ffrench-Mullen, DIG, Burma Military Police to IGP Burma, 17 September 1918.

25 BL, AAC, IOR&PP, IOR/L/PS/10/724: 1917–1920, File No. P-2686/1919: Lt. Col. JLW Ffrench-Mullen, DIG, Burma Military Police to IGP Burma, 17 September 1918.

26 In 1872 Col. Dalton observes that the Kukis are 'a nation of hunters and warriors, ruled as a nation by their principal hereditary chiefs or rajahs, but divided into clans, each under its own chiefs'.

27 Sating is the flesh between the upper side of the ribs and the hide of all animals killed in the ceremonies or in the chase which is customarily the share of, and a share to be paid by a man to his, senior most male next-of-kin till it went up to the clan *Pipa* (clan head). See, Shaw (1929: 65–66).

28 Segmentary societies are based on kinship or cultural ties, therefore, each individual in the society was all the more willing to render military service since it was quite clear that the individual's survival in the face of external aggression, was conterminous with the survival of the society (For details, see Sahlins 1961).
29 Apart from the commoners, even the Kuki chiefs respected the word of their *Pipa* or *Bulpipa* (the senior most in clan lineage). The decision of the Bulpipa in any matter is final and binding and not in question.
30 Interview at Songtun village, dated 30 April 2017.
31 The feeling of fraternalism is expressed especially at times of adversity or tragedy when the fellow villagers or clans sought a helping hand. This is pretty much evident in the context of the Anglo-Kuki War.
32 Interview at Gamnomphai, dated 28 April 2017.
33 For further explanation on military in traditional society, see Fortes and Evans-Pritchard 1940: xiv.
34 The Chassad village constituted of as many as 300 houses, considered to be one of the largest of Kuki villages in the hills during the Anglo-Kuki War.
35 An excerpt from Field Notes recited by Haothang Kilong, a cultural specialist – documented for my doctoral dissertation (Interview at Motbung, dated 19 September 2009).
36 Interview at Songtun village, dated 15 April 2017.
37 Interview at Gelnel village, dated 28 November 2009.
38 Interview at Molsang village, 10 April 2017.
39 Hutton note in Shaw 1929: 23.
40 Panjis, stone-shoots, and booby traps of all sorts are the defensive weapons used by the Thadous [Kukis] (Shaw 1929: 143).
41 BL, AAC, IOR&PP, IOR/L/PS/10/724: 1917–1920, File No. P-4429/1919: Keith to Webb, 2 June 1919.
42 Interview at Wakapphoi village, dated 20 April 2017.
43 Interview at Tujang village, dated 25 April 2017.
44 BL, AAC, IOR&PP, IOR/L/PS/10/724: 1917–1920, 'Extract from the Proceedings of the Chief Commissioner of Assam in the Political Department', 27 September 1920.

References

Carey, B.S. and H.N. Tuck. 1987 [1895]. *The Chin Hills: A History of the People, British Dealings with Them, Their Customs and Manners, and a Gazetteer of Their Country*. New Delhi: Cultural Publishing House (reprint).
Chatterjee, N. 1975. *The Mizo Chief and His Administration*. Aizawl: Tribal Research Institute (TRI).
Chongloi, S. 2009. 'Relevance of Haosa System in Village Administration in Safeguarding the Kukis Cultural and Political Aspiration', *Ahsijolneng*: 16–24. Shillong: Kuki Students Organisation Shillong.
Dalton, E.T. 1960 [1872]. *Descriptive Ethnology of Bengal*. Calcutta: Firma KLM Pvt. Ltd.
Doungel, N. 2007. *Puchon Pachon* (Customary Practices of Thadou Kuki) Part I & Part II. Imphal: Bir Computer Printing Works.

Evans-Pritchard, E.E. 1940. *The Nuer: A Description of the Modes of Livelihood and Political Institutions of a Nilotic People*. Oxford: Clarendon Press.

Fortes, M. and E.E. Evans-Pritchard. 1940. *African Political Systems*. New York: Oxford University Press.

Goswami, T. 1985. *Kuki Life and Lore*. Halflong, Assam: NC Hills District Council.

Guite, J. 2011. 'Civilization and Its Malcontents: The Politics of Kuki Raid in Nineteenth Century Northeast India', *Indian Economic Social History Review*, 48 (3): 339–376.

Haokip, P.S. 2008. *Zale'n-Gam The Kuki Nation*. India: KNO Publication.

Hunter, W.W. 1908. *The Imperial Gazetteer of India*. Oxford.

Hutton, J.H. 1929. 'Note, In William Shaw's 'Notes on Thadou Kukis', *Journal of Asiatic Society of Bengal*, Calcutta: 3.

Lewin, Capt T.H. 1978 [1870]. *Wild Races of South-Eastern India*. Aizawl: Tribal Research Institute (TRI).

Mills, J.P. 1926. *Ao Nagas*. London: Macmillan & Co.

Sahlins, D.M. 1961. 'The Segmentary Lineage: An Organization of Predatory Expansion', *American Anthropologist*, 63 (2) (Part 1): 322–345.

Shakespear, J. 1983 [1912]. *The Lushei Kuki Clans*. Aizawl: Tribal Research Institute (TRI) (reprint).

Shakespear, L.W. 1977 [1929]. *History of the Assam Rifles*. Aizawl: Tribal Research Institute (TRI) (reprint).

Shaw, W. 1929. *Notes on the Thadou Kukis*. Guwahati: Government of Assam.

Turner, J.H. and Alexandra Maryanski. 1979. *Functionalism*. San Francisco: Benjamin and Cummings Publishing Company.

Zou, V.D. 2005. 'Raiding the Dreaded Past: Representations of Headhunting and Human Sacrifice in North-east India', *Contributions to Indian Sociology* (n.s.), 39 (1): 75–105.

Part IV

WOMEN AND THE WAR

9

APHONIC PARTNERS OF WAR

Role of Kuki women in the Anglo-Kuki War

Hoipi Haokip and Arfina Haokip

There are women in history, and there are men in history, and one would hope that no historical account of a given period could be written that would not deal with the actions and ideas of both men and women.
– Gerda Lerner

A century has passed, but where are the Kuki women in the Anglo-Kuki War? As the above quote makes clear, there were both men and women in history, but it was only in 'historical accounts' that the actions and ideas of women are missing. Gerda Lerner also went on to say that women have been left out in history not because of the evil conspiracies of men in general or male historians in particular, but because we have considered history only in male-centered terms (Lerner 1981: 178). Judith P. Zinsser felt that since women had been marginalised for so long that 'to uncover women's past history and to interpret it is a task as enormous as has been that of writing all existing history' (Zinsser 1993: 43). The problem is that most historians, women as well as men, merely paid lip service to the need to include women's experiences, whereas the overwhelming majority continued their research as before (Zinsser 1993: 47–48). Therefore, history is but about men's actions and ideas. Dolores and Barracano Schmidt called this state of history as 'academic sleight of hand', a state of world without women, a world whose existence is clearly denied (Lerner 1981: 15). The history of the Kukis in general and that of their war against imperialism, which invariably attracts historians' taste is also similarly in the same circumstances. Women remain virtually invisible, silenced and void. This chapter attempts to unravel the role and contribution of women in the Anglo-Kuki War, mainly based on something we can excavate from the narrative accounts of women themselves and from those surviving family members, as well as those of the villagers.

A woman's proper place

The reality of Kuki women can be contended aptly from Simone de Beauvoir's statement:

> [E]conomically dependent like the enslaved, subordinate by law and custom, perpetually the 'other': yet privilege when of the dominant race or class, seemingly pleased with the lack of liberty, seemingly complicit in their own subjugation.
>
> (Marks and de Curtivron 1981: 7)

The Kuki society, like most traditional societies, was patriarchal and followed a patrilineal system, which depicts a clear division of labour between men and women, the existence of customary rituals such as *Sa-ai* and *Chang Ai* indicates a clear distinction of labour where men are to hunt while women is to work in the paddy field. Hence, while the men hunt wild games or goes to war the whole burden of daily work falls upon the women, who fetch water, hew wood, cultivate and help to reap crops, besides spinning and cooking (Chambers 2005: 69). Her life is devoted to the care of the family and in keeping the home well stocked. To understand the significance of women's roles during the war years, a precursory look at some of the social customs prevalent in the Kuki society will give a more comprehensive understanding of their absence in all the historical records, whether oral or written during the war years.

Like most women of Northeast India, a Kuki woman from the day she is born until her marriage and death is bound by the customary laws of her society, the ceremonial practice of *Bride price* and *Chang Ai* demonstrate that economic prosperity of the family lies with women (Gangte 1993: 185). Such customary practices symbolically confirm women as the pillar of the family's economy and to her is attributed the sole responsibility for all round growth and development of the family besides affirming her as the progenitor of the family line. Therefore, to preserve the economic importance of the wife and her relatives in the family circle of her husband, a part of the *bride price* is always kept as due, which is yet to be paid in future while as an appreciation of her economic contribution the *Chang Ai* is performed. The performances of the *minlo* rites (Goswami 1985: 164) during the

Chang Ai ceremony substantiate her importance socially. Paradoxi-
cally, it could only be performed during the lifetime of her husband;
consequently, a widow cannot perform it. The lamentation of a widow
and her children's inability to perform the *Chang Ai* ceremony indicates the discrimination prevalent in the society (Goswami 1985: 576).

Theison chun nu gam khaovang khalna
Lam tol changsel dellou lungmong ponge
Amtol cham chung, changsel len
Bon na delnin, jolou thillang mildin
Bou kabol le,
Miltah sangin lungjonthing bang sange
Lhangai nu bang longlhi pilchang bangthei

I have the utmost desire to persuade my mother to observe
the festival of *chang ai*. I would never be content until and
unless I can see a *mithun* brought in the dancing yard during
the festival of *Chang Ai*. By looking at the *mithun* I would try
to forget my grief caused by my father's death which is in fact
is as big as the tallest tree. My tears fall on the ground like
scattered paddy. I weep like the woman named *Lhangai* nu.

Hypothetically, although credit is bestowed on the women during the
performances of *Chang Ai*, in fact the reputation and stature of the
husband is rather enhanced more than of the wife, as is evident from
this folk song:

Jo hang thange jo dalhong komin in
Haocha phunte alaija hungbal lun
Haocha phunte alaija naballe
Jo lun laito lome. (Goswami 1985: 576)

My father is renowned for his paddy, which is stored in the
whole house. All the chiefs come to my house and because
of this the prestige of my father and his big gong is much
enhanced.

On the successful completion of *Chang Ai*, a man is supposed to attain
a state of physical, moral and spiritual transcendence that makes him
not only qualified to perform the *Chon* (feasts of merit) but also eligi-
ble to be a professional priest (TS Gangte 1993: 179). As such, a woman's proper place was to uplift the reputation of her husband docilely

during her lifetime without any grudges. Again, traditional customary burial ceremonies of the Kukis honour men who during their lifetime have performed numerous *chon* rites. Predictably men thus regarded agricultural work as tedious and took pride of their martial quality and appreciate only war and hunting; they abhorred all household and agricultural works and considered them as menial. Consequently, all other works, save hunting and fighting, fall on the shoulders of women and slaves (Kipgen 2005: 158).

Politically a woman has no say in matters pertaining to the village administration, although she could assist her husband in all other matters. Prevalence of such customary practices contradictorily elevates and also demotes her status in the society. Therefore, to uphold her integrity and position befitting the customary laws, she works laboriously for the self sufficiency of the household, shouldering all responsibilities compliantly. In such a scenario, when the Anglo-Kuki War advanced, all available records were written about men of high rank, such as chiefs and warriors. The Kuki world or community was by and large a society of men, and genealogies were traced from the male line only; women were not viewed as an integral part of the historical record. Consequently, the vast majority of women remained silent and invisible; their history subsumed under general descriptions of men's lives, the few women who did appear had predictable roles as the mothers, daughters, wives and mistresses of famous men. Hence, in the few available journals and biographies of the war heroes, one rarely find mentions of women. Women's sole purposes were to sire a number of male children and tend to the hearth, work stoically in the paddy and contribute to the economy of the family. In fact, her laborious agricultural work allowed the Kukis to continue resisting the Colonial rulers for a stretch of three long years and failure for the women to cultivate agricultural fields led to depletion of food stock and thus their eventual defeat and surrender.

It was from this general background that we now look at the role of Kuki women during the Anglo-Kuki War 1917–1919. We would like to see their role from three broad headings: as an invisible confederate, as an implicit ruler and finally with their unspoken sufferings.

Invisible confederate

The Kukis, unbeknownst to many, had a very efficient village administration with systematic division of labours for men and women and boys and girls alike. Being predominantly agriculturists and hunters by nature, they had an organisational system called the *Lom* (youth corps of the village), in which set task are assign to each capable individuals, and within this they also have the female *Lom*, whose main duty was to keep all the wine mugs of the *Lom*. Whenever someone comes after hunting a big animal or after winning a war against the enemies, the *Lom Upanu* (woman leader of *lom*) takes the predominant part in offering the wine of honour to the hero known as *Laiju* (a variety of rice beer). This village *loms* are usually (if not necessarily) founded on the basis of a well established Kuki traditional institution called *Som*. *Som* is a bachelor's dormitory where section of young boys choose a particular house in the village as their training house and dormitory for the night. Each *som* has a leader (*som-upa*) who train and discipline the young ones in the way they should grow up as a Kuki warrior. Interestingly, the existence of or the condition for choosing a particular house as *som* depended on the availability of unmarried woman in that house. It was the duty of the girls of the family to arrange for the materials needed for the boys to sleep upon, offer them tobacco, mend and wash their clothes, prepare their provisions if required and wake them up early in the morning (Goswami 1985; Doungel 1993: 142). At night, she had to remain awake until all the *som* boys arrive. In this way, she had virtually turned into the servant of the *som*. Once the maiden lady of the house married, *som* also had to exit from that house and shift to another house where they can get unmarried woman. If the strength of Kuki warriors depended on the efficient working of *som*, and if *som* depends on the strength and veracity of woman(men), then one cannot really undermine the role of women. This is especially so during the war.[1]

Women, especially unmarried women, were the ones who helped the men in cooking, washing and mending their clothes during the war. They were the ones who acted as the nurses and doctors of men by tending their wounds and giving them body massage so that the men can continue their fight against the enemy. Besides, the whole women of the village will render their invaluable services in aiding the men prepared for the war, say, preparing rice-cake and dry-meat, producing gunpowder, supplying food to the various stockades in the jungle, and so on. Besides, all women had to gather food from fields and jungles, prepare them and supply their men who are in the battle-fields. In the field, the Kukis' provisions consist of yams and rice boiled to a cake in bamboos. Due importance was attached on the women to see that their husbands' requirements are being met before setting out

on the warpath. Women's roles in the war can be taken in hindsight
from T. H. Lewin's (2004: 154) description:

> A woman, who was engaged working in the fields, asked
> another why she had come so late to her sowing. She replied
> that her husband having just started on the war path, she
> had been detained in preparing his food and other necessary
> arrangements, one of the enemies of the tribe heard say this,
> and became very angry at learning that she had thus suc-
> coured one who had gone out to do injury to his people. He
> bethought himself also, that if the women did not take care
> of the house and prepare their husbands' food when going
> on the warpath, there would be considerable inconvenience
> accruing.

Kuki women have always supported and stood behind their men
like rocks. They are regarded as the morale strength of the Kuki
men. Hence, when the men set out for a war, all the women and
aged of the village accompanied the party on an hour's journey on
their way, carrying the provisions and then bading them with loud
wishes for their success, 'May you be unhurt, and bring home many
heads' (Lewin 2004: 149). When they return victory, there will be
jubilation in the village for at least three days where the warriors
will be decorated with headdresses called *thu'pa* and become famed
warriors. Carey & Tuck noted that, on arrival at the village, the
party was met by the entire population, young and old, male and
female, who shouted, cheered and caressed them, and then led them
at once to the liquor pots, where they sat and told them their tale
of bloodshed and pillage to the admiring women and to the men
who were too old and the boys who were too young to carry arms.
The return of warriors was always celebrated by a feast (Carey and
Tuck 2008: 230).

Truly, from both the Kuki fighters' point of view and also from the
enemy's point of view, the role of Kuki women in the war was tremendous and indispensable. In this sense, the defeat or victory in the war,
to a large extent, depends on their role as well. It was in recognition
of this fact that even the mighty British Empire had to indulge on
so much of inhuman and brutal activities against the Kuki villages.
Knowing that the strength of Kuki fighters was due to tremendous
assistance given by their women from the village and realising that
Kuki rising could not be suppressed unless all sources of livelihood

for the Kuki fighters are erased, they not only burnt down the villages but also systematically destroyed all their foods and livestock. Women were also prevented from gathering food in the jungles or taking up their cultivation. The idea was that if they let the Kuki women and children go unharmed, and their village supply undisturbed, then they will not be able to prevent the women from carrying out their duties towards their men, and hence it would be impossible to win the Kuki war. Thus, to punish the men, all the women, children and aged also had to bear the brunt of destruction. The fact that this hapless population was put in the various 'concentration camps' was to prevent them from giving assistance to Kuki fighters. Thus, it is unfair to exclude the role of Kuki women in the Kuki war in which they were one of the central pillars.

All through the Anglo-Kuki War, women assisted the men in supplying food to the men preparing for the attack some distance from the villages; they gave whatever aid they could to the men and bore the brunt of the hardships too. Phabei, an octagenerian woman, told her grandson, that when the chiefs choose the ablest of his men for the war it was the wives who prepared the provisions necessary for them to carry such as rice cakes, called *changlhah*, baked in banana foiled leaves while some in tubes of bamboo known as *changthei*, dried tobacco leaves called *dummom* and their *tuibuh* (nicotine water gourd pouch), dried meat and *anthom* (fermented rice beer).[2] She also said that, besides feeding the children and the elders, women rose early preparing to finish her household tasks and are the last to retire, prudently keeping her ears and eyes alert, she contributed whatever support that was required of her. As the war dragged on, due to the rampant British burning of the villages, property and cattle in the villages, women were neither able to cultivate the paddy fields nor other crops for the next season. Therefore, during the period of calm, women accrued whatever they could find to feed the family in the neighbouring *jhum* fields and community forest. She also narrated how, during the course of the war, women would sometimes forage into the jungles in search of edible roots, leaves, wild fruits, wild honey, yams and legumes. Every family member, both men and women alike, rendered their service in assisting the men. Whatever they collected in the jungles were equally distributed among the villagers. They also make sure that the men were not in short supply of *dummom* (dried tobacco leaf). On one occasion she mentions how her mother visited Pu Tintong at Imphal jail, before his deportation and gave him *dummom*.[3]

Sometimes women who left the villages to acquire food rations from neighbouring villages or bazaar often met firing from the British troops. Onhol Lhungdim recounts his uncle Jillhum narrative:

> While accompanying women and children procuring food rations on our way back from Suganoo, suddenly, we met the retreating troops with their coolies descending from Lonpi, at a place called Komtunglhang, which was halfway between Goboh and Suganoo. The troops on seeing us fired shots and we ran helter-skelter for safety, hiding in the nearby woods. In the ongoing firing fortunately women and children were unscathed but one man by the name of Thangkhopao was shot death and we had to leave his dead body behind. We thence had to take another off beat route to reach the village with barely our life intact and with much fright.[4]

The above statement amplifies that the British were not averse to shooting anyone in sight, irrespective of gender.

The women, along with providing food for the family, also assisted in processing gunpowder, such as in extraction, filtering, boiling, sieving and mixing charcoal. In most cases, pounding of the gunpowder was normally carried out by the men; however, sturdy women were called upon to assist the men when the men needed respite from the hard pounding or there were shortages of men to pound the gunpowder.[5] Although women were not involved directly in waging the war, women too were assigned the task of spying activities, such as the incoming and outgoing of the British troops.[6] Although these spying activities were not assigned formally, they always contributed by alerting the village chief of any suspicious activities or any incidents happening during the course of their journey from one village to another for the purpose of gathering food rations from the friendly neighbouring villages.[7]

The Kuki women loyally supported the cause of the war and when interrogated about the nature of the war or that of the leaders, they refused to divulge any information and remained tenaciously ignorant about it. As such, in April 1917, when J.C. Higgins and Major Croslezh marched to Aishan to capture Changjapao, the villagers were passively hostile, with few exceptions, to give any information of the whereabouts of Chengjapao; rather they gave them wrong information to mislead them.[8] Then again, when J.C. Higgins enquired the Kukis about the disposition of Pache's forces, they merely said that there were none in this direction but that he had a large force and Maokot was helping them.[9] As the Kukis in general denote both men and women, inferences can be drawn that women were also not left behind in interrogation. The fact that they remain silent and ignorant testifies that women patriotically supported the cause of the war. The British were fully aware that women also supported the war as passive resisters; therefore, whenever opportunities arise they were captured. Thus in a letter sent by Coote to Mr. Webster, he wrote,

> a woman was caught and brought back to camp. But too frightened at present to be coherent, but I hope to get information out of her tomorrow morning before letting her go. I will be able to use her as a messenger to Ukha.[10]

Thus, to say that the Anglo-Kuki War was the war fought between men is incomplete and biased in many ways.

In order to understand the mind of Kuki women during the war, it is pertinent to uncover the various songs composed by them to commemorate the war. Kukis were lovers and great composers of folksongs and ballads. These traditional folksongs were sung in harmonic parts. The system of singing in polyphony was known to the Kukis from very ancient times (Goswami 1985: Appendix 4). Whenever they moved to new settlements, they were always accompanied with their musical instruments. Men and women were well versed in composing numerous ballads eulogising the numerous cycles of their social life, transmitted from generation to generation. Paokhomang Haokip stated that Kuki ballads and folk songs are historical sources that recorded the story of Kuki chiefs and war heroes from generations; when these histories are eulogised in the form of ballads and folksongs, the lived memories of Kuki life and lore are never lost (Haokip 1997: iv). As such, each clan have their own numerous folksongs and ballads, from such ballads and folksongs, insightful glimpses of women's role as invisible collaborators during the Anglo-Kuki War could be traced.

In general, social festivities of the Kukis are chronicled and eulogised in the form of well versed poems and ballads. Women of high pedigree such as the wife of chiefs have often composed and eulogised poignant ballads. Such compositions by the chief's wife are considered laurels of honour. One such ode composed by the wife of Haotinkhup, Kamhao chief (Esprit de corps 2010: 3), honouring the fame of Mr. Ngulsong, Chief of Lonpi and father of Ngulbul, the Great War hero of Lonpi goes like this:

Jang toni tuisong peng mi umlou e
Katoi song, O tuilum pholngou
Nangjing jin eim O.

Translation:

A few are born with exception
My beloved Ngulsong, the Pholngou (vaphol)
O . . . are you my guest.

When the cap of the British officer and the musket were presented to the chief of Chassad by the Chief of Longja, Pi Nemjavei, wife of Lhukhomang Haokip (Pache) Chief of Chassad referred with veneration as *Inpinu* (matriarch), in appreciation of being honoured as the head of the Haokip clan, composed a ballad (Esprit de Corps 2010: 8).

Keila khoi ang kakiton
Phung guol laisim lun
Khotin dong nol e.

Free translation:

Despite all my imperfections
My families with a remarkable token
Honour me worthy thy worthwhile
Passing through all the gates
With well wide acclaim.

Below is the folk song composed by the women of Laijang, the village of the great Kuki war hero, Pu Tintong before the commencement of the battle, to boost the moral and spirit of the chief in his battle against the British (Haokip 2014: 103):

Laijang Tintong bullunmang
Pupa khangkuol seh inlang,
Jalai guoldeb'in,
Jalai guoldeptei inlang,
Setccha kai golseh dounan
Kai guol lhing tei hen

Free translation:

Daring Tintong of Laijang
May thou enthral thy ancestors
May thy fame unparalleled

May thy fame unequalled
Against thy foes thou wage
May thy force be reckoned.

Odes were composed during the war period, and these were sung in the villages as marks of respect to those slained. One such Ode composed and sung in the village of Laijang was:

Kalan kho kim dem dem
Noiya galtol dinnom o
Golchim tadim e'
Nanglung songbang kumsot a'
Ka tou lheimo
Goldang kainoi peng pelep
Golngai nahim mo?
Jansot paova nasap sap
Gol hung lou hei mo?
Lung leng peng pa gol ngai.[11]

Free translation:

Thy loving land of yore
Thou wage thee war
Have thou not yet quench
Through thy years of thorny hedge
Thy soul afflicted
As youthful butterfly
Are thou heart bereaved
Soulfully through night thou mourn
Aren't thou friends home yet?
As soulful butterfly thou grieve.

The folksongs composed significantly highlight women's corroboration during the war by glorifying their achievements so that they remained morally strong, and their fame was recorded in the form of folksongs that would be passed down from one generation to another. Therefore, women acted not only as direct assistants to the daily requirements of their fighting men, but also they constituted the bulk of moral agents behind the men who would otherwise have felt demoralised before the modern army of the colonial government. In short, they were the invisible confederate in the war. It may not be an exaggeration, as it used to be in the past head-hunting days, to say that the moral force behind men's ability to withstand against the imperial forces for about two years was women.[12]

From homemaker to implicit ruler

It is a fact that women were never allowed to meddle in the village administration. However, since the house of the Hoasa (chief), known as Haosa Inpi, served as the highest court of justice according to the traditional Kuki society, where cases were decided, she, as the wife of the chief, tacitly partook in the affairs of the administration and was the ears and eyes of the husband. All affairs that were undertaken were noted by her, and she thus acquired the customary laws and skills to run the village. In fact, in the presence of her husband she did not conduct nor consult on political matters. However, at the time of her husband's absence or death, or until the son come of age, she, as the matriarch, overlooked the affairs of the village as a silent ruler, although the authority may be temporarily transferred to the next of kin, awaiting the maturity of the minor son. In all matters regarding criminal and civil affairs of the village, she was consulted and her presence was equally important. All matters were executed with her knowledge and her voice of approval was a must.[13]

Customary law decreed that unless she as a wife remarried or was without a son her position as the chief's wife could not be infringed upon until the son came of age. Thus, when the Chiefs were imprisoned, the next of kin was customarily appointed to look after the affairs of the village. In the case of Aisan village, when Chengjapao Doungel was arrested and to be transported from Imphal jail to Sadiya, the power of chiefship was given to his brother Thongngam Doungel in the presence of his ministers (*semang-pachong*). Chengjapao consoled his wife Douneng that he would return back safely and not to be disheartened (Doungel 1986: 32–34). It is to be noted that since Chengjapao did not have a male issue and only one daughter, named Jamkhoneng, her power as the chief's wife would be undermined by the family male members and hence she was left powerless. But, in the case of Chassad village, when chief Pache was in detention at Sadiya, upon his death after release his wife Nemjavei became *Haosapi* (chieftainess) of Chassad as the regent of her minor son. In the case of Laijang too, although the regency was in the hands of the next of kin, Mrs. Veiphal, the third wife of Pu Tintong Haokip, chief of Laijang, after his death, was consulted in all matters. Neijalhing recounted:

My mother was well versed and skill in the affairs and conducted of the village's customary laws. She presided over all the meetings of the village administration regarding civil and criminal cases and was consulted regarding shifting of the village site to the present location and all other important civil and criminal cases.[14]

The respect shown to Nemjavei Haokip, wife of Chassad chief Lhukhomang (Pache) Haokip, by all the subsidiary clans of the Haokip and the villagers denote the reverence shown to a chieftainess. She was the voice behind her husband in all affairs.[15] She accompanied Pache when he went to the Somra Tract and in most of his hidings. After the fighting at Kongal, when Pache fled the next day to Chahong Khunou, he was accompanied by a young man, his wife and daughter, a woman and a girl attendant and the illegitimate son and his younger brother Kamjadou.[16] This implies that she was the constant partner of her husband during the war. Not only was she much acclaimed for her bearings and wisdom the villagers were awed by her indomitable wit and knowledge in the customary laws and was thus referred as as 'pasal sanga pasal' (more manly than man).[17] Due respect was shown to the Haosapi (chieftainess) by all the subsidiary Haokip clans and the villagers alike. When her husband was imprisoned she took it upon her shoulders to administer Chassad village with the aid of the council of ministers as per the customarily laws, while going on with her normal everyday agricultural activities. And when Pu Lhukhomang (Pache) died, she administered the affairs of the village as the regent of her minor son Tongkhothang with authority and precision. Her fame as an efficient ruler was widely acclaimed by all. She was described to be physically beautiful, fair and taller than the average Kuki man in stature, and possessed indomitable strength and courage. Her knack of solving any disputes that arose was taken with awe and pride among the Haokips.[18]

Despite customary law denying a chieftaincss the right to politically become the head of the village, if the next of kin so appointed to administer the village at the chief's demise misused his power detrimental to the welfare of the villagers, she being the wife of the Haosa (chief) as Haosapi can step in and legitimately take over the administration as a regent of her minor son. When such maladministration occurred, the family clan and the council of ministers cannot raise any objection to her claim. Thus, she is the matriarch, who makes sure that administration of the village is carried out fairly and efficiently for the welfare of the villagers. When some of the principal chiefs were transported away from home after the Anglo-Kuki War, it was the women who shouldered the responsibility of the village amidst much hardship. She sometimes had to travel to Imphal to settle land disputes that often cropped up during many instances after the death of the chief.[19] She even had to travel to Imphal to file complains against the misconduct of the nominal regent so appointed and to exert her authority as the legal regency.[20] Though society refused to acknowledge their power and authority, the chieftainesses were the unvoiced rulers of the villages. Nothing went unnoticed before their eyes.

Unspoken suffering

Traditionally, the art of warfare among the Kukis may be described in one word – surprise (Lewin 2004: 148). Therefore, when open hostilities commenced with some other clan, it is *sine qua non* among them that no woman should know a word about the matter (Lewin 2004: 148). Therefore, matters pertaining to war were the exclusive affairs of men and women were in general excluded; even the wife of a chief literally term as Haosapi is not permitted to meddle in such matters. Whenever war is to commence, children and women are often taken to a safe hiding place. To elucidate this fact, T.H. Lewin (2004: 145) stated that:

> On one occasions my predecessor Captain Graham, was visiting a Kookie village, and he discovered that they held some British subjects in captivity. On demanding their release, however, the chief refused to let them go; and Captain Graham equally refusing to go without them, things began to look mischievous. At length the Chief in a rage betook himself off to his house, and the big gong began to toll. Captain Graham describes the effect as miraculous: every woman and child disappeared from sight as if by magic.

During inter and intra warfare, women were not spared from being killed nor free from being captured as captives. Therefore, the prime duty of the chiefs was to see that women were always evacuated from the villages. Once the war commenced, safe hiding places were always reserved for the women and children so that when the enemy left the villages, the women could come out from their hiding place and continue with their normal daily duties in assisting the men. In some cases, huge pits (*khul*) were dug, or caves in jungles were the normal places where women and children would be hidden from being killed or being held captives. In other cases, unsuspecting neighbouring villages where chosen.[21]

During the Anglo-Kuki War, most Kuki villages took to jungle hideouts, as there was no neighbouring Kuki village to take shelter against the invading British forces. For instance, an octogenarian Neijalhing narrated what she remembers in the case of the Laijang people. The women and children of Laijang under chief Tintong Haokip were initially hiding in the *jhum* fields but when it was also destroyed by the British they were forced to live in the forest hideouts, mostly in the caves. When they were in the cave, they were sometimes supplied with yams (*bal*) from the fallow *jhum* field by Tintong and party although it was not sufficient to quench their hunger. Women had to regularly fan out in the jungles for wild roots and other vegetables and forest products to feed their children and aged inmates of the hideouts. At night, the women would sleep *in a half sitting* position with their knees enfolded by their arms not due to lack of space in the cave but in order to remain vigilant and not fall into deep slumber. They kept themselves alert to avoid any surprise attacks and to wait for information coming from the men. She also narrated that such alertness was necessary not only against the capture of British forces who would take them to concentration camps but also because the Kukis were also alarmed against the attack from the neighbouring tribes who remained hostile to them.[22]

The British method of attack was rampant burning and destruction. In view of these facts, when fighting was to take place, women, children and the aged were relocated to a safe hiding place, so that the British would not be able be lay their hands on women for interrogation. The following excerpt taken from Laura Hardin Carson's memoirs also make mention of such instances: 'that the men of Sakta had secreted their women and children in the jungle and had carried out six months provision for them, and that they were spending their time day and night making ammunition'. (LH Carson 1997: 228). As the war prolonged and the food was depleted, these women and children who had been skirted in the jungle would be at a starvation level, surviving on whatever they could get from the jungle. Thus, when fighting was to take place at Haipi, women and children of Haipi village were evacuated to Sielsit village, a day journey from Haipi, far ahead of the advancing enemy forces.[23] 50 houses were burnt to the ground in Haipi and as a result of the defeat most of the villagers left the village, many never to return again.[24] While in Lonpi, 70 houses were gutted and whatever cattle remain were slaughtered by the British troops who encamped at the village. Meanwhile as news of the impending attack was alerted in Chassad area, most of the Chassad Kukis took refuge at Naohlang, the only Kuki village south of the Nampanga.[25] In Maokot village too, in apprehension of the looming defeat, some 50 individuals including men and women decided to undertake a long torturous journey towards Somaleng on the Somra tract. In the said course of the journey, they faced unpleasant weather hazards and hostility from the earlier inhabitants (Haokip 2005: 73).

Pu Onhol Lhungdim explained what he heard from his grandmother of the hardships faced by the people of Goboh after the British burnt down their village:

> On the day Goboh village was torched by the British, my grandmother along with other women and children witnessed the incident from the nearby hill range with much sorrow. When the British troops torched the village, we could hear the sounds of bullets and shells fired. It was heart wrenching to see our houses go up in flames. After the troops left the village, some of the men went inside the village at night to survey the damage and what property they could be salvage from the wreckage inflicted by the British troops. Whatever poultry, cattle and property we had were burnt to ashes. Nothing was spared, houses burnt, property destroyed, as the village became uninhabitable, we were rendered homeless, cloth less and without food.[26]

Undeterred by the burning of their villages, most of them rebuilt their villages again, for instances, Changbol Khunou, Hemthang, Tuidan were burnt on 11 and 12 February 1918, Changbol Khunou was rebuilt.[27] They had to rebuild their villages again from the wreckages left behind and much of the responsibilities in rebuilding would in all probability be borne by the women since most men were engaged in war activities. Pu Onhol Lhungdim narrated that when the villagers went back to the villages to see if there was anything they could salvage from the wreckages, they found everything charred to the ground.[28]

Concentration camps were established at Ningel, Tengnoupal, Bongmol, Lonpi and Nungba, where they were heavily repressed (Haokip 2008: 169). Lonpi was set up as the centre of the concentration camp for southeastern zone/hills and many Kukis have surrendered or were captured and put into these concentration camps. They were tortured with just a morsel of food, enquiring the whereabouts of Ngulkhup who had managed to escape.[29] The British officials were unsuccessful in their forcible attempts to extract the where about of Ngulkhup from the villagers. Women too were not spared from being questioned or from being confined in concentration camps. The following statement of Higgins clearly elucidates these facts:

> Speaking of concentration camps reminds me that Lieuten-ant Lanktree told us that he had definite information that the Kuki villages on our south border had taken their women and children for safety to the northern villages of the Chin Hills and that the men had returned to Manipur to fight. If this is so, I think it would be a good move to intern these women and children in concentration camp remote from the border, say at Falam, Kalemyo or Kalowa.[30]

The women were witness to the inhuman torture inflicted to the men. The most horrifying was that of Mombi (Lonpi) village, the rebel cen-tre of the south. Here a concentration camp was opened at Kul-Jang, in the vicinity of the present Lonpi village; women and children were kept together in open camps outside the main camps in which men were kept. They also had to witness and suffer silently from the torture meted out to them, where men were tied together with one another in their loins and made to proceed in a long chain. Heavy loads of rice bags were put on their backs or shoulders and then were driven like herds of cattle up the steep hill. This process will be repeated several times from sunrise to sunset and ended with lashes on their back.[31] They witnessed the horrendous torture meted out to the men in silent suffering. Onhol Lhungdim wrote about the harrowing tale:

> After the arrest of the leading chiefs, the men who took part in the war were arrested from all the villages and kept together in Lonpi Kuljang. The men were forced to carve out holes from two planks of wood and in each holes their hands and feet were locked and with cane rope, twisted and knotted for suppleness, each men was flogged thirty lashes on their bare buttocks. If the Gurkha soldier so appointed slag in flogging the men, the British officers would order him to inflict more force. Streaks of blood gush out at the severity of the flogging and even soiled the Gurkha soldier's uniform instructed to flog the men. Such was the excruciating torture; wails and cries echoed in the villages. Women and children watch hap-lessly from a distance, listening to the cries of pain with tears. The men after the punishment couldn't even stand and went limping as if they were dying. They had to crawl on all four.

It was the women who nursed the men with deep sorrows, scurrying around for herbs and whatever means they could rely on to treat the wounds of the men. As a result of such inhuman atrocities some of the men succumbed to it while a few became incapacitated in mind and body.[32]

After the war most of the men were forcibly engaged in constructing bridle paths connecting points in the Manipur and the Chindwin valley and also connecting the various post with each other (Shakespear 1980: 237). As such it was left to the women to borne the task of looking after the household, shouldering dual responsibilities. Neijalhing noted how his brother too went to work as subsidiary coolie for one of the village members, who had no male member in the family that could work.[33]

As the war continued, life became uncertain, with food supply becoming scarce and women surviving on yams and barks of banana trees for survival, with threadbare clothes they had to bear the harsh and chilling winter of the hills.[34] Many suffered various forms of illness due to constant flight for safety. Mr. Ondem recount how his grandfather contacted ailments unknown to them due to constant flight and hiding in the forests.[35] The wife of Leuthang, the Chief of Goboh, died while Leuthang was held in Kuljang Lonpi before deportation to Sadiya via Imphal Jail. She died probably due to psychological ailment and even on the day of the funeral, Leuthang was permitted to pay his last rite for barely a few minutes and was led back in chains, escorted in the front and rear by soldiers. This tragic incident remains an unforgettable tale of emotional suffering among the villagers of Goboh, even today.[36]

The silent sufferings of the women can be well noted from the Ode composed by the wife of Ngulbul, chief of Longja, on the day he was escorted from his village to Imphal. She escorted him as far as the *Guntui* (Imphal River) beyond the village of Lonpi. The Ode was composed on her way back to the village, imploring the river to communicate her message of anguish.

Ka ngai mel a namu le
Mongmo pheiphung ason'e
Hinti'o lhangdam tin twinu.[37]

Free translation:

If you see my beloved,
Tell him that I return with sorrow,
O! thou mountain stream.

254

Nemjavei too often visited Imphal to enquire about the condition of her husband. The task of travelling to Imphal was by no means easy nor was sending a telegram. One had to travel on foot for days amidst rough terrains, but despite these difficulties, during the three years of sentence she constantly travelled to Imphal to enquire about her husband's condition, wiring telegram messages to his beloved husband Lhukhomang (Pache). Notwithstanding her illiteracy as an obstacle, she must have supposedly taken the assistance of officials to wire these messages, which should be appreciated given the political scene during that period when the Kukis were regarded as rebels by the Government. Below is the short polyphonic sonnet composed by Nemjavei concerning her telegram correspondence with her beloved husband and her dealing with government office:[38]

Kahui Borosap koma,
Veigam lekha kathol thot,
Ngaikom thong lhung nam?

Ahung, ahung thong lhung'e,
Amang lungthim guikhaovin tongdon'e,

Laija chin Mang henkolkai,
Achun naovang kap inte,
Mang lung kiheijin,

Mang lung kiheitah sang in,
Lhanga Mangkang sap thim thu,
Choiphal go bang aham'e.

Free translation:

Through the District Officer of Kohima,
I [from Vei land] wired my message.
Have you received it?

Yes! Yes! I have received it,
Your dear message reached me through the Government telegraph.

My beloved is in Government prison,
He will cry like a child,
Government! Please change your heart.

Far from changing heart,
The mind of the white government officer,
Has become stiff like a bow.

The miseries and sufferings of the people, including women, would have been unimaginable. Their morale down, their property lost and with trepidation, many had to flee their old villages and venture out in new areas to start a new life, while the remaining had to start from shreds again against abject hardships. A total of 126 Kuki villages had been burnt down to the ground, 16 villages permanently declared 'barren' and deserted and 140 villages mercilessly punished and coerced to surrender (Shakespear 1980: 236–237). In these villages, apart from the dead and wounded, the Kukis also lost heavily in terms of grains and cattle by forcible confiscation or by burning. The British had no qualms in burning the villages and whatever property and livestock of the Kukis were. The rampant destruction of paddy, cattle, fowls and property impoverished the Kukis to a great extent and the once self-sufficient Kuki villages were destroyed, resulting in famine. In such situation the women took a leading part in making sure that children and men do not suffer the pangs of the adverse situation. With much loyalty and devotion they scurried into jungles collecting whatever wild edible foods could supplement their requirements. Weathering the harsh climate and the onslaught of unceasing monsoon rain, and with children on their backs, they had to travel long distances when information was received of imminent threats and fighting. Rain, heat, shortages of food and chilling winters, stuffy monsoons and so on led to a number of deaths.[39]

The British administration took no measures for the development of the Kukis and the Kuki villages. The Kukis were described as *Dusman* (i.e enemies or hostiles) as opposed to friends (Gangte 2013: 146). Kukis had to work on communal penal labour for the government. No 'Dusman' villages were given any licenced guns during the whole period of the British regime up to the period of Independence (1947). Any report, true or false, against them was welcome by the colonial government, which gave them severe punishment without caring much as to the veracity of the claim. After the death of Tintong, his eldest son was arrested due to false allegations. A *Lambu* was sent to arrest him and Nemjalhing, the third wife of Tintong on hearing this, raised her voice in objection and anger against the incompetent attitude of the village council of ministers. Later, after a year a *Lambu* came again and torched their house and threatened that unless they bailed out the young boy, he would be forced to undergo rigorous hard labour. With no money and living in abject hardship after the war, she sought help from Onkhai, Chief of Vadungdai, who by custom was the nearest kin of the family. The chief gave her one gong, a prized treasure among the Kukis. With the Gong she went to Imphal and bailed the young boy.[40] The post-war years were a period of tremendous hardships, with thousands dead from of starvation and epidemics. Laura Hardin Carson, a missionary women working in the Chin Hills, witnessed these periods of severe famine and recorded that

> after the insurrection, several villages had been burned with large quantities of food. The villages that turned against the Government at the time of its greatest need had to be punished. They were put at making roads and making artificial lakes. When they should have been in their fields they were making ammunition or after doing forced labour. The result was a terrible shortage of food.
>
> (L.H. Carson 1997: 228)

Death from starvation and later influenza was widespread (Ibid.: 239, 240). Over and above these there was the imposition of the house-tax, where inability to pay was punishable by imprisonment, and as such the women therefore in all possibility slaved and toiled so that the government's penalty against their families did not arise. Thus, the sufferings of the women during, as well as after, the war days have been insurmountable in the view of animosities meted out against the Kukis in general.

Aftermath

The historical records of the Anglo-Kuki War 1917–1919, a span of three years, cover mainly the role of men in general. Women were invisible, and their role continues to remain buried and unexplored. Most historians have failed to find value in women's experiences, just as they savour men and believe what is said about men. This is unfair. Truly, any study of the Kuki society will remain incomplete unless women are included. Their untold stories during the Anglo-Kuki War, which have been lost in the sands of time, need to be explored. Existing histories presented 'a world in which men act and women are largely invisible'. There were many Nemjavei among the Kukis whose stories needed to be studied. Unearthing the many unaccounted stories of women during the war has become a mammoth task due to the unavailability of historical records, both in terms of oral or written. Also, the absence of surviving women to narrate their personal experiences further added to the difficulty in reconstructing their roles. Despite these shortcomings, the chapter has been compiled from whatever available information could be accessed through oral, archival, memoirs etc. An attempt has been made to recreate their role during the war years through the limited available resources at hand. It should be remembered that women have always made history as much as men had. It only requires new attitudes and new methods to do justice to this marginalised section of the society.

Notes

1 For details about *Lom* and *Som*, see Haokip (2013: 177–194).
2 As informed by David Tongjam Haokip, Vicar (Sr. Minister) St. George's, Church of England, East Ham, London, who recounted the tales narrated by his grandmother Pi Phabei who died at 91 years of age in 1982. Interview with him on 7 May 2017.
3 Ibid.
4 Personal interview with Pu Onhol Lhungdim, age 85 years of Goboh village, at his son's residence in Games Village, Langol, on 18 June 2017.
5 As informed by Pu Ngamjason Haokip, 85 years, residence of Kholmun village, Churachandpur District, on 5 June 2017. He spent his lifetime in the Chassad village before he shifted to his current residence in Kholmun and was thus well acquainted with the numerous accounts of the Chassad ruling family.
6 As informed by Pu Hemjang Haokip, 95 years, at his residence in Kholmun Village, Churachandpur District, on 24 June 2017.
7 As informed by Pu Ngamjason Haokip, 85 years, residence of Kholmun village, Churachandpur District, on 5 June 2017.
8 Manipur State Archives (MSA), Imphal, R-2/231/S-4: Tour diary of JC Higgins, Political Agent in Manipur from April 1916 upto 1918.
9 Ibid, p. 86.
10 MSA, R-2/85/S-2, Sec. No. 41 (Assam), Pol/B/ March 1919, 'Progress of the Operation against Kukis'.
11 As sung by Mrs. Neijalhing Haokip, daughter Pu Tintong, chief of Laijang at her residence at Salbung Village, Churachandpur District, on 5 June 2017.
12 In the days of head hunting women directly and indirectly participated in the war as the moral agent. Their explicit act of ridiculing men who could not go to war or performed 'manly' activities by refusing any partnership or marriage and celebrating the 'warriors' or men who can take heads or went to war, directly affected the morale of every man in warfare or hunting. See for instance, B.W. Andaya, 'History, head hunting and gender in Monsoon Asia: Comparative and longitudinal views', Southeast Asia Research, Vol. 12(1), 2004, pp. 13–52.

13 As informed by Pu Thonglhun Haokip, 75 years, New Lambuland, Imphal, on 15 July 2011.
14 Personal interview of Pi Neijalhing Haokip, 95 years, daughter of Pu Tintong Haokip, Chief of Laijang at her residence at Salbung Village, Churachandpur District, on 5 June 2017.
15 As inform by Pu Ngamjason Haokip, 85 years, residence of Kholmun village, Churachandpur District, on 5 June 2017.
16 MSA, R-2/231/S-4: Tour diary of JC Higgins, Political Agent in Manipur from April 1916 upto 1918.
17 Mrs. Vahjaneng Touthang, age 85 years, wife of (L) Hemkholet Touthang, INA pensioner, recounted the tales as passed on by her father, at her residence in Police Jail Compound, Old Lambuland, Imphal- West, Manipur on 10 May 2017.
18 As informed by Pu Ngamjason Haokip, 85 years, residence of Kholmun village, Churachandpur District, on 5 June 2017.
19 Pi Lamkhoneng(75yrs) wife of (L) Letsei Haokip, Chief of Waken Village, at her residence in Waken Village, Kangpokpi District on 23 April 2014. After her husband's death, she administered the village as the regent till her son Jamkholun Haokip came of age to administer the village.
20 Pu Thonglhun Haokip, retired INA pensioner, 85 years, at his residence in New Lambuland on 12 June 2017.
21 As narrated by Pu Jammang Haokip, Director of Lamhil, at his residence in Haokip-Veng, Imphal East on 23 May 2017.
22 Personal interview with Pi Neijalhing Haokip, 95 years, daughter of Tintong Haokip, Chief of Laijang at her residence at Salbung Village, Churachandpur District, on 5 June 2017.
23 A Life in service, Biography of Maj. S. Kipgen, SM (retd), first published by family members of the late Major S. Kipgen, SM, Autumn 1998, p. 6.
24 Ibid., pp. 6 & 11.
25 MSA, R-2/231/S-4: Tour diary of JC Higgins, Political Agent in Manipur from April 1916 upto 1918, p. 133.
26 Personal interview with Pu Onhol Lhungdim, 85 years of Goboh village, at his son's residence in Games Village, Langol, Manipur on 18 June 2017.
27 MSA, R-2/231/S-4: Tour diary of JC Higgins, Political Agent in Manipur from April 1916 upto 1918.
28 Personal interview with Pu Onhol Lhungdim, whose grandfather was then a lad during the Anglo – Kuki War, on 18 June 2017.
29 Pu Ngulkhup Haokip: Kuki War Hero, Esprit de Corps, 1917–1919, Patriotic Souvenir 2010: 22.
30 MSA, R-2/231/S-4: Tour diary of JC Higgins, Political Agent in Manipur from April 1916 upto 1918, p. 144.
31 Haokip, The Extent of Sufferings of the Kukis During And after the Rebellion, 1917–1919 and its consequent effects in the Japanese/ INA War, 1939–45.
32 Personal interview with Pu Onhol Lhungdim, 85 years of Goboh village, at his son's residence in Games Village, Langol, Manipur on 18 June 2017.
33 Personal interview of Pi Neijalhing Haokip, 95 years, daughter of Tintong Haokip, Chief of Laijang, at her residence at Salbung Village, Churachandpur District, on 5 June 2017.

34 Mrs. Vahjaneng Touthang, 85 years, wife of (L) Hemkholet Touthang, INA pensioner, recounted the tales as passed on by her father, at her residence in Police Jail Compound, Old Lambuland, Imphal-West, Manipur on 10 May 2017.

35 Personal interview of Pi Neijalhing Haokip, 95 years, daughter of Tintong Haokip, Chief of Laijang, at her residence at Salbung Village, Churachandpur District, on 5 June 2017.

36 Personal interview with Pu Onhol Lhungdim, 85 years of Goboh village, at his son's residence in Games Village, Langol, on 18 June 2017.

37 As sang by Pu Onhul Lhungdim on 18 June 2017.

38 As sang by Pu Ngamjason of Kholmun village & Pu Thonglhun Haokip of New Lambuland at their residence on 8 & 24 June 2017.

39 MSA, R-2/231/S-4: Tour diary of JC Higgins, Political Agent in Manipur from April 1916 upto 1918, p. 105.

40 Personal interview with Pi Neijalhing Haokip, 95 years, daughter of Tintong Haokip, Chief of Laijang, at her residence at Salbung Village, Churachandpur District, on 5 June 2017.

References

Carey, B.S. and H.N. Tuck. 2008. *The Chin Hills: A History of the People – Our Dealings with Their Customs and Means and a Gazetteer of Their Country*. Aizawl: Tribal Research Institute (TRI).

Carson, Laura Hardin.1997. *Pioneer Trails, Trials and Triumphs*. Calcutta: Firma KLM Pvt. Ltd.

Chambers, O.A. 2005. *Handbook of the Lushai Country*. Aizawl: Tribal Research Institute (TRI).

Doungel, T.L. 1986. *Pu Chengjapao Doungel, Hinkho Thusim Bu (In Kuki)*. Dimapur: Private Circulation.

Doungel, T.L. 1993. *Chin Kuki Bulpi Ho Phunggui Thusm Leh Chondan Bu (In Kuki)*. Imphal: Guite Doungel Council (Indo-Burma).

Gangte, P. 2013. 'Kuki Nation Towards Political Unity and Consolidation', in Thongkholal Haokip (ed.), *The Kukis of Northeast India: Politics and Culture*, pp. 141–174. New Delhi: Bookwell.

Gangte, T.S. 1993. *The Kukis of Manipur: A Historical Analysis*. New Delhi: Gyan.

Goswami, T. 1985. *Kuki Life and Lore*. Halflong: NC Hills District Council.

Haokip, David T. ed. 2005. *Telsing Singlunte Thusim*. Yangoon: Private Circulation.

Haokip, Hoipi. 2014. 'Genesis of Kuki-Chin-Zo Women's Political Evolvement', in H. Sudhir (ed.), *Tribal History of North East India: Essays in Honor of Professor Lal Dena*. New Delhi: Concept.

Haokip, P.S. 1997. *Khanglui-Khangtha Lakawi La, in Thadou Kuki*. Imphal: Private Circulation.

Haokip, P.S. 2008. *Zalengam: The Kuki Nation*. KNO Publication.

Haokip, P.S. 2013. 'Reinculcating Traditional Values of the Kukis with Special Reference to Lom and Som', in Thongkholal Haokip (eds.), *The Kukis of Northeast India: Politics and Culture*, pp. 177–194. New Delhi: Bookwell.

Haokip, P.S. n.d. *The Extent of Sufferings of the Kukis During And After the Rebellion, 1917–1919 and Its Consequent Effects in the Japanese/ INA War, 1939–45.*

Kipgen, S. 2005. 'Political and Economic History of the Kukis of Manipur', unpublished PhD Thesis, Department of History, Manipur University.

Lerner, Gerda. 1981. *Teaching Women's History*. Washington, DC: American Historical Association.

Lewin, T.H. 2004. *The Hill Tracts of Chittagong and the Dwellers therein.* Aizawl: Tribal Research Institute (TRI).

Marks, E. and Isabelle de Curtivron. 1981. *New French feminism*. New York: Schocken Books.

'Pu Ngulkhup Haokip: Kuki War Hero, Esprit de Corps, 1917–1919', *Patriotic Souvenir*, 2010. *A Life in Service: Biography of Maj. S. Kipgen, SM (retd.)*. 1998.

Shakespear, L.W. 1980. *History of The Assam Rifles*. Guwahati: Spectrum Publications.

Zinsser, Judith P. 1993. *History & Feminism: A Glass Half Full.* New York: Palgrave Macmillan.

10

HER-STORY IN HISTORY
Women's roles and participation in the Anglo-Kuki War

Hoineilhing Sitlhou

Women have a history; women are in history.
— Gerda Lerner

Though many studies have been conducted on the Anglo-Kuki War 1917–1919, women's roles, their contribution or participation have been excluded from the historical narrative. The tendency of earlier historical writings was to focus on men as actors and active agents in history. This chapter concerns with the interplay of war and gender in the context of the Kuki society. The Kuki people follow patriarchal, patrilineal and patrimonial system of family structure. As a result, the line of descent, law of inheritance and law of residence are appointed to the male line only and the children follow the clan name of the father.

The Anglo-Kuki War was a turning point in the history of the Kukis. Interestingly the war, which went on for almost two years, has been undermined in the historiography and mainstream discourse of India. Though, excluded from popular discourses of the Indian Nation-state, the Anglo-Kuki War is widely discussed in colonial writings of both the British administrators and Christian Missionaries. It is also widely studied by scholars from different social science disciplines. However, women roles, contribution or participation have been excluded from the historiography of the war. The war could not have been sustained without the support of the women in various ways. When their husbands were sentenced to confinement in distant lands by the colonial rulers, some of the wives of the chiefs took over the village administration besides being solely responsible for the upbringing of the children. The chapter aims to recover women's agency as a means of restoring the voices of marginal groups who were excluded from the dominant historical narratives. It will draw attention to the accounts of the Kuki women during and after the war by using oral tradition and oral history in order to unravel the role played by them during the war.

Method, materials and approach

Methodologically, a deconstructive reading and analysis of available materials and records on the Anglo-Kuki War has been deployed by looking into:

1 The official writings like government reports, administrative reports, ethnographic and academic monographs written by colonial administrators,
2 Missionary literature in the form of field reports, socio-cultural life of the tribes in their fields, autobiographies and the proceedings and discussions in various conventions held by the mission society, etc., and
3 The written texts of sociologists, historians, anthropologists, local writers' accounts, scholarly interpretation and analysis of colonial ethnographies in the form of research works, published books and unpublished thesis or monographs.

The critiques on existing literature of the Anglo-Kuki War are supplemented with interviews on selected respondents who are direct descent or relations of the chiefs or their wives or surviving villagers. Recordings of oral tradition and oral history including legends, myths, songs, stories, personal experiences, family stories, memoirs etc. were collected. A narrative approach was used to retrieve hitherto untold stories of women's experiences, roles, contributions, songs and their relationships with those around them, especially their husband.

Where is *her*-story in the history of the Anglo-Kuki War?

History is, and has always been, selective and represents a very narrow account of human past in terms of time, space and numbers. The dominant narrative of those in power often sidelined, undermined or marginalised the voices or stories of the masses, and primarily the women. The reason for the invisibility of women in history could be attributed to the patriarchal domination of society. All historical traditions have been written and recorded by male writers and have been shaped by male perspectives (Hmingthanzuali 2010: 3). As Gerda Lerner rightly writes, 'women have a history; women are in history'. According to her, all the earlier historical writings described men as actors and active agents in the scene of history, therefore it is important to give back women their history' (as cited in Hmingthanzuali 2010). 'If history is the progress and advancement of civilisation, then it is absolutely impossible that progress could have been achieved without the equal participation of the women who form about half the society' (Sharma 1998: 49).

The existing literatures on the Anglo-Kuki War is primarily based on colonial writings of both the administrator and missionary, supplemented by writings of scholars and academicians after India's independence, and published and unpublished monographs. The writings are replete with accounts and reports of the sequences of the war, the possible causes, consequences or ramifications of the war (see Shakespear 1929; Reid 1942; Ray 1990; Gangte 2010; Chishti 2004; Parratt 2005; Bhadra 1975; Haokip 1984; Palit 1984; Haokip 2011). While some simply reproduced the colonial ethnographies, others made a critique to colonial discourse and provided the native viewpoints. Lal Dena (1988), for instance, shows how the defeat of the Kukis in the war affected their receptivity to Christianity and resulted in large-scale conversion. Tarun Goswami compiles some of the songs composed by the chiefs (and their close kin) during the Anglo-Kuki War. The songs reflect the different facets of emotion experienced by them; happiness in victory (initial stages of the war); anguish and bitterness at the thought of life in prison; remorse or sadness at their defeat or because of those who got killed in the war (Goswami 1985). Though they are all detailed and are important contributions to the understanding of the Anglo-Kuki War, there is no mention of women's roles and participation in all their writings.

The reports submitted by the British administrators Higgins and Cosgrave to J.E. Webster, Chief Secretary (Shillong) during the war are an important primary source for many historians and social scientists who write on the Anglo-Kuki War.[1] These reports give an account of the progress during the war and the varied ramifications not just to the parties involved (the British and Kukis) but also to the other communities who were directly and indirectly affected by the war.[2] Likewise, there are many letters of correspondence between the different British officers in the field, including their communication with their higher authorities, and these constitute an important historical source for understanding the nature of the war from European perspectives. These official reports and letters of correspondence did not have any record of the women's voices or activities during the war, even though it did make passing references about the women (and children) on how they were victimised by the harsh effects of the war.

The missionary writings and records were as guilty in failing to include the stories of the women. Christian missionary writer Frederick S. Downs, in his *The Mighty Works of God*, called the Anglo-Kuki War 'the Kuki War of Independence'. He discusses the events and consequences of the war and relates the villagers' large-scale conversion to Christianity after the defeat of the Kukis in the war. A passing reference to the Kuki rebellion was also recorded by Rev. William Pettigrew in his, 'Evangelistic and Educational Report for 1921'. The report reads:

> certain Kuki tribes rebelled on the suggestion to provide a second Labour Corp, and punitive measures, later known as the Kuki Punitive Measures were taken against them ere the year closed and lasted well into 1919, before the recalcitrant chiefs surrendered and the strife ceased.[3]

The 'Mission Progress Report for 1922' recorded how the progress of the leper asylum of the American Baptist Foreign Mission Society at Kangpokpi station was obstructed by the Kuki rebellion.[4] Though not directly related to the war, Mrs. Alice Pettigrew's letter, 'Woman's Work Report for 1923', discussed her mission work among the Kuki women a few years after the war (Pettigrew 2005: 95–97).

An alternative stratagem: orality, life-histories and narratives

Narratives or stories occur when one or more speakers engage in sharing and recounting an experience or event. Margarete Sandelowski (1991) in her article, 'Telling Stories: Narrative approaches in Qualitative Research', considers narrative as a framework for (a) understanding the human being as subject of inquiry; (b) conceptualising the interview; and (c) analysing and interpreting the interview data. It is one of the many modes of transforming knowing into telling. This section of the paper make use of the narrative approach to trace the life-histories of the wives of the prominent rebel chiefs namely: Nemjavei, wife of Lhukhomang Haokip (Pache) of Chassad; Chongneivei, wife of Khotinthang Sitlhou (Kilkhong) of Jampi; Haolhing, wife of Vumngul Kipgen of Tujang; and Lhinghat, wife of Mangkho-on of Tingkai. The war, which lasted for almost two years, could not have been sustained without the support of the women who constituted half of the population. Moreover, when their husbands were deported in distant lands, the bulk of family responsibilities and village administration fell on their wives.

Nemjavei, wife of Lhukhomang Haokip (Pache) of Chassad

Both in the historiography of the war and that of the Kukis, Pache or Lhukhomang is a prominent personality known for his bravery and the crucial leadership played by him during the Anglo-Kuki War. He was one of the most powerful Kuki chiefs who had initiated the war. From the beginning, he vehemently opposed the recruitment of labour corps and was instrumental in persuading neighbouring Kuki chiefs to join the armed uprising.[5] Pache was the leader of the rising in the eastern sector or Chassad area. In fact, there is an interesting documentation of his confrontation with the British army. L.W. Shakespear (1977: 225) writes:

> In the mid March a combined Column of 150 rifles (platoons from the 2nd, 3rd, and 4th A.R.) under Captain Coote with Lieut. Parry and Mr. Higgins left for the Chassadh hills . . . Coote joined hands with Patrick (a commander of a column of Burma Military Police); both Columns then moved on north and attacked Kamjong, Pachei's [Pache] principal village, in which action several casualties occurred and Lieut. Molesworth (Burma M.P.) was killed. The two Columns then proceeded by different routes against Chattik and Maokot, and in the fighting at the latter village Coote had 1 man killed and 6 wounded. Lieut. Kay. Mouatt (Burma) being amongst the latter. Pachei (Pache), evading capture, fled into the Somra hills, an almost unknown tract.

Pache surrendered on 5 March 1919 on the promise that his life would be spared. He served a sentence of three years in Sadiya of Assam.

Although a lot of information can be gathered on the life of Pache, little is written about his wife, Nemjavei, who had a reputation for wisdom and knowledge of the customs and culture of the Kukis. She was both a good composer of songs and poems. She composed this song for her husband just before he was deported to Sadiya.

Amang henkol kaidingin,
Khaovang jinang kalha-e,
Hamjang phan ngaichul lou

Free translation:

To suffer in the government prison,
I release you like a rope,
Let good fortune follows you, my beloved.

Amang thimthu la kanellal hammol,
Henkol kaiding in bangjal jet in kalhaove.

Free translation:

I could not convince the government,
For that prison, we bid you farewell with both the hands.

When her husband was in prison, it was natural that she felt restless and constantly worried about the life of her husband, as every wife in such a situation would have felt. Elite women especially were expected to conceal their sufferings and hardships with grace. Songs and poetry were the only ways to register their stress and loneliness. Nemjavei was gifted with the art of composing popular poetry and lyrics. One of her famous songs is about her correspondence through telegraph with her beloved husband Pache when he was on trial at Kohima jail.

Kahui Borosap koma,
Veigam lekha kathol thot,
Ngaikom thong lhung nam?

Ahung, ahung thong lhung'e,
Amang lungthim guikhaovin tongdon'e,

Laija chin Mang henkolkai,
Achun naovang kap inte,
Mang lung kiheijin,

Mang lung kiheitah sang in,
Lhanga Mangkang sap thim thu,
Choiphal go bang aham'e.[6]

Free translation:

Through the District Officer of Kohima,
I [from Vei land] wired my message.
Have you received it?

Yes! Yes! I have received it,
Your dear message reached me through the Government
telegraph,

My beloved is in Government prison,
He will cry like a child,
Government! Please change your heart,

Far from changing heart,
The mind of the white government officer,
Has become stiff like a bow.

This song unravels the invisible hardship and uneasiness of a woman who felt lonely in the absence of her husband. The yearning for the husband is aggravated by the thought of a beloved one staying in a prison far away. The only way to know about him or communicate was to visit the nearest government office and send words through telegraph. It was also her constant source of worry to imagine the kind of life that her husband was going to endure in prison, in a land that was foreign to him. Her constant prayer was that the government would change their heart. But this had never happened. Days passed by, months gone and years lengthened. When the sight of her husband's homecoming is nowhere she could only curse the government for being heartless and inhumane. She therefore described the 'white government's' heart as being 'stiff like a bow'.

According to D.P. Haokip there was no woman in the history of Chassad so influential and whose presence commands respect and power like Nemjavei.[7] D.P. Haokip once stayed in the village of Chassad and personally met and spoke with Nemjavei. He said that in the history of the Chassad family there was never, and will never be, someone as wise and accomplished as her. She was a great orator, tall and beautiful woman, and her fair complexion was said to be like the colour of milk. It was said that she was well versed on genealogical history, tradition and culture of the Kukis. In her husband's absence, she looked after the administration of the village. She often dictated the proceedings and decisions of her village and sometimes at the level of the Haokip clans. Interestingly she was also brave, courageous and an accomplished hunter.

Nemjavei was so influential that she was involved in the selection of a bride for her father-in-law, a widower. She chose a beautiful lady name Hoikhoneng from Senam village located near present day Moreh. On their way to Chassad, they passed through a village dominated by Sakang people who requested the palanquin bearers to show them the new bride. But they were not willing to do so. It was said that the lady died soon after they reached Chassad due to some ailment. In lamentation, she composed another song:

Senamte cha Hoikhoneng,
Phungmang guiloi dia kalah lengvan sangkalta.

Free Translation:

Hoikhoneng, the daughter of Senam people,
I chose you to mend the lineage, but you have gone to heaven (died).

Nemjavei had one son and one daughter with Pache. When she was about to die, upset with the way other Haokips had treated them, she instructed her son Tongkhothang:

Your brothers (meaning those belonging to the Haokip clans) are rich, wise and talented. They have received the blessings of God. But till today, none of your younger brothers have cared enough to visit us or cross the boundary of our village. Because of their negligence, you ought to give the traditional *Sating*[8] to your big brother Kipgen, and obtain his blessing.

Kipgen and Haokip are the sons of Thalhun. They were born at Layang between 1330 A.D. and 1370 A.D (Doungul 2006: 8). She also declared that the Mangvum sub-clan would be thenceforth considered as the youngest and the last within the Haokip clan.[9]

Chongneivei, wife of Khotinthang Sitlhou (Kilkhong) of Jampi

Jampi area in northwestern hills of Manipur, which is Tamenglong district today, was another important theatre of the Anglo-Kuki War. Khotinthang Sitlhou (Kilkhong) of Jampi was one of the Kuki chiefs who started opposing labour recruitment and the leader of the war for the northwestern hills. He killed a mithun and performed the traditional *sathin-salung-neh* in March 1917 to formally decide not to send men for the labour corps. He then distributed a portion of the meat (called *sajam*) to the Kuki chiefs and thus forming a powerful confederacy of the Thadou-Kuki chiefs.[10] Once the war broke out, he assumed the title of 'Raja' of the hills, collected guns and revenues from those villages that were loyal to the British (Haokip 2011: 140).

Khotinthang surrendered on the 24 September 1918 in response to a *parwana* sent out by Mr. Cosgrave, the Political Agent. The promise was that his life would be spared if he surrender and submit 30 guns before the 1 October.[11] The Advisory Committee under Regulation III of 1818 found that he was one of the earliest to organise oppositions to the orders of the State and of the Government. The Committee consider that his influence and position rendered it necessary for the preservation of tranquillity, that he should be kept 'under restraint' for a certain period.[12] He was released after three years in Sadiya.

Kilkhong was married to Chongneivei who hailed from Singjol village of Naga Hills. She was 25 years old when she was married to Kilkhong in the year 1910, though engaged to a man named Phohpu, but Kilkhong forced her into marriage because of her beauty. She was tall, well built, fair and 'her face was flat' (an important trait of a beautiful women at that time). What people remember of her is that she was endowed with physical strength and was also a gifted and capable administrator. She had three daughters and two sons with Kilkhong. Her youngest child was born in 1927 after the death of her husband.[13] She was very fond of wearing necklace made of cornelian beads (the traditional or customary necklace of the Kuki woman) and used to wear sets of them. It was said that the water spirits (of the Tuilong or Barak River) gave her a '*chinkeng*' for hanging her large collection of cornelian beads. This shows how she was such a popular chieftess among the Kukis. Till today, the *chinkeng* is with her grandson Thangkholen Sitlhou residing in Gunngolphai Village.[14]

Her popularity declined after she remarried to a lower primary government school teacher Tinkhup, at the age of 34 years. She bore him two sons. She was made to relinquish her title as chieftess of Jampi after her second marriage. The people of Jampi used to say about her: '*kichem se hihleh Jampi nu-nu din akilomin alimjong ahoijin chingjong aching in thakhop set ahi vaihop jong athem in*' (If she had not gone wayward, she was fit to be the chieftess of Jampi in terms of her beauty, wisdom, physical fitness or strength, and ability to rule).[15] A second marriage of a woman, especially among the chiefly class, was not well regarded in those days.

Haolhing, wife of Vumngul Kipgen of Tujang

Prior to the proclamation of the war against the British, a meeting was held at Jampi village in the second week of March 1917. Vumngul Kipgen, chief of Tujang[16] and head of the Kipgen clan, along with his eldest son Lunjangul Kipgen, had attended the Jampi Summit. Vumngul is remembered in history as the more realistic and practical chief who foresaw the dire consequences that the rebellion was to bring. In the same meeting, he and his son had expressed their apprehensions that they were all ill-equipped and without sufficient guns and ammunitions to fight the British (Haokip 1984). At that period, the Tujang family had settled at Molvailup village of present day Burma.[17] Though initially reluctant to wage a war, Vumngul actively participated and commanded the Eastern region (Burma) in the war. The trials of the principal Kuki chiefs were held in Burma (Somra Tract) under the Chin Hills Regulation 1896 and punishment was pronounced accordingly (Haokip 2011). Vumngul was one of the ten Kuki chiefs who were detained in Homalin jail and then sent for detention at Taunggyi, in Burma (Myanmar) (ibid: 183). He spent four complete years at Taunggyi jail and was released in 1922. After his release, he joined his relatives at Noneh in Northwest Manipur (present day Tamenglong). He died in the year 1938.[18]

While Vumngul Kipgen was involved in the war, he left behind his wife Haolhing and five sons. The names of the five sons were Lunjangul, Tilkhosei, Letkhopao, Mangpithang and Mangkhovom. It was said that Haolhing had taken care of the children in the absence of her husband. We did not have any record of her administrative capabilities, as their eldest son Lunjangul was already an adult at the time when their father was serving the sentence. What is remembered of her is the song composed by her at the time of her husband's departure to Taunggyi:

Joumang henkol kaijong le,
Ajemtol la kheponte,
Namtin kai dongsa.[19]

Free Translation:

Even if the noble sons of the hills are in prison,
His glory shall not fall on the ground (shall not fade),
He was the man honored by all nations.

The song depicted that she was an exceptionally brave woman who, instead of mourning like other women, glorified the emotional but

historical moment so that the men would not be disheartened. She
believed in the cause her husband was fighting for and seemed to have
no worries or fears at how she was going to take care of herself, her
sons or her village in the absence of her husband.

Lhinghat, wife of Mangkho-on of Tingkai

Mangkho-on was recalled by a villager to be a handsome and fear-
less man. He was of medium height, kept a long hair, wears a *boitong*
(waist-cloth), a loin cloth and a head gear made of cloth. He was a
good administrator and a cultured man. He was also a village priest
and was known to treat his villagers of their ailments. Mangkho-on
was a great hunter and had killed many wild animals including bears,
reindeers and monkeys during his lifetime. He was also good at making animal traps and was known to have wrestled with a bear. He lived
for about 90 years and was buried in Tingkai village.[20] Mangkho-on
was known to be active in the war from the very beginning and participated in the Jampi war conclave (Haokip 2011: 152). Mangkho-
on was no longer at the prime of his life when the war broke out. He
already had three sons and two daughters. He was vehemently against
the recruitment of labour corps and a brother by the name Seithang
Haokip was killed in the process of his opposition to British rule. To
him, being asked to go to France simply as a menial labourer in the
war front was an insult.[21]

Paodong Haokip[22] recalls some of the sayings of Mangkho-on after
his return from Sadiya. On one instance, he said, '*Anu ngaisangin
kachate ngaina asangjoi, kachate ngaina ban ah jamom/dumom
kangaipen'e*' (I missed my children more than my wife when I was in
prison, I missed my tobacco leaf most). This is a true manifestation of
Kuki male chauvinism in traditional Kuki society. It might not necessarily reflect his true feeling towards his wife, but expressing emotion
towards one's wife candidly was considered unmanly. Men, especially
those in leadership positions, therefore refrained from expressing their
emotions about their wife in public. The fear of being branded hen-
pecked was a matter of great consideration. In another instance, he
said, '*Kajanmang in Tingkai khosung ah kana um jin, kahung khah-
doh leh Jail sung ana hi ji'e. Kathang kam na kan ngaiji in chule kaloul-
hona kalou ma kahin ngaiji'e*' (In my dream, I was in Tingkai village,
when I woke up it was in Jail. I missed my trapping and *jhum* field).
He also said that 'imprisonment is not easy, I always wanted to get out
of it'. 'I missed my birthplace Tingkai where I used to go and hunt'.
However, one interesting thing he said was, '*Neh le chahjong Jail sung*

achun atuinai' (the food and drink inside the jail taste good). While he was under confinement, he composed a song which had become very popular in Tingkai area:

> *Mang in henkol eihenna,*
> *Khen cheng toidonnem donte gam,*
> *Kamui lhanlha in gam kamui*
> *Thihpi dongkot neihon in, bolna vangkho lamdang tante*

Free translation:

> When the British put me in prison,
> To that land where my beloved ones live,
> I have always seen in my dream, that lovely country,
> Open the iron gate, so my sadness will fade away.

Not much is remembered about his wife, Lhinghat, except whenever he was about to go in to battle, she used to pack for him tobacco for his journey. But she was also a good composer. When her husband was in prison, she composed one moving song.

> *Mang in henkol abutna senang koi,*
> *Mongmon keimang henkol sung ah.*

Free translation:

> The government keep my beloved one in prison,
> Oh! my beloved Mang would be in grief inside the prison.

Mangkho-on's return from jail was celebrated by his villagers and a grand welcome was given to him. The women of the village in all households brewed rice beer enough for the whole village to partake in drinking outside the chief's house. They danced and sang all night in merrymaking to mark the return of their chief. Interestingly, the villagers were scared to speak directly to him. They were not used to someone who had travelled to a distant land. This is a song composed by the villagers to commemorate the return of their chief:

> *Kumkho sota henkol kibuhin,*
> *Thonglhungta bolna vangkho,*
> *Hung un ning-ju-ai-sa khoppiu hite,*
> *Penna bullun Mangkho-on*

Free translation:

> After long years of imprisonment,
> He comes home where he belongs,
> Come! Let us eat and drink (celebrate)
> For our progenitor/head Mangkho-on

The study has managed to single out the contribution of only four prominent women amongst many others. The limitation of the study is that it gives importance to the accounts and biographies of notable women of the chiefly class who were strong, powerful and more privileged than the average women. The study agrees that women of different social classes are bound to have diverging differences in terms of experiences and perspective (Hmingthanzuali 2010). But, it can be assumed, based on this study, that women did contribute despite the fact that their contributions were not recorded in history.

War and gender: concluding discussion and analysis

> The road is thronged with women; soldiers pass
> And halt, but never see them; yet they're here
> A patient crowd along the sodden grass,
> Silent, worn out with waiting, sick with fear.[23]

This poem by Siegfried Sasson could be used to illustrate the experience of women during the Anglo-Kuki War. The experiences of women are often overlooked or undermined despite the extra pressure that war heaped on them. The reason lies in the fact that war is a gendered phenomenon, one with meaning for the relative status of men and women within any society.[24] There are also social myths that define war as a masculine undertaking and delineate the differential duties prescribed for men and women during wartime. For instance, men are expected to be protectors of their women, homes and families, whereas women are expected to maintain these same homes and families, thereby supporting their men, and waiting for them to return.[25] In fact, this stereotypical vision of war has been persistent in almost all cultures and societies. War is considered to be strictly men's business. They go to the front, do the fighting, take the risks and make the decisions. Women stay at home, take care of the children and keep the home fires burning, waiting for their soldier husbands to come home (Goldstein 2003).

In contrast to the above popular notions about the gendered effects of war, L. Kelly (2000: 61–62) writes:

> women can be empowered during wartime as the traditional "feminine" role is challenged, allowing them to be heads of households, work in the public sphere, and display qualities and skills which are often reserved for men or regarded as "masculine".

In Kuki society, politics has never been considered a woman's domain. This is in line with the discussion by Sherry B. Ortner (1996) of the tendency to associate women with 'nature' and 'the domestic unit', and men with 'culture' and 'the public entity'. Therefore, activities such as politics, warfare and religion are seen as more removed from nature, as superior to domestic tasks, and therefore as the province of men (Ortner 1996: 33). Nemjavei, chieftess of Chassad and Chongneivei, chieftess of Jampi, were cases that were an exception rather than a rule. Both of them were known to be good administrators and commanded authority for a while in the absence of their husbands. They were both strong women physically, well-informed, and Nemjavei was known to be a good hunter too. They exemplify cases in which the stereotypical gender roles and ascriptions are challenged and reversed in times of conflict (El-Bushra 2000: 67) due to the increased rights and responsibilities assumed by women during the war (Kelly 2000).

Nemjavei, Chongneivei, Haolhing and Lhinghat were all good composers. While the contribution of Haolhing and Lhinghat in the realm of village administration and knowledge in customary laws was not recorded, they had singlehandedly taken care of their households in the absence of their husbands during the war and in the years of their imprisonment. This could be due to the customary norms of the male dominated Kuki society, which do not encourage women to govern. According to Mangkhosat Kipgen (1997), women had no place in social organisation and village administration. There are exceptionally few instances of a widow of a deceased chief ruling over the village on behalf of her minor son, until his maturity. In community matters, women were not consulted, and if they volunteered their opinions, they were not given weight. It is a role, which sees them as the centre of domestic life but not actively participating in decision-making (Lloyd 1991; Sitlhou 2015).

The song composed by Haolhing before her husband's departure shows her emotional strength though expressed in a lady-like restraint. She tells him, the villagers and the world that she was supportive and proud of her husband's endeavours. She believed in the cause that her husband was fighting for and seemed to have neither worries nor fears at how she was going to take care of herself, her sons or her village in the absence of her husband. In the same way, the songs of Nemjavei and Lhinghat were filled with concern at the thought of the suffering of their husbands in prison. They were not lamenting about their own misfortune or struggles due to the war or the absence of their husbands. It was evident from all these narratives that they were capable of playing a very significant backstage role in the rebellion off-the-battlefield.

The tendency of the official version of the accounts of wars has always been to focus on 'men in trousers' (Nordstorm 2005). 'Women and girls were not allowed military positions or equipment, but they transported messages, munitions, supplies and food. They were the backbone of the war: running arms, procuring survival necessities, acting as communications systems, doing reconnaissance' (ibid: 401). The Kuki women were also responsible for sheltering, feeding, clothing and couriering messages secretly, often endangering their own lives. There were instances in which the British soldiers interrogated the women regarding the whereabouts of their men. There was also a record of the molestation of a woman relative of Mangkho-on, chief of Tingkai, by the Britishers. She was held in captivity for a whole night to induce Mangkho-on to submit to the authority of the Britishers.[26]

When the British were pursuing Tintong and Enjakhup parties, they were gathering with a large following of men, women and children at a place called Kolkang.[27] 'Finding themselves hard pressed by the Britishers they commenced to drop followers, women and children, who were picked up by their pursuers'.[28] Women and children tend to figure heavily in terror warfare as they tend to be less mobile than men.

> Women are usually responsible for their homes, critical subsistence, and the young, and thus tend to be more directly tied to a set locale . . . women generally search out and try to carry their children (and sometimes the infirm and elderly), and are thus among the slowest to flee. They are thus among the most likely to be caught by troops, by bullets, and by bombs. Home and hearth, mothers and children tend to represent the heart and core of virtually all societies.
>
> (Nordstorm 2005: 402)

Close to the end of the war, Lieutenant H. Rundle, who was based on the Chin borders, and his troops were assigned the task of searching for and compelling the prominent Kuki chiefs to surrender their guns.[29] 'In order to achieve this object the Area Commander collected men, women and children in certain concentration camps, where they were fed and maintained till the guns were surrendered'.[30] The hardships women experienced on the way to the concentration camps and at the concentration camps themselves were clearly as physically, mentally and emotionally exhausting as the experiences of men. One of the reasons for the defeat of the Kukis during the war was due to the depletion of their food rations. The British administrator Sir Robert Reid (1997) wrote, 'the rebellion broke out after the Kukis had reaped the harvest in 1917. Columns operating over a wide area prevented them from sowing and reaping a crop in 1918, and by 1919, resistance collapsed owing to the lack of food'.

This is evident in the surrender of Pache, chief of Chassad. In the words of Brigadier General C.E.K. Macquoid,

> Pachei, his leading men and followers, broken up into small gangs, being now hemmed in, were remorselessly pursued, many being killed or captured, until, worn out and with no supplies and unable any longer to support themselves in the jungle, large numbers of men together with women and children; came into various posts and surrendered. Pachei personally still kept the field and eluded all attempts at capture, until himself worn out and hungry, he slipped with his wife and child through the cordon formed around him, came into Imphal and gave himself up on the 5th March.[31]

Similar in substance is the letter of chief of Mombi, Ngulkhup and Chief of Nungoinu, Kamjathong dated 11 October, 1918, wherein they expressed their desire to make peace with the British government. *Inter alia* they wrote:

> Your honour in anger has burnt our houses and destroyed our mithuns, pigs, fowls and property generally. Now our bodies are entirely unclothed and our women and children about to perish of starvation. If our women and children starve, we men shall be ruined and shall become like wild beasts.[32]

The war, which lasted for almost two years, could not have been sustained without the support of women, who were instrumental in collecting fruits and tubers from the jungle as the British curbed cultivation activities.

The Anglo-Kuki War had devastating consequences on the social and economic lives of the affected villages, which were burned down several times. Epidemics that broke out during and after the fighting eventually killed more people than the operations themselves had (Downs 1971: 169). During about the same years of the Kuki Rebellion, the American Baptist Missionary Crozier had served as a government medical officer. In appreciation for the services he had rendered during the war, the Mission was finally given permission to purchase land for a new centre at Kangpokpi on the Imphal-Kohima road. The site was divided to accommodate an educational institution, roadside dispensary, a cemetery, a hospital, a leper colony and ladies compound (Zeliang 2005). The mission compound encouraged women education and gave shelter to a number of Christian widows and their children around 1923.[33] The compound was under the charge of Mrs. Crozier, who taught them to be self-reliant, educated and well-versed with the scripture, knowledge of medicine, health and hygiene. These women and their children became influential personas in the society (Sitlhou 2011). Widows were actually looked down upon in the society and ostracised. But the mission compound turned them into personas who were indispensable to tackle the epidemic and devastation caused by the war.

All the above points of discussion prove the indispensable role of women during the war. In essence, war can give many women the opportunity to prove themselves as equal and just as capable as men, in turn disproving traditional or stereotypical gender roles that have been ascribed to each sex for hundreds of years (Kelly 2000: 61–62). It is crucial here to highlight the fact that women were not just passive victims of the Anglo-Kuki War, as is habitually the perception. In fact, women's participation in the war challenges conventional notions of power and the stereotypical gender roles in the society.

Acknowledgments: I would like to thank my field assistants Lunminthang Guite and Priscilla Vahneimoi Haokip; all my esteemed respondents for their time and enthusiasm; and my husband Chongroilen Sampar for patiently editing and discussing this chapter with me. I am grateful to UGC-SAP of Department of Sociology for funding the fieldwork for procuring data for the study.

Notes

1 Letter of Mr. W.J. Reid, Commissioner, Surma Valley & Hill Districts, Camp Imphal, 2 January, 1918.
2 Letter of Mr. Cosgrave to Mr. Webster, Camp Shuganu, 5 January, 1918.

3 Pettigrew, Rev. W. Evangelistic and Educational Report, 1921. in History of Christianity in Manipur (Source Materials). compiled by Elungkiebe Zeliang 2005. Manipur Baptist Convention: Imphal.

4 Mission Progress Report for 1922. ABFMS 1922: One-Hundred-eight Annual Report (P. 92–5). complied by Elungkiebe Zeliang 2005. Manipur Baptist Convention: Imphal.

5 Ibid.

6 Thangbawi tous. (Tuesday 10 November, 2015). 'The Kuki War History', http://thangbawitouthang.blogspot.in/2015/11/the-kuki-war-history.html. accessed date: 19 May, 2017.

7 D.P. Haokip, interviewed on 8 May (2017) at New Lambulane, Imphal. Dr. D.P. Haokip is a 70-year-old former finance secretary of Kuki Baptist Convention, a Church in Imphal. He was originally a native of Gilchingnang village and used Nemjavei's house at Chassad as a stopover when going for his place of education. Nemjavei was his distant relative.

8 A customary practice of the Thadou-Kukis in which a portion of the meat of an animal killed in hunting is given to an elder brother as a mark of respect.

9 D.P. Haokip, interviewed on 8 May (2017) at New Lambulane, Imphal. Dr. D.P. Haokip is a 70-year-old former finance secretary of Kuki Baptist Convention, a Church in Imphal. He was originally a native of Gilchingnang village and used Nemjavei's house at Chassad as a stopover when going for his place of education. Nemjavei was his distant relative.

10 British Library, London (BL), Asian and African Collections (formerly Oriental & India Office Collections) (hereafter AAC), Indian Office Records and Private Papers (hereafter IOR&PP), IOR/L/PS/10/724: 1917–1920, 'Burma-Assam Frontier: Disturbances among Kuki Tribesmen in Manipur', File No. P-693/1919: J.E. Webster, CS Assam to Foreign Secy. GOI, 27 June 1919.

11 Ibid, p. 6

12 Ibid, p. 7.

13 Nengchin Sitlhou (Niece of Chongneivei) was interviewed on 21 March 2017 at Keithelmanbi village. She was formally an occupant of Jampi village in Tamenglong district which was burned down by NSCN-IM during the Kuki-Naga Conflict.

14 Thangkholen Sitlhou (grandson of Chongneivei), Interviewed on 21 March 2017 at Gunngolphai Village.

15 Ibid.

16 The name 'Tujang' had been carried on by the Kipgen clan since their settlement in the fertile valley near Tuhmun (present day Burma). Currently, Tujang is located adjoining to the NH-2 in Sadar Hills (West).

17 Nguljalal Kipgen was interviewed on 2 March 2017. He is now 72 years old and is the present chief of Tujang Part II. The original Tujang was in present day Myanmar. He is the grandson of Vumngul Kipgen.

18 Ibid.

19 Further explanation in Thadou-Kuki dialect – Namtinkainesa (leng/hao sakai le don nesaaseinaahi). Jougam a loupitah a umpachusongkul'a um jongleahinachumansah/kemsahponte.

20 Paodong Haokip belongs to Tingkai Village and is now settling in Imphal. He is 83 years old and is an Indian army pensioner. interviewed on 29 March 2017 at Imphal.
21 Ibid.
22 Ibid.
23 The first four lines of the poem by Siegfried Sasson (1983), Written August 1916 – son the way to make a night attack on Quadrangle trench beyond Mametz village.
24 Gender and War, The Oxford Companion to American Military History, 2000, OUP. www.encyclopedia.com/history/encyclopedias-alma nacs-transcripts-and-maps/gender-and-war, accessed date: 20 June, 2017.
25 Ibid.
26 Paodong Haokip belongs to Tingkai Village and is now settling in Imphal. He is 83 years old and is an Indian army pensioner. interviewed on 29 March 2017 at Imphal.
27 BL, AAC, IOR&PP, IOR/L/MIL/17/19/42: 1919: 'Despatch on the Operations Against the Kuki Tribes' Macquoid to Keary, 27 April 1919.
28 Ibid.
29 BL, AAC, IOR&PP, IOR/L/MIL/17/19/42: 1919: 'Despatch on the Operations Against the Kuki Tribes' Macquoid to Keary, 27 April 1919.
30 Ibid.
31 Ibid.
32 Ibid.
33 Alice Pettigrew, 'Women's Work Report for 1923', in Zeliang 2005: 96.

References

Bhadra, Gautam. 1975. 'The Kuki (?) Uprising (1917–1919): Its Causes and Nature', *Man in India*, 55 (January–March): 10–56.

Chishti, S.M.A.W. 2004. *The Kuki Uprising in Manipur: 1917–1920*. Guwahati and New Delhi: Spectrum Publications.

Dena, Lal. 1988. *Christian Missions and Colonialism*. Shillong: Vendrama Institute.

Downs, Frederick S. 1971. *The Mighty Works of God*. Assam: Christian Literature Centre.

El-Bushra, J. 2000. 'Transforming Conflict: Some Thoughts on a Gendered Understanding of Conflict Processes', in S. Jacobs, R. Jacobson and J. Marchbank (eds.), *States of Conflict: Gender, Violence and Resistance*, pp. 66–86. London: Zed Books.

Gangte, Priyadarshni M. and A.K. Singh. eds. 2010. *Understanding Kuki Since Primordial Times*. New Delhi: Maxford Books.

Goldstein, Joshua S. 2003. *War and Gender: How Gender Shapes the War System and Vice Versa*. New York: Cambridge University Press.

Goswami, Tarun. 1985. *Kuki Life and Lore*. Haflong: North Cachar Hill District Council.

Haokip, Doungul Letkhojam. 2006. 'Historical Traditions and Customary Laws of the Chassad', unpublished PhD Thesis submitted to Department of History, Manipur University, http://hdl.handle.net/10603/103831 (accessed 19-05-2017).

Haokip, Jamthang. 1984. *Manipur a Gospel leh Kuki ho Thusim.* Imphal: Private Circulation.

Haokip, Sonthang. 2011. 'Anglo Kuki Relations', unpublished PhD Thesis Submitted to the Department of History, Manipur University, http://hdl. handle.net/10603/103668 (accessed 19-05-2017).

Hmingthanzuali. 2010. 'Women in Mizo History: Changing Roles, Status and Participation from 18th to 20th Century', unpublished PhD Thesis submitted to the Department of History University of Hyderabad, http://shodh ganga.inflibnet.ac.in/handle/10603/103740 (accessed 19-05-2017).

Kelly, L. 2000. 'Wars Against Women: Sexual Violence, Sexual Politics and the Militarised State', in S. Jacobs, R. Jacobson and J. Marchbank (eds.), *States of Conflict: Gender, Violence and Resistance*, pp. 45–66. London: Zed Books.

Kipgen, Mangkhosat. 1997. *Christianity and Mizo Culture: The Encounter Between Christianity and Zo Culture in Mizoram.* Aizawl: Mizo Theological Conference.

Lloyd, J. Meirion. 1991. *History of the Church in Mizoram: Harvest in the Hills.* Mizoram: Synod Publication Board.

Nordstrom, Carolyn. 2005. '(Gendered) War', *Studies in Conflict and Terrorism* (Special Issue: Women and Terrorism, Guest Editor: Cindy D. Ness), 28: 399–411.

Ortner, Sherry B. 1996. *Making Gender: The Politics and Erotics of Culture.* Boston: Beacon Press.

Palit, D.K. 1919 [1984]. *Sentinels of North East India: The Assam Rifles.* New Delhi: Hans Raj Gupta & Sons.

Parratt, John. 2005. *Wounded Land: Politics and Identity in Modern Manipur.* New Delhi: Mittal Publications.

Pettigrew, Alice. 2005. 'Women's Work Report for 1923', in Elungkiebe Zeliang (ed.), *History of Christianity in Manipur (Source Materials).* Imphal: Manipur Baptist Convention.

Ray, Asok Kumar. 1990. *Authority and Legitimacy: A Study of the Thadou-Kukis in Manipur.* New Delhi: Renaissance Publishing House.

Reid, Robert. 1997 [1942]. *History of the Frontier Areas Bordering on Assam from 1883–1941.* Guwahati: Spectrum Publications.

Sandelowski, Margarete. 1991. 'Telling Stories: Narrative Approaches in Qualitative Research', *Journal of Nursing Scholarship*, 23 (3): 161–166.

Shakespear, J.W. 1977 [1929]. *History of the Assam Rifles.* Aizawl: Tribal Research Institute (TRI).

Sharma, Manorama. 1998. *History and History Writing in North East India.* New Delhi: Regency Publication.

Sitlhou, Hoineilhing. 2011. 'Land and Identity: A Sociological Study of the Thadou-Kukis of Manipur', unpublished PhD Thesis, Centre for Study of Social Systems, Jawaharlal Nehru University, New Delhi.

Sitlhou, Hoineilhing. 2015. 'Patriarchal Bargains and Paradoxical Emancipation: Issues in the Politics of Land Rights of the Kuki Women', *Indian Journal of Gender Studies*, 22 (1): 92–115.

Zeliang, Elungkiebe. ed. 2005. *History of Christianity in Manipur (Source Materials)*. Imphal: Manipur Baptist Convention.

Part V

TRIAL AND TRIBULATION

11

KEEPING THEM UNDER CONTROL
Impact of the Anglo-Kuki War

Seikhohao Kipgen

We must endeavour by thoughtful and sympathetic administration to ensure that they shall not again embark on a mad course of rebellion.
– Nicholas Beatson Bell, Chief Commissioner of Assam

Scholars have different opinions on the impact of the Anglo-Kuki War. One general consensus is that it brought about direct administration in the hills of Manipur and Somra Tract in Burma. The introduction of new administration was, however, seen from different perspectives. These perspectives are mainly based to two confusing and unrelated reasons given by the colonial archives. On the one hand, it was said that the new administration was meant to control the turbulent Kukis and prevent them from taking up another uprising against colonial authority. On the other, it also uttered a stereotypical notion of administration as a means to extend 'the benefits of civilisation'. Scholars argued from and between these two lines of colonial thinking but tended to be eventually trapped with the notion of 'civilisation'. It hardly crosses the mind that the new administrative structure, which overshadowed the old system, could be the poorer option for the hillmen. The pre-war situation of Manipur hills makes it clear that there was a massive changeover from a tribal to a colonial system. For the Kukis, the new administration was to eliminate the old political structure and to control and circumvent the spirit of freedom. Although colonial system propped and make use of the old village political structure by superimposing the colonial authority on it, it had at the same time, destroyed the older power structure of the principal chiefs or village which had for long controlled over a large number of villages in the

285

hills. This is especially so to the power of the Kuki principal chieftains who had controlled large part of the hill areas. The destruction of the traditional Kuki political structure is not only significant but also brought subsequent devastation to Kuki polity at large. Besides, there were massive socio-cultural consequences of the war. Its impact on the hill economy hardly pained scholar's field input. This chapter attempts to unravel some of the significant consequences of the war in general and on the Kuki community in particular.

Impact on the administration of Manipur

One of the major consequences of the Anglo-Kuki War was the overall administrative reorganisation of the hills of Manipur. Prior to the war, the hill areas were nominally controlled by the colonial officials through a single British officer stationed at Imphal and were largely under the control of independent tribal chieftains. They have not been integrated within the political structure or a unified administrative network of Manipur state. Apart from the occasional tour of the Political Agent in Manipur and visits by the hill *lambus* (middlemen or peons), there was hardly anything to name administration of the hills. On the other hand, other than their contribution of annual house-tax, porterage (*pothang*) and labour (*beggar*), the hillmen were virtually left alone. Manipur state had given back nothing in return to what it received from the hillmen. The old tribal polity largely remains untouched and one can rather see them flourishing. Occasionally the Maharaja of Manipur received military assistance from the war-like Kukis as mercenaries against his enemies.

In analysing the cause of Kuki rising, the Assam government also felt that lack of administration and the spirit of independence among the hillmen was one major factor. At one level, the hill *lambus* were accused of 'responsible in no small measures for the rebellion'.[1] On the other hand, it is argued:

> One of the causes of the rising undoubtedly was that the President of the Darbar, with his duties in Imphal and in the Manipur valley, could not possibly give adequate attention to tribes scattered over 7000 square miles of all but impassable mountains. The tribesmen had contributed some Rs. 70,000 a year in the form of house-tax, but had received in return practically no benefits: neither roads, nor education, nor medical aid.[2]

Therefore, it went on justifying that the President of the Darbar required the assistance of British officers to administer the hills. Hence, it was eventually decided to station three Sub-Divisional Officers in different parts of the hills, whose duty was to improve roads and provide education and medical aid to the hillmen.

The truth about the new administrative policy was, however, more to do with controlling over the hillmen, especially the turbulent Kukis. The Chief Commissioner of Assam, for instance, clearly spelt out this in his speech before the Manipur Darbar after the war:

> I have been in close conference with His Highness the Maharaja regarding the future administration of the hill tribes of Manipur. We are both agreed that more shall be done for these simple, savage people than has ever been done in the past. We must endeavour by thoughtful and sympathetic administration to ensure that they shall not again embark on a mad course of rebellion. Subdivisions must be opened in the heart of the hills where resident Sub-divisional officers will administer simple justice, will open out roads and communication, will establish schools and will give medical relief. The Government of India are in full accord with the proposals of the Maharaja and myself.[3]

To 'ensure' that Kukis do not embark on another course of 'rebellion' against the colonial authority, new administration was, therefore, introduced in the hills. This announcement heralded a new age of direct administrative control over the hillmen. The hill areas of Manipur were consequently divided into four subdivisions, one being directly administered by the President of Manipur State Durbar. Under the new scheme, the other three subdivisions were made under the British officers. They were:

1 The Southwest area with headquarter at Churachandpur was left to the charge of B.C. Gasper. It covers the areas west of the Manipur river and includes the Manhlun Manchong, Ukha and all areas stretching southwards from Silchar bridle path to the Lushai Hill border, for checking free mobility of the Kuki's to avoid recurrence of the Kuki movement.
2 The Northwest area with headquarter at Tamenglong was left to the charge of William Shaw for better control of the Kukis against the Kabuis and other Nagas;

3   The Northeast area with headquarter at Ukhrul was left to the charge of Lt. Peters with a view to intercepting free mobility of the Kukis in the area (the SDO was made to station at Chassad at least for three months in a year); and

4   Besides, a large area comprising north of Manipur State including the Mao and Maram Naga groups, the whole of Mombi (Lonpi) areas in the Southeast and the various tribes of hills bordering the valley continued to be administered directly from Imphal under the President of the State Durbar due to better transport and communication system and financial implications.[4]

Under the new rules, it was laid down that the President of Manipur State Durbar (a British Officer) had the power equivalent to the District magistrate and so also the Sub-divisional Officers (SDO) had powers equivalent to the sub-divisional Magistrates. Appeals in the civil and criminal cases against the order of SDOs would lie with the Political Agent. In civil cases, no appeal was allowed against the order of the President of Manipur State Durbar. Thus, the Maharaja and the State Durbar were practically eliminated in the administration of the hill areas. It is clear that the Durbar exercised no direct control, but from time to time it tried to claim their indirect control through its power over the budget (Dena 1991; Shakespear 1929; Palit 1984). It shows that only in theory that the tribal people were under the Government of Maharajah. The exclusion of the Maharaja's authority was so complete and thorough that the tribal people tended to forget that they were the subjects of the State of Manipur. In short, the hill people were given separate status though they were in principle within the political state boundaries of Manipur. This was done in order to prevent the rise of any movement like the 'Kuki Rebellion' in future. A long tradition of friendship and alliances maintained by the Manipuris and the Kukis also came to an end.

The British authorities therefore assumed the direct administration of the hill tribes to prevent the Kukis from rising up against them. They justified their action by invoking an absurd idea that they were merely assisting the Maharaja of Manipur and it was an act of preserving peace and providing 'civilisation' to hillmen. Not understanding the deep relationship between Manipur and the hill people, Robert Reid, the Chief Commissioner and official colonial historian, for instance, later claimed that 'Manipuris cannot and will not give the hills an administration of the standard to which they are both entitled and now accustomed' (Reid 1983: 88). In this way, the British policy of keeping the hill tribes under its direct control eventually created 'a barrier of wall' between the hillmen and the plainsmen in a way they could never have come together as friends and allies in the future. The wedges drawn between them gradually increased antagonism and conflict, which directly unfolded under the tutelage of the new colonial administration. On the other hand, the power of the principal Kuki chiefs was destroyed, and now the new administration controlled the hillmen through the petty village chieftains or headmen who were now anointed with colonial blessing and support. Thus, the strong hill administration became the visible impact of the Anglo-Kuki War (Gangte 1993; Chishti 2004; Bezbaruah 2010).

The Manipur Maharaja was under duress to accept the new arrangement otherwise the whole expenditure on the war waged against the Kukis was said to be fought in his favour which he silently denied. Besides, the colonial state also insisted that Manipur should extend direct administration into the hills although they knew that Manipur was lacking the resource and manpower to do so. When the hills of Manipur cannot be taken away from it under the existing treaty, the colonial state in practice took over the hills by indirectly sponsoring its administration financially and with manpower. Therefore, all the required finance to extend direct administration over the hills was funded by colonial GOI. How this administrative arrangement was meant to extend colonial hegemony (not Manipur Maharaja) was clearly discernible in the letter of the Chief Commissioner of Assam to the Viceroy on 19 April 1919:

> We must establish British sub-divisional officers at suitable places in the hills. These men, working under the president, would reside in the areas all the year round, open up roads, administer simple justice, set up schools and hospitals, and generally act as fathers to the hillmen and restore their confidence in the British raj.
>
> (as quoted in Dena 1991: 133)

Positioning 'British sub-divisional officers' who will act as 'fathers of the hillmen' and then 'restore their confidence in the British Raj' (not Manipur Raj) against any further uprising was therefore central to the new scheme of administration.

It was on this ground that the GOI had also finally agreed to the proposal. Therefore, it sanctioned the scheme along with the financial support. The total amount required for the administration of the hills was estimated to be Rs. 1,25,000/- annually. This amount was allocated under different heads as follows: Hill Officer (Rs.20,000/-), three sub-divisional officers (Rs.30,000/-), communications (Rs.30,000/-), education (Rs.l0,000/-), medical (Rs. 15,000/-), and miscellaneous (Rs. 20,000/-). This amount was contributed by the GOI, partly with direct funding and partly through what it called 'concessions'. Thus, Manipur was to provide Rs. 50,000 out of the total house-tax collected from the hills and the remaining amount Rs. 75,000 should be provided by GOI. The GOI share of Rs. 75,000/- will be taken from different sources on which Manipur was to pay GOI. Out of the annual tribute of Rs. 50,000, Manipur should devote Rs. 45,000 for the hills and pay only Rs. 5,000 to GOI. Rs. 30,000 which Manipur annually paid to GOI towards the cost of maintaining its roads to British territory should now be devoted to the hill administration. To relieve Manipur from its financial constraint due to the hill administration, its annual payment of Rs. 60,000 to GOI on its outstanding loans was also reduced to Rs. 10,000 (that is what it spent on the hill administration Rs. 50000 was returned from this amount).[5] Taken together, Manipur state was virtually spending nothing for the new hill administration; the total amount being paid by the GOI. If the hill house-tax was Rs. 70,000, then Manipur state was still getting Rs. 20,000 from the hills, which constituted its additional amount on its state exchequer.

Immediate impact of the war

In the proceedings of the Chief Commissioner of Assam it was recorded that the Anglo-Kuki War shook the entire Northeastern Frontier of India.[6] After fighting for more than two years (1917–1919), most of the Kuki villages had been burnt down and ravaged. Famine and starvation set in motion bringing untold miseries to the people. To avail political amnesty some of the Kuki chiefs in good faith agreed to lay down their arms and stop fighting. In this connection Chengjapao, chief of Aisan along with 48 of his people, firearms and with Rs. 300 as fine were the first to court arrest themselves on 23 August 1918.[7] It was said that he sought general pardon on behalf of the Kuki people (Hangsing 2015). Innocent Kukis who were kept in the concentration camp were subjected to inhuman treatments. Even women and children were not spared for the labour force. They were made to work in constructing roads and bridges between Imphal and Tamu and other roads connecting Ukhrul, Tamenglong and Churachandpur.

Living in unhygienic concentration camps, the Kuki inmates became victims of various diseases like malaria, cholera and small pox. Horrendous torture of inmates, physical beating, starvation and several other forms of abuses were the daily occurrence. It may be noted that even after the Kuki war the British Indian soldiers continued raiding big villages, which consequently led to its disintegration into smaller scattered settlements. The Kukis were further penalised by making them pay war reparation of Rs. 1,75,000. The amount was recovered within five years, partly in cash and partly in the form of penal communal labour like cutting government roads, constructing government offices, engaging as porters and so on. The whole Kuki populace suffered for a long time due to this inhumane treatment. The new administration did not bring any sight of relief, but was harping on to fulfil the colonial objective of putting the hillmen under their direct control permanently (Chishti 2004; Haokip 1998).

As the war lasted for more than two years, it led to total disruption of their cultivation process. This 'tragic inhumanity' and wanton destruction of lives and properties led to the outbreak of all sorts of miseries, including famine. As such, people had to face a hard time in subsisting their edible items found in the forest like wild roots, raw leaves, fruits, etc. for their bare minimum survival. The Anglo-Kuki War shattered the Kuki society and economy so much so that they were not able to stand united like before. It was so severe that it affected the region in different degrees and magnitudes. The war claimed many lives and rendered many homeless. Livestock were killed and crops destroyed. The war constituted the most memorable epoch making event in the history of Kukis in particular and for the region in general. Time can never erase the valour and gallantry of the Kukis, who made supreme sacrifices to defend their freedom and homeland.

Socio-cultural consequences

The socio-cultural impact of the Anglo-Kuki War was also strongly felt. The devastation of the war had caused the Kukis was not only in terms of economic dislocations and their own ways of life but also in terms of their overall social structure. Prior to the war, Kuki social life was mainly centred on their traditional chieftainship institution and its associated bodies such as the village *som* (bachelor's house), village *lom* (cooperate labour organisation) and others. It was under these traditional institutions that the self-sufficient village economy, polity and other social orders were maintained and sustained. It is known that these institutions had worked quite well until about the Anglo-Kuki War. The fact that Kukis could fight the British military forces for almost two years was testimony of the efficient functioning of these traditional institutions. The brutal suppression of Kuki rising was therefore not only about the suppression of the rising; it was also about the destruction of these age-old institutions. The gradual destruction of important traditional institutions draws our attention. For instance, a traditional Kuki village had drawn its art of fighting, *esprit de corps*, cooperation, discipline, social orders and etiquettes much from their *som* and *lom*.

Evidences have suggested that the institution of *som* subside gradually and eventually vanished after the suppression of Kuki rising for reasons difficult to find. One possible reason could be the declining needs of village security after the occupation of the hills by colonial state. Since the basic needs of *som* was based on the military need of the village community, the end of such threat under colonialism could have gradually led to the discouragement of the practice of group dormitory in *som*. The rapid conversion to Christianity also impacted much on the decline of *som*. We can see that most missionaries discourage this system as they saw it as a site of vice and immorality. However, the gradual death of this invaluable institution *som* was injurious to the social health of the Kuki society in many ways. First, it led to the destruction of regimented or military culture of the Kukis. If *som* is the institution where the spirit of cooperation, discipline and social orders and etiquettes, then it makes sense to argue that all these important characters of Kuki village society had also gradually declined in time. On the other hand, it is also possible to argue that the increasing social crimes, conflicts and other forms of evils in the village after the war were also due to this. *Lom* institution survived but it also lost its true spirit of cooperation and community consciousness because the main institution of *som*, that educated and developed such spirit, had died down.

The brutal suppression of the Kuki rising also shocked their cultural foundation. For instance, their defeat at the hands of colonial forces shattered their faith in their traditional God (*Pathen*). Kukis were strong believers in their God and faithful to their religion. For this reason, they strongly opposed Christian missionaries in their villages. During the war, there is evidence to show that they had a strong faith in their God and believed that he would protect them and give them victory over the British. Political Agent in Manipur, for instance, reported about the faith that Kukis had on their God in relation to the 'war' against the British:

> The enemy Kukis are all talking that they have got their God and the said God has been helping them in the present Kuki war. The British Government [would] never be able to bring

them in submission and at the end they (Kukis) would be victorious.[8]

In this sense, their defeat at the hands of the British was seen to be the inability of their traditional God (*Pathen*) to protect them from the large forces under colonial state. In other words, the victory of British in the war was seen to be the victory of Christian God over the Kuki God. This, on the one hand, brought a major crisis of conscience in what they faithfully trusted till then, and on the other, generated a major reorientation of their faith in their traditional God (*Pathen*) and opened up their minds towards Christianity, the religion of the victor. The result of this reorientation was the rapid conversion to Christianity in post-war period. Evidence has also suggested that large numbers of Kukis came towards Christianity and mission works also progress much rapidly than before the war. We can see that the major opposition to Christianity among the Kukis was coming from their chiefs who felt that conversion to Christianity was the first step towards colonial political control. However, such opposition came down after they were defeated in the war (Downs 1971; Dena 1988; Vaiphei 1999).

The Anglo-Kuki War was socially and culturally a watershed in the history of the Kukis not only because of the decline of some of the important traditional institutions but also because the rapid expansion of Christianity in the aftermath of the war have drastically transformed their social and cultural lives. Christianity imparted and infused not only the new religion and belief in Christianity but it had also transformed their ideas, mentalities and social practices in a big way at the cost of their traditions and customs. It is up to the historians to judge whether such changes were for the betterment or for the worse. Yet, it was certain that major change had taken place in the process of becoming a good Christian. These changes might not have taken place had there been no major war such as the Anglo-Kuki War.

Curtailment of chief's power and breakdown of Kuki unity

One of the most striking consequences of the Anglo-Kuki War was the curtailment of the power of principal Kuki chieftains, who were the bedrock of the rising. Before the war, Kuki chiefs were broadly divided in two: village chiefs and principal chiefs. While the principal chiefs were also the chief of their immediate village, their power and dominance also spread over many other village chiefs through clan networks as well as tribute relationship. The unity of Kuki people across the highland region revolved around their power and dominance. This power often extended over the villages of non-Kukis as well. Hence, before the war larger parts of the hills were under the control of some of the principal Kuki chiefs. In fact, the Kuki war of 1917–1919 was one such incident that demonstrated not only the supremacy of some principal Kuki chieftains over large parts of the hills but also the unity they have wielded among all sections of the Kuki society. J.H. Hutton, in his notes on Shaw's book, for instance, vividly explained the position of the principal Kuki chiefs before the war:

> Before the Kuki rising of 1918–19, the administration of the hill areas of Manipur was not very close, and the Thados ruled as they were by well organized chiefs and treated, as they had been in the past at any rate, by the Manipur State as allies almost as much as subjects, managed their own affairs in their own way and had recourse to force only in exceptional cases.
>
> (Shaw 1929: 3)

The brutal suppression of the Kuki rising finally ended the long hegemony of principal Kuki chieftains in the hills of Manipur, which had in turn generated some major consequences on the Kuki society. The prestige and power of the Kuki chiefs was hit hard by the war and was considerably lowered with the end of the war. As the strength and unity of Kukis lie in the authority of their principal chiefs, it was clear to the colonial state that in order to prevent any future uprising such dominance needed to be curtailed. It was from this line of thinking that the new administration was introduced in the hills. In fact, the traditional power and autonomy of the Kuki chiefs was uprooted with the introduction of direct administration over the hills. The destruction of Kuki's principal chieftains was followed by redistribution of power among all the village chiefs who were now anointed and empowered by the colonial regime. Each village chief was now under the direct control of the British sub-divisional officers and was duty bound to serve them. As we noted earlier, the British sub-divisional officers now become 'fathers to the hillmen' by replacing the old principal Kuki chieftains. In this way, the dominance of Kukis over the hills of Manipur was flattened and destroyed. The destruction of the power of principal Kuki chieftains resulted into some multiple destructions on the Kuki society. First, it destroyed the supremacy of Kukis over the hills of Manipur, which had been until then protected and enforced by their principal chiefs. Second, their freedom to 'manage their own affairs in their own way' has ended, and they were now under the oppressive regime of colonial power. Third and most importantly, the unity of the Kukis had been broken down with the destruction of their centripetal force so far revolving around the power of their principal chieftains.

The breakdown of unity among the Kukis after the rising was one major setback under the new colonial administration. Apart from propping the village level chiefs as the tool of colonial power against their principal chiefs, the colonial state also particularly encouraged those Kukis who remained 'loyal' and 'friendly' to the British during the Anglo-Kuki War to take up the leadership of the Kuki community. This section of the Kuki population enjoyed the benefits of colonial state in terms of education, health, job sector. Many of them have also become Christian in the process. Thus, by propping this section to take up the politics of the Kukis against the old powerhouse was one major setback, in so far as unity among the Kukis was concerned. Lacking the spirit of nationalism and the love for country and community, the new leaderships and the organisations they formed were very soon taken over by selfish interests. To gain some petty concessions from the colonial government they all fought over some petty issues like 'name', representations, and so on. This infighting often went beyond the point; sometime even to the point of disowning the very name they were known by: Kuki (Ray 1990: 111–131). The narrow outlook of these new leaderships had set the ground on which Kuki unity was slowly broken, and the pendulum is still swinging.

The breakdown of unity among the Kukis was further enhanced by increasing tensions among the individual villages over the possession of territory, boundaries and resources which now become a reality to survive with under colonial capitalist regime. These tensions developed not only between two or more Kuki villages but also very soon became the core issue in the relationship between Kuki villages and their neighbouring Naga villages. In empowering one village against the other villages, and the destruction of all layers of power structure between the village and the colonial state, tensions over land and boundaries was one major source of conflict in the aftermath of the war. In many cases, Kuki villages that had supremacy over many other villages previous to the war had become the point of attack now in the new scenario. Such scattered tensions and conflicts gradually developed into a sort of ethnic animosity in the later period, as people gradually became conscious about their ethnicity and tribal identity. In short, the breakdown of peace and tranquillity in the hills after the new administration took over the hills was undoubtedly one significant result of the Anglo-Kuki War.

If the principal Kuki chieftains' powers were broken down after the war, their spirits were not. We can see that the primary objective of the new administration was to break down the power of these powerful hill potentates. Their traditional power and influence were taken away, they become a mere chieftain of their own village; they become equal members of the hill society under the British power. Yet, it is interesting to note that a study conducted after the war and some official reports categorically put that their 'tails are not down', and they still aspire to become the 'Raj' one day. William Shaw, who had conducted an official ethnographic survey among the Kukis after the war, found that despite being physically ruined, the Kukis 'do not consider themselves beaten yet and still brood over the future ahead of them', because they still strongly believed that 'they are destined to be rulers of their earth and not to be submissive to any one'.[9] Seeing their pity situation under colonialism, it was obvious that the Kukis, especially those who had fought the British and now being deprived of the care of 'civilisation', would brood over the opportunity to tide over their state of subjugation. They knew that they could not do this on their own although they did so in various small ways. As the spirit of freedom had not died down, many Kukis would do anything to thwart the control of British or refused to obey their orders in tacit. They were still bounded by the promise they made in Chassad conclave to fold together like the clothes and speak in one voice like the birds. They were always on the lookout for their 'messiah' which they expected to come from the east. To their amazement, this came during the Second World War.

The outbreak of the Second World War heralded a new hope for the Kukis. When Mahatma Gandhi launched 'Quit India Movement' in 1942, the Kukis urge for freedom got a new lease on life. Very soon, this hope became a reality when the Japanese army and the Indian National Army (INA) under Subhash Chandra Bose appeared at the eastern gate to fight against the British and Allied forces. To many Kukis who felt disheartened under the colonial regime, the coming of Japanese and INA was seen to be a 'God sent messiah', as some writers would put it. They took every possible measures to reach out the invading forces, joined the rank of the military establishment as fighters, informers, spies, campaigners, guides and coolies. Even before the war began, many Kukis had joined the Japanese and INA establishment. Once the war started, the whole Kuki population did whatever they could to help the invading forces by supplying food, nursing the sick and wounded, providing information and guiding them in the rugged, roadless mountains. Thousands of Kukis also died in the ensuing war (Guite 2010: 291–309; Ghosh 1969; Lebra 1971; Singh 1993). However, the defeat of INA and Japanese forces was another setback for the Kukis' anti-imperialist struggle. Their hope to free themselves from British imperialism was again broken. Onkholet Haokip, who was popularly known locally as *Japan Pakang*, was so upset by the defeat that he had decided to follow the Japanese when they retreated.[10] Hundreds of Kukis were honoured INA pensions by Indian government after independence and given the status of 'Freedom Fighters' of India.[11]

Concluding remarks

Kukis had fought hard to defeat the British military forces at the cost of everything but their rising was brutally suppressed. Apart from all sorts of unimaginable sufferings in the aftermath of the war, the Anglo-Kuki War had also brought many long-term consequences against their erstwhile freedom, power and cause heavy destruction to their institutions, culture and social values which could not be put back to its earlier position. The breakdown of their unity, the trend that set into motion after the war, is still progressing. The colonial policy of dividing them into pieces is alive, even after 70 years of independence. Yet, what the Kukis had displayed was the uncompromising freedom that they valued and the fighting spirit that they had in their culture. Recognising this martial quality during the war, the Kukis had been recruited in large numbers by the colonial armies. If the price of the mighty British Empire was brutal, it always remained a sweet memory to the Kukis for the gallant show. This much is what the frontier tribal people could do for the freedom of the nation.

Notes

1 British Library, London (BL), Asian and African Collections (formerly Oriental & India Office Collections) (hereafter AAC), Indian Office Records and Private Papers (hereafter IOR&PP), IOR/L/PS/10/724: 1917–1920, 'Burma-Assam Frontier: Disturbances among Kuki Tribesmen in Manipur', File No. P-693/1919: J.E. Webster, CS Assam to Foreign Secy. GOI, 27 June 1919.

2 BL, AAC, IOR&PP, Mss Eur E325/13 (1920): 'Extract from the Proceedings of the Chief Commissioner of Assam in the Political Department', No. 8856-P, 27 September 1920 by A.W. Botham.

3 Manipur Secretariat Library (MSL), Cabin No. 32: 'Khongjai Lal Result, 1919–1920'.

4 Administrative Report of Manipur State, 1919–20, p. 2. See also Dena (1991).

5 Manipur Secretariat Library (MSL), Cabin No. 32: 'Khongjai Lal Result, 1919–1920'. See also Dena (1991: 133).

6 BL, AAC, IOR&PP, Mss Eur E325/13 (1920): 'Extract from the Proceedings of the Chief Commissioner of Assam in the Political Department', No. 8856-P, 27 September 1920 by A.W. Botham. See also Shakespear (1929).

7 BL, AAC, IOR&PP, IOR/L/PS/10/724: 1917–1920, File No. 5032/18: Webster, Assam to Foreign Secy. GOI, 12 September 1918.

8 'Statement of Waishon Kuki, Chief of Leirik, Lam No. 4', enclosed with DO No. 30GA: W.A. Cosgrave to J.E.Webster, 13 May 1918, in Assam Secretariat, Appointment and Political Department, Political Branch, Political – A, March 1919, File No. 9C/M-61P of 1918, Proceeding Nos. 1–255.

9 Shaw, Thadou-Kukis, pp. 23 & 50.

10 Onkholet Haokip was a Kuki chief who developed love and affection with the Japanese soldiers for which he was nicknamed as Japan Pakang. The affix Japan in his nickname – Pakang itself suggests a strong bond of relationship or connection with the Japanese. His name is still widely known among elders of the 'Thadou-Kukis'. He followed the Japanese up to Japan during their retreat and refused to come back to his forefather's land until its liberation. The story about Japan Pakang is collected from Pu. Mangpithang Kipgen and confirmed by several octogenarian Kukis. See also Sheikhohao Kipgen, Political and Economic History of the Kukis of Manipur, Akansha, 2014.

11 See for instance 'Bande Mataram' – Freedom Fighters of Manipur who's who. Published by Freedom Fighters Cell/Deptt. of Manipur Pradesh Congress Committee MPCC (I), 1985. Among the 120 INA pensioners (with their photographs), 75 of them were Kukis. Besides, in connection with the receipt of 'Tamra Pattra', a booklet was also issued by the INA Committee in which the names of the recipients were given.

References

1985. 'Bande Mataram' – Freedom Fighters of Manipur Who's Who. Freedom Fighters Cell/Deptt. of Manipur Pradesh Congress Committee MPCC (I).

Bezbaruah, R. 2010. The Pursuit of Colonial Interests in India's North East. Guwahati: EBH Publishers.

Chishti, S.M.A.W. 2004. The Kuki Uprising in Manipur: 1917–1920. Guwahati: Spectrum Publications.

Dena, Lal. 1988. Christian Missions and Colonialism. Shillong: Vendrama Institute.

Dena, Lal. 1991. Modern Manipur. New Delhi: Orbit Publishers.

Downs, F.S. 1971. The Mighty Works of God. Assam: Christian Literature Centre.

Gangte, T.S. 1993. The Kukis of Manipur: A Historical Analysis. New Delhi: Gyan.

Ghosh, K.K. 1969. Indian National Army: A Second Front of the Indian Independence Movement. Meerut: Minakshi Prakashan.

Guite, J. 2010. 'Representing Local Participation in INA-Japanese Imphal Campaign: The Case of the Kukis in Manipur, 1943–45', *Indian Historical Review*, 37 (2): 291–309.

Kipgen, S. 2014. *Political and Economic History of the Kukis of Manipur*. New Delhi: Akansha.

Haokip, P.S. 1998. *Zale'n-gam: The Kuki Nation*. KNO Publication.

Lebra, J.C. 1971. *Jungle Alliance: Japan and the Indian National Army*. Singapore: Asia Pacific Press.

Pahend Hangsing. 2015. 'Brief Account of the Anglo-Kuki War 1917–19', *Manipur Times*, 20 December 2015 (accessed 24–01–2017).

Palit, D.K. 1984. *Sentinnels of the North-East – The Assam Rifles*. New Delhi: Palit & Palit.

Ray, A.K. 1990. *Authority and Legitimacy: A Study of the Thadou-Kuki*. New Delhi: Renaissance Publishing House.

Reid, Robert.1983. *History of the Frontier Areas Bordering on Assam from 1883–1941*. New Delhi: Eastern Publishing House.

Shakespear, L.W. 1929. *History of the Assam Rifles*. Guwahati: Spectrum Publications.

Shaw, William. 1983. *Notes on the Thadou-Kukis, With an Introduction by J.H Hutton*. New Delhi: Cultural Publishing House.

Singh, N.L. 1993. *Manipur During World War II (1941–45): Socio-Economic Change and Local Response*. Imphal: Manipur State Archives.

Vaiphei, Kim. 1999. *Manipur Gamma Christian Hou Hunglut chuleh Kukite lah a Pathen hou kipat thusim*. Private Circulation.

INDEX

Page numbers in *italic* indicate a photograph on the corresponding page.

Durbar 97, 170, 172, 183;
see also Darbar
Dwe, Tsan 83

Eastern Ghats, hillmen of 157–58
economic grievances 175–77
enemies in arms, Kukis as 61
Enjakhup 15, 37, 60, 123, 126–27,
206, 276; capture of 111, 127;
detention of 62, 64; firearm
training 213; quotation 37; during
winter war (1917–1918) 49
epidemics 2, 53, 109, 257, 278
esprit de corps 215, 222
ethnic animosity 295

Falkland, H.L. 134–35
famine 26, 87, 111, 114, 183–85,
256–57, 290–91
Ffrench-Mullen, J.L.W. 22, 51–53,
109; battle at Khailet 215; on
Kuki fighters 67, 136, 211,
215–16; on Kuki morale 215; on
Kuki tactics 66–67, 118–19, 127,
214; on Kuki united actions 168;
on military occupation 53; request
for medals 216
firearms 128–29, 213; *see also* guns
First Anglo-Burmese War
(1824–1826) 79
flying columns *see* 'mobile/flying
columns' tactic
folksongs *see* songs
food supplies, destruction of 2,
9–10, 24–25, 52, 57–59, 87,
100–101, 107, 111, 174, 243,
256, 291
forage 98, 125–26, 243
forced labour 26, 159, 180–82, 257;
see also pothang
fortification of villages 15, 25, 45,
128, 131–33, *132*, 147, 200, 225;
see also stockades
Fowler, E.O. 80
France, labour recruitment for 6,
17, 26, 39, 68, 78–82, 85–87,
95–96, 98, 122, 168–69, 185–86,
188–89, 203–5, 272
French, David 10

friendly villages 3, 6, 20, 24, 38,
41–42, 53–54, 102, 105–6,
109–10, 112–13, 163, 190–91,
205, 244, 295

Gal-an 200
Gal-Ihim 200
Gallou-thu 146
Gandhi, Mahatma 296
Gaothanga 161
Gasper, B.C. 287
Gelnel 226
gender, war and 274–78
Germans, Kuki knowledge of 16–18
Ghee 176
girls, role in Kuki society 241
Gnarjal 126
Gobok 48
God, Kukis and 292–93
gongs 40, 144, 187, 239, 250, 257
Goodall 125
Goswami, Tarun 140, 264
government, village 217
grand chiefs-in council *see* chiefs-in
council
Great War *see* World War I
guerilla warfare 11, 15–16, 25, 66,
68, 100–101, 105, 114, 118–19,
123, 129, 147, 174, 200, 208;
counter-guerilla operations 10, 98,
110–11, 113; objective of 120;
understanding 119–22
Guite, Jangkhomang 24
Guite people 159, 162, 165
gunpowder 45, 121, 130–31, 244
guns 128–29, 189; collection in
preparation for war 44–45;
confiscated from Kukis 18,
128–29, 178, 213; *jangvoh* 129;
Martini rifles 125, 128, 146;
muzzle-loaders 25, 44, 50, 52,
124, 127–29, 146, 213; number
obtained by war end 101, 213;
songchep 129; surrender of 40,
54, 95, 277; *thihnang* 129
Gurkhalis 51, 176–77

Hackett, Major 134
Haika 134

For Product Safety Concerns and Information please contact our EU
representative GPSR@taylorandfrancis.com
Taylor & Francis Verlag GmbH, Kaufingerstraße 24, 80331 München, Germany

www.ingramcontent.com/pod-product-compliance
Ingram Content Group UK Ltd.
Pitfield, Milton Keynes, MK11 3LW, UK
UKHW020935180425
457613UK00019B/409